**WITHDRAWN**

HARVARD LIBRARY

**WITHDRAWN**

# HISTORY, ETHICS AND EMERGENT PROBABILITY

Ethics, Society and History
in the Work of Bernard Lonergan

Kenneth R. Melchin

UNIVERSITY
PRESS OF
AMERICA

LANHAM • NEW YORK • LONDON

Copyright © 1987 by

University Press of America,® Inc.

4720 Boston Way
Lanham, MD 20706

All rights reserved

Printed in the United States of America

**Library of Congress Cataloging-in-Publication Data**

Melchin, Kenneth R., 1949-
History, ethics, and emergent probability.

Bibliography: p.
1. Ethics, Modern—20th century. 2. History—
Philosophy—History—20th century. 3. Probabilities—
History—20th century. 4. Lonergan, Bernard J. F.
I. Title.
Bj319.M45  1987     171     87-10443
ISBN 0-8191-6362-7 (alk. paper)
ISBN 0-8191-6363-5 (pbk. : alk. paper)

BJ
319
.M45
1987

All University Press of America books are produced on acid-free
paper which exceeds the minimum standards set by the National
Historical Publication and Records Commission.

# Table of Contents

ACKNOWLEDGEMENTS.................................... ix

PREFACE.............................................. xi

CHAPTER ONE: Introduction............................ 1

    1.1   Social Ethics: Various Conceptions of
the Discipline..................................... 8
    1.2   The Question of Progress and the
Relevance of World Views.......................... 13

CHAPTER TWO: Ethics and the Philosophy of History.... 25

    2.1   Immanuel Kant..................................... 25
    2.2   Jacques Monod..................................... 33
    2.3   Lonergan: Ethics, History and Religion............ 45
           2.3.1 Chance...................................... 47
           2.3.2 Religion.................................... 49
           2.3.3 Tradition................................... 51

CHAPTER THREE: Probability........................... 59

    3.0   Introduction...................................... 59
    3.1   The Empirical Stance.............................. 61
    3.2   Systematic and Non-systematic Relations........... 64
    3.3   Probability....................................... 72
    3.4   Heuristic Structures and the Complementarity
of Classical and Statistical Inquiry.............. 76
    3.5   Two Probabilities................................. 80
    3.6   Verification...................................... 84

CHAPTER FOUR: Emergent Probability................... 97
    4.0   Introduction...................................... 97
    4.1   World Views....................................... 98
    4.2   Randomness and Scientific Explanation............ 101
    4.3   Conditioned Schemes of Recurrence................ 105
    4.4   Emergent Probability............................. 108
    4.5   Emergent Probability and the Human
Sciences......................................... 111
    4.6   Finality......................................... 113

**CHAPTER FIVE: Ethics and Emergent Probability............ 123**

    5.0   Introduction...................................... 123
    5.1   Skills and Recurrence Schemes.................... 125
    5.2   Mediation........................................ 128
    5.3   The Practical Orientation of Intelligence.......... 134
    5.4   Patterns of Experience........................... 137
    5.5   The Dramatic Pattern and Responsible,
          Moral Practice................................... 141
    5.6   Freedom and Moral Life: Essential
          and Effective Freedom.......................... 144

**CHAPTER SIX: History, Ethics and Emergent Probability I..... 165**

    6.0   Introduction...................................... 165
    6.1   Analytic or Critical Philosophy of History
          and the Speculative Philosophy
          of History....................................... 166
    6.2   Wilhelm Dilthey................................. 172
    6.3   Emergent Probability as an "Upper Blade"
          for a Critical Philosophy of History............... 175
    6.4   History as Meaning.............................. 177
          6.4.1 "Internal" Conditions and the Dramatic
                Subject: Dialectic and Dramatic Bias......... 178
          6.4.2 The Schemes and Series of History
                and Society: Intersubjectivity
                and Dialectic............................. 181
          6.4.3 "External" Conditions and the
                Dramatic Subject......................... 187
    6.5   Ethics and History I: Progress and
          Decline.......................................... 189
    6.6   Ethics and History II: The Foundations
          of Value......................................... 195

**CHAPTER SEVEN: History, Ethics and Emergent Probability II. 209**

    7.0   Introduction...................................... 209
    7.1   The Good of Order and Social Structure:
          Lonergan and Hobbes........................... 210
    7.2   Individual Bias................................... 214
    7.3   Practical Intelligence as Historical................ 216
    7.4   Group Bias...................................... 219
    7.5   Marx and the Cycles of History.................. 221
    7.6   General Bias and Historical Decline............... 227

       7.6.1 Preliminary Clarifications:
            Intellect and Will........................ 227
       7.6.2 General Bias and Decline.................. 233
       7.6.3 Sinful Man and Human Agency............. 236
  7.7 The Possibility for Reversal:
       History, Ethics and Religion..................... 239
       7.7.1 The Higher Viewpoint,
            Cosmopolis, and Moral
            Impotence............................... 239
       7.7.2 Religion and the Human
            Sciences: The Limits and
            Demands of Intelligence in
            the Face of Moral Impotence................ 242
       7.7.3 God's Love as the Wholly
            Transcendent Solution
            Operative Immanently in the
            Lives of Subjects......................... 248

EPILOGUE............................................... 263

BIBLIOGRAPHY......................................... 273

# ACKNOWLEDGEMENTS

Grateful acknowledgement is made to the following for permission to reprint selected passages from previously published material:

Harper & Row, Publishers, Inc.: from *Method in Theology*, by Bernard Lonergan, S.J., © 1972 by Bernard Lonergan. Reprinted with permission.

Philosophical Library, Inc., Publishers: from *Insight: A Study of Human Understanding*, by Bernard Lonergan, S.J., © 1957, 1958 by The Longman Group. Reprinted with permission.

University of Notre Dame Press: from *Randomness, Statistics and Emergence*, by Philip McShane, © 1970 by Philip McShane. Reprinted with permission.

*New Blackfriars*: from "Lonergan's Appropriation of the Concept of Praxis," *New Blackfriars* 62 (1981): 114-26, by Charles Davis, © Charles Davis. Reprinted with permission.

# Preface

While the major ethical crises of our age are forcing an unprecedented degree of interdisciplinary collaboration among human, social and natural scientists, there remains little agreement on a basic framework or on appropriate conceptual tools for such a collective task. Theoretical and ethical pluralism are the norm rather than the exception in the academy. But in the absence of an explanatory context for understanding the concrete meaning of this pluralism, specializations which were pursued in the name of disciplinary competence have become insurmountable obstacles to communication and cooperation towards the good of culture.

Among the more difficult of the problems arising within such interdisciplinary projects is the dispute over foundations and procedures for discovering ethical criteria for the guidance of society. This is so particularly in the fields of economic and political life. The quest for evidence in the empirically-based sciences has been carried out in opposition to the intrusion of more or less arbitrary preferences or "values" championed by ideologically biased interest groups. But in the absence of an agreed set of procedures for gathering and verifying evidence in the field of ethics, the relationship between scientific explanations and the direction of social, political and economic life remains a mystery.

This study proceeds with the conviction that the problems of interdisciplinarity and ethical foundations are interrelated. The crisis of pluralism in interdisciplinarity is not only a crisis of theories and methods in any given science. It is, perhaps more profoundly, a crisis in thinking the relationships among the sciences. This crisis comes to a dramatic point of focus in the debate over the relationship between "fact" and "value." Morality and ethics are a distinctively human enterprise. Consequently a "science" of moral life or moral action, if it is to have any force whatsoever in the shaping of contemporary culture, needs to be understood, in some way, in relation to the other sciences which explain our metabolism, our reproduction, our languages and our wars. The reader may react with caution suggesting that ethics differs *in kind* from the other sciences. But until a precise explanation of this *kind* of difference is forthcoming (an explanation which will need to appeal to some sort of empirical evidence on moral life) the problem of reasonable foundations for values remains in all of its complexity and import. For contemporary Western men and women are committed resolutely to differentiating good ideas from silly or destructive ideas on the basis of some appeal to evidence.

Clearly the full determination of a set of solutions to these problems remains the very goal of the many interdisciplinary projects currently underway. However prior to a theory, a verification procedure, or a research program stands a heuristic — a way of asking questions, a set of insights which preorganize the questions and the data, a signpost indicating where the data will lie, a clue concerning the tools for gathering data. It is the heuristic which is the explicit concern of this study. My intent throughout these chapters is to introduce a heuristic structure called emergent probability into this forum in interdisciplinary ethics. My direct effort will be to show how this heuristic structure can serve as a context for unifying explanatory theories in ethics and in the philosophy of history. But in so doing I will also suggest some possible lines of convergence with the natural sciences, particularly with the field of evolutionary theory.

Clearly this study operates on many fronts. However the principal goal which informs its structure is actually quite modest. Emergent probability was conceived by a Canadian-born philosopher-theologian, Bernard Lonergan, who had achieved some notoriety in theological circles, but whose work remains virtually unknown in the wider academic community. Lonergan's work in ethics has been taken up by a good number of moral theologians. But few have paid close attention to the links between this work in ethics, his writings on emergent probability, and his account of the dynamic structure of history. The route towards my treatment of the problems in interdisciplinarity and in ethical foundations will be an analysis of how emergent probability sets the hermeneutical context for Lonergan's ethical theory and his discussions on history. The relevant texts here are *Insight*, chapters six and eighteen and *Method in Theology*, chapter two for ethics, and *Insight*, chapters seven and twenty for the philosophy of history. While the immediate task throughout is interpretive, a presentation of the wider implications of emergent probability and some debate with alternate approaches to the issues under discussion accompany the exegesis and bring the field of questions beyond those of concern only to Lonergan scholars.

The chapters organize themselves according to the interpretive task. Chapters three and four are an exposition of emergent probability. Chapter five examines how emergent probability is at work in Lonergan's account of the structure of practical, moral action, and most particularly in his notions of essential and effective freedom. In chapter six some relevant prior questions in the field of the philosophy of history are discussed and emergent probability is introduced as a context in which history can be understood in terms of acts of meaning without falsifying the wealth of insights from psychology and sociology on "social structures." Finally the foundations of moral normativity are examined in relation to this explanatory sketch of the structure of historical process. Chapter seven carries the discussions in the philosophy of history into an outline of the dynamic structure of historical dialectics and an introduction to the problem of historical evil. Finally, to introduce the field of questions which emergent probability is developed to answer, the first introductory chapter discusses alternate views on the discipline of social ethics and the import of heuristic world views in social ethics. The second chapter treats the notions of determinism, indeterminism, chance, necessity, empirical knowledge, religion and tradition as they arise in two other thinkers, Immanuel Kant and Jacques Monod. My treatment of Kant and Monod relies on recognized authorities and is, of necessity, quite brief and introductory. Throughout the chapters I have tried to clarify Lonergan's insights by drawing upon reputable sources to compare and contrast his work with those of his critics and with those of other noted approaches.

Discussions of religion, theology, faith and God arise regularly throughout the pages of this study. It was Bernard Lonergan's conviction that while the sciences have been somewhat successful in carving out their own legitimate domain of competence, free from the intrusion of meddling theologians, they have also suffered from their interminable wars with religion. Neither the practitioners of religions nor the intellectuals in pursuit of answers to questions on ultimate reality have been successful in coming to grips with the scientific revolution. But neither have the scientists left room within their explanatory schemata for an intellectually serious appropriation of the insatiable religious hunger which dynamizes so much of human life. Consequently contemporary Western men and women are left divided in, among and about themselves. Lonergan's approach to the problem was to look to the very quest for truth which dynamizes the scientist as the evidence for a link which could unify science and religion. Thus, the problem of science and religion is conceived again as a problem of interdisciplinarity which is met with a heuristic structure, developed on the basis of some evidence on the side of the subject, and proposed as a new way of thinking the very nature of interdisciplinarity itself. The effort here has not been to answer a wide range of concrete questions in the fields of religion or theology; rather it has been to develop a way of thinking about science, ethics, politics and history in a way which is open to thinking and living the love of God and God's love for us.

These chapters have been cast with a view towards an audience familiar with the work of Bernard Lonergan. However chapters three and four, introducing emergent probability, can also be read by the patient, dedicated reader seeking an introduction either to Lonergan's work or to a novel heuristic for questions in evolutionary theory or science and religion. Those who seek a full understanding of Lonergan's work will need to supplement these chapters with some of the other items cited in the notes. However I have tried to include in these two chapters sufficient introductory material to trace the first stretches of a road which Lonergan invites us all to travel. Chapters five through seven are unintelligible apart from a thorough understanding of emergent probability. But the first two introductory chapters sketch a route towards emergent probability in a fashion which might be of some interest to philosophers and theologians in the fields of ethics and the philosophy of history.

Acknowledgments can only begin to recognize the debt which I owe to the countless men and women of Concordia University's Department of Theological Studies and Department of Religion, and St. Paul University's administration and Faculty of Theology. I am grateful for the extraordinary introduction to the work of Bernard Lonergan which I received from Dr. Sean McEvenue of Concordia University, Montréal, Dr. Philip McShane of Mount Saint Vincent University, Halifax, and Prof. Charles Davis of Concordia. It is difficult to imagine the course which my own intellectual development might have taken without their influence. I am indebted particularly to Prof. Charles Davis who was most influential directly from the planning stages of this study, through the research which followed, to the editing of draft materials. I thank Dr. Angelo Mingarelli of the University of Ottawa, Dr. Mark Doughty and Dr. Morris Shames of Concordia's Lonergan University College, Dr. James Pambrun of St. Paul University, Ottawa, Fr. Fred Crowe of Regis College, Toronto, and Messrs. Martin Hubbard and Jack Gammon of Ottawa for providing helpful criticisms. I appreciate the support and cooperation which I have received from Dr. Sean McEvenue in making available to me all the resources of Concordia's Lonergan University College. And Dr. Fred Crowe and Fr. Michael Shields were generous in assisting me in gaining access to the materials of the Regis College Lonergan Centre Library. I have received considerable direction at Concordia's Lonergan University College in living out the invitation extended by Lonergan. And I have received sustained example and encouragement from the faculty members of St. Paul University in taking religion seriously in an intellectually satisfying way. Finally I am pleased to thank my wife, Sandie, for her encouragement, support, her help and cooperation from the very outset. Without her this project would have been impossible.

I wish to thank the St. Paul University Research Centre and the Herbert Glassmacher Fund for their generous assistance in providing financial support towards the preparation of this book for publication.

Ottawa, August, 1986<br>
Kenneth R. Melchin

# Chapter 1

# Introduction

In April, 1968, an Italian industrial manager, Dr. Aurelio Peccei called together a group of thirty individuals from various international backgrounds in the sciences, in economics, in industry, in government and in other disciplines of the academy to discuss what came to be termed a *problématique*.[1] It had become increasingly clear to Dr. Peccei that a complex of interrelated sets of problems, international in scope, was beginning to threaten the present and future generations of mankind. The signs of the times included ever widening gaps between the world's rich and poor, rapidly diminishing resource bases, marked changes in the global ecosystem that foreshadowed deteriorating living conditions for future generations, and generally, an alarming interdependence among areas of life that were thought previously to be unrelated. Existing governments and international agencies lacked a sufficiently comprehensive understanding of such problems to formulate proper remedial policies. Nor did they have adequate means at their disposal to implement measures to control and guide the forces operative in the international economy and in the global ecosystem.

Following Dr. Peccei's April, 1968, gathering an informal organization called the Club of Rome was formed. Its goal would be to initiate research projects, to solicit research funding and to publicize studies and reports on this global complex of problems. And in the summer of 1970 Professor Jay Forrester of the Massachusetts Institute of Technology (M.I.T) presented to the Club of Rome a proposal for the Club's first research project on "The Predicament of Mankind." Forrester's proposal included a preliminary, theoretical model and a methodology for analysing the interaction among world systems. The basis for the model and the method was the computerized System Dynamics approach that had been developing at M.I.T. since 1957. Forrester proposed that a careful and comprehensive study of world systems according to the modeling techniques and the computer assisted analysis procedures of System Dynamics would yield a set of predictions and recommendations for global policy formation in the interest of present and future generations of mankind. The proposal that was prepared for that July, 1970, meeting with the Club of Rome (the world model that came to be known as World2) was published subsequently in a text entitled *World Dynamics*.[2]

The Club of Rome was sufficiently impressed with Forrester's methods and they arranged for Professor Dennis Meadows, a former student of Forrester's and a published researcher and scholar in the methods of System Dynamics, to direct the first phase of the project. Funding from the

Volkswagen Foundation supported the project and three books were published subsequently to present to the wider public the results of the team's research. *The Limits to Growth*, first published in 1972, was written for general readership. It presented the basic premises of the World2 and the subsequent World3 projects and summarized the conclusions derived from twelve initial computer simulation runs. *Toward Global Equilibrium: Collected Papers*[3] presented in some detail the ongoing work of the subsections of World3. And *The Dynamics of Growth in a Finite World*,[4] published in 1974, contains the complete detailed, technical description of the final version of the World3 model. With this third publication (and its subsequent contributions to the revised, second edition of *The Limits to Growth* in 1974) the Forrester-Meadows phase of the Club of Rome project ended.

But the project's conclusions sent shock waves throughout the world. *The Limits to Growth* was powerfully argued; it was translated into several languages and the first edition arrived on the scene immediately prior to the global agricultural and energy crises of 1973.[5] The conclusions from the first trial runs amounted to a prophecy of impending doom for the planet.[6] The authors of the project's first report were emphatic in their call for immediate and wide-sweeping policy changes to curb current rates of growth in all sectors of global life.[7]

In an effort to determine an appropriate set of policy guidelines for reversing the current trends the research team simulated the implementation of a series of sets of policy decisions between 1975 and the year 2000. They selected the policies whose results would be most favourable and their conclusions amounted to a set of minimum requirements for a permanent state of global equilibrium.[8]

The methods of the Forrester-Meadows project, their spectacular publication style, the timing of the first report and their gloomy predictions had the effect of associating a popular image of "doomsday prophecy" with the Club of Rome; an image which, in the words of Barry Hughes ''...largely still prevails [1980] even in the face of considerable diversity within the organization and subsequent reports to the body which differ markedly from the first.''[9] However, and perhaps much more significantly, the Forrester-Meadows project initiated a new type of world model and a new phase in the evolution of a "global management science" that promises to contribute to man's efforts in understanding and guiding his own destiny. The Forrester-Meadows model marked the beginning of a series of comprehensive, long-term global models integrating a multiplicity of world processes; economic, social, ecological and political. In his book, *World Modeling*, Barry Hughes lists more than five further global projects begun since 1972, that carry forward the enterprise initiated by Forrester and Meadows. In addition, he notes no less than six additional models more narrowly focused or less well documented, which continue to search for insights into the interrelations among sets of world processes. What might be termed a new discipline in world process studies began to emerge with the Club of Rome's first project; a discipline driven by a sense of alarming urgency and passionately committed to bringing together within a comprehensive theoretical framework the highly specialized fruits of the labours within a multiplicity of heretofore isolated disciplines.[10]

As a part of this proliferation of global scale models there has begun to emerge a field of literature dealing specifically with the theoretical, methodological and ethical problems involved in devising and applying models to public policymaking. This literature has become a forum for collaboration and discussion among evolutionary theorists in the physical and biological sciences, business and management science specialists, philosophers, engineers, mathematicians, computer scientists, political scientists, sociologists, anthropologists and ethicists.[11] Each group of experts is coming to understand that the most fundamental issues of their own discipline are relevant to the formation and implementation of global models and all understand that the future of the globe is, to one degree or another, at stake. In his book, *Models in the Policy Process*, Martin Greenberger raises some of these deeper issues associated with modeling procedures in general. His concern throughout the book is that models usually embrace sets of assumptions, implications and ideologies which are often not examined critically by modelers or policymakers and which can affect their results and predictions, often quite significantly. When model results are used in the formation of policies such implicit structural features of models can have the effect of shaping the course of policy. Greenberger's interest is in seeing that this impact be examined critically.

> It is not a question of whether models will be used in policymaking. They always have been in one manner or another. The real questions are how well they be used, in what form, for what purpose, within what organizational framework, and with what safeguards.[12]

Greenberger concludes that an institutionalized profession of third-party model analysts needs to be developed to provide a mediating and evaluating link between policy research and policymaking.

> Such analysis would be directed toward making sensitivity studies, identifying critical points, probing questionable assumptions, tracing policy conclusions, comprehending the effects of simulated policy changes, and simplifying complex models without distorting their key behavioral characteristics.[13]

In his analysis a critical, evaluative assessement of models is crucial for maintaining the responsibility of policymaking.

Greenberger's call for a profession or a discipline to mediate between policy research and policy formation echoes the concerns which occupied an American social ethicist, Gibson Winter, during the nineteen sixties. In his 1966 study of the role of social science in public policy, entitled *Elements for a Social Ethic*,[14] Winter proposed that an intermediary discipline which he called social ethics could come to the aid both of social science and of policy formation by making explicit the hypotheses of meaning and value that function implicitly in the theories and methods of various social scientific styles. In his analysis of three schools of sociology popular in North America during the nineteen fifties and sixties, Winter noted how each school or style had an implicit "ordering principle" which organized data on social phenomena. This ordering principle constituted a heuristic which guided the scientist through his or her inquiry and anticipated the form which the discoveries or analyses would take. Integrally related to this ordering principle was a notion of human fulfillment that was to be realized to some degree in the social order. Thus, according to Winter, some conception of the form or shape of human value was an integral part of the scientific theory or style. As the results of social scientific analyses set the basis for policy decisions on social issues, the conception of the structure of society and of human fulfillment implicit in that particular style of analysis became enshrined in the policy legislation. And as long as the ordering principle and the notion of human fulfillment remained implicit in the scientific style the values enshrined in the policies remained uncriticized and unappropriated. Winter conceived social ethics, or in his view religious social ethics,[15] as a discipline whose goal would be to ferret out the ordering principles and the evaluative aspects of scientific models so the values implicit in scientific analyses could be understood, assessed in terms of their adequacy, and then either rejected, modified or critically enshrined in the legislation.[16]

Winter's approach in *Elements* was to draw upon a number of fields of research in the social sciences and in philosophy to explain the relationship between personal, meaningful, responsible activity and the intersubjective bonds and relations which set the context for such personal activity and which are themselves transformed by it. His fourth and fifth chapters of *Elements* develop a fourth social scientific style which Winter proposes as a context within which the first three can be analysed. And to develop this fourth, intentionalist, style Winter drew upon a notion of intersubjectivity from Alfred Schütz, an insightful reconstruction of G. H. Mead's analysis of the structure of human sociality, an account of the self-transcending or intentional dynamism of embodied consciousness drawn from the work of M. Merleau-Ponty, and a development of the notions of "project" and "temporality" drawn from the works of Alfred Schütz and Edmund Husserl.

In Winter's view the ordering principle and the evaluative notions operative in the various social scientific styles were linked integrally to the styles' implicit notions of the relationship between human freedom and the determining contraints of social, historical processes. And to the extent that a style emphasized either the conditioned structure of human action, or the free, creative dimension of human responsibility, that style embodied a corresponding notion of social normativity. His effort in developing the fourth style was to understand human responsible sociality as embracing both the free and the conditioned dimensions.

As will become apparent in the pages here, central epistemological, ethical and religious issues concerning determinism, indeterminism, human freedom, human sociality, social order, human value, and historical progress and decline seem to arise in some of the discussions surrounding the modeling process.[17] Greenberger is not explicit in calling his model analysis discipline a social *ethics*. But his acute awareness of political biases, ideologies, theoretical presuppositions, and general assumptions operative in modeling theories and methods reflects Winter's concern for the normative import of theories in social science and their impact upon policy formation. Because of the interdisciplinary nature of the modeling process, model analysis raises the question of an overarching vision or notion of the structure of world processes, unifying natural, ecological processes with human social, economic and political processes. And such a vision or notion will include, either explicitly or tacitly, some notion of the relationship between human responsibility and social historical processes. Consequently, Gibson Winter's approach to social ethics could contribute significantly to the model analysis enterprise proposed by Greenberger.

The following study of Bernard Lonergan's "emergent probability" is offered as a contribution to this discipline of social ethics so conceived. My ultimate goal is to investigate and to help clarify the role that a rather novel explanatory heuristic can play in unifying natural and social scientific research. As we will see in the next chapter, the relevant issues and problem areas in the social sciences include a range of topics which, at first glance, do not appear to be the direct concern of the social ethicist. Questions about the "lawful" or "random" nature of world processes would appear to be more appropriately the concern of the philosopher of science. And yet these very questions, when asked of human, social and historical processes become questions about the nature and structure of human freedom and determinism; questions that have always concerned the ethicist. What Winter has shown is how social scientific analyses and policy research often contain implicit anticipations of the nature and limits of human freedom, of the locus of responsibility for social processes, and of the possibilities for social and historical change. While the literature analysing the theoretical, methodological and ethical aspects of world models has focussed some attention on such assumptions from the field of ethical theory, as they are relevant to policy research, there remain older fields of literature which have tried to analyse explicitly the nature of ethical foundations and the structure and dynamics of world and historical processes.[18] And so the route towards my ultimate goal will be an extended discussion of Lonergan's heuristic, "emergent probability" in the context of questions and concerns from the fields of ethics and the philosophy of history.

One of the greatest challenges that Meadows' and Forresters' work helped bring to light was the problem of how to think about human systems, social processes, historical dynamics in relation to evolutionary, ecological, physical and biological processes. It was this very concern for integrating an explanatory anticipation of the structure of human, social and historical processes into a wider heuristic reflecting the insights and the operative anticipations from the twentieth-century sciences that animated Bernard Lonergan's work in *Insight*. Lonergan understood that in order to handle adequately questions about the nature of human freedom, the structure and the range of human responsibility for society and history, the nature of intersubjectivity, or the foundations of moral normativity, a prior set of questions needed to be answered. When the sciences explain "reality" in terms of, for example, physical or chemical "laws," what is the meaning implied by the terms "reality" and "law?" It is generally understood that human life processes stand in some continuity with physical, chemical, botanical, zoological and animal psychological processes. What is the meaning of the term "continuity" here? Wherein lie the discontinuities? Lonergan's approach to these prior questions turned to the evidence from the contemporary natural sciences. But in line with Kant's "Copernican Revolution" his focus of attention was not principally upon the content of such sciences but upon the knowing process itself. And in continuity with the operative procedures in the sciences his concern was an empirical attention to the dynamic structure of the knowing operations in act. As we will see in the third and fourth chapters below, the result of this empirical inquiry was the discovery that science works with two distinct heuristic structures, the statistical and the classical, each with its own sets of anticipations. And so an integrated heuristic that would reflect the operative procedures and anticipations of the sciences would have to embrace both structures in a single world view. Lonergan calls this world view "emergent probability."

Emergent probability is an anticipation of the dynamic structure of the genesis, the operation and the transformation of world and human processes. In line with a determinist world view emergent probability admits the operation of recurrently operative laws and processes in which initial conditions and interrelated sets of events determine outcomes. But in contrast to the determinist view emergent probability also admits the fact of coincidentally converging sets of events and processes. Such coincidence is generally chance or random. And as will be discussed later in greater detail Lonergan understands this fact of randomness to play a key role in the structured dynamism of evolutionary emergence. What is most significant about emergent probability is that while Lonergan works out his principal terms and relations in dialogue with questions and issues from the natural sciences, the data upon which his work is based are fundamentally the human acts of knowing. And the evidence from this data would suggest that an isomorphic structure of the knowing and the known unifies the worlds of the natural and the human sciences.

It is my contention that emergent probability has a great deal to offer as a heuristic that could help unify the questions and anticipations of social and natural scientists working on research for policy formation. For emergent probability explains human freedom, human creativity, human responsibility as well as the realities of determining social, economic and historical structures in the terms and relations of a heuristic that is equally applicable to an explanation of natural evolutionary processes. In chapters five, six and seven, I explain how this heuristic is operative in Lonergan's sketches of the foundations of ethical theory, in *Insight* and *Method*, and in his sketch of the dynamic structure of history in *Insight*. But as I note in the introductory pages to these chapters, Lonergan's work in the areas of ethics and philosophy of history remain as introductory sketches and not complete theoretical treatments. Consequently the focus of my attention in these three chapters is upon the power of the heuristic, emergent probability, in clarifying the direction of Lonergan's intended meaning in his writings in these two areas. I have responded to some criticisms raised against Lonergan's work in these areas and I have discussed alternate approaches to the relevant issues in an effort to contribute to this clarification. I have no doubt that continuing research in ethics, in theories of history, and in world modeling will carry far beyond the initial clues presented here, and might conceivably reverse some of the positions worked out in these chapters. But I am equally convinced that only an integrated heuristic like emergent probability can provide the framework for such further research.

Since the focus of this study is upon the heuristic, emergent probability, chapters three and four begin by introducing the relevant terms and relations as they are developed from Lonergan's *Insight*, by Philip McShane, in his book *Randomness, Statistics and Emergence*.[20] This approach is followed here because McShane's presentation is worked out in conversation with other positions in the field of the philosophy of science. And while my study is not intended as a contribution to the philosophy of science, some of the questions and issues dealt with by McShane provide helpful clues and a fuller exposition of the basic insights. Chapter five is an introduction to emergent probability as it is operative in Lonergan's account of the dynamic structure of responsible moral and practical action. And here the power of this heuristic is manifested in Lonergan's account of human freedom, with its twofold structure of essential and effective freedom. In chapter six some relevant prior questions in the area of the philosophy of history are discussed and emergent probability is introduced as a context in which human history can be understood in terms of acts of meaning. Here Lonergan's notion of progress is presented as the foundation for a normative dynamism operative in history and as the foundation for the moral "ought" operative immanently in acts of moral responsibility. Chapter seven carries the discussions in the philosophy of history into a sketch of the dynamic structure of historical dialectics and an introduction to the problem of historical evil. Lonergan's solution to the problem of evil is a religious solution, wholly disproportionate to history but operative salvifically in history.

To provide an introductory context for understanding the specific nature of my concern for Lonergan's work I have summarized, quite briefly, in the second chapter, how two prominent thinkers, one from the late eighteenth century and one from the mid-twentieth century, have worked out explicit accounts of the relationship between the foundations of ethics and the dynamic structure of historical and evolutionary processes. My presentations of the works of Immanuel Kant and Jacques Monod are not intended as exhaustive analyses of their respective theories but as an introduction to a set of questions and issues that have animated my approach to Lonergan, and as an illustration of the far-reaching import of answers to questions in these fields. As should become clear the relationship between Kant, Monod and Lonergan is not purely extrinsic. For the questions that Lonergan sought to answer were questions that were set by the work of Kant and by some research upon which Monod drew. I have chosen these two thinkers because each in his own way has sought to meet the questions from historical or evolutionary theory and ethics with a single integrated explanation. To illustrate the import of issues from these two fields upon debates in world modeling I have included a brief discussion of the notion of "progress" as a prelude to this introduction to Kant and Monod. But before launching into these analyses I would like to situate Gibson Winter's approach to the discipline of social ethics within a field of alternate approaches.

## 1.1 Social Ethics: Various Conceptions of the Discipline

Winter's vision of the discipline, social ethics, by no means represents a consensus view among those who call themselves social ethicists. Recent contributions to the field of social ethics, especially from North American Christian ethicists who have attempted to rethink the foundations of their own religious traditions in the face of contemporary social problems, have reflected widely diverging conceptions of the nature, the scope, the methods, and the tools of social ethics. In 1972, Ralph B. Potter, Jr. tried to render some order out of this chaos by listing what he saw to be the various aspects of an extremely broad view of social ethics which was proposed by Walter Muelder.[21] He pointed out the dangers in conceiving the discipline along these broad lines and then formulated a narrower account of the responsibilities of the social ethicist. Potter invites the social ethicist to attend to areas of disagreement or controversy occurring in the lives of people engaged in working out moral problems in the social sphere of life and to help focus that attention Potter lists four distinct areas of disagreement that could conceivably separate participants in such debates. Disagreement can arise from "alternate readings of the empirical facts of the situation." They can also be "rooted in the 'facts' of the non-empirical theological or quasi-theological realm which determines the wider context of understanding within which men define and ponder their options." A third source of disagreement can be the differences of "fundamental loyalties of disputants." And the fourth potential obstacle to agreement Potter calls the "mode of ethical reasoning." Potter recommends that social ethics restrict its enterprise to the analysis of this fourth area of potential disagreement. And in so doing Potter feels that the discipline could make an essential contribution to mediating disputes on policy issues.

Potter's publication elicited considerable response, both favorable and critical, and in October, 1974, the American Academy of Religion sponsored a Religious Social Ethics Group to study the issues raised by Potter. The results of this original meeting of the Group were a set of six papers revised for publication in the Spring, 1977 issue of *The Journal of Religious Ethics*. Of the six published response essays, only James Childress' is written in the spirit of Potter's proposal. William Everett does not accept explicitly Potter's fourfold categorization of the areas of potential disagreement. But he does address the issue of loyalties and societal commitments of the ethicist as a central problem in "the ethics of ethics."[22] Glen Stassen does an analysis of Potter's four areas of potential disagreement and argues that this proposal itself reflects implicitly a social theory of ethical discourse. Stassen proposes that social ethics should not restrict itself to the analysis of one structural element in one particular ethical or social theory. Rather, social ethics should analyse and evaluate all the relevant elements of various social and ethical theories.

> Religious social ethics works at the theory level, including social and ethical theory, and seeks to relate the ground-of-meaning dimension to more particular levels of judgment.[23]

Stassen's proposal bears some similarity to Winter's view of the field.

Two contributors, Joseph Hough, Jr., and Richard R. Roach, explicitly reject Potter's proposal that social ethics restrict its role to analysing sources of disagreement in issue and policy debates. Their conviction is that social ethics should be "critical advocacy." In the face of a strong conservative tendency in contemporary American churches, Hough urges that Christian social ethics must assume the responsibility for a "relentless advocacy of ethical positions on matters of public policy based on Christian theological criteria," and for a "participation by the ethicists in action oriented toward specific change goals." Roach carries this first recommendation forward with a laudatory analysis of the social goals advocated by some liberation theologians and a critique of their efforts to achieve these goals.[24]

The essays in this set of responses to Ralph Potter can be understood as examples from one of two broad ways of conceiving the enterprise of social ethics. One might name this normative or prescriptive social ethics. For each of the contributors seeks to participate, in some way, in the responsible direction and construction of society. Potter and Childress want to clarify the moral reasoning in debates over policy issues. Everett wants to study the interests of the participants in such debates. Stassen wants to understand the import of social theories in the analysis of the structure of the social and policy decision-making process. And Hough and Roach want to advocate and scrutinize critically positions in the debate. What all have in common is a preoccupation with values and norms as they are operative in shaping and directing society and the contemporary processes in which such shaping takes place. All are interested in the human person as morally responsible for society.

There exists a second way of conceiving social ethics that might be called a descriptive ethics.[25] And whereas the first social ethics asks how the individual can and ought to participate in shaping society this second asks how the society has already shaped morality and the individual. The contributions of Everett, Stassen and, as we shall see below, Pitcher and Winter, reflect a considerable influence from this second social ethics. Gibson Winter notes in his first chapter of *Elements* that the nineteenth-century human sciences emerged as an effort to seek a scientific (and thus legitimate) foundation for social order in an analysis of the "laws" governing social processes.[26] And so in its genesis, social ethics "two" arose as a part of social ethics "one." But as a result of the technical nature of the contributions from the social sciences this second enterprise quickly became a discipline in its own right, though seldom isolated completely from social ethics "one." Contemporary studies in this second conception of the discipline include analyses of extant theories of the sociology of moral life (Ossowska), studies of the import of bodily symbols in constituting notions of social order and social process (Douglas), and more comprehensive analyses of the role that concrete religious and ethical symbols play in reflecting, constituting and transforming cultural life (Geertz). Lawrence Kohlberg has built upon the foundations of Jean Piaget to provide evidence of stages of moral development that cut across cultures. And Jürgen Habermas has sought to integrate Kohlberg's findings into an account of social evolution.[27] While the data bases of these works differ considerably they share a common concern for regularities, patterns, structures that are operative in the genesis, the function and the transformation of moral norms in and across cultures.

Gibson Winter's response to the essay of Ralph Potter was written in collaboration with Alvin Pitcher. And here he restates a more refined formulation of his view of social ethics as a critical mediator between the implicitly lived symbols and values that inform the ordinary life of a people (ethos) and the policies that seek to embody and reflect this ethos.

> Religious social ethics reflects upon the character and source of the ethos of a society, upon the relation of the ethos to public policy, and upon the practices of institutions and persons in the light of the policies and ethos of the society.[28]

Winter and Pitcher can be understood as seeking to bring some of the contributions from social ethics "two" into social ethics "one." Their analysis of the role of paradigmatic views of the structure of ethos in ethical inquiry reflects the attitude of social ethics "two," a descriptive concern for patterns or structures operative in the moral and religious life of cultures. But their direct concern is with making such patterns explicit so that they may be scrutinized critically in the policy-making and the reflective practice of a society.

However, Winter's and Pitcher's descriptive concern has a particular focus to it. Their interest is in the way in which paradigmatic views of the structure of ethos are operative in social scientific theories when such theories are implemented in research for policy.

> In our view, what is essential is a determination of the underlying meaning or structure of a historical situation. However, such a determination cannot be made without attention to the present historical development; and thus it requires some appropriation of descriptions of the present historical situation from the social sciences. There is no simple way to appropriate the social sciences, since each description presupposes a way of looking at reality. Without an assessment of these presuppositions, the descriptive materials of the social sciences become covert prescriptions which determine ethical judgments.[29]

And so their view of social ethics can be understood as a bridge between social ethics "one" and "two," with a remote concern for social policy and a direct concern for heuristics operative in descriptive science that shape implicitly the course of policy.

My own appreciation of Winter's vision of the discipline of social ethics[30] is rooted, fundamentally, in my respect for Winter's grasp of the heuristic function of theories in empirical inquiry. As I will argue in the following chapters, Bernard Lonergan has explained how knowledge is always the answer to a question. Questions intend ranges of possible answers, they suggest the evidence that would verify or refute the answers and they set forth the structure of the explanation and its proof. Because of the synthetic or creative nature of the insight, knowing is not necessarily locked into the determining constraints of available questions. And horizon shifts occur when direct and inverse insights give rise to whole new sets of questions. Theories are integrated sets of insights (more or less probably verified) and questions. When the questions and insights are about man, society and history, the theories both suggest and delimit ranges of possibilities about what man does, what he or she can do, and what he or she ought to do. However one understands the relation between these descriptive and these normative notions, such suggestions and delimitations remain the legitimate concern of the ethicist.[31]

A growing number of people working in the various branches of the social sciences are becoming attentive to this role that normative notions and notions of the nature and limits of human freedom and responsibility play in the social sciences. In his *New Rules of Sociological Method*, Anthony Giddens seeks to give an account of the enterprise of sociology which recognizes that "[t]he production of society is brought about by the active constituting skills of its members, but draws upon resources, and depends upon conditions, of which they are unaware or which they perceive only dimly."[32] In contrast to other schools of sociology which tend to overemphasize either the socially determined character of human action or the autonomy of individual agency, Giddens founds his proposal for the method of sociology on an account of what could be called the intersubjectively conditioned structure of human freedom and responsibility. In the field of economics, Irving Kristol has drawn attention to concrete values which are explicit in the classical economic theory of Adam Smith and to other values which are operative explicitly or implicitly in the three main schools of thought currently in vogue. In the field of world modeling, C. West Churchman and Heinz Von Foerster both advocate the importance of the value of the unique individual person in a theory or method of managing complex systems.[33] Whether or not one agrees with the particular conclusions of any of these authors their very preoccupation with the import of ethical concerns in social theories and methods is evidence that Winter's proposal for a social ethics is already in practice to some extent in the various sciences themselves. With the growing awareness, particularly in the modeling field, that such ethical concerns have a considerable impact on public policies when social scientific analyses become the basis for policies, the need for Winter's form of social ethical analysis becomes more acute. Winter's and Greenberger's call for an independent discipline merely asks that this type of reflection itself become methodologically self-conscious and rigorous.

In this study I do not carry Lonergan's heuristic emergent probability into a concrete analysis of social scientific theories and methods. Such an analysis must be left to an additional study. My principal goal here is to make explicit the heuristic structure operative in Lonergan's account of ethical action, its social, historical locus and import, and its relation to the dynamic structure of history. But just as Winter proposed his intentionalist style as a context for understanding other styles, I would suggest that emergent probability can help in unifying the questions and anticipations in the natural and social sciences. And my responses to criticisms of Lonergan and to alternate approaches are intended as suggested lines along which further dialectical analyses might proceed.

In the field of world modeling or futures research one of the more conspicuous ways in which normative notions are operative in scientific theories and explanations is in the various authors' implicit or explicit assessments of the meaning, the value, the likelihood, the possibilities and the means for securing human progress. To suggest that some social, historical present or future constitutes some form of progress is to imply that, barring the complete irrelevance or impotence of moral action for history, persons are morally bound, in some way, to continue or to begin to participate in effecting this progress. In a historical age which understands itself historically, any social, historical or evolutionary theory will inevitably raise (and will usually suggest some answer to) the question as to whether or not the present constitutes some qualified form of progress. And in this way such theories or explanations usually contain some implicit or explicit normative notions. To argue for complete moral impotence or the complete irrelevance of moral action for history is to engage directly in ethical theory. And so a brief introduction to a number of discussions in the field of world modeling on this notion of progress should serve to illustrate how ethical issues link together with theories and explanations in science in the form of more or less explicitly differentiated world views or philosophies of history.

## *1.2 The Question of Progress and the Relevance of World Views*

Greenberger classifies the responses to *The Limits to Growth* into four groups and he notes how each group differs in its grounds for optimism or pessimism in the face of evidence that growing population, pollution, famine, resource depletion, and overcrowding threaten to overtake the earth's fixed carrying capacity.[34] The first group, which he calls the "Malthusian-pessimists," include Forrester and Meadows. And their reaction appeals to some evidence that continued technological improvements will not keep up to the rates of growth. By the time the crises begin to occur the time for corrective response will have been passed. "Technological-optimists," on the other hand "...feel that technology will continue to evolve fast enough to keep pace with the problems of burgeoning population, pollution, and resource depletion."[35] "Economic-optimists" agree with the "technological-optimists" that rates of technological achievements will keep up with growth crises. But their convictions lie rooted in the economic theory that links technological incentives to economic growth. Crises associated with growth processes are linked, in their view, to flaws in the price system which result in benefits accrued or burdens incurred without the proper payment of costs. The fourth group, "the confrontationists," do not see economic growth as either good or evil, in itself, but approach the evidence and the analyses with a view toward determining which growths could be sustained and which would create problems requiring a response (either in the form of a technological corrective or a policy legislating growth reduction.)

In an article which takes the form of a fictitious conversation between proponents of an optimistic and a pessimistic world view, Richard O. Mason argues that *a priori* paradigms or world views are operative in the field of responses to this issue of growth.[36] And what divides the two participants in Mason's conversation are opposing assessments of the goodness of our recent history of technological control over the world. Mason's point is that the classes of responses to *The Limits to Growth* are not rooted, fundamentally, in a verifiable appeal to facts, but in a set of assumptions implicitly operative in the person's own world view; a world view which is seldom clearly understood and appropriated by the individual him-or herself. Furthermore, in Mason's view, "...there is no sure method to guarantee that the assumptions are correct."[37] The positions expressed in the two world views are summarized, briefly, in the concluding statements of the two characters.

*Adam*: Your plea is eloquent, Bud, but on the basis of the data and this debate I can only conclude that our past land-use policy has not been that bad. With intelligent planning for the future, and with effective world models, man will be able to make better use of earth resources and to continue his dominion over nature. The future of man is assured if he follows this approach.

*Bud*: No, Adam, from the debate one must conclude that our land-use policy has been disastrous. Man must stop thinking in terms of his dominion over the earth and begin to consider his moral obligation to all of creation. He must strive for harmony and ecological balance among all species and things. The hope of world models is that they may provide some insights as to how to accomplish this. Man's survival hangs in the balance. The future of man is *not* assured. It is in great jeopardy. We must adopt a new approach.[38]

Mason's illustration focuses on opposed evaluations of recent efforts to manage the globe through technology and on the differences separating a growth-oriented view from an equilibrium-oriented view. And his point throughout seems to be to affirm the value of a care for the whole of creation; a care that seems to have been lost in a growing "techno-rationalist" preoccupation with environmental "control and domination." However, Mason's sketch also conceals a more profound agreement between the two conversationalists. While the two characters differ in their assessments of the means and measures that would constitute human responsibility for ecology and history, both remain convinced that man can, and indeed must implement responsible measures towards shaping his future. Both are convinced that the course of this future which would follow upon such responsibility is, indeed progress.

*Bud*: Conservation is humanity caring for the future, Adam, not technology and cost/effectiveness. This must become the age of man's service to man. Personal service can continue to grow with a static population and without destroying nature. . . . The alert mind of the future must pay close attention to every state of the body, feeling and mind and attempt to place them in eternal harmony with the environment. This will require reflection and concentration. But the rewards are worth it. It is in this way we will find the infinity and pleasure we seek.[39]

Like the four schools of respondents to *The Limits to Growth* summarized by Greenberger, both of Mason's world views take for granted some vision of progress and some measure of moral obligation and moral potency to participate in and promote this course of historical progress.

A more apt contrast to the views put forward by Mason's Adam might have been the vision of *The Human Prospect* put forward in 1974 by Robert L. Heilbroner.[40] After a summary introduction to current trends in population growth, resource shortages, weapons proliferation, income distribution and climatic changes Heilbroner argues that a short run as well as a long range transformational problem faces mankind, a problem of devising and implementing the necessary political measures and institutions for reversing the current trends. Heilbroner asks whether human nature has a history of meeting such global scale moral challenges. And his answer is that the historical evidence would suggest moral impotence.

There seems no hope for rapid changes in the human character traits that would have to be modified to bring about a peaceful, organized reorientation of life styles.[41]

In view of such moral impotence, the most likely scenario, in Heilbroner's view, is a period of "convulsive change" in which a succession of wars, environmental disasters, crop failures, resource shortages slow down current rates of growth and "...give a necessary impetus to the piece-meal construction of an ecologically and socially viable social system."[42] Thus nature accomplishes what man is unable to do and a long term era of post-industrial, low consumption, highly traditional, communally organized civilization is ushered in. Heilbroner is explicit in insisting that his is not a utopian vision of some secure haven of tradition and stability. While his speculations touch upon some of the virtues in such a future his scenario is not even a qualified vision of progress. And the chances for securing some measure of progress will be lost irretrievably because of a decisive flaw in man's moral nature.[43]

What comes into sharp focus in this contrast between the more optimistic responses to Meadows' and Forrester's question about growth and the gloomier prognosis of Robert Heilbroner is the integral relationship between each author's or each character's view of the nature, the limits and the foundations of moral responsibility and their notions of the structure and outcome of history. Mason's Adam is convinced both that the inevitable orientation of history is towards progress and that moral responsibility consists in participating in this progress through current forms of technological mastery over nature and society. Bud is not convinced that progress is inevitable but he remains confident of some measure of moral power to effect historical progress. And the exercise of such moral responsibility for history consists in reversing certain trends in industry, technology and society. Heilbroner, on the other hand, holds no hope for historical progress. And his despair is rooted in his conviction that (a) man is morally impotent in social and political affairs, and (b) his moral action (or inaction) remains a decisive element in determining the outcome of history. One could add to this list of alternative views a position which held that moral action makes no difference whatsoever to the course of history.

While these views on the possibilities and the route towards progress appear as clear and simple alternatives, in fact their apparent simplicity conceals a complex nest of religious and philosophical questions which have plagued men and women through the centuries. How does human freedom mark a departure from "natural" processes? How can human moral actions shape the course of history? Do historical events reveal a structured course or a trend towards a goal or *telos*? How is this future or goal orientation possible in a universe of "cause and effect?" Is the foundation of the moral norm related to any dynamic structure that might be operative in history? Do contemporary events mark a continuity with or a discontinuity from any normative dynamism that might be operative in history? Do morality and/or history stand in relation to a wider, absolutely or relatively transcendent explanatory context? Could such a context be, in fact, true? The history of past and recent attempts to work out answers to such questions is a history of subtle and sophisticated thought, and of careful as well as imaginative appeal to the arguments and the evidence of the time. And many of these attempts have included, to one degree or another, some reflection on the explanation process itself. What could count as evidence? What is the status of knowledge on such matters? What are the appropriate procedures for knowing? Richard Mason suggests that answers to questions of this nature generally take the form of *a priori* world views, sets of assumptions which are not open to verification.[44] But the following chapter presents samples from this rich body of thought that are at once sophisticated examples of appeals to argument and evidence in support of world views, and at the same time more or less careful accounts of the nature and structure of the knowing process. And so this introduction to two great thinkers is offered as a contribution to this quest for evidence and criteria in support of an adequate contemporary world view.

My specific focus of attention in presenting Kant and Monod will be on how each functions with a distinctive set of questions and concerns which function heuristically to anticipate ranges of possible answers and to designate what could possibly count as evidence or argument for supporting such answers. I have chosen these thinkers because each integrates an ethics into a philosophy of history or an evolutionary theory and each highlights a distinctive and essential aspect of the operation of an explanatory heuristic. I would argue that the contribution of each needs to be a part of an explanatory heuristic which would be adequate to the challenges that arise in contemporary social ethics.

In the succeeding chapters my concern with the work of Bernard Lonergan has this same focus on the structure and operation of a heuristic which gives rise to questions, designates the fields of data and, thus, anticipates the structure, direction and scope of explanatory theories. It will become apparent that I am convinced of the novelty and the importance of Lonergan's contributions in this area. And so my treatment of Lonergan's ethics and his philosophy of history has the single goal of showing how the two are unified in their common foundations in emergent probability. My concern with Kant and Monod, then, is as an introduction to my subsequent chapters on Lonergan's emergent probability; an introduction to the import and operation of an explanatory heuristic and an introduction to some essential elements that are expressly integrated in Lonergan's emergent probability. To experts in the work of Kant or Monod I must apologize for oversimplifications which have been made in accordance with the constraints of time and purpose.

## FOOTNOTES - CHAPTER 1

1. For historical background information on the Club of Rome and the World3 model, see Donella H. Meadows, Dennis L. Meadows, Jørgen Randers, and William Behrens III, *The Limits to Growth*, second edition (New York: New American Library, Signet, 1974), pp. vii-xii; Barry B. Hughes, *World Modeling* (Lexington, Mass.: Lexington Books, 1980), pp. 1-2; Martin Greenberger, Matthew A. Crenson, Brian L. Crissey, *Models in the Policy Process* (New York: Russell Sage Foundation, 1976), pp. 1-7.
2. Jay W. Forrester, *World Dynamics*, second edition (Cambridge, Mass.: Wright-Allen Press, Inc., 1973).
3. Dennis L. Meadows, Donella H. Meadows, eds., *Toward Global Equilibrium: Collected Papers* (Cambridge, Mass.: Wright-Allen Press, Inc., 1973).
4. Dennis L. Meadows, William W. Behrens III, Donella H. Meadows, Roger F. Naill, Jørgen Randers, Erich K. O. Zahn, *Dynamics of Growth in a Finite World* (Cambridge, Mass.: Wright-Allen Press, Inc., 1974).
5. Hughes, p. 1.
6. Meadows, *The Limits to Growth*, p. 175.
7. Ibid., pp. 187-8.
8. Ibid., pp. 178-9.
9. Hughes, p. 2.
10. See Hughes, pp. 8-12; Richard O. Mason, "The Search for a World Model," in *World Modeling: A Dialogue*, eds. C. West Churchman, Richard O. Mason (Amsterdam: North Holland, 1976), pp. 1-2; Christopher Freeman, "Malthus with a Computer," in *Thinking About the Future*, eds. H. S. D. Cole, Christopher Freeman, Marie Jahoda, K. L. R. Pavitt (London: Chatto & Windus for Sussex University Press, 1973), pp. 5-6; Arthur S. Boughey, *Strategy for Survival* (Menlo Park, Calif.: W. A. Benjamin, Inc., 1976), p. x. Greenberger makes it clear that the history of modeling dates back to the nineteen twenties and thirties and that the second world war accelerated the development of models and modeling methods, pp. 85-140. So the modeling process itself is much older than World3. Furthermore, Forrester's was not the first global scale model. An econometric model, project LINK, was begun in 1968 to link together existing regional economic models, see Hughes, pp. 8-9. However, the Forrester-Meadows work was the first in a series of global models that sought to integrate social, ecological, political, as well as economic process. On the importance of these modeling projects for stimulating interdisciplinary collaboration, see Freeman, p. 6.
11. See, for example, Hughes, Greenberger, Cole, Churchman and Mason, Boughey. Hughes lists a number of model review texts, pp. 7-8. See also William Burch, Jr. and F. Herbert Bormann, eds., *Beyond Growth: Essays on Alternative Futures. Yale University: School of Forestry and Environmental Studies Bulletin No. 88* (New Haven: Yale University, 1975); Solomon Encel, Pauline K. Marstrand, William Page, eds., *The Art of Anticipation* (London: Martin Robertson, 1975); Jib Fowles, ed., *Handbook of Futures Research* (Westport, Conn.: Greenwood Press, 1978); E. Jantsch and C.H. Waddington, F.R.S., eds., *Evolution and Consciousness* (Reading, Mass.: Addison-Wesley, 1976); H. A. Linstone and W. H. Clive Simmonds, eds., *Futures Research: New Directions* (Reading, Mass.: Addison-Wesley, 1977); C. H. Waddington, F.R.S., *Tools for Thought* (New York: Basic Books, 1977). Clearly this list is only a beginning.
12. Greenberger, pp. 340-1.
13. Ibid., p. 339.
14. Gibson Winter, *Elements for a Social Ethic* (New York: Macmillan, 1966) (hereafter this work will be cited as *Elements*).
15. In Winter's view, ethics is distinguished from ideology in terms of its broader, ultimate horizon or perspective. Ideology takes for granted the given cultural norms of personal and social fulfillment. Ethics questions this cultural horizon in the light of a

transcendent or ultimate perspective, ibid., p. 67. Religion is defined as "embracing man's ultimate concern for being," p. 277n. So in Winter's view, ethical concern inevitably opens onto religious ultimacy, "ethical discernment is religious in the profoundest meaning of religion," p. 277. This view of the relationship between religion and ethics or between Christianity and ethics is by no means a consensus view among scholars. See, for example, Gene Outka and John P. Reeder, Jr., eds., *Religion and Morality* (Garden City, N. Y.: Doubleday, Anchor Press, 1973); Charles E. Curran and Richard A. McCormick, S.J., eds., *Readings in Moral Theology*, no. 2: *The Distinctiveness of Christian Ethics* (New York: Paulist Press, 1980). For reasons which I discuss in greater detail, in chapter two, 2.3.2, and in chapter seven, 7.7 below, I would agree with Winter on this use of the term "religion."

16  In another essay Winter charts the recent development of social ethics in North America in terms of the shift from relatively stable social forms to rapidly changing societies, and in terms of the separation of ethics from the social sciences as the nineteenth-century sciences of man sought scientific status. In Winter's view the result of this separation was not that human science rid itself of an ethical or normative concern. Rather, ethics merely became an implicit element in social science. And so Winter sees his own work in *Elements* as a contribution to a recent effort to discover this normative element which has become implicit in social science, to reinstate an explicit ethical analysis of social processes, and thus to reunify ethics with social science. See "Introduction: Religion, Ethics, and Society," in *Social Ethics: Issues in Ethics and Society*, edited by G. Winter (London: SCM Press, 1968; New York: Harper & Row, 1968), pp. 3-6. On Winter's view of social ethics as an intermediary discipline between social science and policy, see also B. Lonergan, "The Example of Gibson Winter," in *A Second Collection* (London: Darton, Longman & Todd, 1974), pp. 189-192.

17  See 1.2, below.

18  While literature in the respective areas of ethics and the philosophy of history abounds, to my knowledge a comprehensive treatise on the relationship of ethical theories to world views or philosophies of history has not been written. Alasdair MacIntyre's study of ethical theories since the Enlightenment touches upon some of the relevant issues in ethics, *After Virtue* (Notre Dame: University of Notre Dame Press, 1981). The works of J. B. Bury, Robert Nisbet and Sidney Pollard on the notion of progress contain, implicitly, histories of normative notions in relation to philosophies of history; J. B. Bury, *The Idea of Progress* (New York: Dover Publications, 1955; orig. 1932); Robert Nisbet, *History of the Idea of Progress* (New York: Basic Books, 1980); Sidney Pollard, *The Idea of Progress* (Harmondsworth: Penguin Books, 1971). Detailed studies on the ethics-philosophy of history relationship have been done on individual thinkers. See, for example, Michel Despland, *Kant on History and Religion* (Montreal: McGill-Queens University Press, 1973); Yirmiahu Yovel, *Kant and the Philosophy of History* (Princeton: Princeton University Press, 1980); Eugene Kamenka, *The Ethical Foundations of Marxism* (London: Routledge and Kegan Paul, 1962). Kai Nielsen and Steven C. Patten, eds., *Marx and Morality: Canadian Journal of Philosophy*, supplementary volume VII (Guelph, Ont.: Canadian Association for Publishing in Philosophy, 1981). For an excellent example of a contemporary attempt to integrate an ethics with a theory of history, see Jürgen Habermas, *Communication and the Evolution of Society*, translated by Thomas McCarthy (Boston: Beacon Press, 1979).

19  Bernard J. F. Lonergan, *Insight: A Study of Human Understanding*, revised students edition (New York: Philosophical Library; London: Darton, Longman and Todd, 1958) (hereafter cited as *Insight*); *Method in Theology* (New York: Herder and Herder, 1972) (hereafter cited as *Method*).

20  Philip McShane, *Randomness, Statistics and Emergence* (Dublin: Gill and Macmillan, 1970) (hereafter cited as *Randomness*).

21  Ralph B. Potter, Jr., "The Logic of Moral Argument," in *Toward a Discipline of Social Ethics*, ed. Paul Deats, Jr. (Boston: Boston University Press, 1972), pp. 93-114. Potter's article responds to a proposal of Walter Muelder in *Moral Law in Christian Social Ethics*, see particularly p. 20, cited in Potter, p. 95.
22  See Glen H. Stassen, "Editorial Notes," *Journal of Religious Ethics* 5 (1977): 1-7; James F. Childress, "The Identification of Ethical Principles," *Journal of Religious Ethics* 5 (1977): 40; William W. Everett, "Vocation and Location: An Exploration in the Ethics of Ethics," *Journal of Religious Ethics* 5 (1977): 106.
23  Glen H. Stassen, "A Social Theory Model for Religious Social Ethics," *Journal of Religious Ethics* 5 (1977): 22.
24  Joseph C. Hough, Jr., "Christian Social Ethics as Advocacy," *Journal of Religious Ethics* 5 (1977): 123; Richard R. Roach, S.J., "A New Sense of Faith," *Journal of Religious Ethics* 5 (1977): 136.
25  Maria Ossowska makes this distinction between normative and descriptive studies of social morality in *Social Determinants of Moral Ideas* (Philadelphia: University of Pennsylvania Press, 1970), pp. 6-26. Fundamentally, I would say, the distinction can be understood in terms of Lonergan's third and fourth levels of conscious intentionality. The third level includes intentional activities that are oriented towards judgments of fact and, thus, towards knowledge of something which has already occurred. The fourth level includes activities that are oriented towards a distinct object, a decision to act to realize a future which has yet to occur. While third level intentionality can come to know values which have been held and which have been realized in past actions, it is on fourth level intentionality that subjects must evaluate the actions and the values of the past in the course of deliberating on future actions. See *Method*, chap. 1, particularly p. 9.
26  *Elements*, pp. 3-7.
27  See Ossowska; Mary Douglas, *Natural Symbols* (New York: Random House, Pantheon Books, 1970); Clifford Geertz, *The Interpretation of Cultures* (New York: Basic Books, 1973); Lawrence Kohlberg, *Essays on Moral Development*, vol. I: *The Philosophy of Moral Development* (New York: Harper & Row, 1981), particularly chap. one, "Indoctrination Versus Relativity in Value Education," pp. 6-28; Jürgen Habermas, "Moral Development and Ego Identity," and "Historical Materialism and the Development of Normative Structures," in *Communication and the Evolution of Society*, pp. 67-129.
28  Alvin Pitcher and Gibson Winter, "Perspectives in Religious Social Ethics," *Journal of Religious Ethics* 5 (1977): 70. Clifford Geertz's use of the term "ethos" reflects an intent similar to that of Winter, "Ethos, World View, and the Analysis of Sacred Symbols," in *The Interpretation of Cultures*, pp. 126-7.
29  Pitcher and Winter, p. 70. Here Winter and Pitcher illustrate well how Bernard Lonergan's "functional specialty," "history," leads on to the "functional specialty," "dialectics," in two distinct manners. Not only does an analysis of the past and the present lead to the question of values upon which to build a future, and provide materials for its answer. But such an analysis also leads one to question the values that were reflected implicitly in the theories and methods employed in the analysis. See *Method*, pp. 125-6, 128-30, 235-266, particularly 248-9. See also Lonergan, "The Example of Gibson Winter." The "functional specialties" are distinguished and interrelated as different levels of "conscious intentionality." See note 25 above.
30  Winter's contributions to social ethics have changed slightly from *Elements*, and his 1977 article with Pitcher. In *Elements*, his goal was to discover and assess the foundational and normative views of man and society that were operative in various social scientific styles. In his most recent work, *Liberating Creation* (New York: Crossroad, 1981), his goal is to discover and assess such foundations and norms as they are reflected in "the religious heritage of the West," pp. xiii-xiv. For an account of this transition

as it began to take shape in the articles after *Elements*, see K. R. Melchin, "Gibson Winter on Ethics and Social Science: 'Elements' and Four Later Articles," *Gnosis* (Concordia University, Montréal), vol. 2, no. 2 (Spring 1981): 51-64.

31  While a radical distinction (dating back to the work of Kant) has been maintained in most philosophical circles between descriptive and normative statements, the following chapters should illustrate how such a distinction is not principally a question of statements but, more fundamentally one of types of cognitional acts. In addition, while it has been maintained that an "ought" can never be derived from an "is," the chapters below should indicate how the matter is not quite so simple. See also Kai Nielsen, "Introduction," in Nielsen and Patten, eds., *Marx and Morality*, pp. 1-17; L. Kohlberg, "From 'Is' to 'Ought': How to Commit the Naturalistic Fallacy and Get Away With It in the Study of Moral Development," in *The Philosophy of Moral Development*, pp. 101-189, particularly pp. 178ff; Walter Conn, *Conscience: Development and Self-Transcendence* (Birmingham, Alabama: Religious Education Press, 1981), pp. 214-15; Jürgen Habermas, "Toward a Reconstruction of Historical Materialism," in *Communication and the Evolution of Society*, pp. 175-77. In each case what is exhibited is evidence of an "ought" operative in the very act of performance and in the growth dynamic toward competence and authenticity. Thus, while in Lonergan's terms, truth of fact and true value are the intentional terms of third and fourth level intentional acts, it is the immanent norm (ought) which is the criterion of "objectivity" in both cases. See also 6.6, below.

32  Anthony Giddens, *New Rules of Sociological Method* (London: Hutchinson, 1976), pp. 156-162.

33  Irving Kristol, "Rationalism in Economics," in *The Crisis in Economic Theory*, edited by Daniel Bell and Irving Kristol (New York: Basic Books, 1981), pp. 201-218; C. West Churchman, "A Philosophy for Complexity," in Linstone and Simmonds, eds., *Futures Research*, pp. 82-90; Heinz Von Foerster, "The Curious Behaviour of Complex Systems: Lessons From Biology," in ibid., pp. 104-113. See also Harold A. Linstone and W. H. Clive Simmonds, "Epilogue," in ibid., pp. 262-3; and Denis J. Loveridge, "Values and Futures," in ibid., pp. 53-64.

34  Greenberger, pp. 166-170.

35  Ibid., p. 167.

36  Richard O. Mason, "A World Issue Debate: On Assumptions Underlying World Models," in Churchman and Mason, eds., *World Modeling*, p. 97.

37  Ibid.

38  Ibid., p. 106.

39  Ibid., pp. 105-6.

40  Robert L. Heilbroner, *An Inquiry Into the Human Prospect* (New York: W. W. Norton & Company, Inc., 1975).

41  Ibid., p. 131.

42  Ibid., pp. 132-3.

43  Ibid., pp. 127-144, particularly pp. 130-132. While Heilbroner rejects the prospects of progress, his analysis reveals another structure operative throughout world process, that of a dialectic of forces moving to equilibrium to ensure survival. A further study of Heilbroner would need to ask why Heilbroner believes that this "convulsive change" period should result in the human race's survival rather that its extinction. For a brief introduction to this discussion see chap. seven, 7.7.2 below.

44  Mason, "A World Issue Debate," p. 97.

# Chapter 2

# Ethics and the Philosophy of History

## 2.1 Immanuel Kant

Kant's ethical writings are well known. The champion of the autonomous, rational subject, Kant saw the exercise of practical reason as the sole bastion against a chaos of emotional excess and empirical ambiguity. But what is not so widely known is that Kant sought continually to integrate his moral philosophy into a wider philosophy of history. Four of the essays that are published in L.W. Beck's edited collection, *On History*, were written during the same years that Kant was writing and publishing the *Groundwork of the Metaphysic of Morals* and the *Critique of Practical Reason* (1784-1788).[1] And in the view of Michel Despland the moral and theological problem of theodicy lies at the very heart of Kant's philosophy of history.[2] Kant was explicit in understanding humanity and human moral action within the wider view of a teleology of nature and history.[3] Robert Nisbet argues that in spite of the "many antagonistic elements in Kant's thought," he remained as preoccupied as his contemporaries with the idea of progress.[4] Those who are at home in the world of a "teleological," a "utilitarian," or a "natural law" ethical tradition might be delighted to hear that Kant's austere call for a purely rational, formal commitment to the principle of duty was itself situated within a history oriented towards a *summum bonum*. But Kant was a subtle thinker dedicated to reconciling the distinctively human self-constituting structure of practical reason with a broader structure of natural and historical events. And if some contemporary commentators regard his attempts as unsuccessful his work remains, nonetheless, a brilliant effort at reconciling the problems of the continuities and discontinuities between nature and reason, the problems of contingency and necessity, the problems of moral freedom and historical determinism.

The foundations of Kant's moral philosophy are laid out in the *Groundwork of the Metaphysic of Morals*.[5] In the view of H. J. Paton, Kant's aim is to set forth a secure basis for moral activity that can avoid the ambiguities of an appeal to empirical experience and liberate man from the constraints of natural inclination.[6] The first principle of these foundations is the unqualified, autonomous goodness of the good will. For only the good will is always and everywhere good irrespective of its circumstances and its object.[7]

What does the good will will? It wills to act in accordance with duty, but for no reason other than the sake of duty itself.

An action done from duty has its moral worth, *not in the purpose* to be attained by it, but in the maxim in accordance with which it is decided upon; it depends therefore, not on the realization of the object of the action, but solely on the *principle* of *volition* in accordance with which, irrespective of all objects of the faculty of desire, the action has been performed.[8]

And *"Duty is the necessity to act out of reverence for the law."*[9] In the analysis of Paton this notion of law is the purely formal demand of universalizable reason which remains binding irrespective of individual desires and inclinations. The reverence which the reasonable person feels for the law is "a unique feeling which is due, not to any stimulus of the senses, but to the thought that my will is subordinated to such a universal law independently of any influence of sense."[10]

What is the universal law which commands this respect? It is the categorical imperative. "I ought never to act except in such a way *that I can also will that my maxim should become a universal law.*"[11] As distinct from a hypothetical imperative which determines an action as practically necessary as a means to attaining an end, the categorical imperative calls for an action "... as objectively necessary in itself apart from its relation to a further end."[12] Thus Kant sets out what he understands to be a pure ethics in which reason authors its own laws completely *a priori*, in which the sovereign authority of these laws is derived from nothing other than this *a priori* character, in which the influence of natural inclination or convention is completely circumvented, and in which the principle of action is liberated from "... all influence by contingent grounds, the only kind that experience can supply."[13] This much we learn about Kant's ethics from an introductory course in moral philosophy.

What is less widely known about Kant's ethic is his grounds for establishing the reasonableness of accepting this unqualified, autonomous goodness of the good will as the only appropriate moral foundation for a rational creature.

> In the natural constitution of an organic being — that is, of one contrived for the purpose of life — let us take it as a principle that in it no organ is to be found for any end unless it is also the most appropriate to that end and the best fitted for it. Suppose now that for a being possessed of reason and a will the real purpose of nature were his *preservation*, his *welfare*, or in a word his *happiness*.[14]

Kant proceeds to argue that were this the case nature would have made a grievous mistake. For while natural instinct would have proven competent to secure for man this goal of happiness, reason, in fact, has proven itself to be remarkably inept. Since nature only ordains an organ or faculty to perform what it alone can best perform and since reason remains man's lot in life there must therefore remain

> ... another and much more worthy purpose of existence, for which, and not for happiness, reason is quite properly designed, and to which,

therefore, as a supreme condition the private purposes of man must for the most part be subordinated.[15]

Thus the true function of reason must be to produce a will that is good in itself.

... and for this function reason was absolutely necessary in a world where nature, in distributing her aptitudes, has everywhere else gone to work in a purposive manner.[16]

Carl Becker has argued that the eighteenth century French *philosophes* shared far less of our contemporary world view than popular opinion would lead one to imagine. And he makes a case that their lives and their work were securely planted within the medieval world of natural order and natural purpose.[17] The same can be said of Kant.[18] Michel Despland shows how Kant's view of a teleologically organized cosmos rooted in Aristotelian finality is evident in his first publication, *The General History of Nature and Theory of the Heavens* (1755). In this early stage Kant was evidently aware of the problematical character of *human* development. But it was not until he felt the full impact of Newton and Rousseau (1764) that Kant faced the question of the discontinuity between "the mechanical world of nature and causality" and "the moral world of man, where the notions of human freedom and human destiny assume a central place."[19] In Despland's view this encounter with Newton and Rousseau marked the beginnings of "an original philosophy of history and nature," in which the teleology of nature assumes a distinct form and the autonomous act of reason in moral freedom becomes the central element in the progression of history towards its natural end.[20]

Despland shows that Kant's writings on history indicate that he understood human history as having a structure in which something like a process of social evolution progresses through five stages, and in which the energy dynamizing this evolution is the tension between man's nature and his free will.[21] The first stage, the life of instinct, is pre-political, pre-rational, pre-historical. But the second stage, the age of cultural freedom, witnesses the entry of freedom and rational autonomy. Imagination presents appetites and ends distinct from natural instincts and thereby upsets the spontaneous ordination of world processes towards their natural ends. Wars break out as the result of clashes among the various aims of men and among these aims and natural instincts. In the third stage, the stage of the civil state, the growth of mutual discipline motivated by fear and self-interest begins to secure the possibility for social organization on the basis of laws. As reason begins to curb the excesses of sense and imagination there emerges the possibility for refinement and the arts. This is the age of enlightenment, the beginning of the end to war. It is Kant's age. But before a final peace, wars among nations will "prepare the way for a rule of law governing the freedom of states," in a fourth state of the cosmopolitan republic.[22] A league of nations will unify disparate states on a moral basis. And in the final stage perfect peace is achieved in a moral commonwealth in which all men are moral and legislation and enforcement become superfluous. In the reign of practical reason all ends are mutually compatible.[23]

While nature is governed by the operation of mechanical laws, history is the progressive triumph of freedom from natural necessity. And so while history like nature has an end or a purpose, the goal of a civil union among men, this orientation is in no way a natural necessity. But this raises the fundamental question of freedom and determinism.

> Either freedom is independent of teleological or mechanical necessity and there is no connection between the two, and it is nonsense to speak of a plan of Nature working towards freedom; or freedom is necessitated and hence is not freedom.[24]

Despland turns to Fackenheim for the answer here. Nature poses the problem and man answers it in freedom or dies. Man's perfection can only lie in that which he has created through his own distinctive capacities of reason and freedom (i.e. morality). And so nature could never subvert this purpose and still remain true to itself. But what nature does is to create sufficiently tumultuous responses to man's misuse of freedom that man is forced, not by internal necessity of law, but by rational response to natural situations, to seek his highest good.[25]

The limitations of time and purpose permit only a very brief sketch of Kant's thought, and the Kant scholar will note countless potential if not actual difficulties in this presentation. I can only respond by insisting that my principal goal here is not an analysis of the thought of Kant but an introduction to a set of questions. But even this brief sketch should suffice to show how Kant's life's work was dedicated to integrating a coherent and comprehensive theory of moral action into a philosophy of nature and history.

In the view of Yirmiahu Yovel the key to this integration is Kant's rather novel notion of teleology which differs from the medieval or Aristotelian notion in its focus on the dynamic, changing, developing character of man and his civilizations.[26] Kant's Copernican Revolution placed man at the centre of the universe both as actively constituting agent of knowledge of the universe and, more profoundly, as shaper of the universe through the exercise of practical reason.[27] In the act of knowing the universe, the reflective judgment of purpose — the teleologically structured explanation which understands world processes as oriented towards the fulfillment of purposes or ends — is an essential means for our constitution of coherent, rational explanations of natural and human processes in the areas of esthetics, the organic world, the methodology of science, and empirical history. This reflective judgment does not determine the ontology of the objects of knowledge, as do the categories of the understanding, but they determine, *a priori*, our intersubjective response, our ways of relating to certain classes of objects of experience.[28] In the field of empirical history the sense of purpose which emerges in our study of historical events and which renders rational and coherent our explanation of history, involves the "cunning of nature" — the corrective effects of wars, conflicts, inequalities, self-interest that are discussed above. And this "cunning of nature" operates, in our explanation, to orient the collective exercise of rational human freedom and autonomy towards "the highest good."[29]

But when this reflective judgment of purpose is applied in empirical history a strange correspondence emerges which serves to link the teleology of history with the purely rational, autonomous structure of practical reason. In the sphere of personal morality, the starting point for Kant's ethics was a radical discontinuity between the experiential field of natural desires, and the distinctively human field of the moral will. Thus to ask that man be rationally moral is to raise the further question whether this moral action leads to man's happiness. Kant's answer here is to argue that the object of moral action, "the highest good," is a synthesis of the supreme (*supremum*) good of the rational will and the total (*consummatum*) good, the satisfaction of natural inclination in happiness. The form of the synthesis retains the priority of the categorical imperative of the autonomous rational will and allows man to hope, indeed expect, happiness, not as an end for whose achievement practical reason is a means, but as a correlative historical result accruing to the morally worthy by virtue of the immanent order of things, and guaranteed by God.[30] The principle of "the highest good," thus, becomes the content of that moral nature which man is charged with creating through the exercise of free will. And as a universal purpose or *telos* for all men this principle becomes the regulative idea that guides men through the social, political, legislative, educational spheres of objective moral praxis and serves to unify the realms of nature and freedom in that distinctive teleology that is human history. In the empirical history of human moral praxis the teleology of the rational will and the reflective judgment of purpose in historical explanations harmonize beautifully into a single developmental course of historical evolution.[31] Natural laws with their mechanistic structure of antecedent causes continue to reign in nature, but man's distinctive *telos*, "the highest good," becomes operative in the whole of history as he projects this end upon the course of events in his explanations and in his moral praxis, thus bringing natural laws into the service of history's teleology.[32]

The concern throughout Kant's work in ethics and history is to explain the radical discontinuity between the human order of rationality and morality, wherein actions and events result from the self-regulating, self-constituting action of the autonomous human subject, and the mechanical world of natural causation wherein events are the outcomes of antecedent conditions and necessary laws.[33] Only the self-regulating activity of human reason allows the operation of a teleological or goal-oriented structure of events. For only the autonomously self-actuating capacity of reason can liberate the events of world process from the iron laws of mechanistic determinism.

Linked to this resolute insistence upon the self-constituting autonomy of human reason is Kant's complete repudiation of the legitimacy of any appeal to empirical experience in an account of the foundations of morality or in a moral subject's justification of a concrete value or course of action. Humean empiricism had convinced Kant that an appeal to experience can never yield certain knowledge. Any knowledge which is in any way reliable can only be so by virtue of an *a priori* set of conditions that are universally and necessarily fulfilled by the mind itself.[34] Consequently in Kant's view reason marks a twofold departure from nature inasmuch as reason alone can grasp the necessity in natural processes and at the same time can liberate itself from such necessity by operating reflexively to determine itself in accordance with its own immanent structure.

The fundamental question, then, with which Kant wrestles in his work on ethics and history is the question of the nature and operation of necessary laws. The very problem which set Kant on the road towards his first *Critique* was Hume's argument demonstrating the empirical unverifiability of the necessity of causal relations. Hume inferred that such empirical unverifiability uprooted all knowledge.[35] And instead of questioning the conceptual status of Hume's notion of necessity Kant chose to accept this notion and Hume's demand for necessity and to show how knowing, therefore, must *not* consist entirely of experience.[36] Thus Kant finds the "synthetic a priori" judgment to fill the condition of necessity in knowing.[37] And in natural science the *a priori* concept which yields the necessary connection between antecedent causes and results in physical laws, the modality necessity, is held to be a part of the structure of the mind itself.[38] Consequently, known reality comes to consist of two parts, experience and the categories supplied by the mind.[39]

However, having established how the structure of known physical reality could operate in accordance with necessary laws, Kant faced two problems. First, if natural processes functioned according to mechanical laws in which *antecedent* determinants yield necessary outcomes, then how do you explain the apparent fact that nature as well as history seems to be oriented towards realizing *future* ends or goals? Second, and more significantly, if mechanical *necessity* is the structure of nature, then how do you explain human *freedom*, human moral responsibility, which seems to be characterized precisely by the absence of such determinism? Kant's response to these two problems was brilliant. The liberation from mechanistic determinism lies in reflexively operative self-constitution. And thus the emergence of mind, the moment of radical departure from natural processes, fulfills the conditions for human subjects, first, to project ends or goals into explanations of natural and historical processes, and, second, to order or regulate their own actions in accordance with the immanent structure of mind and, thus, to move the course of history towards a progressively refining vision of such goals. The ensuing course of history is a set of oscillations between nature's conditions and man's responses. And as man refines his own understanding of self and history and progresses in the exercise of practical reason the responses follow more quickly and more accurately upon each situation.

Kant's anticipation of historical progress, then, is rooted in the single normative dynamism of practical reason. The course of history has a structure to it and the stages of history progress in accordance with the progression of collective moral responsibility. This is not a smooth progression for the responses of nature are more or less violent in forcing man dialectically towards collective moral virtue. Human freedom marks a radical departure from natural process, for only mind can operate to order itself and the processes under its control in accordance with its own immanent structure. And it is this reflexive self-constituting structure which is the condition of possibility for teleological or goal-oriented processes to emerge in a natural world of deterministic laws. Into this scheme of history God enters as a postulate of mind whose existence and operation is judged necessary to guarantee that moral action be possible and bear fruit in history.[40]

While Kant's work is infinitely subtle and ingenious, Yovel argues that a fundamental dualism inherent in Kant's dissociation of reason from the empirical world results in what he calls a *historical antinomy*.[41] Kant's complete repudiation of experiential life and natural appetite as a foundation for morality leaves man divided in himself. Man is

> ... a dual creature, belonging at once to opposite worlds, man is torn in his very existence. His natural will has one object, his rational will quite another.[42]

To be true to his own objectives Kant must make the object of the moral will a unification of the two systems, the natural and the empirical. But at the same time this object must be a purely rational object in itself. As a historical succession of events the actual results or outcomes from man's decisions to act in accordance with the categorical imperative are anticipated, by Kant, to fulfill, in fact, man's natural appetite for happiness. And this concrete historical fulfillment is an integral part of the object of the moral will, the *summum bonum*. But this concrete history is itself a part of the concrete empirical history of reason and thus a matter for empirical knowledge. To determine whether such a history is, in fact, the case Kant must either appeal to knowledge of the empirical facts of history or he must postulate a necessary condition, God, which would guarantee that this be the case. Since empirical knowledge of history cannot constitute a part of a foundational ethical system, Kant chose the latter. And in assigning God an indispensable place in his moral system Kant subverted the very Copernican revolution which he sought to bring about. For reason can no longer supply all the required conditions for knowledge, morality and the realization of historical progress.⁴³ As Yovel notes, Kant could not take seriously the question whether

> ... nature, following its own mechanical laws, is primordially such that it cannot lend itself to moral reshaping by man, but must frustrate and negate any such attempt? The basic rules of the critical system cannot preclude this possibility, since it is they themselves which establish it.⁴⁴

And were Kant to face this question his contentless notion of God could supply nothing towards its answer.⁴⁵

I would argue that the root of this problem of dualism in Kant's system lies in the way in which he responded to Hume's demand for some foundation for the "necessity" of causal relations. Yovel situates the origins for Kant's dualism in his quest for "...necessary and universal foundations for knowledge and ethics."⁴⁶ Man's spontaneous sense perceptions and his natural appetites and desires

> ... are particular and contingent elements, which cannot of themselves provide a rational — that is, a necessary and universal — basis for knowledge and action.⁴⁷

And so Kant had to look to a transcendental faculty in man which could supply this necessity and universality by "... subordinating the empirical constituents to its own *a priori* rules."⁴⁸ The result was an *"external reunification of the heterogeneous."*⁴⁹ I would suggest that Kant's flaw was in anticipating necessity and universality as a something-to-be-explained. As we will see below, a significant contribution of Lonergan's work has been to distinguish in knowing (and thus in its correlate, the known) the direct from the inverse insight, the intelligibility from the absence of intelligibility. Hume was right in noting that experience alone cannot yield knowledge of necessity. And Kant was right in concluding that knowing must be "something more" than experience. But by "something more" Kant anticipated knowing to involve an *addition* to experience. And in anticipating necessity as an additional something-to-be-explained Kant looked to the structure of the mind for the source of an intelligible component of the known, the something-to-be-explained, which experience cannot supply. Consequently knowing, and its correlate the known, comes to consist of two parts.

Lonergan meets the problem of necessity with an inverse insight. Empirical necessity is not an additional something-to-be-explained. Rather, it is merely the inertial identity of a concrete intelligible unity or the inertial operation of system, given the fulfilling conditions and the absence of intervening conditions. The necessity of scientific laws is not the unqualified necessity of an absolutely unconditioned but the factual necessity of the virtually unconditioned, the conditioned whose conditions have been fulfilled. While knowing is "something more" than experience it does not involve the addition of something to experience which is not already immanent in experience. Knowing is the (probable) cognitional genesis of the intelligibility which in fact *is reality*. And what knowing does is to sort out and to order appropriately concrete systematic from non-systematic relations. Kant's heuristic did not include any significant role for the non-systematic relation or its subjective correlate, the inverse insight. And so he was forced to anticipate and to explain knowing as supplying an additional (illusory) presence instead of as converting an aggregate into an ordered set of relations (converting an unknown into a known).

While Kant's point of departure, the quest for the foundations of natural *necessity*, leads him to repudiate the reliability of *experiential knowledge* as a solid foundation for an ethics, Jacques Monod looks to the *experiential evidence* of modern biology for a repudiation of natural *necessity* in a quest for an "ethic of knowledge" which conceives man (not unlike Kant) as standing heroically discontinuous from the natural order. And so a brief introduction to Monod is in order.

## 2.2 Jacques Monod

In 1970, Jacques Monod published his essay, *Le hasard et la nécessité: essai sur la philosophie naturelle de la biologie moderne*. In spite of the book's technical complexity, it was extremely popular and became the publishing success of the year.[50] The English translation, *Chance and Necessity*, appeared in 1971 and by 1972 it was widely available in paperback.[51] A biologist, a professor at the Collège de France, the founder of the Institut Pasteur, and a Nobel laureate in physiology and medicine, Jacques Monod sets out to prove, on the basis of a detailed appeal to the most recent discoveries in the field of biology, that man, in continuity with biological evolution, marks a radical discontinuity from the overall structure of universal cosmic processes. For the very origins of teleonomic or purposive processes are purely and simply a matter of blind, mindless chance. His implications for ethics and society, drawn in his last chapter, are that humanity's heroic glory consists in our facing the ultimate irrationality and hostility of the cosmos, recognizing that our hunger for the security of a purposive universe is vain, and founding our life and culture upon an austere ethic which refuses any basis other than the truth of scientific knowledge. Thus, like Kant, Monod champions humanity's daring, our courage, our defiance of tradition and the cosmos in exercising our most precious skill, knowing, to chart for ourselves a road which departs significantly from the overall course of the universe. But unlike Kant, Monod's starting point is the absolute reliability of empirical knowledge which seeks verification in an appeal to experiential evidence. And unlike Kant, Monod's ethics does not unite (or reunite) man to the universe. Rather, it admits that such a unification is a vain hope. For the universe is blind.

Monod's world view is not principally a philosophy of history. Rather, it is a generalized explanation of man and history which is extrapolated from an account of the structure of biological evolution. Monod's principal adversaries in this extrapolation are what he calls the *vitalist* or *animist* theories which seek to explain the apparent fact of teleonomic or purposive structures in biology by appealing to a distinct, unified, primary, goal-oriented principle, universally operative in "living matter" (vitalism), or in the whole cosmos (animism), from which evolutionary ontogeny, invariance and direction are derived, and which is not open to scientific scrutiny or falsifiability.[52] According to Monod, the very cornerstone of all scientific method is the "principle of objectivity,"

> ... the *systematic* denial that "true" knowledge can be got at by interpreting phenomena in terms of final causes — that is to say, of "purpose."[53]

I think we can say that for Monod this "principle of objectivity" means both that any explanation of the universe, man or history which is worth accepting must now meet the demands of scientific explanation and that scientific explanation cannot tolerate the introduction of any principle for which it cannot marshall some experiential evidence and some conceivable (more or less effective or operable) experimental verification procedures.[54] In Monod's view the vitalist or animist teleonomic principles are wholly *a priori*, beyond the range of scientific inquiry, and thus would be radically foreign additions to the scene of universal processes. They are thus repugnant to all who hold to the scientific world view. And three centuries of developing civilization have committed themselves implicitly to this world view.[55] Consequently the difficulty which remains is to explain the apparent fact of teleonomic processes without violating this "principle of objectivity."

The core of Monod's argument is worked out in chapters three through six in an in-depth analysis of the catalytic function of proteins, the structure of their regulatory functions, the epigenesis of complex structures through random or spontaneous associations and bonding stability, and the invariance and chance mutational characteristics of DNA. His analysis aims to show how contemporary biology and biochemistry have sufficient evidence to prove that teleonomic processes in living beings can, and indeed must, be explained as following on and derivative from the more fundamental properties of autonomous morphogenesis (spontaneous structuration) and reproductive invariance.[56] Thus, since autonomous morphogenesis and reproductive invariance involve no contradictions of the laws of physics but rather can be explained completely in terms of physical laws, the derivative principle, teleonomy, need involve no violation of the "principle of objectivity."[57]

The central elements in the teleonomic structure of biological processes are protein molecules. The process of metabolism (the growth and multiplication process of all organisms) consists of a large number of accurately regulated chemical reactions, linked together in complex sequences, along "a great number of divergent, convergent, or cyclical 'pathways'."[58] One particular class of protein, the enzymes, regulates all of these chemical reactions by acting as a highly selective and specific catalyst. In this cybernetically interrelated complex of processes these protein molecules regulate the various reactions by responding with a high degree of specificity to the chemical presence of the intermediate or terminal products of one or more chemical reaction sequences. Thus these regulatory proteins function to maintain a specific pattern of coherence among the reactions. This complex combination of internal reactions, in the presence of specific environmental conditions, results in the spontaneous self-construction of macroscopic structures. And the twofold key to the protein molecule's ability to maintain this channelling activity, to assure coherent functioning, and to allow this self-construction is (1) the molecule's "stereospecific" properties, and (2) the properties of covalent and noncovalent bonding.[59]

(1) Stereospecificity.

All these teleonomic performances rest, in the final analysis, upon the proteins' so-called "stereospecific" properties, that is to say upon their ability to "recognize" other molecules (including other proteins) by their *shape*, this shape being determined by their molecular structure. At work here is, quite literally, a microscopic discriminative (if not "cognitive") faculty.[60]

Proteins can be classified, on the basis of their overall shape, into two types. The "fibrous" proteins are elongated molecules which tend to play only a mechanical role in living beings. The "globular" proteins, on the other hand, are made up of long and complex linear sequences of smaller molecules, amino acids, which fold in upon themselves to form compact, pseudo-globular shapes. Each of the globular proteins is identified by the particular sequence of amino acids in its chain. And each sequence folds into one and only one characteristic shape (with a few exceptions). It is the characteristic shape of each globular protein which accounts for its highly selective catalytic capacity. The complexity of the molecule's shape results in it presenting only one (or a small number of) region(s) active for bonding. This active spot will itself have a characteristic shape, and will thus respond only to another molecule whose bonding area matches the shape of the protein's. This shape specificity is so precise that an enzyme protein will catalyze only one type of reaction, and only one of the various compounds which could undergo that type of reaction. Thus in a region where thousands of compounds are present the enzyme will have the effect of "seeking out" one and only one compound and catalyzing one and only one reaction involving this compound.

(2) Covalent and Noncovalent Bonding. Whereas covalent bonds involve the sharing of electron orbitals between two or more atoms, noncovalent bonds involve no such sharing. The most significant effects of this difference

are a difference in stability between covalent and noncovalent chemical structures and, more important, a difference in the "activation" energies of reactions involving the two types of structures. In reactions with a high activation energy the mere proximity of the two or more constituent compounds is insufficient to condition the reaction's immediate occurrence. For the atoms in the compound need to take up, momentarily, unstable bonding arrangements in order to allow the subsequent bonding to follow. This requires an initial input of energy. This energy is subsequently given off in the reaction itself as the reaction proceeds to a final stable state. But the course of the reaction will have an intermediate, high energy state to which the reaction must be raised if it is to take place or if it is to be reversed or modified in a subsequent reaction. The function of a catalyst (such as an enzyme protein) is to "stabilize" this intermediate, activated state and thus to lower the potential energy difference between this and the initial state. Thus under the appropriate conditions the presence of the catalyst is sufficient to condition the immediate occurrence of a reaction which would otherwise take place much more slowly if at all.

Now the significant difference between covalent and noncovalent bonds is the fact that covalent bonds have a considerably higher activation energy. Noncovalent reactions, on the other hand, occur spontaneously and rapidly at low temperatures in the absence of catalysts. Thus noncovalent reactions normally are unstable for they are reversed as easily as they are formed. A certain stability can be achieved, however, if the reaction involves multiple noncovalent interactions. In this case, though, the molecules involved need to be complementary in their *shape*. For noncovalent bonds can acquire the necessary energy for activation only if the two molecules are in close proximity, virtually touching each other, *at each bonding site*; thus the molecule's stereospecificity.

While enzymes catalyze, and thus regulate, covalent reactions, they nonetheless are able to form noncovalent, stereospecific (shape specific) bonding reactions with the principal substance in these reactions (the substrate). Since this enzyme-substrate complex which is formed remains noncovalently bonded, the enzyme can usually disengage relatively easily from the substrate to allow the reaction to proceed once the catalytic function has been accomplished. Thus the enzymatic reaction involves two steps: the formation of the stereospecific complex (enzyme-substrate), and the catalytic activation of the reaction with the substrate. But because the enzyme-substrate complex is noncovalently bonded and formed only between molecules of complementary shape, there results the potential for a threefold specificity in reactions involving globular proteins. (1) An enzyme will "seek out" and form a stereospecific complex with one and only one substrate; the one with the proper shape. (2) The formation of the stereospecific complex results in the substrate being presented or positioned in a specific way to allow only a small range of possible reactions to follow. (3) Depending on the number of noncovalent bonds involved in the enzyme-substrate complex — when a large number of noncovalent bonds are involved the complex achieves the stability of a covalent association — the relative stability of the complex results in an additional propensity or resistance to subsequent reactions of specific types, and thus a further specificity.

In Monod's view it is these two properties of stereospecificity and noncovalent bonding that make possible the elective discrimination of living things, their ability to pass on an extremely complex body of "information." It is this information-transfer capacity that explains the regulatory function of proteins in complex systems, the spontaneous ontogenesis of such systems, and the invariance and mutational properties of macro-level systems.

Enzymes operate to regulate the occurrence or non-occurrence of specific reactions and to coordinate the pattern or coherence of interactions among a number of reactions. And they do so by virtue of their ability to respond (stereospecifically) to the presence of one or more other compounds whose presence has the effect of heightening or inhibiting the catalytic effect of the enzyme with respect to the substrate. When this other compound is the end-product of a chain of reactions which the enzyme's catalysis initiates, then the resultant regulatory structure is a feedback activation or a feedback inhibition loop. When this other compound is the end-product of a parallel or a previous reaction or reaction-chain the resultant regulatory structure is a linking function, connecting and regulating the occurrence of one reaction-chain in accordance with the performance of another. When this compound is the substrate itself then the activation of a reaction-chain is heightened by the effect of the initial enzyme.[61] Most usually a number of modes of regulation are involved to coordinate the functioning of a number of reaction-chains. The presence of a number of compounds can have the effect of regulating a branching in a number of chains of reactions at a number of distinct locations along the various branches. And in this way a number of weak chemical variations in a complex system of branching chains can have the effect of regulating, in an extremely precise way, the pattern or order in a system of reactions involving much greater energy transfers.[62] A further regulating function is accomplished by some proteins' ability to undergo discrete changes in shape. Such changes in shape will result in changes in its regulating function. And so a kind of threshold effect can be achieved as the activity of a population of molecules will vary in proportion to the relative concentrations of the compounds (ligands) to which the protein responds in its two states and in proportion to the state of equilibrium between the two states.[63] All of these regulatory effects occur as a result of the stereospecific and noncovalent bonding properties of protein molecules.

The dramatic consequence of the structure of these various regulating functions, according to Monod, is that there need be no chemical relationship whatsoever between a complex system of reactions and the origins of the processes which regulate it. Fundamentally it is the protein's shape which gives it its regulatory power. And the chemical processes which determine its shape are chemically foreign and indifferent to the reactions which it regulates. To this chemical independence between an enzyme's function and the controls governing it Monod applies the term *gratuity*. It is this gratuitous or *arbitrary* relationship which breaks the chain of causation, allows an organism both to obey physical laws as well as to transcend them, and fulfills the conditions for the autonomous self-determination of living things. For given this independence between the processes which "inform" an enzyme's behaviour and the processes which it regulates, selection will occur spontaneously as certain patterns of "information" confer a heightened degree of coherence and stability on the organism in accordance with the demands of the physiological environment.[64]

In his fifth chapter Monod explains how this gratuitous or arbitrary relationship between the processes determining a protein's shape and the processes which it controls figures into the teleonomic structure of autonomous morphogenesis at the macroscopic level. And in the sixth chapter he shows how the same mechanisms are operative in the invariance and mutational characteristics of DNA. In both cases Monod's point is to argue that at the root of both molecular ontogenesis and genetic mutation is the element of chance or randomness. In his last three chapters he draws out what he believes to be the necessary implications of this phenomenon of chance for evolutionary theory, for human history and society, and for ethics.

The epigenesis of complex biological structures occurs through the spontaneous association of smaller subunits. And the only necessary conditions for the occurrence and for the variety of forms of such structuration are the stereospecificity of proteins and the random intermingling of a large array of subunits. Consequently Monod asks how the globular protein comes to take on its specific shape and why this shape is stable. The fact is that while a particular globular protein is defined in terms of a unique sequence of amino acids in a long chain, that chain could conceivably fold into a large number of possible globular shapes. But it doesn't! Rather, each sequence folds into one and only one shape (or in some cases a small number of shapes). Monod explains this folding process in terms of the "hydrophobic" properties of about one-half of the amino acids which make up the chain. Like oil in water, these amino acids tend to collect together, expelling water molecules, seeking the most compact shape, and at the same time bonding noncovalently to stabilize this shape.

> Among the many different folded shapes accessible to a given polypeptide sequence only a very few, if not just one, will permit realization of the most compact possible structure. This structure will therefore be favored over all others. Simplifying a little, we may say that the

"chosen" structure will be the one corresponding to the expulsion of the maximum number of water molecules.⁶⁵
Consequently the only significant determinant of the protein's shape will be the order or sequence of amino acids in the chain. And since the amount of "information" required to determine the molecule's shape is far larger than the amount needed to specify the amino acid sequence, the folding process results in a significant "information enrichment"; the amount of "information" that a protein can pass on by its shape is far larger than the amount of "information" required to construct it.⁶⁶

It is this "information enrichment" capacity which is at the root of the heightening of order or "negentropy" which characterizes the epigenetic development of organisms. With the fulfillment of a set of initial conditions "(aqueous phase, narrow latitude of temperatures, ionic composition, etc.)" the mere occurrence of a specified sequence of residues (for whatever reason) results in a unique, complex structuration with stereospecific bonding properties.⁶⁷ Indiscriminate associative interactions among various proteins and various other compounds results in the spontaneous formation of cellular organelles, because of the peculiar stereospecific bonding properties of the proteins. And cellular interactions will both constitute tissues and organs and assure coordination and differentiation of chemical activities among cells, tissues and organs.

At each stage more highly ordered structures and new functions appear which, resulting from spontaneous interactions between products of the preceding stages, reveal successively, like a blossoming firework, the latent potentialities of previous levels. The determining cause of the entire phenomenon, its source, is finally the genetic information represented by the sum of the polypeptide sequences, interpreted — or, to be more exact, screened — by the initial conditions.

The *ultima ratio* of all the teleonomic structures and performances of living beings is thus enclosed in the sequences of residues making up polypeptide fibers.⁶⁸

And what is the law governing the sequence of amino acids in any protein? It is the "law" of *chance!*⁶⁹

Monod is quite precise here in differentiating between our absence of knowledge of a governing rule (ignorance) and the absence of rule. For the actual sequence of residues in any polypeptide chain passes the appropriate tests for natural randomness.⁷⁰ Thus while the mechanism of invariance preserves the products of chance, and while the "information enrichment" process allows this chance product to begin the successive stages of higher order structuration, Monod suggests that the initiating event, the ultimate source of living beings, is purely random, totally blind.⁷¹

Given the characteristics of molecular stereospecificity and non-covalent bonding, the process by which DNA transfers information can be explained in terms of physical laws. What is interesting, in Monod's view, is that the actual code which DNA employs is itself chemically arbitrary. But given the fact of the code (any code for that matter), the physical structure of the system is such that it can replicate the sequence of residues in a polypeptide chain (thus replicating the specifically shaped globular proteins), and this replication process is impervious to alteration from other chemical agencies. This explains the stability of genetic invariance in species.[72] However, because the replication process is fundamentally a *physical* transfer process, it is as susceptible as any microscopic entity to *accidental* quantic perturbations. Such perturbations will be purely and simply a matter of chance or accidental mistakes in the physical "copying" process. But because the copying process itself is "blind" to its content, each accident will be preserved faithfully by the process itself.[73] It is this absolute independence between the processes which bring about genetic variations and the functional consequences of these variations that Monod highlights as essential for our understanding teleonomic evolutionary processes. For it is this realm of "absolute coincidence" which accounts for the creation of "absolute newness" in living beings. Monod sees this realm of "absolute coincidence" not as a property or characteristic of living things, but as an imperfection in the conservation mechanism which defines their living character.[74] And it is this view of the role of chance in originating processes and Monod's interpretation of chance variation as an "imperfection" of life processes which tends to lead Monod towards understanding man as a radical departure from the overall course of universal process.

Monod carries the implications from these discoveries in modern biology into the field of general evolutionary theory. He provides evidence to show how physical environments have the effect of selectively reinforcing and stabilizing the results of chance variation, and how human language created an environment which both favoured brain development and was itself enhanced by such development.[75] Where the relative frequencies of chance variations are usually extremely low the frequent recurrence of relevant biological processes virtually ensures an ongoing succession of such "accidents."[76] This ensuing evolutionary development involves no violations whatsoever to the laws of thermodynamics.[77] And with the chance emergence of such defensive proteins as antibodies the defensive and survival characteristics of organisms are enhanced significantly.[78] In this interaction between organisms and their environments the movements of organisms into different sets of conditions has the effect of regulating evolutionary pressures for or against the survival of different mutations, thus ordering the effects of chance into successful adaptations.[79]

The frontiers of general evolutionary explanation exist at the beginning and at the point of greatest complexity in biological evolution, the original genesis of life and the origins of the human central nervous system. Regarding the first frontier John A. Miles has summarized Monod quite neatly.

The formation of the chemical constituents of life (nucleotides and amino acids) is not implausible in a "prebiotic soup" of methane, simple carbon compounds, ammonia, and water. Equally plausible is the development of protein-like macromolecules containing a polypeptide chain. What is most implausible is the spontaneous occurrence of even a single actual replication. DNA, essential for the transmission of a genetic code, is itself transmitted. *Omne vivum ex ovo.*

The solution again can only be sought in the development of DNA or some substance with similar code-transmitting properties by chance. Though the *a priori* likelihood of this was infinitesimal, it had only to happen once.[80]

At the other frontier, while the miracle of the operation of the central nervous system still remains a mystery, the role of projective simulation seeking confirmation by concrete experience is well enough verified as operative in animal and human cognitional processes that the dualism of mind/brain, matter/spirit must stand as objectively untenable. Monod's suggestion is not that we reject such notions as "spirit" but that we rethink them in terms of the miracle of our biological heritage.[81]

In his last chapter Monod's evolutionary theory becomes an ethics and a philosophy of history. The first phase of man's distinctively cultural history begins when the neurological evolution of the central nervous system, in dialogue with the selective pressures of the physical environment, gives birth to "the development of the [cognitional] power of simulation and of the language that conveys its operations."[82] At this point a corner is turned as the significant conversation among evolutionary forces ceases to be that between genetic mutation and environmental conditions. With the emergence of the human world of ideas a new conversation partner is introduced, and selective pressures come to favour "the expansion of races more generously endowed than others with intelligence, imagination, will, and ambition."[83] However, with man another novelty is introduced, that of wide-scale mortal intraspecific strife. And as tribal or racial warfare becomes commonplace, evolutionary forces come to favour another trait within the world of ideas, that of "cohesion within the horde ... group aggressiveness ... respect for the tribal law."[84] Monod's implications here are twofold. First, it is human behaviour, mediated by the world of *ideas*, and not *genetic* evolution, which becomes significant in orienting selective pressure. Cultural evolution has taken a radical step away from the course of biological evolution.[85] And second, the process of selection of ideas is a twofold process involving (1) the practical performance value of new ideas, and (2) their "spreading power," their accessibility to the minds of existing populations. Because of the fact of intraspecific conflict and the ensuing pressures towards group coherence, both of these selective pressures favour the proliferation of ideas which increase the group's security.[86] And it is this second fact which, in Monod's view, brings us to the current situation, a situation of grave danger.

Because of this twofold selectivity, the process of cultural evolution both "facilitated acceptance of the tribal law," and more significantly "created the *need* for the mythical explanation which gave it foundation and sovereignty."[87] It is this need which, in Monod's view, explains the philosophical and mythical "ontogenies" (stories of the origins of the group that link these origins to the overarching structure of the whole cosmos). For the ideas that were most successful were those which assigned man a secure place "in an immanent destiny, in whose bosom his anxiety dissolves."[88] However, the terrible danger in the contemporary world situation is that scientific knowledge, the set of ideas which has won favour in the operative life of three centuries of civilization (principally because of its practical performance value), demands rejecting these ontogenies which protect man's sense of security and found his values. For scientific knowledge demands man's recognition that, far from occupying a secure place in the center of a benevolent universe which rationally founds a set of values to which man can assent, in fact man is a chance deformation in an indifferent, even hostile universe, which authors no values save those which man himself creates. The "modern soul's distress" is an agonizing contradiction, a radical heteronomy operative in the lives of men. It is the tension between the lived commitment to the "principle of objectivity" which has marked the course of three centuries of civilization, and the inertial adherence, in the mind and heart of contemporary culture, to the values rooted in the natural and religious ontogenies which stand completely repudiated by this principle. To break out of the stranglehold of this tension, this fundamental contradiction, man must now wake up and admit the terrible truth about himself. His world, his universe has no orientation. It has no goal for itself or for man. It neither commands nor rewards man's obedience. Nor does it yield secrets about man's well-being.[89] His world is "deaf to his music, just as indifferent to his hopes as it is to his suffering of his crimes."[90]

In the face of this terrible distress Monod's answer is "the ethic of knowledge." First, value judgments and judgments of scientific knowledge must clearly be distinguished (not separated) so as to preserve the purity of the principle of objectivity. Knowledge is ignorant of values but without "objectivity" values corrupt knowledge. Second, values and knowledge must be recognized as always and necessarily associated in action and discourse.[91] Third, a principal, axiomatic value, "the ethic of knowledge," founds the very principle of objectivity itself and thus the truth of all scientific knowledge.[92] The commitment to the principle of objectivity is not itself a product of knowledge but an initial (arbitrary)[93] ethical choice which conditions the possibility for true knowledge. It is an ethic which man prescribes for himself. In contrast to an animist ethic which claims natural knowledge as the foundation for values, Monod's proposal claims that only an *a priori* ethical commitment to the principle of objectivity (a free choice) can yield truth. Knowledge of evolutionary processes demands that we recognize no natural foundation for values, save the mere fact of their being chosen by humanity. In Monod's view, only this order of priority between values and knowledge can lay the proper foundation for science, can return the power of values to the hands of humanity, and thus, can heal the tensions which are ripping humanity apart.[94]

The history which stands before humanity, if we choose the ethic of knowledge, is a history of freedom which is founded in the recognition that only humanity can author its own future. This ethic is a transcendent value because it sets forth a goal which we must drive beyond ourselves to attain. But at the same time this transcendence is truly self-transcendence (and nonsubservience) because men and women recognize that we are its sole source. Finally, this human future is truly a socialist future because it is based upon the sole authentic foundation for social and political institutions, that of freedom of choice.[95]

Monod shares with Kant a central preoccupation, to explain the structure of teleological or goal-oriented processes without violating the operative laws of physics. And, as with Kant, the liberation from the determinism of physical laws lies in a form of reflexively operative self-constitution. In the field of biology the most complicated problem in an explanation of teleonomy is the question of how complex structures remain invariant over time. And it is here that Monod stands closer to Lonergan than to Kant in his account of necessity. Invariance is simply the fact that the "information" transfer processes (DNA) are themselves resistant to intervention from the chemical processes which constitute and delimit their environment. The necessity of invariance is not principally a presence but an absence of chemical relationship (both actual and potential) between the transfer process and the "information" and its environment. And as with all other processes involved in biological teleonomy the initial occurrence of this transfer mechanism was itself a result of an autonomous morphogenesis.

The teleological structure, in both Kant and Monod, involves the possibility of autonomous structuration, some measures assuring the continuity of this structuration, and the dialectical engagement with environmental forces allowing a selection process to reinforce those trials which adapt successfully. This selection process is fundamentally the fact that only successful adaptations survive. And since only success survives, the ensuing structure is teleologically ordered towards that flexibility which ensures success in shifting environments. Both Kant and Monod understood that a principal locus of this teleology was human society and history. And both understood the normative act of history to be humanity's courageous defiance of nature in the free act of moral choice which constitutes the normative direction of history. *Sapere aude!*[96]

The significant difference between Kant and Monod here entailed

Monod's radical recognition of the presence of chance, randomness, a basic absence of intelligibility, as an essential part of the structure of world processes. Kant's teleology, operative in the mind, involved the operation of a set of categories, themselves a part of the structure of the mind, and identity of moral action with this immanent structure. Monod's teleonomy, on the other hand, operative throughout the whole of biological process, involved the chance or random occurrence of order or system through the *coincidental* convergence of conditions, and the continued recurrence of this identical order or system through the routine operation of another system which is resistant to interference (whose initial genesis was itself a matter of chance). In both cases the development process involves selection and survival. But in Monod's view, the teleological operation is the chance emergence of ordered structure from coincidentally interacting conditions. Given the initial occurrence of the DNA replication mechanism, a continuation of this emergence is virtually ensured. And given the organism's interaction with shifting environments the ongoing genesis of more and more complex structures will continue as existing structures are modified successively. The evolutionary operator, in Monod's case, is not a set of categories but a "higher order" operative structure — the chance emergence of system from coincidentally interacting processes — whose functioning structure is "non-systematically"[97] related to the immanent structure or pattern of the systems or processes which it begets. It is this absence of systematic relation which is the central element in the meaning intended here by the term "higher order." And it is the fact of chance or coincidence in the ongoing genesis of the biological processes which accounts for this absence of systematic relation.

Because of a radical difference in their respective points of departure, their respective sets of questions, anticipations, concerns, and the counterarguments which they set out to refute, Kant and Monod come to quite different conclusions on the overarching rationality or intelligibility of the universe and its relationship to man. Kant's self-constituting man is reunified with a universe which is teleologically ordered towards God. Monod's self-constituting man, on the other hand, is alone in an indifferent, hostile universe. The origin of their differences rests, in large part, in their respective attitudes toward empirical or experientially based knowledge. Kant's move towards the subject as constituting agent of morality and history (and knowledge) was the result of his search for the origins of necessity in empirical knowledge. His heuristic excluded the fundamental adequacy of empirically verified facticity and sought the necessity of pure logical coherence. Such necessity was absolutely essential and so empirically based knowledge could not be a fundamental *a priori* point of departure. Monod, on the other hand, moved towards the subject as constituting agent of morality and history as a result of his absolute confidence in the reliability of empirical knowledge. Such confidence forced him to admit the reality of randomness, chance, brute coincidence, as a fact of world process.[98] And since his heuristic allowed no third alternative to the two poles of pure chance *or* a vitalist or animist necessity, his *a priori* commitment to the reliability of knowledge led him to pronounce the overarching structure of evolutionary teleology to be a matter of pure chance.

It is interesting to note that while Kant claims to leave man united to natural processes, in a more basic sense Kant's man remains equally isolated from empirical reality. For the categorically constituting activities of the mind in knowing are so overwhelming in Kant's system, that "... no legitimate link is available between pure reason and the ultimate foundations of the universe."[99] And so while Monod's commitment to the rational unity of knowing and the known in science results in his seizing upon a fundamental irrationality in world process to explain the evolutionary genesis of novelty in teleological processes, Kant's commitment to the unity and coherence of logical system led him to seize upon the fundamental duality of knowing and reality and to appeal to the constituting activity of the mind in his account of teleology. In the final analysis, both theories leave man in their own form of limbo.

As we shall see, below, Lonergan, working in the wake of Kant and of some of the scientific knowledge upon which Monod draws, provides a real third alternative. With Monod, Lonergan trusts the unity of knowing and reality.[100] But like Kant he understands that knowing is not simply to be taken for granted, rather, it must be explained as the cognitional genesis of reality. Such an explanation will not assume the form of a deduction of *a priori* logical principles which must be true necessarily, but a methodologically differentiated and rigorous implementation of the operations of empirical knowing, in act, which seeks identity with its own operative structure. Like Monod such an inquiry discovers the reality, the facticity of randomness as an essential element of world process. And like Kant and Monod, Lonergan explains teleology in terms of autonomous morphogenesis and environmental selection. But unlike both, Lonergan leaves man in continuity with the structure of the physical and biological orders, and in continuity with a dynamic orientation operative throughout the whole of reality.[101] The structure of this dynamic is worked out with tools that are similar to those of Jacques Monod. But Lonergan's novel understanding of the structure of "statistical laws" provides a third option to chance and necessity, an option which integrates the two in the structure, emergent probability. And in a way which is unlike both, emergent probability leaves man and the universe open to God.

## 2.3 *Lonergan: Ethics, History and Religion*

This brief introduction to the works of Kant and Monod should serve to illustrate how the route towards adequate answers to questions of progress, questions of ethical foundations, questions of the structure and dynamics of history, inevitably involves a complex set of problems in the areas of cognitional theory and scientific methodology. What I have tried to show is how the concerns which animated these two authors, the questions which they set out to answer, the positions which they sought to refute, the possibilities which they envisioned as acceptable candidates for answers, the possibilities which they actively or tacitly excluded, all constituted a heuristic which informed the nature and the course of their projects. And it is this set of anticipations, as much as the data which the two studied, which accounts for the results of their respective inquiries. It is as if knowing were an appetite whose specific requirements we can both satisfy and modify through the raising and answering of questions. This study of the work of Lonergan aims at making the appetite itself the object of critical inquiry so as to heighten the degree to which we can not only satisfy existing appetites but also cultivate more appropriate appetites.

Clearly this approach to cognitional and theoretical issues betrays a number of indentifiable assumptions in the very area which it seeks to investigate. But as will be discussed in greater detail in later chapters the questions relevant for assessing the truth of an explanation do not concern the mere fact of assumptions operative in the insights but their adequacy in framing a field of data and anticipations which is in some sense isomorphic with the immanent context of reality, and their adequacy in meeting and settling the relevant questions. In both cases the word adequacy is defined not in terms of some *a priori* theory but in terms of a norm that is operative immanently in human subjects who have cultivated the cognitional and responsible skills. It should have become apparent by now that the more traditional form of separating descriptive from normative statements has been left far behind. And it will also become apparent that this cultivation of skills does not and cannot exclude religion.

Before launching into Lonergan's emergent probability a number of issues need to be addressed in a preliminary way. There are a number of key areas in which Lonergan differs from both Kant and Monod which set the framework for a discussion of the relationship between science and religion. The first of these concerns the meaning of the term "chance." Monod has made a good deal out of the fact that the emergence of the DNA structure was a "pure chance" event. And for Monod this apparent fact utterly precludes any overarching meaning or purpose (and thus any legitimately religious dimension) to the structure of evolutionary history. The second concerns the very meaning of the term "religion." Finally, the third concerns the role which traditions have played within religious, and indeed within all human understanding. Lonergan's approach to the relationship between ethics and history recognizes the importance of the religious dimension of human life and the important role which religious traditions play in promoting the historical good. While recognizing that a vast literature exists on each of these topics my hope here is to clear up some confusions, in a preliminary way, and at the same time to sketch an outline of the rather novel approach which will be treated in greater detail in the chapters which follow.

### 2.3.1 Chance

While my brief introduction to Jacques Monod, above, noted the positive contributions which his discovery of the role of chance could make to an account of the teleological structure of world process, the implications which he draws for ethics and history have come under some criticism. In dealing briefly with one of these criticisms here I will indicate how Lonergan's emergent probability presents a third alternative to the two options of chance or necessity, in a heuristic which integrates the absence of intelligibility into an intelligible explanation.

In 1978 A. R. Peacocke, Dean of Clare College, Cambridge, England delivered a lecture at Oxford University which was expanded and published subsequently in two forms, in the journal *Zygon* (1979) and in his book *Creation and the World of Science* (1979).[102] In his lecture Peacocke draws on an additional body of research by Prigogine and Nicolis and by Eigen in the field of biology to launch a qualified critique of some research conclusions and some implications drawn by Monod. In 1979 similar criticisms of Monod were raised by John Bowker, from the Department of Religious Studies at the University of Lancaster, England, in a paper which he delivered at the Oxford International Symposium held at Christ Church.[103] The thrust of both critiques runs as follows.

The centre of Monod's presentation lies in his account of the origins of the first organism with the self-replicating DNA mechanism. The macromolecules which translate the DNA code and thus replicate the basic elements of biological life are themselves coded in DNA. And so since the only thing that can translate the DNA code is itself the product of translation, the problem remains to explain how the first code emerged and survived (as the only survivor, for all living things utilize the same code) with no apparent purpose or survival value, until a primitive translation mechanism emerged that could replicate it and thus ensure its survival.[104] Monod's conclusion is that the occurrence was a single, chance, zero-probability event. As a one-time event the occurrence had no precedent. And so the probability of its occurence (understood as frequency probability)[105] was virtually nil. In Monod's view it is this element of pure chance, pure unlikelihood, which renders the entire consequent course of biological teleonomy irrational, lacking in any intelligibility, as a radical deviation from the normal course of universal process towards entropy.

However, there is other evidence to suggest that far from being a freak event, this emergence of the DNA mechanism was virtually ensured, not as the result of a single physical or chemical law or set of laws, but as one possible outcome from a larger set of probable structure-transmission mechanisms. The work of Prigogine and Nicolis has demonstrated how the relevant structures could possibly have emerged in an environment in which a set of chemical and physical oscillations occur spontaneously when the environmental systems are out of equilibrium. Given the continued input of energy and given the fulfillment of a number of other environmental conditions, such oscillations in the system will stabilize, first temporally as a sequence of events, and then spatially as a distribution of shapes.[106]

Subsequently the work of Eigen has shown how such laws in chemical kinetics can link with the statistical (stochastic) "laws" governing the probable recurrence of specific mutations and the growth of population sizes of particular molecular species. Eigen and his colleagues have conducted their investigations far enough to conclude that given the fulfillment of a wide range of possible sets of fulfilling conditions, some form of coding and translation replicative mechanism can be regarded as not only possible but quite probable. Eigen's conclusion is:

> That the evolution of life, if it is based on a derivable physical principle, must be considered an *inevitable* process despite its indeterminate course. ... The models treated ... and the experiments discussed earlier ... indicate that it is not only inevitable "in principle" but also sufficiently probable within a realistic span of time. It requires appropriate environmental conditions (which are not fulfilled everywhere) and their maintenance. These conditions have existed on Earth and must still exist on many planets in the universe. There is no temporal restriction to the continuation of the evolutionary process, as long as energy can be supplied.[107]

What Eigen shows is how the fact of randomness, the reality of coincidental convergences of conditions, the absence of intelligibility or rule governing individual outcomes, can itself become integrated into an account of aggregates of such occurrences which displays an overarching intelligibility. The fact of a single or a set of actual, objectively real, chance occurrences (as opposed to occurrences for which sufficient understanding is lacking) does not render the whole of world process irrational. Quite the contrary, as I will show in the next chapter, there is an essential absence of intelligibility which is correlative with every intelligible unity. Eigen's discovery is that statistical laws, operative in randomly interacting processes, given an appropriate set of fulfilling conditions, are themselves a form of intelligibility and can function in the context of a wider explanatory structure, to render intelligible the emergence of system or order from randomness. And Peacocke goes on to speculate how this dynamically creative "exigence," which is the fundamental structure of world process, could be understood as the agency of God's ongoing creation.[108]

Lonergan's emergent probability, which generalizes an explanatory structure incorporating and integrating the facts of randomness, statistical laws and classical (or deterministic) laws, is in continuity with these experimental results and these explanations in the field of modern biology. However emergent probability is also an open-ended heuristic structure which admits of possible higher order integrative levels which would stand beyond the limits of currently verified theories in the natural and human sciences. In fact emergent probability demands that the very dynamic towards emergence become the object of empirical study. And in the work of Lonergan it is this dynamic, as operative in the questing spirit of humankind, which is both the religious hunger itself and the principal datum for the unrestricted (or transcendent) character of its object, God.

## 2.3.2 Religion

While Monod rejects a religious dimension or context for a truly "scientific" explanation of ethics and history his own work has come under some criticism for embracing, in an uncritical fashion, an essentially religious character. John A. Miles has argued that: (1) in appealing to an ethical imperative to found the complete and utter universality of a cosmic explanation, Monod's result is what is usually referred to as religion; and (2) throughout Monod's account there can be identified a set of essential elements of religion which are operative in his explanation to inform the shape and to betray the true nature of his project.[109] Miles quotes Clifford Geertz:

> The heart ... of the religious perspective ... is the conviction that the values one holds are grounded in the inherent structure of reality, that between the way one ought to live and the way things really are there is an unbreakable inner conviction [that] what sacred symbols do for those to whom they are sacred is to formulate an image of the world's construction and a program for human conduct that are mere reflexes of one another.[110]

Miles does not rule Monod's project out of court for its (essentially religious) claim to universality and its demand for moral assent. Quite the contrary. His approach is to recognize Monod's project for what it is and to assess its adequacy, first by identifying the religious heritage within which its symbols stand (a heritage within the Greek and Christian West, ranging from Democritus and Epicureanism, through various avenues, to Nietzsche and Existentialism),[111] and second, by noting which questions it has left unanswered. In Miles' view, the essential question excluded by Monod was how one might remain committed to living in accordance with his natural philosophy while holding sincerely to the possibility that it might be radically inadequate. It is this serious question about the adequacy of ultimate explanation which in Miles' view a religion recognizes and accepts. And in rejecting religion out of hand (in the tradition of hostility which science *qua* religious vision has had towards religion) Monod fails to understand his own enterprise.[112]

What is interesting about Miles' critique here is his analysis of how questions of foundations in ethics, in natural science, and in the human sciences, inevitably drive towards an essentially religious scope, bringing forward and implementing elements from older and existing religious and ethical traditions, and at the same time unifying descriptive (is) statements with normative (ought) statements. This analysis of religion is by no means original, and Miles' debt to Clifford Geertz is recognized. But while such figures as Peter Berger, Clifford Geertz and Eric Voegelin have argued that questions in the social sciences give rise to religious issues and that religious phenomena appear to be universal elements of culture,[113] Miles' critique of Monod serves to remind us how pervasive and acute such religious issues are. In his 1982 Presidential Address to the American Academy of Religion, Gordon Kaufman notes that the contemporary threat of nuclear war brings humanity to the essentially religious questions of ultimacy.[114] But he also notes that traditional religious responses may very well be inadequate to this religious question.

> The point I am suggesting here, that changes in the historical situation in which we find ourselves — empirical historical changes — themselves call for, indeed force upon us, changes in our religious symbolism and in the frames of reference within which we make our value judgments and moral choices, goes counter to a central assumption of many in this room, I suspect.[115]

Kaufman is stressing that the contemporary religious questions which arise in the heart of the great social, historical, economic, cultural problems of our age, are indeed religious *questions*. Responses to these questions, *as essentially religious*, remain to be grasped and formulated (or from another viewpoint we remain to be grasped by them in a form of conversion) in a way which is adequate, concretely, to the demands of contemporary life. It is this dynamic view of the cultural context of religious questions which explains Lonergan's preoccupation with theological method. When the context of culture has changed sufficiently so as to demand a reformulation of religious questions then theology must shift from reflecting upon the known to reflecting upon the unknown with a view towards arriving at answers to new questions.[116]

As this shift takes place the search for answers to new questions gives rise to questions as to how best to conduct such a search. And this subsequent concern is with method in theology.[117] Lonergan would agree with Gordon Kaufman that this revised understanding of theology as reflection upon a tradition of religious experience in search of responses (that must be both known and lived) to the great religious questions of our age, must break down the barriers between the study of religion and theology.[118]

## 2.3.3 Tradition

Recent studies of the history of the notion of progress suggest that many of our current convictions about the goodness of industrial and economic growth are rooted in an older world view which has its proximate origins somewhere in the eighteenth century. In the view of Robert Nisbet[119] the growing skepticism about progress in the West is a result of the recent collapse of widespread confidence in a set of axioms about the value of the past, the nobility of the West, the worth of economic and technological growth, faith in reason and belief in the intrinsic worth of life on this earth; axioms which were linked to Western religious traditions and which, together, had constituted a foundation for Western civilization. In another analysis Alasdair MacIntyre has drawn attention to what he understands to be a radical crisis of foundations in ethical theory. The inability of ethics to escape from what he argues to be an all pervasive "emotivism" is rooted in the loss, since the Enlightenment, of an older Aristotelian teleological view of humanity and our relation to God and the cosmos. Whereas earlier ethical statements derived their meaning and validity from a wider vision of human purpose, rooted in this classical world view, the loss of this world view has spelled the loss of ethical foundations.[120] The suggestion of both Nisbet and MacIntyre is that the attainment of appropriate responses to contemporary ethical questions will require some return to our past, some recovery of a traditional element or context which we once had and which we have lost. And the implication of both scholars is that this recovery of tradition is at once a conscious recognition of a context of principles operative implicitly in the genesis of contemporary civilization and an essential condition for its continuation.

But if we have learned anything from Marx it is that we must remain suspicious of any call for a return to an authoritative "tradition" (particularly a religious tradition) which cannot marshall hard evidence for its contribution to contemporary human welfare on the basis of a critical appeal to the facts of history. In a recent collection of articles in the 1981 Supplementary Volume VII of the *Canadian Journal of Philosophy*, entitled *Marx and Morality*, the question is reopened asking how Marx's theory of the dialectics of history influences or even permits the possibility of a moral theory. And in his article on "Scientific Socialism and the Question of Socialist Values," Andrew Collier proposes a defence of the view that radical political differences can be settled in an appeal to historical fact.[121] Collier argues that Marx's social, political and economic theories do not rest, ultimately, upon independently founded or non-rational value judgments. In Marx's work (as in all the human sciences) there is no clear-cut distinction between objective statements and emotive/prescriptive statements; such a distinction is neither warranted nor is it possible. Rather, in Collier's view, what Marx provides is an appeal to the empirical evidence of history to support a theory which fixes, with precision, the exact meaning of the technical terms that carry the emotive/prescriptive force. Thus, according to Collier, Marx's work sought to do what any scientific socialism must do; it progressively weeded out any prescriptive or evaluative terms which did not derive their exact meaning and foundations from a historical theory which stood verified by fact.[122] In this view such a critique of the ideological tendencies of traditional moral or ethical notions is the only way to guard against minority interests operating to oppress the common person.

These two sets of arguments and their apparently contradicting claims, pose a significant methodological problem for anyone seriously engaged in the quest for comprehensive responses to contemporary theoretical and moral issues. Is there a material content, rooted in an older, perhaps religious, tradition, implicitly operative in our very act of choosing, which we must recognize and appropriate in our contemporary view if we are to remain intellectually honest? Or can we and, indeed, must we seek out and critique our every material supposition in the name of emancipation from the dominating and oppressive tendencies of all tradition? Can this critique tolerate a religious dimension? The debate between these two sets of positions is expressed in one of the best contemporary forms in the discussions between Hans-Georg Gadamer and Jürgen Habermas.[123] And while a detailed introduction to this debate is neither possible nor necessary here, Fred Lawrence has indicated how the apparent contradictions in the two views need not necessarily lead to an impasse.[124]

Working from foundations which have been laid down by Lonergan, Fred Lawrence argues that the route beyond this impasse lies in recognizing that the controls of meaning (the cognitional and responsible mediators of cultures and cultural transformations) are not universally fixed for all time but are themselves engaged in an ongoing process.[125] In other words, the attainment of what Lonergan calls a truly "modern philosophic differentiation of consciousness"[126] involves recognizing that neither a return to traditional norms (or a traditional explanatory context for normativity) nor a new "science" of man and society (in the fashion of contemporary sciences) which fixes a new normative context, will be adequate to the challenges of contemporary culture.[127] What is required is the grasp that the normative basis for meaning and value is operative immanently in the spontaneity of intentional subjects and that an adequate explanatory context requires an active appropriation of this dynamic structure as it is operative personally in one's life. Such an appropriation reveals that the relationship between the materials of culture which are traditional at any point in time and the critically selected goals and values that would humanize culture, is a relationship of "sublation" (whose structure is that of emergent probability and) whose successful achievement is a function of personal authenticity. Such a sublation both brings forward and critically transforms the traditional materials. And far from ratifying either the traditional or the new materials as *fundamentally* normative, self-appropriation grasps that what is normative is authentic subjectivity. Thus self-appropriation moves beyond itself to discern the personal and social characteristics and conditions for wide-scale authenticity. And such discernment discovers that central to these conditions is the subject who is grasped by the love of God.[128]

It is my contention that the generalization of the explanatory heuristic structure, emergent probability, synthesizes the profound contributions of Kant and Monod, and at the same time resolves many of the problems which both men encountered in accounting for the foundations and dynamics of ethics and history and the role of religion in ethical and historical processes. The following introduction to this work of Lonergan is offered here as a proposal for an explanatory heuristic which seeks to reorientate the raising and answering of questions in the fields of ethics and the philosophy of history in a way which is both faithful to the demands of empirical inquiry and which is open to the significance of God's love in our lives.

## FOOTNOTES – CHAPTER 2

1. L. W. Beck, "Sketch of Kant's Life and Work," in *Kant on History*, edited, with an introduction by L. W. Beck, translated by L. W. Beck, R. E. Anchor, and E. L. Fackenheim (Indianapolis: Bobbs-Merrill, 1963), p. xxvii.
2. Despland, *Kant on History and Religion*, pp. 6-7.
3. Ibid., pp. 17-24.
4. Nisbet, *History of the Idea of Progress*, p. 221.
5. Immanuel Kant, *Groundwork of the Metaphysic of Morals*, translated and analysed by H. J. Paton (New York: Harper & Row, Harper Torch Books, 1964).
6. H. J. Paton, "Translator's Preface," in ibid., p. 8.
7. Kant, in ibid., pp. 61-4.
8. Ibid., pp. 67-8. Emphases are in Paton's translation.
9. Ibid., p. 68. Emphases are in Paton's translation.
10. Paton, "Analysis of the Argument," in ibid., pp. 21-2.
11. Kant, in ibid., p. 70. Emphases are in Paton's translation.
12. Ibid., p. 82.
13. Ibid., p. 93.
14. Ibid., pp. 62-3. Emphases are in Paton's translation.
15. Ibid., p. 64.
16. Ibid.
17. Carl Becker, *The Heavenly City of the Eighteenth-Century Philosphers* (New Haven: Yale University Press, 1932), chap. 1.
18. See Despland, p. 17. Yirmiahu Yovel cautions against equating the medieval teleology with that of Kant, see *Kant and the Philosophy of History*, pp. 3-5, 128-9. While Kant's teleology is dynamic, he nonethless shares with the medievals an overall, teleologically structured explanatory context.
19. Despland, p. 20.
20. Ibid., pp. 20, 22-3.
21. Ibid., pp. 43-4.
22. Kant, *Critique of Judgement*, p. 433, quoted in Despland, p. 43.
23. Despland, pp. 42-3.
24. Ibid., p. 45.
25. Ibid., pp. 44-7.
26. Yovel, pp. 128-9.
27. Ibid., pp. 136-7.
28. Ibid., pp. 159-61.
29. Ibid., pp. 161-8, 194-8.
30. Ibid., pp. 56-8, 66, 81-2.
31. Ibid., pp. 167-8.
32. Ibid., p. 79.
33. See ibid., pp. 135-6.
34. See Justus Hartnack, *Kant's Theory of Knowledge*, translated by M. Holmes Hartshorne (New York: Harcourt, Brace & World, Harbinger Books, 1967), pp. 5-16.
35. Ibid., pp. 8-10.
36. Ibid., p. 32.
37. Ibid., pp. 12-14.
38. Ibid., p. 44.
39. See Yovel, pp. 299-300.
40. Ibid., pp. 81-2, 121.
41. Ibid., pp. 272, 21-2.
42. Ibid., p. 273.

43  Ibid., pp. 21-3, 60-1, 271-6.
44  Ibid., p. 274.
45  Ibid., p. 276.
46  Ibid., p. 299.
47  Ibid.
48  Ibid.
49  Ibid. Emphases are Yovel's.
50  John A. Miles, Jr., "Jacques Monod and the Cure of Souls," *Zygon* 9 (March 1974): 22.
51  Jacques Monod, *Chance and Necessity*, translated by A. Wainhouse (New York: Random House, Vintage Books, 1972).
52  Ibid., pp. 24-5, 21.
53  Ibid., p. 21. Emphases are Monod's.
54  See, for example, ibid., p. 165.
55  Ibid., p. 170.
56  Ibid., pp. 23-4.
57  Ibid., pp. 23-4.
58  Ibid., p. 45.
59  The following summary is drawn from ibid., chap. III.
60  Ibid., p. 46. Emphases are Monod's.
61  Ibid., pp. 62-5.
62  Ibid., pp. 66-8.
63  Ibid.,pp. 68-70.
64  Ibid., pp. 77-8.
65  Ibid., p. 93.
66  Ibid., p. 94.
67  Ibid.
68  Ibid., p. 95.
69  Ibid., p. 96.
70  See ibid., p. 96-7.
71  Ibid., p. 98.
72  Ibid., pp. 105-111.
73  Ibid., pp. 111-113.
74  Ibid., pp. 114-117.
75  Ibid., pp. 118-19, 126-9.
76  Ibid., pp. 120-1.
77  Ibid., pp. 123-4.
78  Ibid., pp. 124-5.
79  See J. Miles, p. 25.
80  Ibid., p. 25. See Monod, pp. 140-6.
81  Monod, pp. 154-9.
82  Ibid., p. 161.
83  Ibid., p. 162.
84  Ibid., pp. 161-2.
85  Ibid., p. 162.
86  Ibid., pp. 165-6.
87  Ibid., pp. 167.
88  Ibid., p. 166.
89  Ibid., pp. 169-173.
90  Ibid., p. 173.
91  Ibid., pp. 173-4.
92  Ibid., p. 173.
93  By being a completely arbitrary choice, not necessitated by any "law" other than the

"law" of chance, the commitment to this principle of objectivity is itself a chance occurrence, and thus, stands in continuity with the overall structure of teleonomic processes. And so like all teleonomic processes the very processes of rational knowledge itself are as blind, as mindless, as irrational, as every other evolutionary deviation from the overarching march of the universe towards entropy.

94  Ibid., pp. 176-7.
95  Ibid., pp. 178-80.
96  Kant, *On History*, p. 3.
97  See chap. three below.
98  Clearly this analysis is not complete. For Monod's work reflects a French existentialist philosophical orientation and this tradition is noted for what Paul Ricoeur has called a "hermeneutics of suspicion," with its correlative philosophical gesture of defiance. On this fundamental gesture in philosophy, see Paul Ricoeur, "Hermeneutics and the Critique of Ideology," in *Hermeneutics and the Human Sciences*, translated and edited by John B. Thompson (Cambridge: Cambridge University Press, 1981), p. 63. Monod reflects this tradition's vision of man's heroic self-affirmation in the face of absurdity. And a complete study of Monod's ethics would need to analyse how this vision operated historically to shape his normative foundations. But while this analysis would reveal the suggestive power of images and traditions in culture and the import of this suggestion in shaping the concrete *genesis* of Monod's work, the fact remains that Monod's principal foundation, operative throughout his study, is his confidence in the reliability of empirical knowledge. Without this confidence Monod would have had no book, indeed no career. Perhaps it is the influence of existentialist philosophy that would explain why Monod stopped short of seeking an intelligibility immanent in statistical knowledge. See Section 2.3.1 and chaps three and four below.
99  Yovel, p. 298.
100 In Lonergan's work this is not an assumption. Rather, such a trust is empirically verifiable as an operative stance in any and all cognitional acts. Indeed, even to posit a "reality" distinct from knowing involves the subject in a contradiction. See, for example, Philip McShane, *Wealth of Self and Wealth of Nations* (Hicksville, N. Y.: Exposition Press, 1975), pp. 39-46.
101 Clearly Lonergan recognizes significant discontinuities on the various "levels" of evolutionary process. And the significant discontinuity on the human level involves the ability of intelligence to grasp and fulfill conditions for historical emergence. But the brilliance of emergent probability is its ability to explain the precise forms of various evolutionary discontinuities within the terms and relations of one continuous operative structure. See chap. four below. See also *Insight*, pp. 210-211, 227 on the discontinuities at the human level.
102 A. R. Peacocke, "Chance and the Life Game," *Zygon* 14 (December 1979): 301-322; *Creation and the World of Science* (Oxford: Clarendon Press, 1979), chap. 3.
103 John Bowker, "Did God Create This Universe?" in *The Sciences and Theology in the Twentieth Century*, ed. A. R. Peacocke (Stocksfield: Oriel Press, 1981), pp. 98-126.
104 Bowker, p. 112. See Monod, pp. 142-5.
105 See chap. three below.
106 Peacocke, "Chance and the Life Game," pp. 310-312; Bowker, pp. 116-117.
107 Peacocke, ibid., p. 314; see also Bowker, pp. 117-119.
108 Peacocke, ibid., pp. 315-320.
109 J. Miles, pp. 31-38.
110 Clifford Geertz, *Islam Observed*, p. 96, quoted in J. Miles, p. 31.
111 J. Miles, ibid., pp. 32-8.
112 Ibid., pp. 38-41.
113 Berger and Geertz argue for the generality of religion while Voegelin discusses the

import of religion for political science. See Peter Berger, *The Sacred Canopy* (Garden City, N.Y.: Doubleday, Anchor Books, 1967); Clifford Geertz, *The Interpretation of ultures*, particularly chaps. 4 through 7; Eric Voegelin, *The New Science of Politics* (Chicago: University of Chicago Press, 1952).

114 Gordon D. Kaufman, "Nuclear Eschatology and the Study of Religion," *Journal of the American Academy of Religion* 51 (March 1983): 7. For an account of religion which stresses "ultimacy" as its central element, see F. J. Streng, *Understanding Religious Life*, second edition (Encino, Calif.: Dickenson Publishing Company, Inc., 1976), pp. 5-9. See also Lonergan, *Method*, pp. 101-103.

115 Kaufman, p. 9.

116 I am not presuming here that no distinctions exist between religious studies and theology. But I would agree with Kaufman and Lonergan that when both face the great religious questions of our age, they participate in the same enterprise. See note 118 below.

117 See *Method*, p. xi.

118 Kaufman, p. 13; Lonergan, *Philosophy of God, and Theology* (London: Darton, Longman & Todd, 1973), chap. 1 and p. 59; Lonergan, "Lectures on Religious Studies and Theology," *A Third Collection*, ed. F. E. Crowe (N.Y.: Paulist Press, 1985) pp. 113-168.

119 Nisbet, *History of the Idea of Progress*, pp. 317, 352.

120 MacIntyre, *After Virtue*, see p. 57.

121 Andrew Collier, "Scientific Socialism and the Question of Socialist Values," in Nielsen and Patten, eds., *Marx and Morality*, pp. 121-154.

122 Ibid., pp. 135-6, 146-8.

123 See, for example, Ricoeur, "Hermeneutics and the Critique of Ideology."

124 Fred Lawrence, " 'The Modern Philosophic Differentiation of Consciousness' or What is Enlightenment?" in *Lonergan Workshop*, vol. 2 (Chico, Calif.: Scholars Press, 1981), pp. 231-279.

125 Ibid., pp. 273-4.

126 Ibid., p. 231.

127 Ibid., p. 265-6.

128 Ibid., pp. 266-274.

# Chapter 3

# Probability

## 3.0 Introduction

In a set of lectures delivered in Halifax, Nova Scotia, one year after the first publication of *Insight*, Bernard Lonergan introduced his discussions on probability with these words:
> I do not attempt to offer a theory of probability in *Insight* but a heuristic structure that heads toward the determination of a theory of probability.[1]

The tone of presentation in these Halifax lectures is certainly consistent with this exploratory posture.[2] And Lonergan's treatment of questions raised from the perspective of other theoretical positions is evidence that he considered the development of a full-blown theory of probability on the basis of his clues in *Insight* as work which remained to be done.[3] Anyone who is familiar either with the mathematical and theoretical literature on the calculus of probabilities or with the practical and theoretical literature in the field of statistics will recognize this development to be a massive task requiring in-depth engagement with the existing positions. Such engagement occurs slowly, on many fronts, involving many scholars. And in cases where a foundational issue in science or the philosophy of science is involved, the result of the engagement is often not a complete acceptance of one or another position. Rather, a new direction of development often results from an initial period of chaos, after a new position or set of positions has successfully undercut the commonly held views without itself being accepted as a completely developed alternative. This, at least, has been the recent history of accounts of the structure of scientific theories, in the eyes of Frederick Suppe.[4]

Twenty-five years after the first publication of *Insight* it would seem that the development of thought on probability and statistical knowledge among mathematicians, scientists, statisticians and philosophers of science has, for the most part, bypassed any consideration of the clues presented by Lonergan. A few works make passing reference to Lonergan's notion of statistical knowledge in the course of other considerations.[5] Shortly after the appearance of *Insight*, James Albertson devoted two and one-half pages of a book review to discussing some problems that he saw in Lonergan's presentation.[6] One article was published on Lonergan's views on probability in an Irish students' philosophy and theology journal in 1973.[7] A few doctoral dissertations have included some restatement of the clues published in *Insight*.[8] Four articles have appeared recently, written by Patrick H. Byrne of Boston College, which introduce and develop Lonergan's clues in a wider field.[9] But along with Byrne, only one author, Philip McShane, has attempted to engage in a serious discussion on probability with mathematicians, scientists and philosophers of science. And while the reviews of *Randomness, Statistics and Emergence* have been, for the most part, favourable, none appear in main-line science or mathematics journals.[10] In a 1972 review of *Randomness*, William Mathews laments that no references to Lonergan's work can be found in *Beyond Reductionism, The Alpbach Symposium*, edited by Koestler and Smythies.[11] And the same can be said of Frederick Suppe's *The Structure of Scientific Theories*, and of A. R. Peacocke's *The Sciences and Theology in the Twentieth Century*.[12]

One could speculate on the reasons why this engagement with existing positions in the field of probability has not occurred. But unless such speculation included a decisive engagement with extant theories it would not settle the issue as to whether or not it should occur. What seems to be required is an introduction of Lonergan's clues into various areas and levels of contemporary debate, areas where other positions currently dominate. A public discussion of the relative merits of Lonergan's clues and insights on probability could only help the refinement of current thinking. And should some of his clues prove fruitful perhaps the theoreticians and foundational thinkers might find *Insight* to point towards a subtle but fruitful shift in the direction of future thought on empirical method and scientific theories.

In any case, whatever the outcome, the engagement needs to occur. Unfortunately the chapters that follow do not include full debates with other positions in the fields of mathematics, science or the philosophy of science. But they do represent an attempt to show how issues and theories on probability and statistics inevitably arise within debates in the fields of ethics and the philosophy of history. I am in no position to take up Lonergan's invitation to carry the clues in *Insight* forward towards a full-blown theory of probability. However, my hope in presenting these next two expository chapters is that the fruit that Lonergan's clues seem to bear in other areas will constitute evidence and perhaps motivation for someone else to take up the invitation extended by Lonergan.

The procedure followed throughout my investigations of probability and emergent probability has been to do what was necessary to understand McShane's book *Randomness, Statistics and Emergence*. Thus the order of topics covered here corresponds, very roughly, to the order of presentation in *Randomness* rather than to that in *Insight*. But in an effort to direct the reader's attention to a somewhat novel aspect of Lonergan's approach (an aspect which I have come to regard as among the most important contributions that Lonergan has made to the human sciences) I have begun with a few pages on "The Empirical Stance."

## 3.1 The Empirical Stance

In his 1958 Halifax lectures Lonergan talks a little on the background surrounding his treatment of probability in *Insight*. In many introductory text-books in statistics or probability theory the author includes one definition of probability as a limit of a proper fraction expressing a proportion of occurrences of an event $i$ to a total number of cases as $n$ approaches infinity.

$$\frac{n_i}{n} = \lim_{n \to \infty} \frac{n_i}{n} \quad [13]$$

Such a definition is an operational definition of probability inasmuch as it defines a probability as something that can be determined through the performance of a set of experimental operations. However it is not actually operational because an accurate determination requires the performance of an infinitely large number of operations. This definition has led to a host of debates concerning the actual existence of probabilities, the possibility of their accurate calculation and the epistemological status of knowledge gained through the execution of contemporary techniques in statistics.[14] And it is to some of these problems that Philip McShane has devoted a good number of pages in *Randomness*.[15] But what is significant here, at this introductory stage, is that Lonergan is concerned with probabilities as *some sort of knowledge* which can be gained about a state of affairs through the implementation of a set of experimental procedures. His concern is with the *a posteriori* case of probabilities.[16] Statistical procedures are being employed massively in the natural and human sciences. Conclusions are being drawn from experiments that involve their implementation. And such conclusions are held, to one degree or another, as claiming something about the world of human experience.[17] Lonergan is curious as to what kind of knowledge, if any, the implementation of statistical techniques yields about the world of human experience.

Following the approach of Lonergan, McShane likewise is concerned with the nature of acts of knowing as they are performed in the application of statistical techniques to the solution of empirical problems. Thus his stance or approach in *Randomness* is empirical in the sense that his questions about probability pertain to the implementation of probabilities in empirical science. But there is another sense in which both Lonergan's and McShane's approach to probability is empirical. To investigate any matter empirically is to attend to instances of human experience with questions about the "nature" of such experiences. But when the object of investigation is the act of empirical inquiry itself, the curious subject is faced with a difficulty. To marshall evidence from previous experiments is to attend spontaneously to the content or term of such experiments. But rather than helping the investigation such attention inevitably constitutes an obstacle. For what is sought is not knowledge about what came to be known through the performance of the experiments but knowledge about the knowing. The alternative might seem to be to ask questions, from an *a priori* perspective, about the very possibility, the logical possibility, of any and all acts of knowing. But such questions bring the subject no closer to answering his or her questions about the nature of knowing. For their answers can only pertain to what *might possibly* be the case and not to what *in fact* is the case. A question of fact can never be settled *a priori* by an appeal to logic but only *a posteriori* in an appeal to evidence. What then constitutes evidence in an empirical investigation into empirical knowing? Lonergan suggests that we turn to instances of our own empirical inquiry as they occur when we encounter any unknown.

Empirical method has a curious and backward way of moving towards the understanding of its object.[18] A customary way of answering the question "what is it?" is to say "it is an $x$" when $x$ designates the name of a class of objects, when such a class is to be distinguished from other classes in a field, and when the characteristics of that class can either be described or explained by experts in the field.[19] But when there arise questions about the distinctions between the classes, or about the obscurities of the central insights that define the procedures for classification or when there are discovered objects or data that seem to fit into none of the classes then the question "what is it?" takes on a new meaning. The answer cannot be found by appealing to stock names, distinctions, insights and verification procedures, for there continue to arise questions that just cannot be answered intelligently in terms of the stock conceptual tools. It is in this case that empirical method implements its curious and backward way of investigating its object.

The investigator can name the object. But initially the name has no meaning, no familiarity, no intelligibility. The function of the name is heuristic. The name does not serve to classify the object but only to point to it as an object that can be experienced in some way or another but remains to be understood. "Let the object be named $a$," where $a$ can be any set of marks, squiggles, letters, or characters as long as it is not presupposed that we know what $a$ "means." The next step is a little more complicated. The investigator must turn his or her attention to the empirical occurrences of $a$ and to whatever experiential evidence can be gathered about $a$ that will give clues to the appropriate context or perspective in which $a$ is to be understood. Is $a$ an operation or the result of an operation? Is it a unity or a manifold? Does it have a structure? Where does it begin and where does it end? Can first hand sensory operations yield the necessary data or will microscopes, computers, or chemical test equipment be necessary? Is $a$ to be understood in relation to $b$ or in relation to $c$? Will we need interviews, questionnaires, frequency tables, statistical testing? By shifting contexts and perspectives, trying to bring one or another set of questions to bear on *a*, listing the data, juggling it around, rejecting one perspective in favour of another, performing endless operations in controlled settings to test possible sets of questions and answers, the investigator moves more or less slowly towards a discovery.[20]

That discovery, when and if it occurs, is an insight, an "internal" psychological event in which something *new* becomes psychologically present to a human person. It is a personal event which only occurs to one who has travelled the road of questions, operations and rejected answers. Its initial occurrence substantially reduces the obstacles to its successive occurrence in other persons. For, once the appropriate road of questions, procedures and answers has been charted the endless manifold of blind alleys can be avoided. But still the insight occurs only to one who treads the charted path.

The insight grasps a relation or set of relations that define *a* in terms of its appropriate context of other elements. And if it is correct[21] the insight can be formulated into a definition that fixes its relations to other elements such that progressive steps in the manipulation of that definition and the drawing of corollaries brings more of the relevant experiential data to bear on *a*. Thus gradually *a* becomes less obscure and more intelligible and meaningful. And this meaning, while certainly born of old elements and data is nonetheless a new meaning.[22] Everyone has experienced some of these stages in the "logic of discovery"[23] (or the learning process). And so many of us can recall moments when we have been startled to find that something quite familiar was in fact quite obscure and unintelligible.[24] The once-familiar object or event is given an ill-fitting or singularly inappropriate name. And then it is manipulated and juxtaposed with other objects of experience which seem to have nothing whatsoever to do with it. But by such manipulations and juxtapositions the object or event comes to be "seen" in a strangely new context of relations and other terms. By asking and answering appropriate questions we acquire the relevant set of insights that serve to reorient habitually our attitude towards the object. And when these insights are correct[25] the daily operations of implementing the understanding continue to yield data which are explained by and which serve to verify and re-verify the insights.

Following the approach of Lonergan, McShane's procedure in *Randomness* is to apply this empirical method, this set of stages in the "logic of discovery," reflexively, to the personal, "internal" discovery process itself as it occurs in the application of statistical techniques in empirical science. Thus while his data base is to be found in references to experiments in the natural sciences and in other philosophers' attempts to understand statistical knowing, the data themselves are psychological events which occur when human persons travel the charted (or uncharted) path described briefly above. The experiments are thus public in the sense that we all have experiences of acts of knowing. But they are private in the sense that *my* attention to *your* acts of knowing will most often fail to bear fruit.

## 3.2 Systematic and Non-Systematic Relations

The terms "systematic" and "non-systematic" have specific meanings in the works of Lonergan and McShane, meanings that will not be intelligible immediately to anyone who is not familiar with their works. As a first step towards these meanings McShane provides a set of examples.

1 2 3 4 5 6 7 8 9 10 11 12 . . .
6 7 5 6 4 7 6 7 5 5 6 4 . . .
5 1 8 4 3 9 2 7 4 6 9 3 . . .

> One understands immediately — and this is usually taken to be the full meaning of the dots at the end — how the first series would be continued. The series is systematic, with a formula for the nth term. The behaviour of the series is lawful and that lawfulness is 'mathematically expressible' in an elementary way.[26]

"Systematic" is defined in terms of the performance of the cognitional act noted above, the act of insight.[27] And in an effort to help turn attention to that public but oddly private data base upon which his definition draws, I will reproduce, here, some of the features of insight noted by Lonergan.

What we have to grasp is that insight
(1) comes as a release to the tension of inquiry,
(2) comes suddenly and unexpectedly,
(3) is a function not of outer circumstances but inner conditions,
(4) pivots between the concrete and the abstract, and
(5) passes into the habitual texture of one's mind.[28]

The stages in the genesis of understanding include clues, concepts, images, questions and anticipations. Women and men ask questions, we wonder, we seek to understand, we look for clues, we check out the clues. We conjure up images and draw diagrams, write sentences, tear up paper, erase sketches, rewrite, suppose and manipulate the suppositions. And then suddenly we have insights that answer the questions.

> The answer is a patterned set of concepts. The image strains to approximate to the concepts. The concepts, by added conceptual determinations, can express their differences from the merely approximated image. The pivot between images and concepts is the insight. And setting the standard which insight, images, and concepts must meet is the question, the desire to know, that could have kept the process in motion by further queries, had its requirements not been satisfied.[29]

What is grasped or "abstracted"[30] in an act of insight Lonergan names intelligibility. And the characteristic that is common to acts of insight, the characteristic that constitutes the basis for his distinction between systematic and non-systematic relations, is the fact that intelligibility regards the essential as essential, the significant as significant, the important as important, and it excludes and disregards the incidental as incidental, the irrelevant as irrelevant, and the negligible as negligible. The terms "essential," "significant," "important," "incidental," "irrelevant," and "negligible" always have a concrete meaning that is particular to each act of intelligence. But while their concrete referents are always particular the relations among these terms themselves are generalizable as either identity (or similarity) or nonidentity (or opposition). And so the constitutive characteristic of an insight is that somehow, the performance of a psychological act called insight results in the fixing of concrete elements in an experiential manifold in the relations of identity and non-identity such that what is fixed in the identity constitutes a unified psychological presence called intelligibility. Thus insight and intelligibility are defined "implicitly" as, respectively, the act whose occurrence specifies an object and an object whose nature is defined in terms of the occurrence of an act.

Hence, relative to any given insight or cluster of insights the essential, significant, important consists
(1) in the set of aspects in the data necessary for the occurrence of the insight or insights, or
(2) in the set of related concepts necessary for the expression of the insight or insights.

On the other hand the incidental, irrelevant, negligible consists
(1) in other concomitant aspects of the data that do not fall under the insight or insights, or
(2) in the set of concepts that correspond to the merely concomitant aspects of the data.[31]

At first glance it might seem that the approach proposed by Lonergan entraps him in what might be called a "hermeneutic circle." And so it would be useful here to describe more clearly what this approach involves. Lonergan never asks whether acts of understanding occur. To ask such a question is to give evidence of the prior occurrence of a set of acts of understanding *of some sort or another*. His question is always about the empirically verifiable *characteristics* of intelligent acts and their contents or terms.[32] The fact is that acts of intelligence *of some sort or another* are experiences that are within the horizons of all human subjects. But although we experience such acts, prior to our investigating their distinguishing characteristics we do not know how they occur, what constitutes the essential characteristics of their objects, or what might constitute the difference between such acts competently executed and others incompetently executed. So intelligent inquiry is conceived[33] by Lonergan as an appetite for "intelligibility" and an act of understanding is defined as that act whereby the appetite for "intelligibility" is satisfied.[34] Implicitly, then, "intelligibility" is defined as that which satisfies the appetite of inquiring intelligence. And at this point the procedure again becomes empirical. Lonergan turns his attention (inviting the reader to do the same) to actual occurrences of instances of investigation and discovery in an effort to discover if there are further distinguishable characteristics, classifiable stages, common orientations to various instances of acts of intelligence.

Thus it stands that Lonergan points to an appetite in humans, he notes that this appetite is for answers to concrete questions, he observes that the appetite is satisfied and its satisfaction is signalled when a psychological act occurs whose object meets the conditions of the question, and he attends to various occurrences of the psychological act in order to study its structure, its characteristics, and those of its object. He discovers that the single, universally distinguishable feature of acts of understanding (and of their respective intelligible contents) is that they include the essential as essential and exclude the incidental as incidental. And so the meaning of the term "systematic" is to be understood in terms of what is included as essential in an insight.

Let us define systematic processes by the already enumerated properties that, other things being equal,

(1) the whole of a systematic process and its every event possess but a single intelligibility that corresponds to a single insight or single set of unified insights,

(2) any situation can be deduced from any other without an explicit consideration of intervening situations, and

(3) the empirical investigation of such processes is marked not only by a notable facility in ascertaining and checking abundant and significant data but also by a supreme moment when all data fall into a single perspective, sweeping deductions become possible, and subsequent exact predictions regularly are fulfilled.[35]

Thus McShane's first numerical series above can easily be extended to the nth term.[36]

But there is a curious feature to this account of insights, a feature that links the definition of an insight with the definition of what Lonergan calls an "inverse insight."[37] Systematic relations are defined not only in terms of what is included as essential for the occurrence of an insight, they are also defined in terms of what is *excluded* by this psychological act. The data, the relations, the other possible answers to the question were rejected as mistaken or irrelevant because they did not qualify in meeting the demands of the question or the intent of the inquiry. When intelligence grasps the unity in, let us say, the meaning of words in a written sentence and the meaning of such sentences in a paragraph in a book, then the size of the page, the style of the print, the various alternate dictionary meanings of the words are all rejected by the spontaneously selective reader as not significant or essential to that meaning. To give another example, if one has left one's car lights burning over a cold winter's night and if one wants to know, the next morning, why the battery does not start the car, the answer would be formulated as an explanation (a unified set of insights) relating the electro-chemical properties of a lead acid battery to the magnitude of the resistance of the car's incandescent headlamps and the fact of a closed switch over eight hours at a temperature below zero degrees Celsius. In this case the single intelligibility that unifies the data systematically is the set of chemical equations that explains the conversion of lead oxide and sulphuric acid to lead sulphate under certain determinable conditions. Neither the colour of the car, the address of its location nor the income bracket of its owner are related systematically to the process that resulted in the battery discharging.[38]

It would seem, then, that some questions can be answered with insights that include and relate some data and exclude others.[39] In other cases, however, questions need to be met with the admission that there is insufficient data to answer the intent of the question. And currently the natural and human sciences abound with questions of this type. But there remains a third type of case, distinct from the two above, that also seems to occur within the range of our experiences. Some questions deserve to be answered with the "insight" that there is no answer; there is no intelligible unity to the data that satisfies the intent of the investigation. This brings us to consider the third series of numbers in the above citation from *Randomness*.

> 5 1 8 4 3 9 2 7 4 6 9 3 . . .
> . . .
>
> The third series ends also with dots. But the dots added to it have no other significance than as indicating that the series be continued. There is no rule for its continuation in so far as there is no rule relating the first eleven members given. In so far as there is no law relating to it, it may be described as totally random. The terms follow each other in a non-systematic fashion and one does not expect to arrive at a systematic formula governing them or at a generating formula for further members.[40]

Lonergan has named the act which grasps that there is no single intelligible unity to be grasped in data an "inverse insight."[41] Personal experiences of a devalued sort of such an inverse insight[42] would include instances when what one grasped was not the answer to a question but the fact that one has asked the wrong question. Inverse insights are not simply the admission that the question cannot be answered at present, or that one's level of intellectual development in the relevant fields is insufficient. Neither are they an admission that relevant data are missing. An inverse insight is not the absence of an act of understanding. Rather, it is itself an act of understanding. And what it grasps is that there is no unified intelligibility to be understood that will meet the demands of the inquiry. There is no systematic unity to the selected body of data.[43]

Before going on to consider some of the problems associated with inverse insights and with randomness that are treated by McShane in *Randomness, Statistics and Emergence* it might be helpful to note here that there is a kind of inverse intelligence corresponding to every direct insight. The term "abstraction" is often taken to refer to an act of intellect whose performance results in a unified experiential manifold being wrenched apart or torn from its proper context for the purposes of empirical or analytic scrutiny. The image associated with the term might be that of a student of biology dissecting a frog without any regard for the wonder of life. Or perhaps the term might evoke the image of a "scholar" making up his mind (usually the image is of a male) on what the world is like or on what it *ought* to do, in "abstraction" from any real concrete, detailed knowledge of human experience. It is certain that far too many examples of either image can be found in our world of experience. But let us consider for a moment another, not so popular meaning for the term "abstraction." Here the image might be that of a mechanic troubleshooting a failure in the electrical system of a car. When the solution is found the diagnosis "abstracts" from all the aspects of the car's operation which were not relevant to an understanding of the malfunction. The abstraction, in this case, is an enrichment in understanding and not an impoverishment. And the enrichment involves both the fact that the relevant data on the car's malfunction were identified and correctly interrelated and the fact that the irrelevant data were rejected. Anyone who has needlessly paid seventy dollars for a new battery only to find that the problem was a defective starter motor is in a good position to appreciate this difference between relevant and irrelevant data (and thus this "enriching" sense in which Lonergan uses the term abstraction).[44]

Corresponding to every direct insight there would seem to be a kind of inverse intelligence which rejects those elements in experience which are not relevant to the insight. And so the very possibility of any act of intelligence, in this analysis, would seem to rest upon the capacity of intellect to select and interrelate, on the one hand, and, on the other, to reject as irrelevant, at the same moment, data which do not constitute a part of the unity that is the insight. The distinctive feature of the *inverse insight*, then, would be not that it represents a departure from what usually occurs in a direct insight, but that it involves a focus upon something that is essentially but not obviously present with a direct insight.[45] However this focus comes as a surprise in the case of the inverse insight because, unlike the inverse dimension to the direct insight, the inverse insight grasps the absence of an intelligibility which previously was expected to be present.

The first chapters of *Randomness, Statistics and Emergence* are devoted to raising and answering questions about the objects of inverse insights, non-systematic or random relations in data. And this discussion inevitably leads into the distinctions between a naive realist and a critical realist cognitional theory.[46] For the purposes of this introduction I will state here simply that Lonergan's cognitional theory affirms that knowing does, in fact, know reality but that knowing reality and experiencing reality are two different but inevitably interrelated ways of relating to reality. Thus the question that Lonergan poses is always the "nature" of knowing and its relative correspondence with reality. It is never the question as to "whether" knowledge ever "knows reality."[47]

One of the prevailing theories on statistical knowledge discussed in *Randomness* affirms that there exists no objective correlate in being for an inverse insight. The whole of being is systematically interrelated. Knowledge is only of "classical" laws (laws which express a unified set of direct insights). And thus randomness, or the absence of a systematic, intelligible unity to data or to a process is merely an illusory appearance resulting from insufficient data. Hence statistical knowledge, knowledge which paradoxically grasps a sort of "intelligibility" in randomly occurring events, is merely an imprecise substitute for complete knowledge of systematic relations.[48]

McShane works towards developing a response to this challenge by introducing two examples, the movement of billiard balls on a table and the movement of a penny through a fair toss.[49] I will discuss briefly this second example. When a fair coin is tossed the outcome of heads and tails from a succession of tosses would appear to be randomly or non-systematically distributed. In view of our contemporary knowledge of the laws of physics one might ask why the outcome of each toss could not be predicted successfully. But the fact remains that such prediction, under normal circumstances, is not possible. This resistance to prediction is in some way related to an absence of reason governing the processes involved in a succession of coin tosses. And this absence of reason manifests itself in the absence of system in the distributions of heads and tails in a succession of tosses. How can this be? If the tossing of a coin is fully determined by the laws of physics how can there be an element of randomness in a series of tosses?

McShane's answer involves a distinction between the terms "non-systematic" or "random" and "indeterminate."[50] The toss of a coin is in no way an indeterminate process. Given enough time and enough data on (a) the initial position of the coin, (b) the precise motion and force imparted by the toss, (c) all the intervening motions and operative forces, and (d) the characteristics associated with the fall of the coin, the exact motion of the coin and thus the outcome of the toss conceivably could be accounted for. Thus the process is determinate inasmuch as it is determined by a complex of factors that can be understood in each case.

But there is something queer about the way that the process is understood.[51]

(1) The toss consists of a succession of stages each of which involves the operation or intervention of a complex of conditions. There is no way of

knowing prior to any toss (except under controlled conditions) what conditions will be operative at each stage. The very presence of any one of the conditions can be decisive for the outcome of that toss. And so *no single act of understanding* can grasp a generalizable pattern to the conditions operative throughout *every occurrence of a succession* of coin tosses.

(2) The reason why such a single act of understanding is impossible for a succession of tosses is because each condition of each toss is itself conditioned by a multiplicity of further conditions. As each condition is listed in terms of its own complex of conditions the list yields a diverging series. Each condition may be intelligible in terms of its own complex of preconditions. But the mere presence or absence of any one condition in the process is decisive for the outcome of the toss. Such presence or absence alters not simply the particular values and magnitudes in the toss but rather the entire intelligibility of that instance of the process. Each individual toss can only be understood by: (a) performing a succession of acts of understanding of each possible condition in terms of its own complex of preconditions; (b) judging whether and how the results of each successive act of understanding brings its respective condition to bear on the process; and (c) grasping the resultant interaction among the particular operative conditions in that instance of the process in a subsequent act of understanding. This subsequent act of intelligence, far from grasping an intelligible unity proper to the generalized act of "tossing a coin" grasps only the particular, unique relations among all the previous insights that were required to understand *this particular toss*. To understand this toss requires not only this one final act of understanding but all the previous acts which determined what conditions were operative in the toss. And the relationship among all the individual acts of understanding is *not* a generalizable intelligibility *proper to all instances of* tossing a coin.[52]

(3) Continued attempts to grasp an intelligible unity common to a succession of instances of coin tossing quickly brings an intelligent investigator to conclude that such attempts do not and can not lead towards a generalizable understanding of all instances of tossing a coin. There are too many conditions and pre-conditions that operate differently in each toss. And extremely small variations in each condition and pre-condition have a decisive impact on the outcome. Each toss seems to have a pattern of interrelated conditions that is for all intents and purposes unique. Consequently intelligence is led to conclude that, in any sequence of tosses *there is no reason why one result should prevail recurrently over another*.[53]

This final act of intelligence is not a failure to perform an act of intelligence. It is itself an act of intelligence. And what it grasps is an absence of *a stable intelligible unity governing recurring instances of the process*, and consequently an absence in intelligible reason why one or another result should regularly prevail. The process is named a non-systematic process and this final cognitional act which grasps the absence of stable, recurrent system is the devalued inverse insight. Like all acts of intelligence the content of the inverse insight goes beyond the data to affirm a generalization that is verified in instances of performance of the experiment.[54] And somehow even though we admit the possibility of a long run of heads in a *fair* coin toss we tend to doubt whether any single intelligibility would be found to explain such an unlikely occurrence. The fact is that the continued operation of gambling casinos and lotteries never ceases to verify this particular absence of reason that is at the root of the laws of probability.

The difference, then, between the discharging of a battery as an example of a systematic process and the toss of a coin as an example of a non-systematic process rests in the difference between what can be generalized about a succession of occurrences of a class of events or processes.

(A) The insight that grasps the intelligibility of any *one* instance of a systematic process is the *same* insight that grasps the intelligibility of *all* instances of that process. The insight is *generalizable* because the intelligibility governing the process is *stable* (invariant) under ranges of environmental conditions.

whereas

The insight that grasps the intelligibility of any *one* instance of the non-systematic process is *different* from the insights that understand *each other* instance of that process. The insight is *non-generalizable*. And a generalizable intelligibility is not to be found because the intelligibility governing the process is *not stable* under ranges of environmental conditions. This fact, *this lack of a unified, generalizable intelligibility in all instances of the process, is what is generalized as relevant to that class of process.* This grasp is the inverse insight.

(B) The intelligibility that is *common* to all instances of the systematic process *decisively relates* what is *particular* to each instance of the process.

whereas

The intelligibility that is *particular* to each instance of the non-systematic process *decisively interrelates* what is *common* to all instances of the process. And so there is no generalizable intelligibility associated with the outcomes of a succession of occurrences of the process.

It is interesting to observe, here, how the act of classifying events and processes and the act of understanding their intelligibility are interrelated differently in systematic and non-systematic processes. In a systematic process there is a set of insights which distinguishes this class of process from another. But there is also a set of insights which understands the systematic operation of each instance of this class of process. The classifying insights and the insights that understand the process both apply to each and every instance of the process. However, in a non-systematic process there is a set of insights which classifies the process and which applies or corresponds to every instance of the process. But there is no common set of insights which understands the outcome of each trial in terms of its conditions. And this absence of correspondence between classification and explanation in non-systematic processes will be a key element in understanding what Lonergan means by probability.

## 3.3 Probability

This brings us to consider the second of the three series of numbers listed above and the curious interrelation between direct and inverse insights which grounds probability.

6 7 5 6 4 7 6 7 5 5 6 4 . . . .[55]

. . .

Turning now to the second series we can note immediately that it too is irregular, the terms follow each other in non-systematic fashion, and a general formula for the nth term is not to be expected. Yet the dots at the end of this series indicate more than an arbitrary continuation of the series. The series is less irregular than the third series, and to appreciate that additional meaning is to reach the basic insight of statistical science.[56]

Thus the rule which we arrived at with the second series was that it oscillated around the value 6: the rule says nothing about the values of the particular terms although these are obviously part of the object of inquiry. Moreover this omission is a knowing omission: the fluctuations about the number 6 are acknowledged to be lacking in significance.[57]

With regard to the coin toss example, above, a succession of groups of ten toss trials could easily be carried out and the relative proportion of the occurrence of a heads, in each group of trials, could be expressed as a proper fraction. In this case the series of proper fractions would resemble the series of counting numbers above in that the terms in the series would oscillate about one-half. In both cases there is to be grasped an absence of system in the succession of terms. But at the same time this absence of intelligibility is not the whole story. There is a difference between these two series and the third, totally random series of numbers considered above.[58] In these two series the terms oscillate or fluctuate about a number. And while there appears to be no way of knowing how far and in which direction each number will diverge from the norm, still there is a certain intelligibility to be grasped in the fact that this oscillation occurs and is expected to continue occurring. The value of each number in the series cannot be determined by a general formula, but there still remains something intelligible that can be affirmed about all the elements in the series. And it is this "something intelligible" that is the object of the investigation which follows.

In the practical application of statistical techniques the first steps usually include a classification of the events which make up the population and

Probability 73

which are to be found in the sample. It was noted above, in the example of the coin toss, that the process "tossing a coin" could be classified as a generalizable process regardless of the fact that no common intelligibility linked the outcomes to determining conditions in a succession of tosses. But there was a further set of classifications that had to precede the investigation into the presence or absence of system, the classification of outcomes into the two groups, heads and tails. The identifiable characteristics common to all occurrences of outcomes in each class can generally be listed so as to ensure that an outcome can be judged either to qualify or not to qualify as an occurrence of one or another class. And examples of such classifications can easily be found. Insurance companies identify types of losses for which they will sell protection and types of customers to whom they will sell it. They compile actuarial statistics and levy premiums on the basis of the frequency of occurrence of losses of one type or another among drivers in one or another age group. Such classifications involve insights, but these are not initially the insights that grasp the relations between an occurrence of an event and its conditions. Rather, they are the insights that grasp some initial intelligibility that is common to two different occurrences of an event of a class.[59]

A second feature worth noting is that events of a defined class occur a number of times or in a number of places. And it is the frequency of their occurrence that is counted and tabulated. Whether this frequency is a temporally distributed succession or a spatially distributed set of simultaneous occurrences it is nonetheless the number of occurrences of events of a class that is the concern of the statistician. Pollsters count the frequency of instances of an opinion favourable to the government. Educators establish intervals in the range of marks from lowest to highest and they count the frequency of instances of marks in each interval. And actuaries count the frequency of occurrences of automobile accidents among male drivers between ages eighteen and twenty-five.[60]

The probability of occurrence of an event of a certain class is expressed in a proper fraction. And this fraction has a curious feature to it, a feature that echoes the relations among determining conditions in a non-systematic process. The probability of a heads occurring in a succession of tosses is one-half. But if in fact I flip a coin three times and if tails appears three times I am not overly surprised. Likewise if I roll a die ten times and fail to roll a six I do not conclude that the die must be loaded. In each case the particular deviation from the probability is not only tolerated; it is expected. When a succession of "relative actual frequencies"[61] of occurrences of various classes of events is calculated the deviations from the probabilities do not simply occur occasionally. *Rather, they are the norm.* Indeed the probability itself may never occur at all in the list. In statistics the particular case is expected to deviate from the probability[62] whereas generally, in classical science, the particular case is expected, all things being equal, to coincide with the result that is anticipated by applying the law.[63] Furthermore this divergence in statistical science is expected to be random or non-systematic. And when such deviations are not random, when there appears a pattern to the deviations, the investigator stops looking for a norm of the statistical type and starts looking for an explanation of the classical type.[64]

It should be noted at this point that in the normal application of statistical techniques to empirical problems the goal of the investigation is to discover *a posteriori* a statistical norm or a probability in the occurrence of classes of events. Unlike the toss of a coin or the roll of a die there is usually no antecedent symmetry discernible in the structure of a population or experimental field. Thus there is a sense in which the insights gained from an investigation of probabilities as they apply to coin tosses will not be identical to the insights gained in an understanding of the acts in which probabilities come to be known empirically. However, following the approach of Lonergan, McShane looks to cases like coin tosses and rolls of a die for the central insights that characterize statistical knowing and then turns to the empirical application of statistical techniques for an account of an attitude or set of anticipations operative in the sciences that intend or head towards this type of knowledge expressed in the pure case. The point here is that reality never displays only the pure characteristics either of the systematic or of the non-systematic process in isolation. But in order for actual acts of knowing to be understood correctly the two "pure" types of classical and statistical knowing need to be distinguished so that their respective contributions to any actual act of knowing can be appreciated.[65]

The cognitional acts involved in understanding the probabilities in a coin toss would seem to break down into two stages or phases. The first stage concerns individual tosses. Here the outcome of one toss is considered in terms of its determining conditions. The second stage concerns not individual tosses but sequences of tosses and, finally, all coin tosses in general. The pages above were devoted to discussing this first stage. The conclusion here was that if there is anything to be understood about the generalized act of tossing a coin, that understanding would not be a general account of particular tosses in terms of their conditions. The second stage, then, has a difficult mandate to fulfill. It must understand something common to all tosses but this something must not only respect the absence of system relating outcomes and conditions, it must, at least implicitly, embrace this absence of system in its own insight. How is this accomplished?

First,[66] it is noted that each toss yields only one outcome and there are only two possible outcomes. The results fall into two classes. The ratio of actual outcomes to possible outcomes is, thus, one-half. And if it can be shown empirically that the two outcomes are equally possible — that there is no reason why one should prevail over another — then the probability of each could be said to be one-half. Thus there is an essential "absence of reason" in the very meaning of probability.

Second, it is noted that whatever the outcome of a toss, that outcome would have been reversed if the initial position of the coin had been reversed. Thus the set of all possible combinations of conditions determining the outcome divides into two equal subsets each of which can be associated with a class of outcomes.

Third, "the relative actual frequency of 'heads' is the fraction obtained by dividing the number of times 'heads' occurs on any given succession of tosses by the number of tosses in that succession."[67] Lists of such relative actual frequencies can be compiled and it can be observed that the proper fractions differ from one-half and they oscillate about one-half. But the sequence of differences is not orderly. This can be observed. And this observation can be explained in terms of the absence of system relating outcomes to conditions in individual tosses; in terms of the inverse insight which was the conclusion of the first stage discussed above. If the differences from one-half formed an orderly series then the results (the lists of relative actual frequencies) would form an orderly series. And this order would have to be accounted for in terms of an insight grasping something common in the relation of each outcome to its conditions. It will be seen below how the presence of evidence of order in statistical data functions as a clue directing the scientist towards a discovery of functional or systematic relations between conditions and outcomes.[68] But here the inverse is the case. The absence of order in the statistics is understood to correlate with and verify the inverse insight which grasped an absence of system relating outcomes to conditions.

Thus (1) since each toss yields one of two possible classes of outcomes, (2) since each class of outcomes can be associated with one of two possible subsets of combinations of determining conditions, (3) since observed relative actual frequencies oscillate irregularly about one half and since this oscillation is explained in terms of the absence of rule relating conditions to outcomes,

> ... intelligence, then, can grasp a regularity in the frequencies by abstracting from their random features and by settling on the centre about which they oscillate. That abstractive grasp of intelligibility is the insight that is expressed by saying that the probability of 'heads' is one-half.[69]

It is interesting to note how the inverse insight functions as the bridge effecting or enabling the transition from the first stage of acts to the second. What is common to all instances of tossing a coin is precisely the lack of a single intelligible unity relating outcomes to conditions in all cases. And so intelligence is led to "look elsewhere" for something that can be understood about all tosses. Since there is no single intelligibility governing the relationship between conditions and outcomes in all the tosses there will be no significance, no intelligibility to be understood, in the aggregate of actual deviations from the probability. And it is this absence of intelligibility in actual deviations from probabilities that is the key to Lonergan's definition of the meaning of probability.[70]

The two stages in the acts of understanding concern different "levels" of explanation. That is to say that they concern different sets of correlations among data. The first concerns the correlations between results and conditions in individual cases. The second concerns the correlations between the frequency of occurrence of classes of events in a succession of cases where the classes of events constitute a unified population with empirically demonstrable features. In the first stage the event is considered in terms of its own particular determinations. In the second, the event is considered as a constitutive part of a larger whole, the population. In the first, the individual occurrences of the event are considered. In the second, successions of recurrences of the event are considered. In the first, no common intelligibility is discovered in the relation of events to conditions in a succession of cases. In the second, what is discovered to be intelligibly common to a succession of cases is the relation of this class of events to other classes of events that make up the population. And, finally, in the second, what is centrally significant to the event's relationship to the other events in the population is the absence of common intelligibility or system linking individual outcomes to conditions. Thus, the possibility exists that a number of different classes of events can define a unified population in terms of regularities in their respective probabilities. Consequently because of the absence of recurring system generating events there can occur a unified intelligibility called a population whose "state" is constituted by a determinate set of classes of events recurring with relatively stable probable frequencies. And it is this possibility that is the key to understanding Lonergan's account of "emergence."[71]

## 3.4 Heuristic Structures and the Complementarity of Classical and Statistical Inquiry

As was noted above, an account of probabilities as they are discovered in the course of applying statistical techniques in empirical experiments is not as straightforward as this brief account of the coin toss example might suggest. In most research there is neither evidence nor a possible explanation for any antecedent symmetry in the experimental field. Furthermore there usually occurs in scientific inquiry an oscillation between the scientist's anticipations of randomness and his or her anticipations of system. Thus the goal of the experiments is rarely a simple matter of marshalling evidence for the absence of system. Rather, it is through the performance of the experiments that the scientist must discover the presence or absence of system. It is usually the case that the experiments yield insights and v-probable[72] verifications for the operation both of system and of the absence

*Probability* 77

of system on different "levels" or in different quarters of the experimental field.

As a brief introductory example, if an American quarter is used in a coin toss experiment there is good reason for expecting an absence of symmetry in the distribution of relative actual frequencies about one-half. This anticipation is based upon the knowledge (an insight of the direct or classical type) that the coin is minted with two metals of different weights and that the two metals are distributed in layers through the thickness of the coin. This imbalance is not expected to result in every toss turning up a heads (or a tails). And experiments can verify that this anticipation is correct. But one does expect that one of the outcomes will turn up more frequently than the other. And so the application of statistical techniques has the goal of fixing the probability of one outcome at something more than one-half. There still remains an absence of intelligibility associated with the *complete* set of conditions governing each toss. Were this not the case the set of relative actual frequencies would not distribute randomly about some probability and the absence of randomness (the presence of order) would continually be discernible in continued sets of trials with that coin under those experimental conditions. There is a shift in the probability associated with a succession of heads (or tails) from one-half to something more than one-half. And this shift is accounted for in terms of the direct insight into the alloy composition of the coin. There remains the problem of determining the probability associated with a heads. But this is a problem of procedures for testing and verification in statistical science. It would seem that the problem is not insurmountable for statistical procedures do, in some cases, yield dependable results that are known to be dependable.

In a case where the presence of a biassed coin is not known prior to the test, the issue still remains a problem of which procedures are appropriate for distinguishing biassed coins from inadequate samples and improper tests. The act of understanding an actual probability is in no case *a priori*. It must always be determined empirically. Whether the coin is biassed or unbiassed the actual probability associated with a heads will always be understood in terms of (1) an inverse insight grasping an absence of intelligibility associated with the complete set of conditions whose operations are decisive for the outcome, (2) a direct insight grasping the regular occurrence of classes of outcomes, (3) a direct insight grasping a norm in a succession of relative actual frequencies of occurrence of each class of outcomes, (4) an inverse insight grasping the absence of regularity in the divergences of the relative actual frequencies from the norm, (5) a direct insight grasping the correlation between this fact of non-systematic divergence and the absence of a single, recurring intelligibility linking conditions to outcomes in a succession of tosses, and, finally, (6) a direct insight grasping a correlation between the divergence (or non-divergence) of the probability from one-half and the unequal (or equal) alloy distribution of the coin.[73]

What becomes evident in this example is that a significant element in empirical science is the anticipations of the scientist. The investigator begins by formulating a set of questions that reflects a pattern of anticipations, that specifies a particular field of data, that heads toward an explanatory goal and prescribes a set of operations and techniques that facilitate the attainment of this goal, i.e. the answer to the questions. The statistical scientist, or the natural or human scientist who implements statistical techniques, implements a statistical heuristic structure. Lonergan's section 2.4 of *Insight* develops an account of the characteristics that distinguish the heuristic structure of statistical inquiry from that of classical inquiry.[74] And McShane devotes his fifth chapter of *Randomness* to showing how the two heuristic structures complement each other in the overall procedures of investigation in empirical science.[75]

Empirical science involves an initial anticipation of what is to be known, and such an anticipation can be called an "open heuristic concept."[76] This anticipation is an intentional operation. It is an operation which, by virtue of its performance, the "open heuristic concept" becomes present as a notion or a question to a subject.[77] This initial intentional operation is the formulation of the question "what is it?" And in classical and statistical sciences this question takes two different forms. Classical science seeks knowledge of "the nature of ..." whereas the statistical inquirer seeks to know "the state of ..."[78] The classical scientist sets out to discover the nature of $x$ by adverting to different kinds of data and by looking for sensible similarities and differences that will serve to classify and distinguish different natures. The characteristics of these natures might be known beforehand in whole or in part or they might be discovered or revised throughout the investigation. In any case the ideal towards which classical science proceeds is "the discovery and verification of determinate functional relations"; of unified intelligibilities that relate conditions to outcomes and parts to wholes.[79]

The statistical scientist, on the other hand, adverts to the occurrence of events (a unity which has been classified in terms of direct insights) with a concern for knowing the events that constitute a population and, most important, the frequency of their occurrence. The scientist looks for regular and abnormal patterns in the distributions of frequencies of events of kinds where the precise meanings of the terms "regular" and "abnormal" may be specified beforehand or they may be redefined in the investigation. The goal, the knowledge of the "state" of a population, is reached when sets of classes of events are associated with corresponding sets of probabilities. En route towards this goal the scientist borrows classifications from classical science, he specifies appropriate volume intervals of events, she tabulates relative actual frequencies and implements elaborate statistical techniques derived from the mathematics of probability to aid the leap from relative actual frequencies to ideal frequencies. But while such a leap goes beyond the data it is nonetheless a legitimate leap of intelligence that can be verified in a procedure that is analogous to, but subtly different from that in classical science.[80]

What is significant here is that Lonergan's account notes a difference in the classical scientist's and the statistical scientist's concern with events. The classical sciences seek to understand an event as the outcome of determining conditions. But the statistical sciences seek to understand the event in terms of its relations with other events whose recurrence defines the state of a population. Such statistical understanding may pave the way or provide clues to explanations of the classical type which account for the stabilities in probabilities in terms of classical laws. And such classical laws may explain the distributions among the probabilities of the events that make up the population in terms of a condition or a set of conditions operative in the environment. But this explanation does not violate the absence of system linking the full set of conditions that are relevant in determining individual outcomes. Rather, it is principally an explanation of the relations among probabilities of aggregates of various classes of events rather than an explanation of individual events.

McShane provides a brief example of this oscillation between the two heuristic structures of empirical science.[81] In a set of buttercup experiments, the act of classifying buttercup types involved insights and formulations developed in classical science. Without such classifications statistical inquiry could not begin. The initial hypothesis was one of a random distribution of defined plant types. But as the frequencies of occurrences of types in randomly chosen meadow quadrants came to be tabulated and the relative actual frequencies calculated, what became obvious was a correlation between the distribution of types of buttercups and one specific environmental condition, land drainage. A set of controlled experiments succeeded in verifying this correlation and such verification served to clarify further the definitions of the three classes of flowers. The initial hypothesis of randomness was based upon an anticipation of a non-systematic relationship between the various habitat conditions and the probable distributions of aggregates of flowers of each type. But lists of distribution figures soon suggested some presence of system. The hypothesis of randomness was replaced by a classical hypothesis correlating water table levels and field drainage conditions with the probable distributions of aggregates of buttercups of each type.[82] And this second hypothesis was subsequently verified. It is worth noting that while the investigation proceeded on the basis of a set of initial statistical anticipations these anticipations did not determine in advance either the results or their "interpretation." Rather, a particular hypothesis and a particular set of anticipations made possible the accumulation of experimental results and it was such results that eventually overturned the hypotheses. What occurred was a transformation of the scientist himself or herself. The accumulated experimental evidence served to steer him or her away from the original anticipations and towards the intelligibility immanent in the data.[83]

## 3.5 Two Probabilities

A distinction has been drawn between two schools of thought on probability. Taro Yamane distinguishes the objective approach to probability from the subjective approach. The first includes the principle of insufficient reason and two forms of the frequency theory of probability.[84] And this objective approach corresponds, very roughly, to the approach to probability discussed here. The significant difference in the approach that is based upon Lonergan's insights is that the principle of insufficient reason is here integrated into a frequency theory that conceives a probability as a norm from which actual cases diverge non-systematically instead of a limit approached by a finite or an infinite sum. The subjective approach to probability is introduced with a quote from L. J. Savage:

Personalistic views [Yamane would substitute here the term "subjectivist"] hold that probability measures the confidence that a particular individual has in the truth of a particular proposition, for example, the proposition that it will rain tomorrow.[85]

In his book *Randomness*, Philip McShane discusses some of the questions associated with the meaning of the term "probability" when it is used to denote degrees of certainty or verification in what has been called the "subjectivist" approach.[86] He finds that the two schools do not, in fact, offer conflicting interpretations of the same thing. Rather, there are two distinct types of "probability" and each school offers some insights toward an account of each type. The questions associated with the probability of verification, which McShane calls "v-probability," and the subjective theory, deal with the different types of verification and the status of verified knowledge in both statistical and classical science. McShane's discussion of v-probability leads into an account of verification and of the "critical realist" cognitional theory which (he and others[87] would argue) is implicitly operative in the empirical sciences.

McShane begins by noting the distinction between two types of questions:

There is the what- or why- question, with which we mainly dealt in the last section, and there is the is-question, 'is it so?', 'is it the case?', which is our present concern. It is the is-question which drives the relativity physicist halfway round the earth to observe an eclipse. It presupposes some answer to the what-question — the eclipse-observer has at his fingertips both theory and expected sensible consequences — and its answer adds nothing more to the what-answer than a Yes or a No.[88]

The is-question proceeds from an exigence, a drive or appetite, of inquiring intelligence whose existence is granted in the practice of empirical science.

Most simply the exigence is the desire for empirical evidence to support a theory. "Perhaps we might make a start to our discussion from the commonly-accepted fact, that a theory is not acceptable without some possible empirical checking."[89] The generality of the exigence accounts for why this fact is commonly accepted.

McShane's distinction between is-questions and what-questions is based in Bernard Lonergan's account of the second and third types of cognitional operations.[90] In performing the second type of operation the subject wants to understand natures and states. But the product of such a set of acts initially is nothing more than a good idea. To move beyond good ideas requires a shift in one's mental attitude. The ideas are viewed with what might be called here a "hermeneutic of suspicion," (to borrow a term from Ricoeur). Can the ideas be verified? Are they the case? And this new mental stance with its concern for evidence characterizes the third type of cognitional operation.

The term or object of this operation is not principally the consistency of logic, the unconditional necessity of the hypothetical syllogism. Rather, the object is "v-probable" facticity. The scientist wants to know as best he or she can what is so, in fact, and not what could conceivably be otherwise. It is this concern with facticity, with particular times and places, that distinguishes the third from the second type of cognitional operation. The second type of operation seeks intelligibility, whether of the classical or the statistical type (with its curious element of absence of intelligibility). The third type of operation seeks to go beyond the intelligibilities grasped in insights and to establish whether these insights integrate all relevant experiential data and thus correspond to the recurrent intelligibility immanent in the ongoing routines of human experience. Do the insights completely satisfy the demands of the question, and do they "fit" with the data of experience? This is the concern of the third type of question.

In the common practice of empirical science answers to is-questions include an indication of a degree of certainty, of a "probable" certainty. But the term "probable" here means something quite distinct from the probability that I have been discussing so far. Thus McShane coins the term "f-probability" to denote the probability proper to statistical science and "v-probability" for the probability of confirmation or verification in both statistical and classical science.[91]

Most simply, f-probabilities and v-probabilities concern respectively what-questions and is-questions.[92]

> The first and basic step is to distinguish between probability as an answer to a what-question and probability as a quality of an is-answer: the former is f-probability, the latter is v-probability. To distinguish them, as we shall see, is not to separate them; they are in many ways interlocked. But without the distinction, which is based on the two different mental stances, the character of their interlocking would be

permanently obscured.[93]

F-probabilities concern distributions and patterns of distributions of frequencies of events. And the f-probability answers the question "what is the pattern?", "what is the ideal frequency?" V-probabilities, on the other hand, concern judgments about the correctness or truth of the answers to what-questions. And these judgments answer is-questions: "is the law verified?", "is the distribution normal?" In addition, f-probability does not pertain to an individual case. F-probabilities (in terms of this analysis) are ideal frequencies from which individual cases will always diverge non-systematically. And so when applied to individual cases an f-probability is only a guess.[94] The inverse insight "there is no reason why" which is at the basis of the meaning of f-probability affirms the absence of evidence relevant to individual cases.

V-probability, on the other hand, affirms not the absence of evidence relevant to individual cases but the relative sufficiency of evidence available for affirming the truth or falsity of both laws and individual cases.

> Both a guess and a probable judgment are based on incomplete knowledge: intelligent reflection in either case shows that evidence is insufficient for certainty. In the case of the probable judgment that insufficiency is partial: there is some approximation towards sufficiency which can be grasped as such, leading to the modest commitment of a probable judgment, a judgment which is probably true, which converges in a non-statistical sense on true judgment.[95]

At this point two possible confusions can arise. First, some debates about the subjectivist school on probability, noted above, arise as a result of the implementation of f-probabilities in the formulation of v-probable judgments of truth. Thus the role of probabilities in statistical and classical science is doubly confusing. It is common practice to perform a succession of verification tests, both in classical and in statistical science, and to express the v-probable truth of an hypothesis in terms of the f-probable frequency of occurrence of test results that fall within a commonly accepted range. The fact that test results cluster around statistical norms bears witness to the fact that testing procedures cannot completely isolate interferences, inaccurate readings, poorly controlled tests, etc., etc. But the statistical norms in the test results are to be understood in terms of a reflective act of intelligence correlating the accepted f-probability of favourable test results with the intelligibility expressed in the insight, to pronounce a v-probable judgment of truth on the hypothesis.

The second possible confusion concerns the role of f-probabilities in reasonable betting on individual cases.[96] Thus the question can arise whether an f-probability can be the v-probable certainty of an individual occurrence. Clearly, given the option, it would be "reasonable" to bet on drawing a face card from a euchre deck. And the proper fraction two-thirds that expresses the f-probability associated with the appearance of a face card in a succession of draws figures heavily in the explanation why such a bet would be "reasonable." Nonetheless two-thirds is not the v-probable certainty that a face card will be drawn in a single case. This is so firstly because v-probabilities (as defined here) are predicates of judgments of matters of fact. They are not relevant to predictions. We might want to use the term "likelihood" to designate the relevance of prior evidence to predictions in statistical experiments. Secondly, the proper fraction two-thirds does not affirm that one-third of the available evidence is missing. The fact is that this f-probability does not express the relative sufficiency of evidence bearing upon this case. The f-probability is one hundred percent of the available evidence bearing upon this case but because the event is the outcome of a non-systematic process all the available evidence still tells nothing about the outcome of this particular draw. There is no reason why any one of the twenty-four cards in the deck should prevail over any other. And it is this "no reason why" that accounts for the fact that gamblers do not regularly lay fraud charges against casinos when improbable occurrences result in their financial destruction. Individual cases diverge non-systematically from probabilities.

How then do f-probabilities figure into reasonable betting on the likelihood of outcomes in particular cases? The answer suggested here has three parts.

(a) The question "is it reasonable to bet on drawing a face card from a euchre deck?" is not properly a question of the truth of fact of an occurrence or explanation but a question for deliberation. "Should I act in this way or not?" The question is on Lonergan's fourth level of cognitional operations.[97] And while such a question for deliberation demands empirical facts, it is not answered by them. Questions for deliberation intend future prospects, goals, values, and actions that will realize such prospects.

(b) Assuming that I have decided to place one bet on drawing a face card from a euchre deck the question becomes one of anticipating the possible results of an individual outcome of a non-systematic process armed with an f-probability. "Is it likely that I will draw a face card?" The occurrence or non-occurrence of the likely outcome will not verify or falsify the f-probability. And so there is neither an f-probability nor a v-probability applicable to the anticipation of drawing a face card.

(c) But there is an imprecise but relevant meaning to the term "likely" and this meaning is integrally related to the f-probability, two-thirds, associated with a succession of such draws. The likelihood or the reasonableness of the bet consists in the recognition that (i) there is no knowledge available to predict individual cases, (ii) the best available knowledge is the f-probability, two-thirds, which is the mid-point from which a large number of relative actual frequencies of drawing a face card will diverge non-systematically, and (iii) this f-probability is to be accounted for in terms of the fact that a euchre deck has twice as many face cards as numbered cards.

## 3.6 Verification

Verification of hypotheses is done differently in classical science and in statistical science. But underlying such differences there is a common structure to the cognitional operations that are involved in both sets of procedures. And Lonergan has listed and interrelated the elements of this structure.

To grasp evidence as sufficient for a prospective judgment is to grasp the prospective judgment as virtually unconditioned.

Distinguish then between the formally and the virtually unconditioned. The formally unconditioned has no conditions whatever.

The virtually unconditioned has conditions indeed but they are fulfilled.

Accordingly, a virtually unconditioned involves three elements, namely:

(1) a conditioned,
(2) a link between the conditioned and its conditions, and
(3) the fulfillment of the conditions.

Hence, a prospective judgment will be virtually unconditioned if

(1) it is the conditioned,
(2) its conditions are known, and
(3) the conditions are fulfilled.

By the mere fact that a question for reflection has been put, the prospective judgment is a conditioned; it stands in need of evidence sufficient for reasonable pronouncement. The function of reflective understanding is to meet the question for reflection by transforming the prospective judgment from the status of a conditioned to the status of a virtually unconditioned; and reflective understanding effects this transformation by grasping the conditions of the conditioned and their fulfillment.[98]

This summary is dense and loaded with terms that have precise meanings. And so this study can hope neither to explain these precise meanings nor to bring forth the empirical evidence that serves to verify the accuracy of this account. Rather, I will discuss only briefly how the verification procedures in statistical and classical sciences differ in the ways that they link a conditioned with its conditions. While this discussion may seem unsatisfactory it should become clear that a satisfactory treatment would involve a detailed examination of a number of cases of verification procedures as they occur in the natural and human sciences and an in-depth engagement with other accounts of verification. As was noted earlier, such a treatment has not been done on the basis of the foundations set forth by Lonergan.

It is worth noting that empirical science concerns theories verified in an appeal to instances in accordance with procedures judged acceptable by the science. Thus the problem is always one of specifying appropriate procedures.[99] But an integral part of the procedures is an attitude of care for the object under investigation. Anyone can recall cases in which an urgent matter spontaneously called forth the implementation of verification procedures appropriate to the issue. "How badly are the children hurt?" "Why is the business going under?" "Is that my house that's burning?" The criteria for selecting relevant data, relevant questions, and relevant test procedures varies from field to field. But the orientation of care and the corresponding appetite for true answers to questions is common to all fields. Just as the orientation of care and the appetite for truth are, given the right circumstances, spontaneous, so too the selection of relevant data, relevant questions and relevant procedures are spontaneously a function of the structure of inquiring intelligence. As will be noted below,[100] inquiring intelligence involves the cultivation of skills. But such skills are not a foreign imposition on the mind but a cultivation and a systematization of a spontaneous capacity of the human intelligence.

There is a sense, then, in which verification involves both the performance of techniques and the developed competence, or maturity of the human subject. There is no way that verification yields results that are universally convincing. Rather, verified results convince only those who are appropriately developed, appropriately skilled and, in many cases, even appropriately disposed[101] to performing the acts required to affirm a virtually unconditioned with some v-probable qualifications. This inability universally to convince with appeal to evidence could lead one to feel that truth is not to be had by anyone. But since there continue to be developed, in some sciences, generally accepted criteria both for pronouncing a practising member competent and for specifying the relevant data, questions and procedures for verification in that field, empirical science has not universally given up the quest for v-probable truth. When the data base of a field expands, when new procedures are discovered, when new questions arise in a field, that ask about the existing limits of horizons of the field then the generally accepted criteria for verification and for pronouncing a member competent also must change. But these changes do not constitute evidence that verification is impossible. Rather, it is the probable truth of the newly verified evidence that forces the refinement of procedures.[102]

The verification procedures of classical science will differ from those of the statistical sciences principally because particular occurrences can be predicted with the application of classical laws and the theoretical results can be compared with actual measurements. But since statistics do not apply to individual cases such a procedure cannot be a part of verification in statistics. At first glance it might seem that this constitutes an obstacle to any verification of statistics. But this conclusion arises from a misunderstanding of verification in classical science. Even though theoretical results can be compared with actual results in individual cases in classical science it is not the individual result that verifies the hypothesis. Rather, such a result when combined with a host of other such results in the context of an intelligently conceived and defined set of verification procedures fulfills the particular experimental conditions necessary for the v-probable judgments of that field of science.[103] And so there occurs that leap of constructive intelligence — the enriching abstraction — from individual cases to general laws, from data to determinate intelligibilities, that characterizes all forms of human knowing. It is the intelligently conceived set of verification procedures proper to that science which specifies the particular experiments needed to verify a theory. And the performance of this set of procedures is the link between the conditioned and its conditions. The actual performance of the experiments yields the sets of results that mutually confirm each other and at the same time fulfill the specified conditions.[104]

In statistical science there exist comparable and equally complex sets of intelligently conceived verification procedures that specify what constitutes a representative sample and what test results serve to verify a statistical hypothesis. Predictions cannot be compared to measured results in particular cases in statistics. However, it is possible to employ a range of techniques that will generate separate sets of mutually confirming test results, and to specify criteria according to which distribution patterns can be accepted or rejected. And it is these sets of statistical techniques and criteria relevant to the various applications in different disciplines that constitute the link between a statistical hypothesis (a conditioned) and its conditions. The performance of the actual experiments and the accumulation of results that satisfy the relevant verification criteria constitute the fulfillment of the conditions and permit the affirmation of the v-probable truth of the hypothesis.[105]

The range of problems associated with the status of verified knowledge cannot be discussed here for this would involve a concrete dialogue with the history of philosophy and with the actual practices of current scientists. This preliminary sketch presented by Lonergan, discussed in some further detail by McShane, and introduced briefly here is offered as an invitation for further dialogue and dialectical analysis. But the following concluding paragraph drawn from *Randomness, Statistics and Emergence* should suggest the direction towards which Lonergan's account of probability is headed. A critical realist stance is not merely an incidental part of Lonergan's thought. It is an integral element of his emergent conception of humanity, who is a part of developing world process, and headed towards God.

> On this view the real is what is known or to-be-known in true judgment, or in terms of scientific practice it is what is known or to-be-known by Theory Verified in Instances. This clearly does not make the real a function of what is known in contemporary science and com-

mon sense. Reality is neither a Kantian Ideal nor a dependent of the mind. It is there to-be-known and we move asymptotically towards its knowledge through the true judgments of science and common sense. Reality is not a function of what is known: rather, knowing is a function of the real, where the word 'function' has a dual sense. It has the mathematical sense of isomorphism. But it also has the biological sense — and here we might fit our assumption into the context of the evolutionary hypothesis to be discussed later. Knowing is a process which takes place in the human organism. It is, one might say, a higher process of digestion with questions for appetite. It is a process which has evident survival value — witness Western science, the arms race, or merely man against beast. Had that process emerged as Plato or Plotinus described it, we would long since have become extinct. It is its adaptation to the environment, material reality, which ensures its organic possessor survival, and that adaptation is the one we described as an isomorphism.[106]

## FOOTNOTES – CHAPTER 3

1   B.J.F. Lonergan, *Understanding and Being*, eds. E.A. Morelli and M. Morelli (New York: The Edwin Mellen Press, 1980), p. 87 (hereafter cited as *Understanding and Being*).
2   While Lonergan remained convinced that with *Insight* he had "hit upon a set of ideas of fundamental importance," he nonetheless realized throughout *Insight* that these fundamental ideas remained to be developed into a fully explanatory, verified theory. *Insight*, p. xxx.
3   *Understanding and Being*, pp. 87-91.
4   Frederick Suppe, "Introduction" to *The Structure of Scientific Theories*, second ed., edited with a Critical Introduction and Afterword by F. Suppe (Urbana, Ill.: University of Illinois Press, 1977), pp. 4-5.
5   Joseph Flanagan, S.J., "From Body to Things," in *Creativity and Method*, edited by Matthew L. Lamb (Milwaukee: Marquette University Press, 1981), pp. 495-508; Matthew L. Lamb, *History, Method and Theology: A Dialectical Comparison of Wilhelm Dilthey's Critique of Historical Reason and Bernard Lonergan's Meta-Methodology*, A.A.R. dissertation series 25 (Missoula, Montana: Scholars Press, 1978), pp. 401ff; Leo J. O'Donovan, "Emergent Probability and the Method of an Evolutionary World View," *The Personalist* 54 (Summer, 1973): 250-273; idem, "Lonergan: Emergent Probability and Evolution," *Continuum* 7 (1969-70): 131-42; Hugo A. Meynell, *An Introduction to the Philosophy of Bernard Lonergan* (New York: Barnes & Noble, 1976), pp. 9-47. A larger number of works have been written on Lonergan and the philosophy of science but these listed above touch on the distinctiveness of statistical knowledge. Works written on Lonergan and the philosophy of science include Langdon Gilkey, "Empirical Science and Theological Knowing," in *Foundations of Theology*, edited by Philip McShane (Dublin: Gill and Macmillan, 1971), pp. 76-101; Patrick A. Heelan, "The Logic of Framework Transpositions," in McShane, ed., *Language, Truth and Meaning*, pp. 93-114; idem, "A Realist Theory of Physical Science," *Continuum* 2 (1964): 334-342; Mary Hesse, "Lonergan and Method in the Natural Sciences," in *Looking at Lonergan's Method*, edited by Patrick Corcoran (Dublin: The Talbot Press, 1975), pp. 59-72; J. Kroger, "Polanyi and Lonergan on Scientific Method," *Philosophy Today* 21 (1977): 2-20; idem, "Theology and Notions of Reason and Science: A Note on a Point of Comparison in Lonergan and Polanyi," *The Journal of Religion* 56 (1976): 157-161; Matthew L. Lamb, "Towards a Synthetization of the Sciences," *Philosophy of Science* 32 (1965): 182-191; Edward M. MacKinnon, "Cognitional Analysis and the Philosophy of Science," *Continuum* 2 (1964): 343-368; Philip McShane, "The Foundations of Mathematics," *The Modern Schoolman* 40 (1962-3): 373-387; idem, "Insight and the Strategy of Biology," *Continuum* 2 (1964): 374-388; R. Eric O'Connor, S.J., "A Dialogue on Learning Mathematics," in Lamb, ed., *Creativity and Method*, pp. 509-525; idem, "From a Mathematician," *Continuum* 2 (1964): 313-315; Gerard Watson, "A Note on Lonergan and a Greek Conception of Science," in Corcoran, pp. 55-58.
6   James Albertson, S.J., review of *Insight*, in *The Modern Schoolman* 35 (1958): 242-244.
7   John Humphreys, "What, If Anything, is Probability?" *Horizons* (a journal of the students at Milltown Institute of Philosophy and Theology, Dublin) 7 (Summer, 1973): 91-103.
8   Anne Marie Martin Brennan, "Bernard Lonergan's World View: Emergent Probability and the God-World Relation," unpublished Ph.D. dissertation, Columbia University, 1973; Rocco Cacòpardo, "A Study of Ongoing Social Processes," unpublished Ph.D. dissertation, Brunel University, Uxbridge, Middlesex, 1974; Gerald V. Kohls, "The Evolutionary Source: A Study of Evolution Based on the Philosophy of Bernard F. Lonergan," unpublished Ph.D. dissertation, University of Fribourg, Switzerland, July, 1969; Leo J. O'Donovan, "Evolution as a Systematic Concept in Recent Catholic

Thought," unpublished Th.D. dissertation, Westfälische Wilhelmsuniversität, Münster, 1971.
9   Patrick H. Byrne, "God and the Statistical Universe," *Zygon: A Journal of Science and Religion* 16 (1981): 345-363; "Lonergan and the Foundations of the Theories of Relativity," in Lamb, ed., *Creativity qnd Method*, pp. 477-494; "On Taking Responsibility for the Indeterminate Future," in *Phenomenology and the Understanding of Human Destiny*, ed. Stephen Skousgaard (Lanham, Md.: The University Press of America, 1981), pp. 229-238; "The Thomist Sources of Lonergan's Dynamic World View," *The Thomist* 46 (1982): 108-145.
10  Reviews of *Randomness* include G. Barden, *Philosophical Studies* 20 (1971): 344-6; R. J. Blackwell, *The Modern Schoolman* 49 (1971-1972): 89; W. Mathews, *The Heythrop Journal* 13 (1972): 319-321; W. Newton-Smith, *Bibliography of Philosophy* 18 (1971): 34; P. Quay, *Review for Religious* 30 (1971): 30; D. Ryan, *The Furrow* 22 (1971): 596-598; John Heywood Thomas, *The Clergy Review* 56 (1971): 310-312.
11  Mathews, p. 319.
12  Suppe, see note 4 above; A.R. Peacocke, *The Sciences and Theology in the Twentieth Century* (Stocksfield, England: Oriel Press, 1981); the same can also be said of Ian G. Barbour, *Issues in Science and Religion* (New York: Harper & Row, Publishers, Harper Torchbooks, 1966).
13  *Understanding and Being*, p. 87ff. An example of this type of definition can be found in Taro Yamane, *Statistics: An Introductory Analysis*, 3d ed. (New York: Harper & Row, Publishers, 1973), p. 108.
14  Ibid., pp. 87-96.
15  *Randomness*, chap. 8.
16  *Understanding and Being*, p. 87.
17  On the majority consensus among empirical scientists on a qualified "realist" stance, see A.R. Peacocke, "Introduction," in Peacocke, ed., p. xi. On an emerging consensus among contemporary philosophers of science on a qualified "realism," see Suppe, "Afterword — 1977," in Suppe, ed., pp. 652, 716-728. However, the novelty of Lonergan's account of empirical knowing as a *critical realism* is not to be underestimated.
18  This introductory account of empirical method might seem to beg the question of an investigation into empirical understanding and to short-circuit the debates that fill the pages of books like that of Suppe. However, this example is merely a brief illustration of an account that is developed in greater length in *Insight*. And the intent of this illustration is to highlight the role played by "implicit definition" in empirical understanding. Eric O'Connor was convinced that this was one of Lonergan's most important breakthroughs, R. Eric O'Connor, S.J., "From a Mathematician," pp. 313-14.
19  On the distinction between "nominal" and "explanatory" definition, see *Insight*, pp. 10-11, 12-13. See also Flanagan, pp. 502-507; Heelan, "Realist Theory," pp. 336ff.
20  An amazing chronicle of this journey from occurrences of events through questions, clues, alternate perspectives and endless experiments to discovery can be found in June Goodfield, *An Imagined World* (London: Hutchinson, 1981). Of course, this chronicle also includes verification, see 3.5, 3.6 below.
21  Insights are accepted as correct or rejected as incorrect in a subsequent cognitional act called "judgment," see *Insight*, chaps. 9, 10, 11. In fact, most judgments are only v-probably correct, see 3.5 and 3.6 below.
22  This "newness" of meaning in an insight is a key element in Lonergan's "enriching" sense of "abstraction." See 3.2 below. Of course, an insight need not be a truly original discovery for it to be a "new meaning." The point here simply is that with an insight there becomes psychologically present to a subject a meaning which was not present prior to the insight.
23  On the particularly odd meaning that this expression takes on within Lonergan's approach, see *Randomness*, pp. 10-12, 86-90. It would appear that "discovery" has little

to do with "logic."
24  I would suggest that J. Hillis Miller's efforts at "deconstruction" in the field of literary criticism can be understood as attempts to bring the reader around to viewing the familiar as, in fact, something quite foreign. See "The Limits of Pluralism III: The Critic as Host," *Critical Inquiry* 3 (1977): 439-447.
25  On the notion of judgment, see 3.5, 3.6 below, *Insight*, chaps. 9, 10, 11.
26  *Randomness*, p. 20.
27  Ibid., pp. 22, 35.
28  *Insight*, pp. 3-4.
29  Ibid., p. 10.
30  On the term "abstraction," see note 44, this chapter below.
31  *Insight*, pp. 30-31. On the notion of "implicit definition," see *Insight*, pp. 12-13, and note 18, this chapter above.
32  Ibid., p. xvii.
33  This conception or definition is by no means *a priori* but rather from experiential data and clues.
34  On Lonergan's notion of the "eros of the spirit," see *Method*, p. 13.
35  *Insight*, p. 48. This account may seem somewhat romantic to a contemporary philosopher of science whose attention, in recent decades, has been focused almost undividedly upon the massive fact of failure in the application of empirical techniques, and upon the radical "paradigm shifts" that have occurred in the sciences during this century. But while attention to the limits and the failures of empirical knowing must be understood as a welcome corrective to an earlier *hubris* and an essential stage in the ongoing genesis of self-knowledge, it must not be allowed to obscure the characteristics of empirical knowing which are most responsible for the very genesis of this preoccupation with failure. Science and technology have been so successful in the past century that revolutionary discoveries have become a matter of course. Consequently when limits to operative heuristic structures (which are derived from previous discovery) are encountered in the study of new data, then failure becomes alarming precisely because it is an exception to the massive rule of success. Subsequent attention of philosophers becomes focussed almost exclusively upon such failures and, thus, the acknowledgement of limits and deficiencies in empirical knowing becomes elevated to a principle of suspicion over the very possibility of knowledge. I would suggest that this feeling of alarm and suspicion animates Mary Hesse's counsel that theology avoid looking to science for its own foundations. See Mary Hesse, "Retrospect," in Peacocke, pp. 284-291.
36  *Randomness*, pp. 20-22.
37  *Insight*, pp. 19-32.
38  This is not to say that such factors are not related *at all, in any way*, to the discharging of the battery. Rather, the point here is to draw attention to two things. (1) Direct insights relate data systematically in response to single particular, concrete questions. (2) There are different kinds of relations one of which is the systematic relation. The high income bracket of the owner and her ability to replace cars at will might operate as a condition for her careless attitude towards automobiles. The fact that the owner has always hated the colour of his car might contribute, in some way, towards his unexpressed wish to destroy it. And either of these factors might play a part in answering the question "why were the lights left on?" But this is a different question from our original question "why does the battery not start the car?" Only the *fact* that the lights were left on and not the *explanation* of why they were left on is necessary for answering the question why the battery does not start the car. The pages and chapters that follow explore some of the elements and empirical characteristics of the various other types of relations that might exist between, say, the income of a car owner, the colour of a car and a dead battery. But to answer, concretely and precisely, what relations in fact exist among such events, would require a detailed study of one such case.

39  In most cases such insights are only v-probable, see 3.5 and 3.6 below, and *Insight*, pp. 300-304.
40  *Randomness*, pp. 20-21. Technically speaking there is a rule operative here. However the rule only relates to the type of numbers (integers), not their order.
41  See *Insight*, pp. 19-25, 53-58.
42  It would appear that the difference between pure inverse insights and devalued inverse insights lies in the presence or absence of statistical residues. Lonergan uses the term, devalued inverse insights, for those cases wherein intelligence anticipates systematic relations in data and then discovers statistical laws to be operative. Pure inverse insights, on the other hand, leave no statistical residues. For examples, see *Insight*, pp. 19-25, 53-58.
43  The discovery that one has been asking the wrong question of a body of data is a good example of a devalued form of inverse insight. However the most powerful and the most significant inverse insights are those which follow upon the best line of scientific questioning of the age and which, consequently, lead either to a whole new direction in scientific inquiry or (when statistical residues are present) to the study of distinct "levels" in the structure of reality. On the meaning of the term "levels" here see chap. four below.
44  On this "enriching" sense of "abstraction," see *Insight*, pp. 87-89; *Verbum: Word and Idea in Aquinas*, edited by David Burrell (Notre Dame: University of Notre Dame Press, 1967), pp. 141-181 (hereafter cited as *Verbum*).
45  Lonergan uses the term "residues" to designate the defect in intelligibility that is associated with various instances of a generalized insight, on the one hand (the empirical residue), and with the coincidental manifold which allows the operation of statistical laws, on the other (the statistical residues).*Insight*, pp. 25-32, 54-58, 86-102.
46  See *Method*, p. 76.
47  *Insight*, p. xvii. See also 3.6 below, and *Randomness*, p. 145.
48  *Randomness*, pp. 37-8. See also Byrne, "On Taking Responsibility," pp. 231ff.
49  Ibid., pp. 32-37, 40-43, 51-3. On the coin toss, see also *Insight*, pp. 60-62.
50  Ibid., pp. 37, 53.
51  The following account is my own reconstruction of some of the insights discussed in *Randomness*, pp. 32-37, 40-43, 51-53.
52  It is interesting to note that while a toss of a coin is characterized by factors that intervene throughout the toss and cannot be identified with any precision prior to the toss, the discharging of a battery is characterized by factors that *can* be identified precisely prior to the process. If other factors intervene to change the normal process that is expressed in the chemical equations for a discharging battery, the battery is not discharged, it is broken. The normal process of discharging a battery precludes the operation of intervening factors that are decisive for the outcome. It is this *regularity* associated with decisively operative factors in a succession of occurrences of a process that is a key element in the distinction between systematic and non-systematic processes.
53  See *Randomness*, pp. 18, 20; *Insight*, pp. 60-62. For a good example of this distinction between absence of intelligibility in a non-systematic process and absence of knowledge, see Monod, *Chance and Necessity*, pp. 96ff.
54  On verification, see 3.5 and 3.6 below.
55  *Randomness*, p. 20.
56  Ibid., p. 23.
57  Ibid., p. 29.
58  See 3.2 above.
59  On the complementary roles of classical and statistical scientific operations, see *Randomness*, chap. 5, particularly pp. 72, 80-81.
60  McShane responds to objections to this frequency theory of probability in *Randomness*, pp. 100ff, 149ff. His procedure is to distinguish v-probability from f-probability in

terms of the distinct cognitional operations involved in each. F-probabilities are predicates of answers to "what-questions" while v-probabilities are answers to "is-questions." See 3.5, 3.6 below.

61 "Relative actual frequencies" are defined by Lonergan in *Insight*, p. 58. "Consider a set of classes of events, P, Q, R, ... and suppose that in a sequence of intervals or occasions events in each class occur respectively $p_1$, $q_1$, $r_1$, ... $p_2$, $q_2$, $r_2$, ... $p_i$, $q_i$, $r_i$, ... times. Then the sequence of relative actual frequencies of the events will be the series of sets of proper fractions, $p_i/n_i$, $q_i/n_i$, $r_i/n_i$, ... where i = 1, 2, 3, ... and in each case $n_i = p_i + q_i + r_i + ...$ ." See also p. 61.

62 See *Randomness*, pp. 25, 26, 28-29; *Insight*, pp. 58-62.

63 On this blanket proviso "all things being equal," see *Randomness*, pp. 40ff; *Insight*, p. 65. See also verification, 3.5, 3.6 below, and Byrne, "On Taking Responsibility," p. 232.

64 On the complementarity of statistical and classical heuristic structures and the oscillations between them, see 3.4 below, and *Randomness*, chap. 5.

65 This is the point of Lonergan's account of "heuristic structures" in *Insight*, pp. 62-6.

66 The following is a reconstruction of the presentation in *Insight*, pp. 60-62.

67 *Insight*, p. 61.

68 See 3.4 below.

69 Ibid., p. 62. The stucture of the proof can be schematized as follows:

The ratio of actual to possible outcomes in a toss is the probability of occurrence of the outcomes in a sequence of tosses if the possible outcomes can be shown to be equally possible, (insight expressed in a definition, formulated on the basis of an appeal to initial evidence).

The absence of order in the succession of deviations of relative actual frequencies from the probabilities is observed, (inverse insight based upon an appeal to experiential evidence), "and correlated with" the absence of common intelligibility relating conditions to outcomes of individual occurrences, (the conclusion from the earlier experimental appeal to evidence, 3.2 above), "thus explaining and verifying" the equi-possibility of the two outcomes and thus the fact that the ratio (in this case one-half) is the probability.

It may be argued that the structure of this proof, the correlation between explanations and cognitional operations, represents a naive view of the structure of scientific theories. It is certainly true that this proof makes an explicit appeal to a realist cognitional theory and thus a realist account of scientific explanation. But the goal of this study is not to present an explicit defence of Lonergan's critical realism in the face of the prevailing theories of explanation in science. This defense is carried out in part in McShane's *Randomness*, pp. 144ff. But this defense in no way constitutes a definitive response to the contemporary field of positions. Similarly no definitive rejection of Lonergan's critical realism has been formulated to date. What is worth noting here is that any account of the structure of scientific explanation and proof will necessarily make some appeal to the actual (realist) truth about experimental operations (experiential evidence). Thus any account of scientific explanation that concludes by refuting the possibility of knowledge of being, gained from an appeal to evidence has cut its own throat. On the structure of verification of hypotheses, see *Randomness*, pp. 90-99; Byrne, "Lonergan and the Foundations," pp. 481-88. On the role of correlation in explanation in science, see Byrne, "On Taking Responsibility," pp. 232-4.

70 Lonergan's definition of probability runs as follows: "Consider a set of classes of events, P, Q, R, ... and suppose that in a sequence of intervals or occasions events in each class occur respectively $p_1$, $q_1$, $r_1$, ... $p_2$, $q_2$, $r_2$, ... $p_i$, $q_i$, $r_i$, ... times. Then the sequence of relative actual frequencies of the events will be the series of sets of proper fractions, $p_i/n_i$, $q_i/n_i$, $r_i/n_i$, ... where i = 1, 2, 3, ... and in each case $n_i = p_i + q_i + r_i + ...$. Now if there exists a single set of constant proper fractions, say p/n, q/n, r/n, ... such

that the differences

$$\frac{p}{n} - \frac{p_i}{n_i}, \quad \frac{q}{n} - \frac{q_i}{n_i}, \quad \frac{r}{n} - \frac{r_i}{n_i}, \quad \ldots$$

are always random, then the constant proper fractions will be the respective probabilities of the classes of events, the association of these probabilities with the classes of events defines a state, and the set of observed relative actual frequencies is a representative sample of the state." *Insight*, p. 58. The "absence of intelligibility" is expressed, in the definition, as the random differences between the relative actual frequencies and the probabilities. Further on this absence of intelligibility, see *Randomness*, pp. 26-7, 43.

71  See chap. four below, particularly 4.4. See also *Randomness*, chaps. 9, 10, particularly pp. 208ff.
72  On the meaning of v-probability or verification-probability, see 3.5 below.
73  Of course these acts of understanding are rarely performed in this order and they are rarely differentiated. Knowing, as it is operative both in statistical and in classical science, is a skill and like all skills the characteristics of competence include smooth and even performance. But like all skills its elements can be differentiated and further development usually requires such a differentiation at some point in time. See 5.1 and 5.2 below.
74  *Insight*, pp. 53-67.
75  *Randomness*, pp. 68-94. See also *Insight*, pp. 103-114.
76  *Insight*, p. 63.
77  See *Method*, p. 7.
78  *Insight*, p. 63.
79  Ibid., pp. 63-66.
80  Ibid., pp. 63-66. On verification, see 3.5, 3.6 below.
81  *Randomness*, pp. 71-76. McShane's example is drawn from J. L. Harper and G. R. Sager, "Some Aspects of the Ecology of Buttercups in Permanent Grassland,"*Procedures of the British Weed Control Conference* I (1953): 256-63.
82  While the relationship between the occurrence of *each flower* and the whole range of conditions that are relevant to its growth continues to exhibit evidence of an absence of system (and anyone who has tried to grow grass from seed can attest to the fact that one can seldom count on every seed sprouting), there exists nonetheless a systematic relationship between the distribution pattern of *aggregates of flowers* and one specific condition. As will be seen in the discussion of emergence this distinction between single occurrences and distribution patterns of aggregates of occurrences is crucial.
83  This transformation in the scientist which results in his or her approaching the data with different sets of questions and anticipations is discussed in *Method* with reference to the historian. In this case the shift is not from the classical to the statistical heuristic structure but from the set of meanings experientially operative in one cultural or historical setting to that of another. Lonergan uses the word "ecstasis" to designate this transformation of the historian. See *Method*, pp. 187-8. See also 6.3 below. This transformation of the subject is the condition of possibility for liberation from the "hermeneutic circle" in which theories beg the question of data. On the "hermeneutic circle," see H. G. Gadamer, *Truth and Method* (New York: Seabury, 1975), pp. 235ff.
84  Yamane, pp. 100-108.
85  L. J. Savage, *Foundations of Statistics*, p. 3, quoted in Yamane, p. 109. On the two approaches to probability, see also Suppe, p. 626 n. 25. There remains a third approach in the field of probability and statistical theory, the Bayes' decision theory, see Yamane, pp. 287ff. I would suggest that whereas the subjectivist approach can be understood as a predicate of answers to "is-questions" (operations on Lonergan's third cognitional level, judgment or verification), and whereas frequency theory can be understood as

a type of answer to a "what-question" (an operation on Lonergan's second cognitional level, understanding), so Bayes' procedure could be understood as the integration of a frequency theory of probability into a "moral" or "practical" decision procedure for calculating proportional outcomes of multiple effect situations. Bayes' decision procedure operates on the fourth cognitional level. For more on this fourth level, see chap. five below.

86  *Randomness*, pp. 131-148.
87  See note 17, this chapter above.
88  *Randomness*, pp. 132-3.
89  Ibid., p. 135.
90  On judgments and is-questions, see *Insight*, chaps. nine and ten; *Verbum*, chap. two.
91  *Randomness*, p. 137.
92  Of course the matter is never quite as simple as this for f-probabilities are used frequently in the process of verification. It would seem, here, that the procedure involved is a matter of performing the appropriate f-probable frequency of tests whose results correspond to predictions based on statistical or classical laws to v-probably verify the laws. For an elaboration, see the pages which follow here.
93  *Randomness*, p. 138.
94  See paragraphs following.
95  *Randomness*, p. 138. For a good example of this distinction between incomplete knowledge and absence of system, see Monod, *Chance and Necessity*, pp. 96ff.
96  On reasonable betting, see *Randomness*, chap. four.
97  See chap. five below.
98  *Insight*, p. 280.
99  *Randomness*, pp. 140-141.
100  See chap. five below.
101  This, of course, is the issue at stake in the concern for the "interests" of the scientific community. See Ian Miles, *"The Ideologies of Futurists,"* in Fowles, pp. 68-72.
102  I would say that this is reflected in Thomas Kuhn's analysis and development of the notion of scientific "paradigms." See "Postscript 1969," in *The Structure of Scientific Revolutions*, 2nd enlarged ed. (Chicago: University of Chicago Press, 1970), pp. 174-210, particularly pp. 203, 205-6, notwithstanding the two paragraphs on pp. 206-7.
103  The work of Imre Lakatos reflects a similar appreciation for the "methodology of research programs" in the development and verification of scientific theories. Single experiments in his view, neither verify nor falsify insights and theories. Rather, sets of related theories are linked in a "research program" and Lakatos' "methodology" is an account of a set of procedures that should be followed if a plurality of research programs are to be allowed to flourish so as to correct and build upon each other. See Suppe, pp. 659-670, particularly pp. 660-662.
104  This is not to suggest, by any means, that such a set of procedures has been developed *completely* in any field.
105  *Randomness*, pp. 140-141.
106  Ibid., p. 145.

# Chapter 4

# Emergent Probability

## 4.0 Introduction

As was suggested in the last chapter's closing quotation from McShane's *Randomness, Statistics and Emergence*, Bernard Lonergan's attempts to grapple with the foundations of probability and statistics had a very specific aim in view. Quite generally one might say that his aim was to develop a structured world view which had its foundations in the methods and procedures of twentieth century empirical science. But this would not be the whole story. For as well as being a philosopher, Bernard Lonergan is a theologian who has spent not a little of his time studying the thought of St. Thomas Aquinas. Thus his aim, throughout his life's work, has been not only to develop a contemporary world view but also to discover if such a world view could be open to an understanding of man's orientation towards the transcendent, and at the same time be in continuity, in some sense, with the Thomistic foundations upon which his own religious tradition perennially has sought to build. This might seem, at first glance, a courageous but somewhat futile attempt to harmonize radically distinct dimensions of history and reality. But in my estimation Lonergan's endeavours are not to be written off quite so quickly.

In an article published recently in *The Thomist*,[1] Patrick H. Byrne provides evidence that Lonergan's clues regarding the relevance of probability and statistics for an emergent or development-centred world view came from within the very works of Aquinas himself. In other words Lonergan did not first work out a world view and then attempt to harmonize it with Thomistic and contemporary theology. Rather, it was in attempting to discover what Thomas Aquinas meant and what he sought to understand that Lonergan found the clues that he would later develop into a contemporary world view in an analysis of the procedures of empirical science. This should not be so unlikely as it might at first seem. For much of Aquinas' own work was devoted to studying the operation of human understanding and conceiving understanding as an analogy for the Trinitarian processions. Lonergan argues, and not unreasonably, that Aquinas' own acts of understanding constituted the evidence upon which his analyses were based.[2] Thus conceivably there could be clues gained from Aquinas' work that might shed light upon the operations of understanding as they are implemented in contemporary science. Professor Byrne provides evidence that this, in fact, was the case in Lonergan's work on Thomas.[3]

The issue of world views is at once exhilarating and staggering. It is becoming increasingly clear that there is no getting around a world view of some sort or another.[4] The question would seem to be not whether a world view but which. And it is this question that animates the host of contemporary attempts to grasp the implications of recent scientific dicoveries into the origins, the dynamism, the structure and the direction of the universe.[5] But to arrive at an adequate world view at this time in history would seem to involve a monumental integration of insights and methods from every quarter of the natural and human sciences.[6] Many current attempts at interdisciplinary collaboration seem to be striving towards this integration.[7] Yet the sheer immensity of the body of knowledge and the subtlety of the insights that demand integration continually obscure the road towards its achievement. The pace of recent centuries of cultural, economic and scientific change seems to have outstripped our capacity to gain an appropriate perspective or viewpoint on humanity, on our origins, on our world of culture and on our futures. And so we are left with vast capacities and skills without a broader perspective on who we are or where we are going.

This problem of world views is not going to be settled easily or quickly. And so this fourth chapter, like the third is not offered as a definitive solution to the problem. Rather, like the previous chapter, the following pages are presented as a sketch of a possible set of clues that have been developed after a period of considerable reflection by a thinker who is recognized in philosophical and theological circles as demanding great respect.[8] This chapter does not represent a detailed engagement with other contemporary attempts to formulate a world view. And where other views are introduced in this chapter, their purpose here is only to illustrate some aspect of Lonergan's approach. The dialectical engagement of Lonergan's thought with the views of others in the philosophy of science still remains to begin on any large scale.[9] The hope here is that this presentation will not function as an obstacle but as an impetus to this engagement.

## 4.1 World Views

In an effort to gain some preliminary foothold on this mountainous issue of world views I have summarized, quite briefly, Bernard Lonergan's provocative sketch of four other world views that can be contrasted with emergent probability.[10] There is no claim here that this summary represents in any way an adequate account of the thought of any of the great men or women who can be identified with these views. But I think that Lonergan'sketch can help to call attention, again, to the import of notions of randomness and system both for one's anticipations of the structure of reality and for one's view of the status of cognitional operations and objects in relation to this reality.

In the two introductory chapters, above, this issue of world views was introduced, first with a brief discussion of the notion of "progress" in the field of world modeling, and then with an introduction to the ways in which Immanuel Kant and Jacques Monod sought to integrate an ethics within a philosophy of history or an evolutionary theory. The concern at this early stage was to provide examples of theoretical attempts to wrestle with the questions of human responsibility for history and the benevolence of world processes. But what became clear in the works of Kant and Monod was the fact that the two differed sharply on matters of cognitional theory and that these differences were foundational for their differences in the fields of ethics and history.

I think it can be said reasonably that what separated Kant from Monod historically was the introduction of the empirical evidence of randomness into scientific accounts of world processes and the widespread appreciation of the import of this experiential evidence among philosophers and scientists alike. Lonergan's sketch of four world views in *Insight* is an initial attempt to chart what was "going forward" through the scientific revolution's preoccupation with empirical evidence and through this discovery of the reality of randomness in world processes. And so the shift from the second to the third and fourth examples, below, can be seen as the historical watershed which separated Monod from Kant.

While this sketch of Lonergan's remains introductory, I think that reproducing this sketch in summary form can accomplish a number of worthwhile results. First, this summary can give some evidence of what sort of thing is meant by the term "world view." World views have a scope, a depth and a pervasive, almost ineluctable impact on the thought of a culture. And until some introduction is made this influence can hardly be appreciated. Second, Max Weber introduced the notion of the "type" and discussed its usefulness in analysis.[11] Basically a "type" is an ideal or pure form that does not usually exist in fact but which functions as a sort of benchmark against which actual cases can be compared. In Lonergan's terms the "type" functions as an image against which insights can be fixed in the specific ways that they differ from the image. These four world views are offered here as "types" against which the insights of emergent probability can be fixed. Thirdly, it is not immediately apparent how classical or statistical knowing relate to world views. These four illustrations provide some clues as to how cognitional theories and acccounts of the structure of the known constitute the foundations upon which world views can be and are built.

The first two of the four world views presented for comparison are the "Aristotelian" and the "Galilean" views. Both types seek understanding of systematic relations, of classical laws, but both conceive the meaning of the term "law" so as, finally, to preclude statistical knowing as a distinct type of knowing. The "Aristotelian" view regards world process as consisting either of cause and effect or of mere coincidence. The regularities of the heavenly bodies explain the coincidental operations and interactions of terrestrial causes. And thus all relations are finally systematic when understood in terms of the motions of the eternal heavens. The "Galilean" view, on the other hand, pronounces earthly contingency an illusion by distinguishing merely apparent secondary qualities presented in sense experience from the "reality" of primary qualities that are grasped in mathematical equations based on this experiential evidence. In this view the acts of scientific understanding expressed in these mathematical equations do not omit or leave behind (as unexplained) the particularity or contingency of concrete times and places (the coincidences that were omitted by the "Aristotelian" laws but subsequently explained away in terms of the eternal laws of the heavens). Rather, natural laws, in the "Galilean" view are immediately attached to or embedded in the basic "prime matter," the stuff of the universe which is perpetually in motion. Thus the natural laws yield a complete and thorough account of all of reality.

The key difference between these two views lies in the meaning of the term "abstraction."[12] In the "Aristotelian" view it is understood that laws grasp and express what is intelligibly similar in two or more cases of an object, an event, or a process. But the law says nothing about the particular locations, the particular magnitudes, the particular times of occurrences of two or more instances of the same class of object, event or process. The law "abstracts" from what is particular or coincidental about the two instances. And such coincidences are explained as resulting from multiple convergences of other operative laws. The operations of all terrestrial laws could, ultimately, be traced back to their originating cause in the heavenly motions and thus the contingencies that are "abstracted" from in the natural laws are explained away finally in terms of a first cause. In the "Galilean" view, however, no such appeal to heavenly first causes can be made and so the particularities of two instances of the same class of object, event or process has to be accounted for. This is done by positing a basic prime matter which takes the "form" of the intelligibilities expressed in mathematical laws in various different times and places. The laws do not "abstract" from particular, contingent times and places but constitute the "form" which prime matter takes on in different times and places. Thus the laws, finally, explain both generalities and particularities in a perfect, classically understood, mechanistically determined universe of basic, prime matter.

The "Darwinian" and "Indeterminist" world views, on the other hand, both grasp that mere coincidence or contingence is not to be explained away in classical laws. Statistics and the probabilities of aggregates yield explanatory knowledge of reality. But the "Darwinian" statistical laws apply to species of "things" and like the "Galilean," the "Darwinian" view conceives such species in terms of observable variations in basic matter and not in terms of intelligibility that "abstracts from" or disregards the particularity of times and places. Reality is not intelligibility but "matter" taking on "form" in place and time. Thus like the "Galilean" the "Darwinian" conception of classical knowledge of species demands an intricate, mechanistically determined web of interrelating classical laws fixing the times and locations of species of things in basic matter. This materialist conception of reality finally precludes the possibility of randomness and the operation of statistical laws. But this contradiction is obscured by the overwhelming emphasis upon the evident *fact* of randomness and its explanatory import for chance variation and natural selection. The "Indeterminist" world view recognizes this paradox and resolves it by pronouncing the macroscopic classical laws which yield the appearance of material and of regularity to be mere illusion. The real is the microscopic and the random on the subatomic level. And only the statistical distributions of Quantum mechanics constitute knowledge of reality. Thus all processes are essentially non-systematic or random. Classical or systematic relations are creations of the minds of scientists and observers and are imposed upon data. Without classical unities and processes the non-systematic processes cannot be conceived as randomly interacting classical laws and so all process is conceived as essentially indeterminate.

## 4.2 Randomness and Scientific Explanation

This introductory presentation of world views might seem like a "set up," presenting straw men that can be knocked down. This is, in no way, the intent here, and again I must emphasize that these sketches should not be taken as responsible analyses of any thinker's work. Rather, the informed reader may recognize the problems introduced by one or more of these "types" as a problem that he or she has had to grapple with in his or her own discipline. The following represents an introduction to the way in which Bernard Lonergan has tried to grapple with such problems and, again, the work of McShane in *Randomness, Statistics and Emergence* has set the general order of presentation of topics here. It will be left to the reader to compare emergent probability with the four views presented here.

Having formulated a definition of randomness and of probability, Lonergan's next step is to ask if these notions can be employed to explain the fact that different "levels" or branches of the natural and human sciences seem to explain recurring patterns of events and processes without always tracing these explanations back to a set of common determinants on some basic "level." An introductory example here might illustrate the problem more clearly.

The weather at a given time and location is defined in terms of the categories and relations of meteorology: in terms of rainfall and other forms of precipitation, in terms of wind speeds and directions, in terms of classes of air masses and types of turbulence occurring at fronts where air masses meet, in terms of air pressures, air temperatures and countless other categories

We all know that meteorological phenomena are determined by the laws of chemistry and physics as they apply to atoms and molecules of chemical compounds in terrestrial geography and atmospheric fluid and thermodynamics, given the contemporary state of world conditions in the ongoing dynamics of the universe. And yet meteorological categories and processes do not correspond to physical or chemical categories in any direct sense but rather they represent correlations and convergences of particular ranges of values in specific combinations of units of physics and chemistry.[13] And with respect to explanations in physics and chemistry the particular patterns, magnitudes and combinations of physical and chemical elements that constitute the meteorological categories and relations are coincidental or without significance. For example, with respect to the fundamental laws and categories of physics and chemistry the value of thirty-four percent as an expression of the percentage of light radiation reflected by a surface has no relevance or significance. But when it is recognized that this value represents the approximate average annual sunlight radiation reflected by the earth[14] and when this fact is linked to such other facts as the twenty-three and one-half degree inclination of the earth's axis, the nineteen percent of sunlight radiation that is absorbed into the earth's upper atmosphere, the dynamic properties of the particular combination of gases which make up the earth's atmosphere, the mass of the earth, the fluid-dynamic properties of that curious molecule, $H_2O$, and the speed of the earth's rotation, then the particular value, thirty-four percent radiation, begins to take on a significant role in explaining the climatic conditions experienced, let us say, at Montréal, Québec. It is not simply the physical and chemical principles of radiation and absorption of light which are relevant to understanding the earth's climatic and weather patterns. Rather, it is the *particular combinations* of physical and chemical principles that are operative in the atmosphere and at the surface of this particular planet in space, that converge to result in a general average sunlight reflection of thirty-four percent. And this *fact*, and its relative stability, are relevant to the terms and relations of meteorology and incidental to the basic terms and relations of physics and chemistry. Hence meteorological explanations do not try to explain a given day's average temperature in Montréal in terms of the subatomic physics of light absorption and reflection, but they begin with the fact that a certain conjunction of conditions tends to yield a relatively stable solar light reflection rate of around thirty-four percent per annum at a particular time and place of world process.[15]

This illustration serves to introduce an issue which looms much larger when we come to trying to explain the relationship between chemistry and biology or between zoology and psychology. There seem to be "levels" or strata of scientific explanations. And while the explanations on a "higher level"[16] of explanation inevitably appeal to laws and processes on a "lower level" they are nonetheless not conceived usually as being reducible to those "lower level" laws. Science seems to divide into physics, chemistry, botany, zoology, etc., each with its own set of terms and relations, and each involving a further number of more specific strata of explanatory correlations (e.g. hydrology, astronomy, geology, etc., etc.). A world view that would reflect the procedures and results among and within these various "levels" and strata would need some understanding of the relationships between these various sets of explanatory correlations and some understanding of the ways in which the processes of the various sciences have interacted throughout the ages of world process. Following Bernard Lonergan,[17] Philip McShane begins his approach to this problem by asking if the notions of probability and randomness, as he has understood them, could contribute a clue towards an answer.[18]

In his ninth chapter of *Randomness, Statistics and Emergence*, McShane draws upon some evidence gained from experiments performed by N. Rashevski in the field of mathematical biophysics to point towards the significance of randomness in relating scientific explanatory "levels."[19] The relations between the processes of biology and the laws of physics and chemistry can be illustrated in contemporary accounts of the life processes of the amoeba. The amoeba consists of atoms and molecules within a certain spatio-temporal range and distribution. But the biological accounts of amoeba-processes, such as digestion, excretion and reproduction, while rooted in physical and chemical explanations, concern a system of characteristics and relations that supervene upon the physical and chemical phenomena. If these biological processes ultimately can be explained completely in terms of the physical and chemical laws then what is the status of the distinct terms and relations of biology? How are we to understand the relation between biological laws and physico-chemical laws?

One approach to the problem among philosophers of science has anticipated a systematic or functional relationship between the physical and chemical conditions associated with an amoeba and the biological processes of that amoeba.[20] That is to say the philosophers anticipate a unified set of functional relationships which grasp and express a single pattern of interactions among all of the relevant physical and chemical processes associated with every amoeba. And this unified pattern, expressed in the terms of physics and chemistry, would decisively account for all the biological functions which distinguish each amoeba as an instance of the generalized class, amoeba. The particularities of each individual amoeba, in this physico-chemical explanation, would be irrelevant to understanding each amoeba as an amoeba.[21] But McShane notes that this anticipation leads to a dilemma. Since biological explanations concern a completely different set of terms and relations from those of physics and chemistry, the philosopher of science is forced either to conclude that the higher, biological level, distinguished by non-deducible characteristics is an epiphenomenon (Pepper) or to accept the overwhelming power of the biological explanations and to account for them by introducing non-scientific factors that could neither be measured nor verified (Meehl and Sellars).[22]

McShane approaches this dilemma by noting that the working hypothesis among serious biologists is of distinct levels of science; levels that concern different sets of terms and relations.[23] He notes, too, that evidence from the work of such scholars as H. Kaeser,[24] and N. Rashevski leads one to conclude that this hypothesis of systematic or functional relationships is not empirically tenable.[25] Rashevski's attempts to discern common patterns at the molecular level among groups of amoeba cells yields only explanations of individual cells as particular and unique.

> But, since there are no two cells perfectly alike, the exact solution of the problem for a given case would contain a tremendous amount of detail which is biologically insignificant because it applies *only to the given case*.[26]

Similarly H. Kaeser remarks that:

> ... the complete enumeration, even if it were possible, of all the molecules within an organism would not account for any but its most trivial aspects.[27]

McShane finds that the evidence points to the fact of randomness, in some way or another, operative at the physical and chemical levels.

> ... the processes involved within the amoeba form a coincidental aggregate which can be understood concretely only through a coincidental aggregate of equations and conditions.[28]

When amoeba processes are explained in terms of physics and chemistry it would seem from the evidence that it is the pattern that is particular and unique to the processes of each amoeba that decisively interrelates what is common to all amoebas. If there exists a single set of generalized explanations of the biological processes operative in all amoebas it cannot consist of classical explanations of biological processes as outcomes of determining physical and chemical conditions.[29]

McShane takes the evidence of randomness or absence of system as a clue to the relevance of a statistical element in explaining the relationship between "levels" of explanation. In terms of the definition of f-probability developed in the previous chapter, a statistical norm or an f-probability neither precludes the determinate operation of classical laws nor explains classes of outcomes in terms of determining conditions. Rather, in a random or non-systematic process a converging coincidence of laws whose pattern or intelligibility may be unique in any single occurrence of the process, nonetheless can yield an event or an outcome that can be classified in a direct insight. This outcome is recognized as an instance of a class of events which recurs and which, together with other types of events, defines a population. The event recurs not because of an identical pattern or intelligibility in a set of classical laws. Rather, because a set of initiating and boundary conditions forces a randomly interacting set of classical processes to yield one or another from a determinate set of classifiable outcomes, the classes of outcomes recur with a more or less stable frequency that is expressed in an f-probability, and this f-probability can be explained in terms of a few initiating, environmental or boundary conditions without violating the absence of system relating the conditions to outcomes. Thus a succession of events of one particular class can recur without any common systematic or intelligible explanation in terms of determining conditions but with a relatively stable frequency that is explained in part in terms of a few selected conditions and in part in terms of the other events that make up the population.[30] The introduction of Lonergan's notion of f-probability makes at least possible or *conceivable* an explanation of f-probably recurring classes of events in terms other than a complete functional or systematic correlation between events and conditions. Whether this clue can constitute an element in an adequate explanation of the relation between explanatory levels in science depends upon whether f-probably recurring events can link up with other f-probably recurring events to yield new systematic patterns and "laws." And Lonergan's notion of the "recurrence scheme" is an attempt to conceive this possibility.

## 4.3 *Conditioned Schemes of Recurrence*

The basic insight at the center of Lonergan's notion of the recurrence scheme is that of reflexivity.[31] The recurrence scheme is reflexive in the sense that the functioning or operation of the scheme has the effect of curling back upon itself and fulfilling the conditions for the scheme to recur. And this reflexivity is a part of the internal structure of the scheme. Most simply a recurrence scheme is a series of events that occur in a specific pattern or order of succession. But not any pattern or order will do. For what is significant about the scheme is that the events recur over and over again in the same pattern or order of succession. And Lonergan proposes, in the reflexive character of the structure of the scheme, a possible or conceivable explanation for this recurrence of a patterned set of events. In a first type of scheme, the relationship between the events making up the scheme is such that each event in the scheme fulfills the conditions for the occurrence of the next event, and the occurrence of the last event fulfills the conditions for the recurrence of the first, thus beginning the scheme anew. In a second possible type of scheme, the events are all conjoined in an interdependent combination pattern such that once all are functioning the scheme continues to function. In any case, the point of Lonergan's notion of the recurrence scheme is that events conceivably can link together in such a way that it is not an antecedent line or string of conditioned events that accounts for the recurrence of any event but a circular or reflexive structure linking a determinate set of events into an ordered pattern. Lonergan provides a few examples of recurrence schemes.

In an illustration of schemes of recurrence the reader may think of the planetary system, of the circulation of water over the surface of the earth, of the nitrogen cycle familiar to biologists, of the routines of animal life, of the repetitive, economic rhythms of production and exchange.[32]

The recurrence of a scheme can be ensured further by defensive circles of events such that any event which tended to upset the scheme would fulfill the conditions for a succession of further events to occur that would terminate in eliminating the intruder. Again the structure of the defensive circle is the set of links between the events in the circle. Each event fulfills the conditions for the next event (or in a circle of the second type one event conditions the occurrence of all the others).

In illustration of schemes with defensive circles, one may advert to generalized equilibria. Just as a chain reaction is a cumulative series of changes terminating in an explosive difference, so a generalized equilibrium is such a combination of defensive circles that any change, within a limited range, is offset by opposite changes that tend to restore the initial situation. Thus, health in a plant or animal is a generalized equilibrium; again, the balance of various forms of plant and animal life within an environment is a generalized equilibrium; again, economic process was conceived by the older economists as a generalized equilibrium.[33]

The key to understanding the relevance of the notion of recurrence scheme for an account of the relationship between scientific "levels" and strata lies in Lonergan's definition of probability. Within a particular region or environment there can be occurring a host of types of events. If these events are the outcomes of processes which exhibit an absence of recurring system, then the events will recur irregularly in accordance with a certain f-probability. For each event to occur there will be required the fulfillment of a determinate set of conditions. But because that set of conditions is, in fact, fulfilled in a coincidental convergence of laws and processes, the event occurs irregularly (in accordance with an f-probability). However, given the environmental stability of a certain set of factors or conditions, there are types or classes of events that require only the fulfillment of one or a few conditions for them to occur. And when this one or these few conditions are themselves events of another type which are already recurring within this environment (with a certain f-probable frequency) then the coincidental occurrence of the conditioning event(s) in the right time and place is systematically followed by the occurrence of the conditioned event. Given the stability of the conditions of the environment, non-systematically recurring events can link together in a string or group so that the f-probable occurrence of the first event is systematically followed by the certain occurrence of the others.

When the string is extended finally to include an event which conditions the occurrence of the first in the sequence, then the string becomes a loop. In this case the mere occurrence of any one event in the loop sets off a chain that simply continues recurring until something intervenes to break the links. The *complete* set of conditions associated with the occurrence of any single event in the loop will certainly form a non-systematic aggregate and reach far beyond simply the occurrence of the previous events in the scheme. But given the stable fulfillment of these environmental conditions, for whatever reason in whatever chain of circumstances, it is the set of internal relations linking the events in the scheme that explains the *fact* that the scheme recurs once it has begun. The initial occurrence of the scheme is in accordance with the coincidental convergence of conditions. But once this occurs the recurrence of the scheme is systematic, and the system is constituted by the terms or events, and the relations linking the events into a scheme.

Lonergan expands his hypothesis to include a notion of "emergence" that is defined in terms of the calculus of probabilities. Since probabilities — the reference throughout here is to f-probabilities — can be calculated for a succession of occurrences of events of a class, a single f-probability can be calculated for successive occurrences of a set of classes of events. This single probability for the occurrence of the whole set is the product of the individual probabilities. And since probabilities are proper fractions, the product of a set of probabilities is smaller than any of the individual probabilities. But if a set of conditions were fulfilled such that the classes of events began to function as a scheme of recurrence, then, if any one event occurred the whole scheme would occur and would continue recurring. In this case the probability of the whole set would no longer be the product of the individual probabilities. For in the case of a scheme of recurrence whose conditions are fulfilled the occurrence of *any one* of the events would ensure the occurrence and recurrence of *all the others*. The f-probability of the whole scheme would then be a new combination (a form of summation) of the individual probabilities which, because of the interlocked character of the events in a scheme, would be much higher than the original product of the events' individual f-probabilities. Lonergan concludes that there will be a leap in the probability of the combination of events, constitutive of the scheme when the prior conditions are fulfilled, and that this new probability will be the probability of the scheme's emergence.[34] The jump in the probability of recurrence of a scheme is the key element in the meaning of the term "emergence."

In addition to the probability of emergence Lonergan introduces the related notion of a probability of the survival of schemes. Insofar as all the related conditions for the operation of a scheme continue to remain fulfilled, a scheme ensures its own survival. And within limited ranges defensive circles can arise to take care of the occurrence of conditions that would otherwise interfere with a scheme. But the continued operation of a scheme depends, finally, on the non-occurrence of any condition or event that would spell the end of the scheme.

> Accordingly the probability of the survival of a scheme of recurrence is the probability of the non-occurrence of any of the events that would disrupt the scheme.[36]

Recurrence schemes involve a conditioned series of events. But Lonergan goes on to suggest that the recurrence of schemes can constitute the fulfilling conditions for the occurrence and recurrence of further schemes. Just as the occurrence of one or more events can fulfill the remaining conditions necessary for a scheme to begin and continue, so too the functioning of that scheme can fulfill the remaining conditions for another scheme to begin and to continue. Schemes can combine such that earlier schemes can function independent of later schemes but later schemes require the functioning of earlier schemes. The result is what Lonergan calls a "seriation," a conditioned series of schemes which, like the scheme, continues once begun.[37]

## 4.4 Emergent Probability

Emergent probability is Lonergan's proposal for a world view that could account for the evolution or emergence of new intelligible unities onto the scene of world process and thus account for the relations among explanatory "levels" or strata of science. Emergent probability would understand world processes in terms of conditioned series of schemes of recurrence that emerge, continue functioning and disappear in accordance with successive schedules of probability. And it is the acts of intelligence which grasp the *absence of system* in the coincidental manifold of laws operative in the environment, on the one hand, and the *operation of system* linking the events of the scheme and explaining its recurrence, on the other hand, which distinguish the explanatory structure of this account.[38]

Sets of laws interact randomly and this interaction results in classes of events recurring with certain f-probable frequencies. At any stage, world process consists of a huge number of sets of variously interacting classical laws yielding lists and lists of classes of events recurring with corresponding schedules of f-probability. At a certain point a given set of types of events recurs, but because the events do not occur within an appropriate temporal or spatial range or succession, they interact only minimally. However, given subtle changes in the boundary conditions of the environment, or given the coincidental occurrence of the events in an appropriate time and place, the types of events in the set are such that they would form a chain or a conjoined set. Thus the first occurrence of the scheme ensures the continued recurrence of the scheme. The pattern recurs because each event conditions the occurrence of the next, or a single event conditions the occurrence of them all. When the complete set of environmental conditions is arranged so as to permit the events linking into a scheme, then the

*Emergent Probability* 109

probability of the whole set of events occurring jumps from the product of the original probabilities to a new, higher probability. For at this point the occurrence of any one event ensures the occurrence of the whole set.[39]

Two bodies moving through space will continue at relatively constant velocities in relatively straight lines until they come within a particular distance of each other. If their masses are in the proper proportion and if their directions of approach are suitable, then, granting the absence of other masses of significant proportion, the two bodies will begin to orbit around each other in any of a large number of possible (more or less perturbed) elliptical orbits. Thus a systematic process or recurring scheme of events emerges where previously none functioned. A particular set of selected physical laws and numerical values explains the shape of the particular ellipses and thus the schematic or systematic relationships among the events which constitute the recurring pattern of motions. The initial velocities and directions of the two masses and the absence of other masses conditioned the initial occurrence of the patterned motions. But they do not explain the pattern. It is this difference in types of conditions and relations that characterizes emergent probability as an explanatory heuristic. The initial conditions of masses, velocities and directions are one set from among a very large number of possible and probable sets of outcomes of antecedent conjunctions of laws and conditions. The occurrence of any one from this very large number of sets of masses, velocities and directions would suffice to condition the emergence of one or another elliptical orbiting pattern. But it is the *fact* of this particular fulfillment and not its *explanation* that is relevant to the system which defines the recurring motion. And this fact is understood not in terms of another classical explanation but in terms of the probabilities associated with the occurrence of the fulfilling conditions.[40]

In another example the presence of liquid water on the earth's surface and the presence of suitable levels of solar heat will result in the occurrence of the events, evaporation and condensation. But when the atmosphere has stabilized within a suitable range of mean temperatures, when glaciated depressions on continental land masses have been filled to overflowing, when the accumulation and melting of glacial ice have settled into one of a large number of relatively stable patterns, and when the movements of global air masses have settled within a relatively stable range of patterns around and over land forms, then the overall global rates of evaporation, precipitation, surface and underground runoff will settle into a systematic equilibrium arrangement. And this stable hydrological cycle or scheme can itself operate as one of the fulfilling conditions for the emergence and survival of various terrestrial life forms. A complex set of physical, chemical, geological and meteorological laws will explain the particular set of values and relations that define the systematic operation of the water cycle. But only the laws of probability will account for the fulfilling conditions that made possible the actual cycle as it has operated at various moments in the earth's geological history.

The explanation of any stage of world process seeks to conceive that stage in terms of the possibilities and probabilities present in the conditioned series of schemes of the previous stage. The events that recur systematically in the future stage recur only non-systematically in the previous stage, and the movement from the earlier to the later stage consists in the fulfillment of the conditions that enable the events to form a scheme and thus to recur in a certain pattern or order of succession with some regularity. Thus there will be a succession of distinct types of acts of understanding that will be involved in the understanding of any stage of world process.

First. A direct insight or a unified set of direct insights grasps the particular systematic relationships among events in schemes and among schemes in a seriation. The intelligibilities defining systematically recurring patterns of events during any stage of world process will be classically unified sets of laws, events and particular values. But the fact that this stage operates in accordance with these particulars and not others is not to be explained entirely in terms of the systematic intelligibilities defining the schemes and seriations. For with respect to previous stages of world process, this stage was merely one among a large number of possible and probable next stages. Thus the account of the systematic relations defining schemes and seriations, far from constituting a complete account of that stage of world process, constitutes only a partial account. The immanent intelligibilities of the schemes and seriations of this stage were one set among a range of alternatives awaiting realization through the fulfillment of conditions. And the alternatives presented by the previous stage of world process are to be understood in terms of the f-probabilities associated with the recurrence of respective ranges of constituent events and conditions.[41]

Second. The actual schemes and series are conceived as one among a number of f-probable next stages in a succession of conditioned series of recurrence schemes. Among the possibilities presented by the previous stage some will be f-probable for some possible seriations will have their constituent schemes and events actually functioning with some f-probable frequency. Some schemes have sets of conditions fulfilled within appropriate spatial and temporal ranges and so will have an f-probability of emergence. And other seriations have the disadvantage of requiring the sufficiently frequent recurrence of defensive circles to disarm actually occurring events or schemes that would interfere with their systematic operation. The point here is that while a scheme or seriation consists in the systematic operation of its constituent events or schemes, still in cases such events or schemes will be recurring in relative isolation with some f-probable frequency before they begin to function together systematically. Whether or not they begin to function as a scheme or seriation depends upon whether or not a set of conditions essential to their systematic interlinkage is fulfilled. And so the various f-probable next stages will be the various patterns in which actually recurring events or schemes could combine to form a system. They will be probable next stages because there will be (f-probable) frequencies associated with the actually recurring constituent events. And there will be f-probabilities associated with the occurrence or sufficiently frequent recurrence of other conditions which would permit the events to form schemes.[42]

Third. But while at any stage there is a manifold of f-probable next stages, only one of these next stages actually occurs. The final act of intelligence which completes the understanding of the actually occurring seriation is that form of inverse insight which is the basis for the statistical form of knowledge. The set of conditions which is actually fulfilled for a set of events and schemes to form a seriation is so fulfilled in accordance with a particular set of numerical values. Similarly the event or scheme which initiates the operation of one of the schemes or seriations that has achieved a probability of emergence, occurs itself in accordance with a particular set of values. But particular cases diverge non-systematically from probabilities and so there will be a residual divergence of such particular values from the statistical norms associated with the various f-probable next stages. This residual divergence corresponds to the absence of system in the complete set of environmental conditions associated with the operation of the actual seriation. And so this third and final act of intelligence, the inverse insight, will complete the understanding of the conditioned series of schemes of recurrence.[43]

The result of such a succession of stages of fulfilling conditions and schematic interactions of probably recurring events would be the emergence of a higher order genus of "things."[44] And contrary to the anticipations of the determinist or the naive realist, such a higher order genus of things would be irreducible. For the various evolutionary species can only be explained completely in the terms and relations of their own laws which grasp the intelligibility in the systematically recurring schemes and series of schemes operative in their own physical, chemical or biological sphere. The "matter" common to all such species would not be conceived as some aggregate of prime particles, but as the concretely intelligible set of recurrence schemes which can be understood in all instances of their specific life form and which alone suffices to explain their functioning.[45]

## 4.5 Emergent Probability and the Human Sciences

Emergent probability would conceive man as the locus of the realization of a set of successively higher order systematic integrations of the materials and schemes of the four levels of physics, chemistry, botany and zoology. Like the plants, man possesses the capacities to systematize biologically various aggregates of chemical compounds, to adapt to environmental conditions, to develop, and to reproduce single cells and ordered manifolds of cells. With the animals man shares the sensitive appetites and schemes that systematize the lower order organic materials. But unlike the animals, man is characterized by the capacity to effect further systematic integrations of the outcomes of such sensitive schemes in acts of insight, judgment and decision. In short, man is that instance of world process wherein what is intelligible becomes intelligent. With man there occurs the possibility and the probability that the intelligibility immanent in every systematic process, every probability, every scheme of recurrence and every series of schemes can become cognitionally present to a knowing subject intentionally oriented to probably emergent world process. Acts of knowing are probably emergent, higher order systematic integrations of non-systematic manifolds of images and sense data. And as with all schemes and seriations, the higher order system realizes an intelligibility possibly immanent in the lower order manifold in accordance with probabilities. The intelligibility grasped in an insight, the truth affirmed in a judgment, and the value realized in a decision to act all emerge in dynamic processes whose operations are indentical in structure to probably emerging world process. It is this isomorphism which is the basis for Lonergan's affirmation that acts of knowing grasp and affirm the intelligibility immanent in being. The concrete actualization of possible and probable intelligibilities immanent in the non-systematic manifolds of world process constitutes the structure of the dynamic movement of world process. And the cognitional actuation of such intelligibilities immanent in the sensory and imaginative experiences of human subjects engaged in world process constitutes the structure of the dynamic acts of knowing world process.[46]

Emergent probability can offer to the human sciences a structured heuristic which could explain both the continuities and the discontinuities between the human order and the "natural" orders of physics, chemistry, botany and zoology. Armed with such an explanatory heuristic the human scientist can carve out a domain of inquiry which is both distinct from those of the "natural" sciences and linked to them within the context of an overall evolutionary structure. And since the most dramatic dimension of human activity is the act of cognition itself, a human science, so conceived, will have within its proper field of inquiry, the very activity of the natural scientist him- or herself and the relationship between this activity and its results.

However there is also a second way in which emergent probability can be of service to the human sciences. In addition to knowing intelligibilities immanent in world process humans also implement cognitional skills to constitute new events onto the scene of world process. The isomorphism between the structure of world process and the structure of knowing gives rise to the possibility of subjects coming to understand, not only something which has already occurred, but also the fulfilling conditions for the occurrence of something new, something which has not yet occurred. With the development of some level of cognitional and sensorimotor skills humans no longer need to wait for the appropriate convergence of conditions for an event to occur. Rather we can come to know what conditions need fulfilling and we can coordinate and implement a range of motor skills from our own repertoire (as well as from those of others) to bring these conditions into being. The emergence of cognitionally actuated meaning onto the scene of world process introduces a new class of events onto this scene, a class of events which are constituted by meaning. Consequently the study of world process, when it shifts its focus to include humanity, must now be alert to this new type of event, to the new complex of conditions for its occurrence and recurrence, and to a new set of emergent schemes and series in and of such events. For human history is not simply understood in acts of meanings. It is constituted by acts of meaning and by the structures which condition the recurrence of such acts.

Finally there remains a third contribution which emergent probability can make to the human sciences. This contribution comes to light when it is understood that there stands a profound link between the understanding of history in acts of meaning and the constitution of history by acts of meaning. The fact is that we constitute our future history in accordance with our current understanding of ourselves and our history. Our interpretation of ourselves and our history informs the actions in which we shape our future. Consequently emergent probability applied to the field of human history, recognizes that central to the fulfilling conditions for ranges of human futures will be the accounts of human life, human pasts and possible human futures which are generally operative in culture. As human scientists seek to provide tools and materials for the responsible direction of history they discover, to an ever greater degree, that the way people understand themselves sets the ranges of possibility for their future responsible actions. Consequently emergent probability directs the human scientist to an increasing degree to the study of the world of human meaning, to the conditions for the wide scale transformations of meaning, and to the limitations imposed upon possible futures by the ranges of extant meanings operative in culture.[47] It is to this constitutive function of meaning in practical intelligence and in history that the following chapters are devoted.

## 4.6 Finality

As an evolutionary hypothesis emergent probability includes some implications about world process that would be open to verification. Since schemes operate only when and where their conditions are fulfilled and since the conditions for higher order schemes are the operation of the appropriate lower order schemes, the successive realization of schemes will involve spatial concentrations. Later schemes will be found only where earlier schemes are functioning. But since the later schemes are only probable, not every set of earlier schemes will lead to sets of later schemes. So the occurrence of later and later schemes will be restricted to fewer and fewer places. And until their conditions are fulfilled the probabilities associated with the occurrence of later and later schemes will be lower and lower. However, such low probabilities for later schemes can be offset by large numbers of instances and long intervals of time. For what occurs only once in a million years or once in a million places will occur a thousand times in a billion places or a billion years.[48] Furthermore since the emergence of higher and higher order schemes is the movement towards increasing intelligibility or system (for the realization of every recurrence scheme is the emergence of system where previously none existed) it would seem that, at least to date, the dynamism of world process is precisely this movement towards higher intelligibility. At least to date the fact of such large numbers and long intervals of time seems verified. And, granted that sufficiently large numbers and sufficiently long intervals of time remain fulfilled, it would seem that the continued, increasingly systematic character of the universe could be assured. For with large numbers and long intervals of time the occurrence of the probable is only prevented by systematic intervention. And actual frequencies do not diverge systematically from probabilities, so while interventions do occur they do not recur systematically. Granted the continued absence of such intervention, the large initial numbers and the long intervals of time would guarantee the ever higher realization of system.[49]

Since the probabilities of emergence and survival are distinct there will be stability and development as well as breakdowns and blind alleys. And so sufficiently large numbers and long intervals of time conceivably could assure at least one situation in which development occurred. Later schemes generally need earlier schemes for their emergence and survival. While the disappearance of such earlier schemes would lead to the breakdown of the later schemes, the continued operation of such earlier schemes, their development of defensive circles, and their monopolization of materials would tend to secure the stability of the later and more developed schemes. When such defensive circles and imprisoned materials occur, the stability of the developed schemes can have the added negative effect of preventing any further development or the continued development of higher and higher order schemes. Thus there occur blind alleys. But development beyond such blind alleys would be possible if earlier schemes with high probabilities of emergence and low probabilities of survival formed floating populations on which later schemes could depend. Sufficiently large numbers and sufficiently long intervals of time could conceivably ensure that at least one situation would prevail in which world process realized continued development. For despite breakdowns, blind alleys and the consequent need for new starts in both new and old locations, the large initial numbers and long intervals of time would allow development to progress beyond such obstacles.[50]

The presentation so far might seem a wild and farfetched speculation

*Emergent Probability* 115

moving far beyond the presented evidence, leaping gaily to conclusions about evolutionary processes on the basis of suppositions about knowing. It is certainly true that any kind of careful verification of an hypothesis such as emergent probability would demand a detailed study of evidence in every sector of the natural and human sciences. And there is no question that this detailed study remains to be carried out. But the value of this speculation so far can only be appreciated insofar as some implications of the world view, emergent probability, are investigated and understood. The fact remains that the implementation of heuristics in world views does not await verification and no world view to date would seem to stand up very well under careful scrutiny by a community of scholars.[51] Furthermore, the power of world views in uncovering and obscuring data and insights in every branch of the sciences is well known.[52] If there is recognized some place for a branch of the human sciences which studies our dynamic orientation to truth, to beauty, to value, to love and to God, then there will be required a structured account of world processes which understands this dynamic orientation as, in some way, in continuity with the structure and orientation of all of reality. In addition, if we are to hope for some possibility of life for our children in an age which seems to present a number of blind alleys in the set of alternative historical futures, then some ground for this hope needs to be investigated. And these grounds will need to be understood, again in some way, in continuity with the dynamic structure of all of being. Emergent probability represents one man's attempts to recover an element in the procedures of contemporary natural and human sciences (the statistical element) and to integrate that element into a world view which, at least conceivably, could explain both this dynamic orientation and some grounds for hope, in a world view whose structure is equally applicable to any dimension of world process. The verification of the relevance and truth of emergent probability remains to begin on a grand scale. The possibilities suggested here are presented as evidence that it ought to begin.

One final aspect of emergent probability remains to be discussed, the notion of finality. There is considerable evidence that world process is not static but dynamic. Evolutionary development to date provides evidence of at least one instance of world process wherein higher orders of integration have emerged from lower orders. And every instance of human cognition would seem to provide further evidence that this direction towards higher order integration is in fact continuing. Lonergan names this structured orientation towards higher integration, this upward dynamism, finality.[53] Evolutionary development has progressed, at least on this planet, through successively higher systematic integrations of lower order manifolds and each higher integration has been the realization of new intelligibility or system. The fact is, too, that men and women are neither emotionally, intellectually nor responsibly static or satisfied. We are curious, we spontaneously gravitate towards other life forms, we ask questions, we make discoveries, we organize our lives around practical projects, we love and care for ourselves and each other through the responsible development and implementation of cognitionally mediated skills. And in all such acts the drive is towards the actuation of the intelligibility immanent in being or the realization of new being in intelligible projects and plans of action. Finality expresses the fact that the directed dynamism that has been operative in probably emerging world process continues to be operative in the cognitional acts of women and men. Thus finality is as applicable to human history as it is to biological evolution.[54]

While finality makes a limited claim about world process, it is nonetheless not an insignificant claim. Finality excludes a static world process, a world view that has the structure of the logical syllogism, an axiomatic system of postulates and deduced conclusions. It also excludes an indeterminate or totally haphazard movement to world process. For despite breakdowns, blind alleys, spatial constrictions and infrequent leaps forward, the successively higher integrations of lower order manifolds occur and recur according to probabilities. And while a systematic intervention could conceivably prevent what is probable from occurring, such an intervention would constitute a radical change in the structure of world process.[55]

Finally, while finality is a predicate of proportionate being, being whose intelligibility is conceivably proportionate to the potential capacities of human cognitional skills,[56] it is also a datum for and the occasion for a question about the term or objective of this dynamism of world process, transcendent being. Thus when an answer to this question about the objective of dynamically oriented world process is formulated and affirmed, such an answer would also expand upon the notion of finality. It is not the purpose of this study to investigate the answer to the question of transcendent being. But it is widely known that Lonergan's *Insight* chapter nineteen formulates and affirms such an answer.[57] And while intelligence moves quickly and spontaneously to further questions the reader is asked to stop, for a moment, and to consider two facts. (1) The spontaneous movement to the further question about transcendent being, whether to understand Lonergan's answer or to prove him wrong, is itself evidence of what is meant here by finality. (2) Since an answer to the question of transcendent being will need to be intelligent and reasonable to satisfy inquiring intelligence, it will have to take into account this empirical evidence of the finality of world processes and the particular case of finality that occurs in the spontaneous drive of men and women towards insights, truth, goodness and love. The fact that intelligence spontaneously anticipates the complete intelligibility of being is neither an easy fact to refute nor is it a small matter in the face of the question about transcendent being. The fact is that this anticipation is the prime evidence upon which Lonergan affirms the fact of transcendent being.

For the purpose of this study it is sufficient to note that Lonergan's proposal, emergent probability, is a world view which opens onto a consideration of transcendent being. Lonergan treats transcendent being, in *Insight*, as a question for intelligence. But this is by no means the only way in which man relates to transcendent being. And Lonergan's view of religious experience in *Method in Theology* as God's love flooding our hearts, expands somewhat upon this consideration of transcendent being.[58] What remains to be understood, in the chapters that follow, is how Lonergan understands human moral, responsible action in continuity with the structured world view, emergent probability, and how human history evinces a structure which is itself a probable emergence, and which far from precluding the operation of human responsibility and freedom, requires its exercise as the agent of its own dynamism, the upward dynamism of the finality of being, oriented ultimately towards God.

FOOTNOTES – CHAPTER 4

1   Byrne, "The Thomist Sources," particularly pp. 110-119.
2   See *Verbum*, pp. ix-x, 94-5.
3   One might conclude, here, that Lonergan's view of science must be nothing more than a Thomistic, or even Aristotelian view of science. If one's view of cognition precludes the possibility of discovery, and demands an account of the "determining conditions" for a theory or hypothesis in an analysis of the historical or cultural conditions influencing the subject, then one might be led to argue that Lonergan's Thomistic heritage "explains" his world view. However, if one's cognitional theory accommodates the possibility of discovery, then "sources" or historical/cultural influences can be understood as clues or heuristics leading towards a more or less successful cognitional integration of distinctively new materials. This latter alternative is the way in which I would understand the matter. And my judgment is not based simply upon my allegiance to Lonergan, but more significantly upon the results gained from endless hours of experiments like those outlined in McShane's *Wealth of Self and Wealth of Nations* (Hicksville, N. Y.: Exposition Press, 1975).
4   This, I would suggest, is the point made by Pannenberg in his critique of Lonergan, see "History and Meaning in Bernard Lonergan's Approach to Theological Method," in Corcoran, ed., *Looking at Lonergan's Method*, pp. 88-100; reprinted in *The Irish Theological Quarterly* 40 (1973): 103-114. It would seem that the difference between Pannenberg and Lonergan on the relationship of world views and the certainty of knowledge is that Pannenberg demands a knowledge of everything before anything can be known for certain. Lonergan, on the other hand, provides some evidence that we move towards knowledge of everything by v-probable knowledge of some things. Considerably more needs to be said on Pannenberg's critique of Lonergan but it cannot be said here. On the generality of world views, see the "Introduction," above.
5   See, for example, Mark Doughty, "This Impossible Universe," *The Tablet* 235 (Sept. 19, 26, 1981): 906-908, 928-930; John D. Barrow and Joseph Silk, "The Structure of the Early Universe," *Scientific American* 242 (April 1980): 118-28; George Gale, "The Anthropic Principle," *Scientific American* 245, no. 6 (December 1981): 114-122; Erich Jantsch, "Modelling the Human World: Perspectives," in Churchman and Mason, eds., *World Modeling: A Dialogue*, pp. 89-96; idem, "Evolution: Self-Realization Through Self-Transcendence," in *Evolution and Consciousness*, edited by E. Jantsch and C. H. Waddington (Reading, Mass.: Addison-Wesley, 1976), pp. 37-70.
6   I would include in the human sciences such fields as philosophy, literary criticism and theology.
7   See the "Introduction" above, for a brief discussion of this inter-disciplinary collaboration.
8   Such respect is reflected not only in the annual "Lonergan Workshops" devoted to studying implications of his work but also in the world conferences and symposia in Florida, 1970, in Maynooth, Ireland, 1973, in Milwaukee, 1980, and in Santa Clara, California, 1984, all devoted to a critical analysis of his thought. See Corcoran, ed., *Looking at Lonergan's Method*; McShane, ed., *Foundations of Theology*; idem, ed., *Language, Truth and Meaning*; Lamb, ed., *Creativity and Method*; P. B. Riley and T. Fallon, eds., *Religion and Culture: Essays in Honor of Bernard Lonergan, S. J.* (Albany, N. Y.: SUNY Press, forthcoming 1986); Fred Lawrence, ed., *Lonergan Workshop*, vols. 1 to 5 (Missoula, Montana and Chico, California: Scholars Press, 1978, 1980, 1982, 1983, and 1985).
9   While notes 5-9 in chapter three above list a fairly large number of works written on Lonergan and the philosophy of science, such works have had little or no impact on the community of practising scientists and philosophers of science. See chapter three, 3.0 above.

10  *Insight*, pp. 128-139.
11  Max Weber, *The Methodology of the Social Sciences*, pp. 89ff, cited in *Method*, pp. 227-9. See also Weber, "Religious Rejections of the World and Their Directions," in *From Max Weber*, edited by H. H. Gerth and C. W. Mills (New York: Oxford University Press, 1946), pp. 323-4.
12  On the odd meaning of the term that is employed here and its differences from more common usage, see above, chapter three, 3.2 and note 44, chapter three.
13  Indeed, known physical and chemical laws are themselves correlations of more elemental terms and relations which are themselves a matter of considerable dispute.
14  See Richard Schotland, "Meteorology and Climatology," in *Collier's Encyclopedia*, editorial director, W. D. Halsey (New York: Crowell-Collier Publishing Company, 1964), pp. 45-46.
15  Schotland, pp. 40-65.
16  The term "higher" with regard to levels of explanation or evolutionary levels can lead to a certain triumphalism and a certain misunderstanding of the relationship between the "higher" and the "lower." For example, in the past centuries man's status as "higher" than the animals has led to a profound misunderstanding of humanity which has only begun a reversal as a result of the work of such scholars as Darwin, Freud and Konrad Lorenz. The precise meaning of the term "higher" is what is at issue in this account of explanatory levels.
17  *Insight*, pp. 115-128.
18  *Randomness*, pp. 170ff.
19  Ibid., pp. 178ff. McShane's reference is to N. Rashevski, *Mathematical Biophysics*. See also the work of Monod, discussed in chapter two, 2.2 above.
20  Ibid., pp. 175ff. McShane's reference here is to Stephen Pepper, "Emergence," *Journal of Philosophy* 23 (1926): 244, and to the criticisms which have been levelled against Pepper by Meehl and Sellars, "The Concept of Emergence," *Minnesota Studies in the Philosophy of Science*, vol. 1, cited in *Randomness*, pp. 170, 171.
21  *Randomness*, pp. 173ff.
22  Ibid., pp. 173-5.
23  Ibid., p. 203. Among scholars who affirm such levels and attempt to explain their interrelationships he cites Bertalanffy, *The Problem of Life*, in *Randomness*, pp. 186-7, 190, 194, and Waddington, *The Nature of Life*, in ibid., p. 190.
24  Ibid., p. 182. His reference here is to H. Kaeser, "The Kinetic Structure of Organisms," in R. Harris, ed. *Biological Organization at the Cellular and Subcellular Level*.
25  Ibid., pp. 183-4. In support of such a conclusion, McShane also quotes F. A. Hayck, "The Theory of Complex Phenomena," in M. Bunge, ed. *The Critical Approach to Science and Philosophy*, cited in ibid., pp. 193-194.
26  Rashevski, cited in *Randomness*, p. 183, italics are those of Rashevski.
27  Kaeser, cited in ibid., p. 182.
28  Ibid., p. 183.
29  McShane discusses various alternate attempts at systematizing the relations between physico-chemical conditions and biological processes. He finds that such broad and general regularities as can be grasped in, for example, topological relations abstract from the aspects of the processes that are specifically relevant to biology, ibid., p. 184. And explanations attempted at the biochemical level, accounts involving DNA, RNA, etc., end up similarly concluding with non-systematic processes on the lower levels, p. 185. Standard appeals to the example of quantum mechanics as a successful reduction of chemistry to physics fail to grasp that quantum theory is not a systematic account in terms of classical laws but a statistical account, p. 186.
30  See ibid., pp. 199-202.
31  Lonergan's introduction to recurrence schemes is found in *Insight*, pp. 117-18.
32  Ibid., p. 118. For further examples, see Monod, *Chance and Necessity*, pp. 64ff.

33   Ibid.
34   Ibid., p. 121.
35   A note on Lonergan's presentation in *Insight* is in order here. His account runs as follows:
     It follows that, when the prior conditions for the functioning of a scheme of recurrence are satisfied, then the probability of the combination of events, constitutive of the scheme, leaps from a product of fractions to a sum of fractions. *Insight*, p. 121.
     Technically speaking this presentation is not entirely correct. First, the fulfillment of the conditions of the scheme will not leave the f-probabilities of the original events unchanged. Once the occurrence of events within the scheme become conditioned, not simply by events lying outside the scheme, but also by other events within the scheme then their individual f-probabilities change. At this point the calculus of the f-probability of any one event occurring (and thus the whole scheme occurring) must treat the events as dependent, and consequently the calculation becomes quite complex. Second, if the complex of conditions lying beyond the scheme remained unchanged for each event after they have conjoined, then the f-probabilities associated with each event's being conditioned by this set of conditions could be said to remain the same as before. In this case the original f-probabilities would not, in fact, represent the new, actual probabilities of the individual events. However they would represent the probabilities of the events being conditioned by events beyond the scheme and, consequently, the events could be considered to be independent as long as they were independent before the conditions for schematization were fulfilled. This would seem to be the case referred to by Lonergan and in fact the probability of any one event occurring now would be a form of summation. However such a summation is calculated, not as a simple sum of proper fractions, but as the complement of the probability of none of the events occurring.
     Probability of any one event occurring
     $= 1 -$ Probability of none occurring
     $= 1 - [(1-P_a)(1-P_b)(1-P_c)\ldots]$
     My debt here is to Messrs. Martin Hubbard and Jack Gammon.
36   Ibid., p. 121.
37   Ibid., p. 119. McShane's tenth chapter of *Randomness* introduces recurrence schemes by discussing alternative answers to the question put forward by T. A. Goudge, "What ... are the units of evolution?", *The Ascent of Life*, cited in *Randomness*, p. 215. McShane rejects such answers as "species," "organisms," "living things," "chemical compounds," for the more recent notion of "populations." But he finds a host of problems associated with this alternative, pp. 215-18. He summarizes briefly Lonergan's notion of the recurrence scheme, and proceeds to show how Oparin's work in "Biopoesis," pp. 218-19, Odum's work in ecosystems, p. 220, Waddington's, Darwin's and Beckner's works in biology, pp. 221-3, Talcott Parson's work in sociology, all make some implicit or explicit appeal to an explanatory notion with the structure of the recurrence scheme. Each work illustrates a different example of the explanatory power of this notion.
38   See *Randomness*, pp. 220-1.
39   See *Insight*, pp. 121-128; *Randomness*, chap. 11.
40   See *Randomness*, p. 230.
41   See ibid., pp. 221-229.
42   See ibid., pp. 231-235; *Insight*, pp. 119-120.
43   *Insight*, pp. 120, 125.
44   On this odd meaning of the term "thing," see *Insight*, chap. 8, particularly pp. 259-262.
45   See *Randomness*, pp. 201-202, 218-220, 221-222, 231, 232-235, 239-242, 243-245. For other examples of such an explanation, see Monod, chap. 8, and Bowker, pp. 111ff.
46   See *Insight*, pp. 189-191, 210-211, 226-227, 455-458, 467-469, 698.

47  See ibid., pp. 210f, 227.
48  Ibid., pp. 122-123. See also Monod, p. 120.
49  Ibid., pp. 126-7. For a response to Albertson's criticisms of Lonergan on this point, see *Randomness*, pp. 235-236. At the centre of McShane's response lies the inapplicability of probabilities to single cases. World process is never simply a single instance but a manifold of events, schemes and seriations occurring on many fronts realizing a range of actualities from a much larger range of possibilities. See J. Albertson, Review of *Insight*, *The Modern Schoolman* 35 (1958): 236-44.
50  Ibid., pp. 123-124, 127-8.
51  See, for example, the debates presented in Suppe and Peacocke.
52  Thomas Kuhn's chapter ten, in *The Structure of Scientific Revolutions*, second edition, enlarged (Chicago: University of Chicago Press, 1970), contains many examples of such power.
53  One need only read *Insight*, pp. 121-128, particularly the last paragraph of sub-section 2.5 on p. 128, alongside pp. 444-451, particularly the first full paragraph on p. 448, to realize that the earlier account is an account of finality.
54  This will be discussed in greater detail in chapters six and seven, below. For now, see *Insight*, pp. 448-449.
55  See ibid., pp. 126-7.
56  Ibid., p. 391.
57  Ibid., pp. 447, 534, 665.
58  *Method*, pp. 105-107; see also *Insight*, chap. 20.

# Chapter 5

# Ethics and Emergent Probability

*5.0 Introduction*

As I noted in the "Introduction," above, the goal of this study is to introduce the reader, not principally to a theory, but to a heuristic which, in my view, promises to contribute significantly to the ongoing genesis of theory in the human sciences and, more particularly, to a unification of theory in ethics, the philosophy of history, and in evolutionary theory. In an age in which we are discovering, to our alarm, that social, political, ecological, psychological and economic processes are interdependent and mutually informing, the challenges to national and international policymakers in the private and public sectors are demanding an unprecedented degree of interdisciplinary collaboration. And if the experiences of Maurice De Wachter, in the field of bioethics, are an indication of the state of collaborative efforts in other fields, the principal difficulty in such interdisciplinarity is arriving at a common question, a common formulation of the problem, a common set of anticipations or expectations of what would constitute an answer or a solution and what would constitute evidence and procedures for verification.[1] Lonergan's work in ethics, begun in the *Grace and Freedom*[2] essays, and developed in *Insight* and *Method*, was an attempt to probe to the roots of foundational issues in ethical theory with a view towards reunderstanding such foundations within the context of a world view which reflected the insights and operative anticipations of the twentieth century sciences. And so his chapters on the structure of moral, responsible action, the nature of human freedom, and the foundation of moral normativity are introductory attempts[3] to step beyond the immediate range of questions in the field of ethics, to work out a route towards solutions to these problems that reflected the insights and concerns from the fields of evolutionary theory, biology, neurology, psychology, sociology and the philosophy of history. While anyone who knows his work must regard his achievements as impressive, what is most significant, in my view, is the power of his heuristic.

The following introduction to Lonergan's ethics is an attempt to show how he worked out his account of the structure of practical, moral action, and the meaning of the term "freedom," as it applies to human moral responsibility, with the terms and relations of emergent probability. The first point that must be emphasized is that in Lonergan's view, ethics does not pertain principally to statements, to codes, to laws, to social customs, symbols, norms, or even to concrete values. While ethics includes all of these, Lonergan understands them as the objects or terms of human operations. Lonergan's interest was in understanding the dynamic structure of the operations whose performance yielded the genesis of moral norms, codes and customs. Furthermore the key to understanding his account of the structure of moral action is in the word "dynamic." For what is significant about human practice is its flexibility which allows the concrete genesis, combination and implementation of ranges of operative norms in an endless array of concrete conditions, and, more important, its reflexively operative, self-constituting structure in which the performance of operations contributes towards their transformation. I will note very briefly how Lonergan's account is not a naive supposition that individual persons author their own moral practice in complete and autonomous isolation. But if the word "freedom" means anything in the field of ethics it means that subjects play some minimal role in participating in their own self-constitution and in shaping courses of action. And I hope to sketch, very briefly here and in chapters six and seven below, how emergent probability might provide a framework for integrating an account of the structure of practical, responsible operations with the wealth of research that is currently available on the conditioning structures of language and economic practice.

My order of proceeding here has been to begin with Lonergan's most explicit account of the dynamic structure of responsible operations. This is laid out in chapter two of *Method*, in his introduction to the second chapter on "The Human Good." There is considerable evidence (including an admission by Lonergan) that some development occurred from the writing of *Insight* to that of *Method*.[4] There is in *Method* an account of "the good" that moves from an explicit acknowledgement of a broader base for the analysis of moral life, a base which recognizes a type of feeling as an essential and legitimate apprehension of value. In addition *Method* has differentiated a transcendental notion of value that is distinct from the transcendental notions operative in the understanding and judgment of truth. Consequently *Method* remains the clearest beginning for this study. But *Method* implements the heuristic structure worked out in *Insight*, in the context of a new terminology. And in chapters six and eighteen of *Insight* Lonergan laid some of the foundation for this later work in *Method*. So while it is recognized that many of the insights in the earlier work remain incomplete, still the elements of the more developed notions are to be found there. And what I hope to show is that the continuity is to be found in the operative heuristic. My point of departure, then, is an exposition of Lonergan's analysis of Piaget's account of skills.

The next topics, "Mediation" and "The Practical Orientation of Life" are introduced here in an effort to show how the cognitional operations, in Lonergan's account in *Insight* (and briefly summarized in *Method*, chapter one), must be understood as a particular type of skill whose overall genesis and operation is identical in dynamic structure with the full range of skills within the human repertoire. But because of the unique character of the insight, the cognitional operations play a key, mediating role in the various patterns of experience, and in the development and execution of all types of skills. The various ways in which this mediating function operates in the biological and aesthetic "Patterns of Experience" is discussed in 5.4, in an attempt to bring out the way in which terms and relations of emergent probability are operative in *Insight*, pages 181-186. But it is with his account of "The Dramatic Pattern of Experience" that Lonergan begins his account of responsible, practical (moral) action. And so in the last two sections, 5.5 and 5.6, this account of the genesis and development of skills focuses upon those skills that could be called distinctively moral or responsible, and upon the particular meaning that the term "freedom" has when predicated of human responsibility. In my view Lonergan's distinction between "essential" and "effective" freedom, rooted in the distinction between the structure of a scheme and the conditions associated with its recurrence and development, is the key to an eventual integration of theories in ethics which emphasize human responsibility with theories which emphasize psychological, social, economic, historical conditions that limit or effectively preclude its exercise.[5]

While an ethical theory needs, at its center, an account of the foundations of value, of the moral "ought," this topic will be treated in chapter six below. For like Kant and Monod, Lonergan understood that the question of moral value and the question of historical progress or decline need to be answered together in the context of a single framework. And a number of prior questions on the philosophy of history must be answered before the notion of progress can be introduced.

## 5.1 Skills and Recurrence Schemes

Lonergan's four pages in *Method* on the topic of skills[6] represent an introduction to what might be called a "descriptive" ethics. The effort here is to come up with a general account of the structure of human acts whose performance constitutes distinctively moral action. His concern with "the structure of the human good" is a concern for those dynamic elements in human life which are operative in the creative or transformative capacity of man which Marx sought to understand in his account of the practical activity of labour.[7] The question that Lonergan asks of the human good intends the general characteristic structure of those operations whose performance constitutes human life as, in some way, "practical," "responsible," or "moral." And so the notion of "skills," introduced in *Method*, is a basic category that will be operative recurrently throughout this "descriptive ethics."

The development of skills, according to Piaget, consists in the "increasing differentiation of operations" and the "ever greater multiplication of different combinations of differentiated operations."[8] The first clue to a discovery of how Lonergan is understanding Piaget, here, is to be found in Piaget's notion of "groups of operations." The "group of operations" is an instance of the "scheme of recurrence."

> Skill begets mastery and, to define it, Piaget invoked the mathematical notion of group. The principal characteristic of the group of operations is that every operation in the group is matched by an opposite operation and every combination of operations is matched by an opposite combination. Hence, inasmuch as operations are grouped, the operator can always return to his starting point and, when he can do so unhesitatingly, he has reached mastery at some level of development.[9]

The essential feature of this account is that the set or sequence of operations and their opposites can return the operator to his or her starting point. The skill is acquired when a symmetrical succession of oral, visual, manual and/or bodily events or sets of events can be performed in a wide range of possible situations. The cycle can be repeated precisely because the end of the cycle brings the subject back to the point where the first operation or the group can begin again. And whether the skill consists of a sequence of distinct operations or a set of operations performed simultaneously, the characteristic feature of the skill is the fact that it can be reversed and, thus, begun again at the same point. Given the health of the subject, the interest and opportunity (the fulfilling conditions), the cycle or scheme can recur again once it has begun. Lonergan recognized in Piaget's notion of the group of operations an instance of the fundamental building block of emergent probability, the recurrence scheme.

The second relevant aspect of Lonergan's presentation of Piaget concerns the pattern in which skills are learned.

> Jean Piaget analyzed the acquisition of a skill into elements. Each new element consisted in an adaptation to some new object or situation. In each adaptation there were distinguished two parts, assimilation and adjustment. Assimilation brought into play the spontaneous or the previously learned operations employed successfully on somewhat similar objects or in somewhat similar situations. Adjustment by a process of trial and error gradually modified and supplemented previously learned operations.[10]

The clue words here are "trial and error." In the child's encounter with a new object or situation there is an element of randomness.[11] Whatever the object lying within the child's reach, be it a stone, a stick, a toy, and whatever the range of skills within the child's repertoire, the curious child can bring any available skills to bear upon the object in any combination of operations (assimilation). The complete set of conditions associated with the presence of this particular object, the child's current repertoire of developed skills, and the particular combination of operations initially performed, is surely non-systematic. But given the fact of curiosity (the significant fulfilling condition) the child need only stumble upon any new combination of new or old operations whose constituent elements arrange symmetrically (fingers open and close, wrists turn and straighten, elbows bend and unbend) for the performance and reperformance of that group to transform an initially foreign and awkward skill into an effortless routine (adjustment). The two-stage cycle of adapting to new situations consists in non-systematically occurring events starting to recur systematically in symmetrically arranged groups or schemes. Lonergan recognizes in Piaget's account of development the probable emergence of schemes and the conditioned series of schemes wherein newer schemes build upon the old. Trial and error operations occur sufficiently frequently to ensure their routine recurrence in schemes (groups of operations and their opposites) and the trial and error recombination of learned and new groups in ever new situations ensures the routine recurrence of successively larger numbers and wider circles of skills.

It would not be unreasonable to ask what conditions need be fulfilled in order for this process to occur. The answer would involve, in part, an explanation from the field of neurology. It is the complex system of afferent and efferent nerves that links tactile and visual sensory receptors. It would be a neurological explanation which would account for the possibility of distinct sensations and sensorimotor operations grouping into a unity in a complex process involving feedback cycles. But in terms of the heuristic structure, emergent probability, the neurological conditions would constitute a manifold on the explanatory level of neurology, which is ordered or regulated in accordance with the classes of stages and elements in Piaget's analysis of skills. The electro-chemistry of firing neurons would constitute the materials which are ordered in the acquisition of skills but they would not explain in what a skill consists. Piaget's analysis, on the other hand, identifies the elements and the interrelations among the elements of a skill which constitute the intelligibility immanent in the recurring skills and learning routines of a growing child.

All the elements of emergent probability are present in Piaget's analysis. Skills consist of sets or cycles of operations and their opposites that occur, at first, non-systematically. And once they occur sufficiently frequently they can then recur systematically because each cycle can end back where it began. The successive recurrence of each cycle of operations fulfills the conditions for the further expansion of wider circles and more complex combinations of both newer and older schemes. The sufficiently frequent, non-systematic occurrence of the schemes at each stage fulfills the conditions for the jump in f-probability (the ideal frequency of recurrence)[12] of the scheme. Thus once all the appropriate conditions have been fulfilled (the neurological makeup of a healthy, curious child, and the opportunity for exploration) the non-systematic occurrence of the child's most primitive capacities is sufficient to ensure the continued development of successively higher stages of skills.

There can be drawn, here, a distinction between two types of recurrence schemes in Lonergan's presentation of Piaget. The first is the concretely recurring and developing skill consisting of operations combined symmetrically in each group. The second is the general developmental scheme of assimilation and adjustment which brings any acquired or improvised skill into play in any new situation, modifies it according to the demands and opportunities of the new situation and thus ensures the continued development of any and all skills. Both types of schemes occur in accordance with f-probabilities. But while the first type is the concrete, particular group of operations, the second type constitutes the general operative pattern in which the first type emerges and develops. The general adaptive scheme of assimilation and adjustment is the pattern of the child's routine engagement with its environment. And the regular recurrence of this scheme fulfills the conditions for the learning and development of all concrete skills.

## 5.2 Mediation

The notion of "mediation" links the presentation of Piaget's account of skills with the account of the cognitional operations developed in *Insight* and presented very briefly in *Method*, chapter one.

> Finally, there is the notion of mediation. Operations are said to be immediate when their objects are present. So seeing is immediate to what is being seen, hearing to what is being heard, touch to what is being touched. But by imagination, language, symbols, we operate in a compound manner; immediately with respect to the image, word symbol; mediately with respect to what is represented or signified. In this fashion we come to operate not only with respect to the present and actual but also with respect to the absent, the past, the future, the merely possible or ideal or normative or fantastic. As the child learns to speak, he moves out of the world of his immediate surroundings towards the far larger world revealed through the memories of other men, through the common sense of community, through the pages of literature, through the labors of scholars, through the investigations of scientists, through the experience of saints, through the meditations of philosophers and theologians.[13]

The import of the notion, here, is that the performance of groups of sensorimotor operations can stand in a "controlled" and thus recurrently conditioned relationship with the performance of other types of human operations and groups. Motor skills can fulfill the conditions for the occurrence of a whole new class of events, imaginative and cognitional events, to yield the complex operations in what Lonergan calls "the basic pattern."

Operations in the pattern are seeing, hearing, touching, smelling, tasting, inquiring, imagining, understanding, conceiving, formulating, reflecting, marshalling and weighing the evidence, judging, deliberating, evaluating, deciding, speaking, writing.[14]

Vocal utterances, hand motioning, page marking (groups of sensorimotor operations and their more or less durable objects) can mediate (and be mediated by) the occurrence of a distinct, higher order, type of event, the cognitional or imaginative genesis of meaning.[15] Since specific classes of such sensorimotor operations can condition recurrently the genesis of specific classes of higher order imaginative or cognitional events, the assimilation and adjustment structure of skill-learning can yield complex, multi-level skills whose constitutive events extend beyond the range of the merely sensorimotor. The performance of the motor skills involved in speaking words conditions (and is conditioned by) the systematic recurrence of memories, images, feelings, insights, because the scheme of acts extends beyond the movement of the relevant muscles to link such movements and their audible correspondences with emergent intelligibilities which unify and define implicitly elements of a much wider and more diverse experiential manifold.[16] In this way the sensorimotor operations can be performed to yield (to intend) the cognitional genesis of specific meanings (and vice versa) even when the original experiential conditions for such specific meanings remain absent. And it is the complex, multi-level structure of such skills, ensured by the learned and thus systematically recurrent correspondences, which makes possible this mediating function of meanings. Since there is a symmetry to the structure of the correspondence within the complex scheme or skill, the order of mediation can be reversed so that images and insights can evoke words.[17] The recurrent general learning and developmental scheme of assimilation and adjustment ensures the expansion of ranges and combinations of such correspondences. And since mediation moves two ways, the child's world of meaning expands not only with its repertoire of experiences but also as the control of images and insights allows the combination, juxtaposition, and generation of new possibilities in imagination.[18]

The recurrence schemes linking both sensorimotor and intentional events into wider skills are expanded through language to include the control over memories and insights from one's own experiences, images and insights of scholars, and the habitual meanings and expectations of the community.[19] And as with all skills the general developmental scheme would ensure that the operations and groups can be combined, recombined, brought to bear on new objects in new situations and developed so as to yield not only new patterns of old cognitional objects but new insights and new judgments of truth and value. Thus insights are not only into the present data of one's own sensory experience but, more frequently, into the linguistically controlled recollection of data and previous insights and judgments from one's own experience and (most frequently) from the experience of others.[20] Mediation links together groups of operations of various types into wider circles and the heuristic structure operative throughout this analysis is the probable emergence and development of schemes of recurrence.

There follow from the introduction of this notion of mediation a set of implications which Lonergan does not explore explicitly at this point in *Method*, but which concern the structure of operations in "the intellectual pattern of experience" to which he devotes a good part of *Insight*. It might be worthwhile, here, to discuss some of these implications in an effort to link the first pagges of chapter three above, with the general framework of emergent probability developed here and in chapter four. The point to be illustrated is how Lonergan conceives the constitutive elements in the act of empirical understanding and judgment in terms of groups (or schemes) of operations, emerging and developing in accordance with probabilities.

It was noted how Lonergan understood the role of mediation in evoking wide ranges of images, experiences, insights, meanings, memories, hopes and anticipations through the performance of complex, multi-level skills. But this expansion of the "horizons" of experience of the subject is a minor result of this capacity. A more significant result is the capacity for such skills not only to evoke the object of operations in the basic pattern but also to control the recurrent performance of the various cognitional operations themselves such that the operations in the pattern can link together into a larger scheme. The operations in the basic pattern intend objects and each has its own type of object.[21] But certain operations can function as links to other operations when their objects are controlled. One such linking operation is involved in the act of "inquiring." Wondering and asking questions frequently leads nowhere. But when the objects of the experiential operations are controlled through language and images, the recurrent asking of a single question or set of related questions of a controlled body of data significantly increases the f-probability of answers occurring in insights. Thus one need not stumble over data. One can seek and assemble data through such recurring operations as opening books, breaking rocks, pouring liquids into vials, counting events which have been classified, filling out questionnaires and doing mathematical puzzles.[22] The routines of empirical inquiry can focus and refocus a determinate set of questions on a delimited body of data so that discoveries or insights emerge more and more frequently from the data at hand rather than from data or images that are irrelevant to the intent of the questions. Experimental procedures can specify appropriate operations for verifying or rejecting these particular insights on the basis of that relevant body of data. Pedagogical techniques can specify appropriate procedures, contexts and clues so that children can learn with considerable speed a body of insights and skills which has been accumulated and found relevant by a culture. In short, the event, mediation, makes possible the regular (systematic) recurrence of an ordered sequence of sensorimotor, imaginative and cognitional operations in which the object of each earlier operation in the sequence becomes the material upon which the next operation operates. Thus the operations in the pattern link together in a flexible series of schemes such that the later schemes go beyond and build upon the results of the earlier schemes.

Cognition is thus conceived by Lonergan as a succession of groups or schemes of operations whose development and sufficiently frequent execution increases the f-probable occurrence of insights and judgments of v-probable truth. The occurrence of insights is an experience that is common to everyone. But the f-probable recurrence of insights increases as the various operations of the basic pattern of experience are grouped systematically into multi-level skills and as the level and range of the skills' performance are expanded in the general developmental scheme of assimilation and adjustment. As the scheme of operations is expanded to include the question for reflection, the preoccupation with conditions for verification, and the developed capacity for judgments of v-probable truth, then insights come to integrate wider ranges of experience and thus to correspond more closely to the intelligibility immanent in reality. It is apparent that Lonergan conceives the flexible set of cognitional operations involved in understanding and judgment as a complex skill whose structure is that of a series of recurrence schemes, whose emergence and development occur in accordance with f-probabilities, and whose objects correspond to reality in the measure that the skills are executed competently.[23]

One further point remains to be raised in connection with Lonergan's treatment of the notion of mediation. A number of objections have been raised against Lonergan's focus upon the subjective operations in his account of meaning. Fergus Kerr argues that Lonergan's account fails to integrate the contemporary scholarship on the intersubjective structure of symbol, language and meaning. Consequently his treatment of language and meaning is "extrinsic" and "non-participatory," and elitist in its "Western" emphasis upon "rationality."[24] In the view of Nicholas Lash, Lonergan lays the burden of interpreting meaning on the skills and experiences of individual subjects, and in so doing he fails to recognize the extent to which the individual shares cultural and historical meanings that are public.[25] Edward MacKinnon draws upon the work of Wittgenstein to argue that while a child first learns to use words through the performance of cognitional operations, the complete process of learning language involves the child "assimilat[ing] the public meaning of the terms and accommodat[ing] his own usage to this."[26] His conclusion is that "the meaningfulness of language is essentially public and derivatively private."[27]

Lonergan has responded to MacKinnon, in *Method* by arguing that what is true of ordinary meaningfulness is not true of original meaningfulness of any language.

For all language develops and, at any time, any language consists in the sedimentation of the developments that have occurred and have not become obsolete. Now developments consist in discovering new uses for existing words, in inventing new words, and in diffusing the discoveries and inventions. All three are a matter of expressed mental acts.[28]

And here Lonergan discusses, briefly, the intersubjective structure wherein original meaning is shared, transformed, developed, and thereby made public. This structure which draws upon Gibson Winter's reconstruction of the work of George Herbert Mead will be discussed in greater detail in chapter six, 6.4.2 below. But I would suggest that more can be said here about the way in which public meaning is transformed, in accordance with operative schemes, such that recurrent and shifting imagery functions to condition the f-probable recurrence of the cognitional actuation of specific classes and ranges of meanings.

When MacKinnon states that the child "assimilates" public meaning and "accommodates" his usage to this public meaning, he merely transposes the problem of the relationship between language and mental acts. For what are the acts of "assimilation" and "accommodation" if they do not involve an integration of experiential spontaneity and a reorientation of the child's sensitive flow with its anticipations of further experiences, images and insights. Such integrations are subjective acts that usually involve some mediating operation of one or another of the cognitional acts. I would suggest that MacKinnon's point is that the cognitional emergence in most cases, is not a *new* discovery, proceeding in accordance with the systematically regulated skills of the "intellectual pattern of experience," but an actuation of a publicly recurrent system of relations and schemes of relations in the context of a structure of intersubjective exchange. Furthermore there is considerable evidence to suggest that there is a dynamic structure to language and that the elements and processes of this immanent structure interrelate dynamically to inform and to transform meanings within as well as independent from the scheme of marshalling evidence which gives rise to judgments. In the light of this evidence ordinary language is understood as operative dynamically to shape and to shift the meanings that mediate the practice of culture in a way which usually prescinds from (but also can operate within) the process of empirical inquiry which Lonergan explains in the first five chapters of *Insight*.[29]

I would suggest that the clue to understanding the relationship between such dynamic patterns discernible in the operations of language and symbols, and the various subjective operations involved in the skills of cognition, is to be found in the relationship between the image and the insight. Images are essential conditions for insights but insights move beyond images to integrate sets of images and to fix the interrelations among images and the anticipations of questions, in terms and relations that cannot be imagined. Inasmuch as there can be discerned statistical laws operative in the socially, culturally and perhaps universally recurrent patterns of images, and inasmuch as recurring patterns in such statistical laws can be understood in terms of recurring events and schemes of the imagination, such statistical and classical laws will contribute to an explanation of the f-probabilities associated with trends and transformations of practical and theoretical insights which mediate the routines of cultures. For images shift the f-probabilities associated with classes of insights. But such an explanation would also recognize that while the immanent structure of language tends to shape the operative meanings of culture, such shaping does not exclude the higher order integrations of cognitional acts, it only explains the f-probable recurrence of classes of objects of such acts.[30]

This account would also explain why the operative meanings of culture are related non-systematically to truth and to value when they are implemented wholesale and in an undifferentiated fashion in the solution of concrete problems. The tasks and challenges of everyday living involve coincidental convergences of sets of conditions and, as such, are unique in their concrete particularities. To meet these tasks and challenges human subjects select from operative ranges of meanings, images and skills to understand the demands made by each situation and to respond with integrated sets of actions, mediated by more or less differentiated cognitional acts. To the extent that such selection, understanding and response are carried out with some measure of developed competence (attention to detail, openness to others, willingness to consider alternatives, wider horizons, etc., etc.), to that extent the unique demands of each individual situation will be met. While many of the operative images and meanings of culture can be agents of human and cultural value they are so only when selected and integrated appropriately in concrete contexts. Consequently Lonergan's account of the role of cognitional acts in the intersubjective world of human meaning is relevant, not only as an explanation of the original genesis of common meaning but also as explanation of the concretization of meaning in individual acts of intelligence and responsibility. Meaning is public and is transformed in accordance with recurring structures of symbol and image. But unless some measure of selection, differentiation, evaluation and attention (all of which involve some measure of cognitional "re-presentation" and mediation) are a part of the routinely operative *skills* of common culture, current meanings and the suggestive power of images supplant the concrete exigences of human situations, and values are transformed randomly into agents of destruction. One implication of this analysis would be that what is most significant for ethics is not so much the currency of *knowledge* of concrete values (although such knowledge remains important) but rather the developed competence of *skills* whose performance results in the cognitional genesis and actuation of value in concrete circumstances. I would suggest that Lonergan's analysis of the structure and development of cognitionally mediated skills can be understood as a contribution to ethics so conceived.

## 5.3 The Practical Orientation of Intelligence

Lonergan's presentation of Piaget's account of "skills" has the effect of introducing the heuristic structure, emergent probability, in a different terminology, a terminology that might be more familiar or accessible to a reader who has not studied the first five chapters of *Insight*. In addition this introduction has the added effect of drawing upon a body of evidence in developmental psychology where the insights of emergent probability would see to be verified. But I would suggest that there is a further value to Lonergan's way of proceeding here. The effect of *Method*, chapters one and two, is to introduce the cognitional operations, the operations of insight and judgment, as skills and sets of skills whose structure is no different from that of other skills which children and adults learn, and as human activities whose relations and contributions to the whole of human life remain to be explored. The operations of cognition are not isolated from what might be called the "affective" or "practical" dimensions of life. Rather, they are themselves "practical" in the sense that they are acts and groups of acts which are practised and performed on the "materials" of human experiential life and which can be developed to a greater or lesser degree of competence. And they are "affective" in the sense that their performance or development is oriented towards satisfying a human appetite, and their effect is to order the habitual affective orientation of the human subject. The question which stands to be answered is what role these particular skills and sets of skills play in relation to the other appetites and skills which constitute the regular life activity of human subjects and human societies.

Throughout *Insight* there is considerable emphasis upon the pure, detached, disinterested, unrestricted desire to know.[31] Lonergan conceives the dramatic bias of the human subject as the refusal of insight. He speaks of egoism as the "interference of spontaneity with the development of intelligence."[32] His answer to "the general bias of common sense," the long term generative principle of cultural and historical decline, is universal allegiance to the norms of detached, disinterested intelligence. His conception of the "good" is "the intelligibility that is intrinsic to being." And the implication of this conception for ethics is that the pursuit of value and its realization are understood as by-passing human feelings and sentiments, taking their foundation in "intelligible order" and "rational value."[33] It would seem from these examples in *Insight* that Lonergan conceives these cognitional skills as occupying a central role among the various skills and appetites of human life. Indeed it might seem that Lonergan would like to see the other feelings and emotions, the practical concerns of life, the liberation of the psyche in aesthetic experience to be eclipsed by the arid life of rationality.³⁴ I think two comments are in order here.

First. The whole seven hundred and forty-eight pages of *Insight* are devoted to developing an account of human understanding as a set of acts in which there occurs an emergent, transformative integration of an *entire human subject*. This account is developed, in large measure, in opposition to a trend which has conceived knowledge as a commodity and understanding after the analogy of deductive logic. This account has sought to develop a structured world view, emergent probability, which could conceive human intelligent activity, to a greater or lesser degree, as self-regulating or reflexively operative.³⁵ And the goal of the book has been to find some possible, empirically verifiable grounds for distinguishing between human life appropriately or constructively lived, and its terrible, inhumane and criminal deformations which overwhelm our daily experience. This account reflects such current insights as Clifford Geertz's definition of culture in terms of "meaning,"³⁶ R.G. Collingwood's definition of "History as Knowledge of Mind,"³⁷ and Wilhelm Stekel's account of psychotherapy as requiring a mediating act of insight.³⁸ That is to say Lonergan's account has sought to find in an empirical account of human acts of meaning, acts of intelligence, the centrally constitutive element which distinguishes human life from that of the other animals. But Lonergan's approach has been to try to discover the distinctive nature and the peculiar dynamic structure of the acts and skills whose performance constitutes the *genesis* of meaning. In so proceeding, Lonergan has sought to follow up on a number of clues from the work of Aquinas.³⁹ And this concern with the genesis of meaning marks a significant discontinuity from the general trend of scholarship on meaning. If his narrowly focused attention has resulted in his excluding a wealth of insights available from this scholarship I have tried to show how his heuristic could provide a framework for integrating his work with many insights from this field.

Second. There is some evidence in *Insight* that Lonergan's incessant pounding on the theme of detached intelligence, at least in his discussions of the practical and moral application of intelligence, is to be understood as a response to a pervasive "emotivism" or "non-cognitive" approach to ethics and moral life.⁴⁰ There is a recent study of the contemporary import of "emotivism" in ethics, by Alasdair MacIntyre.⁴¹ And while Lonergan's reactions to "emotivism" would seem to manifest themselves in an excessive rejection of emotional life in *Insight*, MacIntyre shares Lonergan's fear of the terrible destruction "emotivism" has wrought during its reign. Fifteen years after *Insight*, in *Method*, Lonergan modifies his notion of "the good," and integrates into his notion of "value" the affective apprehension of values in intentionally-oriented feelings.⁴² Furthermore, as will be argued, Lonergan's notion of "cosmopolis" (the response to the general bias of common sense) is only to be understood adequately in terms of his chapter on "Special Transcendent Knowledge," and his notion of "grace."⁴³ The effect of these additional contexts and these modifications to the original presentation of his ethics in *Insight*, chapters six, seven and eighteen, is to explain much more fully the elements operative in moral life, the materials integrated in the exercise of human responsibility, and the conditions and probabilities associated with the recurrence of acts of human responsibility in history. But the core of Lonergan's account of "The Possibility of Ethics" remains, in my judgment, untouched by these modifications and developments. That is to say that the subsequent modifications remain genetically (and not dialectically) related to the central insights of *Insight*, chapters six and eighteen.[44] The evidence supporting this judgment is what I will attempt to present in this and the following chapters.

In his Halifax lectures, delivered one year after the first publication of *Insight*, Lonergan provides a clue for the role which he sees the cognitional skills playing throughout the general course of daily life.

> The real world is what corresponds to ones *Sorge*, one's concern, and one's concern is not exclusively a matter of the pure desire to know. One's concern includes all of one's affectivity. It involves the whole man, not just this tiny thread of the pure desire to know that is found in us at times. When you are arguing and proving, it is there, and the real world corresponds to it. While familiarity with the real world is also had by the animals, it is had by us in a more elevated fashion by use and by wont and by intellect when necessary. When absolutely necessary we will get down and think out a problem, but that is just an interruption of normal living.[45]

Lonergan's reference to the "pure desire to know" here is to the role that this desire plays in what he calls "the intellectual pattern of experience." And this pattern will be discussed below. But what is relevant here is that Lonergan recognizes that the "intellectual pattern of experience" (that particular mode of application of intelligent skills to which he devotes sixteen of his twenty chapters of *Insight*) is a relatively *infrequent* element in human life. By far the most frequent application of the intellectual skills is in the practical application of common sense. And it is in his account of common sense, most particularly in its dramatic pattern of experience, that we come to see the intelligent acts and skills as elements in a larger series of schemes or recurrence whose object or term is the transformation of the materials of experiential life in the practical routines of an economy, a polity, a culture.[46]

Most of our lives are spent solving an endless set of practical problems, meeting the myriad of exigencies that arise in the concrete course of intersubjective life and executing the routine tasks of a culture in ever changing contexts of problems and opportunities. Most of our lives involve the application of intelligence in the service of practice. Indeed, as is evident from his comment during the Halifax lectures, cited above, while the application of intelligence in the light of the pure desire is itself not immediately practical, still Lonergan recognizes that the demand for such a theoretical application of intelligence arises not simply out of this pure desire but most usually as practical life encounters problems which cannot be met by common sense.[47] And because the objects of this theoretical knowledge are abstract and universal (they are things as related to one another) their application to concrete situations requires a return to the practical orientation of common sense.[48] Furthermore, even in the most theoretical inquiry, the development of appropriate investigation and discovery procedures requires the practical orientation of common sense to devise concrete contexts for the emergence and verification of insights.[49] Most fundamentally, Lonergan's whole approach to cognitional theory is itself an analysis of the practice or performance of acts and schemes of acts through which human subjects come to know.[50] Knowing does not stand alongside practice. Rather, it is an instance of a particular type of practice. And so David Tracy can rightly argue that, for Lonergan, knowledge (the object or term of acts of knowing) does not stand opposed to practice, but is itself founded in practice.

> Rather praxis is theory's own originating and self-correcting foundation since theory is dependent, minimally, on the authentic praxis of the theorist's personally appropriated value of intellectual integrity and self-transcending commitment to the imperatives of critical rationality. In that sense, praxis sublates theory, not vice-versa.[51]

Lonergan's analysis of skills as recurring schemes of acts or operations, including cognitional skills, is proposed as a heuristic structure for an account of instances of human practice. As a heuristic structure it is a part of an overall world view, emergent probability, which invites verification. And as an account of cognition it raises the question of the interrelationship between the related but distinct types of acting or doing: acting intelligently and acting responsibly.

## 5.4 Patterns of Experience

In *Insight*, chapter six, Lonergan drafts a very brief sketch, a notion,[52] of human action or practice in terms of an account of what he calls "patterns of experience." Chapter two of *Method* retains this characterization of patterns of human experience and refers to chapter six of *Insight* for a fuller exposition.[53] It would seem that this sketch of the patterns of experience is an attempt by Lonergan to chart a course towards a contemporary understanding of the relationships among what the scholastics called the vegetative, the sensitive, and the rational faculties, including the two rational faculties of intellect and will.[54] But at the same time, this sketch clearly seeks to identify the limited role that intelligence plays in *all* the experiential patterns. In other words, there is no sense in which Lonergan conceives intelligence as operating in isolation from the other elements or dimensions of human experience. Rather, this account of the biological, the aesthetic, the intellectual, and the dramatic patterns might be regarded as Lonergan's effort to sketch the various different ways that intelligence functions as a mediator throughout the course of human life. This, at least, is the view which is reflected in Lonergan's own answer to a question put to him during his 1958 lectures on *Insight*.[55]

I think that an initial clue to understanding Lonergan's intent throughout these two chapters on common sense, is to be found in *Method*.

> This distinction between immediate and mediate operations has quite a broad relevance. It sets off the world of immediacy of the infant against the vastly larger world mediated by meaning.[56]

From the time that children learn the most basic linguistic skills their entire world of experience becomes mediated by the performance of acts in the basic pattern, acts whose occurrence conditions the psychological presence of intelligently grasped unities in sensible and imaginative experience. Thus there is an element of intelligence, understood in this broad sense, in every aspect of human life. But the role of the controlled scheme of operations which yields insights and judgments is markedly different in the various patterns of experience. In fact it would seem that what distinguishes the biological and the aesthetic pattern is precisely the absence of this particular schematic interlocking of the operations of sense, imagination and intelligence. This is not to say that the biological and aesthetic patterns are not intelligent. It is only to say that the schemes linking sensations to images, sensations and images to intelligently grasped unities, and the sensitive, imaginative and intelligent schemes to the motor skills do not regularly arrange themselves so as to focus and refocus questions on a controlled body of experiential data. Their structure of arrangement differs in the various patterns of experience and these differences correspond to the different intentional orientations of the various patterns.

The biological pattern is characterized principally by its orientation towards securing the continued life of the organism and its species.[57] And here we begin to see how Lonergan starts building a foundation for an ethics. The most primitive biological operations of human persons would seem to have a structure that is oriented recurrently towards a set of goals. The routines or recurring schemes of "sensations, memories, images, conations, emotions and bodily movements," themselves intricate combinations of more elemental biological events and schemes, "converge upon terminal activities of intussusception or reproduction or, when negative in scope, self-preservation."[58] The schemes take up the materials of the organism's environment and transform them in the "interest," so to speak, of the organism's well-being. When the organism becomes "conscious"[59] the schemes remain, nonetheless, more successful (more rapid, more effective, more efficient) means for attaining these biological ends.[60] And while the biological ends concern principally the immanent aspects of the organism's functioning, the greater success of the conscious operations is to be accounted for in terms of the organism's new-found capacity for systematic or controlled attention or "concern" for the "external" environment.[61]

> Thus extroversion is a basic characteristic of the biological pattern of experience. The bodily basis of the senses in sense organs, the functional correlation of sensations with the positions and movements of the organs, the imaginative, conative, emotive consequences of sensible presentations, and the resulting local movements of the body, all indicate that elementary experience is concerned, not with the immanent aspects of living, but with its external conditions and opportunities. Within the full pattern of living, there is a partial, intermittent, extroverted pattern of conscious living.[62]

There is a very narrow role played by the operations of intelligence within the biological pattern, a role that can be illustrated by any recollection of an occasion of hunger and the subsequent steps that were taken to procure food. But the point to be made here is that the organism in the biological pattern spontaneously brings into play any skills within its repertoire and integrates their performance in any one of a large number of possible schemes oriented towards relieving a state of biological distress or achieving a biological goal.[63] It is this orientation that distinguishes the biological pattern, and it is this structured relationship towards the materials of the organism's environment that qualifies the routines of the biological pattern as a first, most basic instance of a practice or transformative activity.

The aesthetic pattern is characterized by Lonergan as a liberation "from the drag of biological purposiveness."[64] And the essential, fulfilling condition for this liberation is the organism's capacity for focussed attention upon the objects of experience in "conscious" life.[65] The aesthetic pattern may involve nothing more than a child taking pleasure in the wiggling of fingers and toes. But it is the control over the intentionally-oriented operations of sense that fulfills the conditions for the child's focussed gaze and attention on the subjective experience of such movements. Once some control over the imaginative and intelligent operations of the basic pattern has been achieved through the mediation of sensorimotor skills, the human subject need not await the occasion for aesthetic experience but he or she can fulfill the conditions for its occurrence in himself or herself or in others.

What distinguishes the aesthetic pattern in Lonergan's account is its orientation towards heightened subjective experience and the feelings which flow from such attention. And as with the biological pattern the structure of the elements of aesthetic experience usually includes mediating operations of imagination and intelligence. Thus the aesthetic experiences can be characterized as flexible schemes and series of schemes intentionally ordered towards heightened experience for its own sake. Lonergan describes the biological pattern as ordered towards a term or goal. But the successful realization of this goal fulfills the conditions for a conscious subject's emancipation from the constraints of biological purpose. Thus the stable recurrence of the schemes and series of the biological pattern (with some time remaining during waking hours) constitutes the fulfilling conditions for the emergence of the events and schemes of the aesthetic pattern. The heightened experience in the aesthetic pattern is spontaneously sought as preferable (more joyous, more delightful) to the constraints of the biological pattern.

The aesthetic pattern involves not only the controlled attention to experiences and the heightened feelings that follow, but also the creative exploration and combination of patterns of images and the feelings that they evoke.[66] The effect of this capacity to control images and feelings of the aesthetic pattern is not an enslavement of feelings and image but their liberation both from biological purpose and from the constraints of the questions and anticipations of the intellectual pattern.[67] The aesthetic pattern includes some straining for truth and some drive towards value, but what results is not knowledge of truth or value but, I would argue, what Lonergan comes to call in *Method* the feeling as intentional response to value.[68]

> The aesthetic and artistic are symbolic. Free experience and free creation are prone to justify themselves by an ulterior purpose or significance. Art, then, becomes symbolic, but what is symbolized is obscure. It is an expression of the human subject outside the limits of adequate intellectual formulation or appraisal. It seeks to mean, to convey, to impart something that is to be reached, not through science or philosophy, but through a participation and, in some fashion, a re-enactment of the artist's inspiration and intention. Pre-scientific and pre-philosophic, it may strain for truth and value without defining them. Post-biological, it may reflect the psychological depths yet, by that very fact, it will go beyond them.[69]

Man is oriented towards being, towards truth, towards value. Being is approached and pointed towards in emotions, symbols, images. And such affective and imaginative thrusts toward truth and value are profoundly significant and essential dimensions of human life. The schemes or routines of cognition, the controlled and mediated skills described by Lonergan in terms of Piaget's analysis, are involved in the aesthetic pattern. But their object is not theoretical knowledge, judgment and decision, but the liberation and heightening of feelings that strain toward what is fundamentally of worth in human life.

As the successful performance of the routines of biological life fulfills the conditions for the events and schemes of the aesthetic pattern, so too the liberation of sensations and images in the aesthetic pattern fulfills the conditions for their integration in acts of insight in the intellectual pattern.

> The aesthetic liberation and the free artistic control of the flow of sensations and images, of emotions and bodily movements, [do] not merely break the bonds of biological drive but also generate in

experience a flexibility that makes it a ready tool for the spirit of inquiry.[70]

While the biological pattern presents the objects of experience simply as the means for securing the life of the organism and its species, it is the aesthetic pattern that liberates the subject from this narrow orientation. The aesthetic pattern shifts the subject's attention to the object for its own sake; for the sake of its heightened experience. This shift away from a biologically utilitarian preoccupation with the object of experience permits the subject's recurrent and focused attention on experience for its own sake. And this fulfills the conditions for the emergence and recurrence of the schemes of the intellectual pattern. For only a focused preoccupation with the question and the data on their own terms can yield the insights that answer questions.[71] While the aesthetic and intellectual patterns are distinct the former constitutes a condition for the occurrence and controlled recurrence of the latter. It would seem that Lonergan's presentation of the relation between these two patterns necessarily implies that the competent performance of the schemes of operations in the intellectual pattern requires a regular return to experience in the aesthetic pattern.

## 5.5 *The Dramatic Pattern and Responsible, Moral Practice*

In his account of the dramatic pattern of experience Lonergan begins to lay the foundations for an account of moral, responsible practice. While the biological and the aesthetic patterns of experience involve some measure of cognitional operation mediating practical routines or skills, it is in the dramatic pattern that the object or intentional term of such skills is the ongoing actuation and reconstitution of the pattern of relations of the subject in his or her "external" and "internal" environments. The goal of the presentation in this chapter, to this point, has been to indicate how emergent probability sets the terms and relations of Lonergan's account of the various types of practical skills within human life, and to indicate how the cognitional acts play a limited but nonetheless effective and potentially transformative role in the practical skills of the various experiential patterns. From here on my object is to begin to assemble the foundational elements of the meaning of the term "responsibility." And my approach will be to outline some of the similarities and the differences between the dramatic pattern and the other patterns, and then to highlight the distinctive elements of a type of practice in which the human subject transforms and sustains the transformation of his or her life through the differentiated and coordinated application of all ranges of skills. To speak of human freedom and its correlate human responsibility is to suggest that such differentiating and coordinating acts involve some measure of reflexively operative self-constitution. And so the last section of this chapter is devoted to a discussion of Lonergan's rather novel distinction between essential and effective freedom.

Where the scientist seeks the relations of things to one another, common sense is concerned with the *relations of things to us*. Where the scientist's correlations serve to define the things that he relates to one another, common sense not merely relates objects to a subject but also *constitutes relations* of the subject to objects. Where the scientist is primarily engaged in knowing, common sense cannot develop without *changing the subjective term* in the object-to-subject relations that it knows.[77]

First. Lonergan's characteristic distinction of common sense is its preoccupation with the elements of experience insofar as they have an import or a bearing on the subject. In this sense, the dramatic pattern of common sense shares with the routines of the biological pattern an orientation towards the "sustenance" and the "nutrition," so to speak, of the subject. Certainly the mediation of the meanings and routines of a culture, an economy and a civilization vastly expands the meaning of the terms "sustenance" and "nutritition" so as to introduce a notion of human "well-being" that is in no way constrained by the limits of biological purpose. But the orientation of the dramatic pattern remains subject-centered. Theoretical knowing in the intellectual pattern, on the other hand, suppresses this concern for the immediate import of knowledge. The dramatic operation of common sense is concerned with knowing, but knowing inasmuch and insofar as it makes an immediate practical difference to my life.

Second. Lonergan introduces here the first significant instance wherein the performance of acts of intelligence has the effect of ordering decisively the performance of sense and motor skills towards the attainment of an object. The dramatic pattern is not satisfied merely with knowing intelligible relations, it is oriented towards *constituting* and *reconstituting* common and new relations. And such relations are constituted as events and plans of action, conceived by intelligence (whether the intelligence of the subject him or herself, or that of the members or founders of the community) and actuated as the integrating principle of complex schemes of skills. The common sense concern or appetite for changing the conditions of life is integrally related to, and a natural upshot of the concern for the import of things for us. Inasmuch as we care about things that make a difference for us, the common sense understanding of such things fulfills the conditions for our application of intelligence and imagination to devising and executing strategies that relate us to such things in the interest of an ever-expanding notion of well-being.

Third. The routine operation of common sense *changes the subject*. In the dramatic pattern this change, a subtle yet significant transformation in spontaneity, emerges in the course of devising and implementing projects, developing roles, and intelligently adapting to new situations (the various ways in which new and old subject-object relations are constituted). While the cognitional operations are decisive in ordering behaviour in the dramatic pattern, still the execution of projects, the development of roles and routines and the adaptation to new situations have the principal effect of transforming ourselves in our habitual way of relating to the objects of experience. Such relations or orientations operate as routine or recurring attitudes, anticipations, expectations, routine patterns for organizing materials and projecting courses of action, and spontaneous feelings and images that are evoked in connection with people, places, insights and environments. Lonergan is quite aware that these habitual orientations to the objects of experience are not directly the products of deliberation and choice. Rather, they are by-products or results of one's whole life of common sense decisions and actions. While common sense intelligence has moved on to new matters the subject's orientation to his or her experience has been constituted by previous experiences, insights and decisions. Intelligent reflection and decision decisively order the materials and activities of experience. But it is the spontaneous relation of the subject to the objects of his or her experience that selects and assembles the materials to be ordered and provides the clues that will condition the probable emergence of insights and programs of action.[78]

There stands here in this account of the common sense operation of intelligence in its dramatic pattern, many of the elements that Lonergan will develop into his prolegomenon to an ethics in *Insight*, chapter eighteen, and his partial sketch of moral life in *Method*, chapter two. And it would be worthwhile here to identify precisely what these elements are.

First. This account of Lonergan's includes the possibility of a mode of human performance that is not determined *entirely* by biological, or social or psychological conditions. The relationship between the neurological conditions and the emergence of acts of intelligent control over sensorimotor skills includes an element of randomness.[79] The neural manifold of the human subject can be so ordered through the performance of sense and motor operations that a determinate set of images, sensory experiences, and linguistically controlled insights can become present to his or her attention at a given time. This set of images, sense experiences and insights can be ordered or integrated in any of a number of ways in an original or a common act of imagination or insight. Likewise a set of insights can so order this flexible neural manifold that imagination and intellect can be called to attention and sense and motor skills can be ordered or integrated in complex set of operations like those involved in playing the piano. The neural manifold clearly presents an exigence in a certain direction in accordance with the demands of the moment and the habitual orientation of the subject. But this exigence generally is not completely decisive. Rather, there is usually some measure of flexibility to the neural manifold that permits a number of possible forms of psychic integration. It is this flexibility and the absence of completely and universally determining system – this element of randomness – that grounds the possibility of practical action becoming responsible. And it is this element of randomness that is developed as an essentially constitutive element of Lonergan's ethics presented in *Insight*, chapter eighteen, and discussed in the pages that follow.

Second. The structure of this relationship between a flexible neural manifold and its emergent integration in psychic acts reflects a dynamic orientation towards a higher order intelligibility and Lonergan has named this orientation finality. This dynamic orientation is manifested both in the integration of experiential elements in insights and in the coordination of sensorimotor skills into programs or routines of action in accordance with acts of intelligence. But the dynamism of finality is further manifested in the relations among the various patterns of experience, in the developmental scheme of assimilation and adjustment wherein the child or adult acquires and perfects skills, in the subject's spontaneous preference for more developed satisfactions and values, and most generally, in the subject's whole care-ful orientation to being. Most fundamentally the dynamic orientation of finality is towards emergent intelligibility, towards the probable realization or actuation of intelligibility as its conditions are fulfilled. While this dynamic notion of finality is heuristically operative throughout this account of common sense in its dramatic pattern it is this notion of finality which will become the key element in the distinction between true and false values and between genetically related values in *Insight*, chapters seven and eighteen, and *Method*, chapter two. These are discussed below in chapter six, 6.5 and 6.6.

### 5.6 Freedom and Moral Life: Essential and Effective Freedom

There is no doubt that any discussion of moral life will require as a centrally constitutive element some account of the notion of freedom. And since the Enlightenment there has been an especially concerted effort and find in the notion of freedom that particular aspect of human nature which qualifies human practice as distinctively moral or responsible. In the first chapter of this book on *Hegel and Modern Society*,[80] Charles Taylor introduces briefly the ethics of Kant as background for a subsequent analysis and evaluation of Hegel's political philosophy. Taylor characterizes Kant's moral thought as a protest against an earlier Enlightenment view of man as driven by desire. And in striving to find an *a priori* basis for moral action in the self-actuating or self-regulating activity of the rational will, Kant hoped to discover the grounds for man's liberation from the bondage of passion and natural inclination. In Taylor's view Kant saw in man's exercise of autonomous, self-regulating, rational will the act which constitutes man's life as free.[81] In another introduction to Hegel's social theory, Herbert Marcuse describes Hegel's own account of freedom in similar terms, as the reflexively operative, self-regulating activity which lifts man above a final capitulation to externally determining conditions.

But freedom is for Hegel an ontological category: it means being not a mere object, but the subject of one's existence; not succumbing to external conditions, but transforming factuality into realization.[82]

The term freedom has had a variety of different meanings, meanings that have been developed differently in various historical ages and which have manifested themselves in a variety of ethical theories.[83] In one usage what is emphasized is the absence of restrictions. For example, a dog that is not caged or tied on a leash is considered free in this usage of the term. In another usage freedom is conceived in terms of its determining conditions. Here, to be free would mean that an event is not the result of the decisively determining operation of a unified set of antecedent causes or conditions. In Lonergan's terminology freedom here indicates the absence of system or pattern in a unified set of classical laws.[84] In this sense the movement of electrons is considered free and a coin's movements throughout a fair toss is regarded as free.

Lonergan's efforts to develop a concept of freedom can be seen in continuity with Kant's and Hegel's attempts to understand freedom in terms of man's self-regulative capacities. The argument or debate to which all three are opposed affirms (either explicily or implicitly) the pre-destined or determined character of human life which would preclude any notion of the subjective locus of human responsibility. Like Kant and Hegel, Lonergan sought to find in an understanding of man's reason, his rationality, his understanding, the key element of this reflexive or self-regulating capacity. The similarities and differences between Lonergan's account and those of Kant and Hegel cannot be explored here. But it is sufficient to note, at this point, the fact that all three thinkers set out to conceive the notion with similar objectives.

Accordingly, an account of freedom has to turn to a study of intellect and will. In the coincidental manifolds of sensible presentations, practical insights grasp possible courses of action that are examined by reflection, decided upon by acts of willing and thereby either are or are not realized in the underlying sensitive flow. In this process there is to be discerned the emergence of elements of higher integration. For the higher integration effected on the level of human living consists of sets of courses of action, and these actions emerge inasmuch as they are understood by intelligent consciousness, evaluated by rational consciousness, and willed by rational self-consciousness....[85]

Man is free essentially inasmuch as possible courses of action are grasped by practical insight, motivated by reflection, and executed by decision.[86]

Freedom in this usage is not an absence but a presence; the presence of an actuated capacity to mediate the performance of sensorimotor acts and skills through the schemes or skills of intelligence. It is the actuated capacity to perform a scheme or groups of acts of cognition. But this cognition is not the knowing that terminates in a judgment of truth. Rather, it is the set of acts which grasp a possible course of action among a range of possibilities presented to the subject at a moment in world process, and which constitute an order or a pattern in a manifold of skills within the repertoire of a subject, in accordance with this conceived course of action. Some knowledge of fact is certainly necessary in the exercise of human freedom. But Lonergan's account of freedom in *Insight* does not define freedom in terms of knowledge of fact.

The curious and distinctive feature of Lonergan's account of freedom is not his emphasis upon the role of intelligence. Rather, it is his integration of the statistical element, his definition of f-probability and his related notion of emergence, into his accounts of intelligence and responsibility which is most original.[87] In itself the notion of randomness, understood as the absence of a decisively determining, systematic unity of classical laws, is unsufficient to explain human freedom. For randomness does not explain the reflexive or self-regulating character that Kant and Hegel knew to be operative in human freedom. What is required is an explanation which includes some element of randomness in the relation between the freely performed act and its determining conditions, but which nonetheless recognizes the act as decisively self-regulating or self-integrating. Thus the explanation, in Lonergan's view, would require an emergent integration of a lower order manifold and a possible means for such an emergent integration to control its own form in a succession of reflexively operative recurrences. The neural manifold, its flexibly recurring aggregate of neurological events, the capacity for system or scheme to emerge and order or pattern such events in accordance with f-probabilities, the exigence for certain forms of integration, and the reflexive capacity to coordinate sense and motor skills in accordance with such an order or pattern are the essential elements in such an explanation. The condition of possibility for the emergence of new order or pattern Lonergan explains in terms of f-probably recurring events of a skill linking together in mutually conditioning sets or chains at the psychic level. And in this view the intricate set of neural pathways would seem to allow the capacity for emergent psychic patterns to operate on acquired sense and motor capacities, coordinating sets of skills in accordance with the emergent psychic order. It is the *occurrence* of such a set of acts (the actuation of this particular capacity, the performance of this skill) which designates a human action as essentially free.

A number of qualifications would be in order here to specify more clearly Lonergan's intent. The first qualification concerns the relation between knowledge of fact and intelligent, responsible grasp and actuation of a possible course of action. In chapter eighteen of *Insight*, Lonergan explains rational self-consciousness (what he later comes to call responsible decision)[88] as the demand for a consistency between knowing and doing.[89] His formulation here is misleading. For it is rooted in a failure to make an adequate distinction between knowledge of fact and knowledge of value, a distinction which is operative implicitly in *Insight* but only differentiated explicitly in *Method*.[90]

An insight about a matter of fact is a possibility inasmuch as what is understood in the insight might or might not be so. Such an insight grasps an intelligibility in a manifold of experential data and that intelligibility might or might not correspond to the intelligibility immanent in world process. The question as to the correspondence (or v-probable correspondence) is only settled in the judgment of fact which assembles the conditions for rejecting incorrect insights and accepting correct ones. And so the word possibility here denotes what is grasped at a relatively incomplete stage in a chain or scheme of acts whose intentional object is the cognitional actuation of an intelligibility already actuated in world process. The possibility of the insight is the possibility of a more or less complete cognitional correspondence; a possibility which is actualized only in another type of intelligent act further on in scheme and which, when actualized, transforms the subject (the person) but not immediately the object (the known).

A possible course of action, on the other hand, is a possibility inasmuch as the relevant conditions for the emergence (the performance) of the course of action are, in part, fulfilled, inasmuch as such conditions are known to be fulfilled (more or less completely), and inasmuch as the course of action is grasped or actuated in an insight or unified set of insights which extrapolates from present and past stages of world process to constitute imaginatively and cognitionally one or more alternative future stages. While such possibilities are occasionally somewhat original, most usually they involve the re-actuation of socially, economically, culturally current routines. The cognitional act which grasps the possibility stands to be followed by a further set of acts in the chain which reflect on the possibility, judge it to be worthwhile, and actuate the intelligibility immanent in the projected course of action in an integration of the skills of the subject (or of the group of subjects if it is a collaborative effort). Such reflection is generally more or less expeditiously executed. The final act, the decision, completes the chain; it constitutes the next stage in that sphere of world process, and thus transforms the objects of world process (the known or to-be-known) as well as the subject(s). The word possibility here denotes what is grasped at a relatively incomplete stage in a chain of acts whose intentional object is the intelligent actuation of a next stage in world process. Consequently inasmuch as the performance of acts of understanding and judgment of *truth* are themselves intelligent actuations of a next stage to world process, the program or plan which outlines a project of empirical inquiry into matters of fact is a possibility of the second type designed to lead to and actuate a possibility of the first type. And inasmuch as knowledge of fact yearns to be integrated into action programs oriented towards improving the life conditions of people around the world, possibilities of the first type are dynamically ordered towards integration into possibilities of the second type. In this sense knowing is a subset of praxis.

The second qualification concerns a possible confusion about what distinctively constitutes human action as free. Men and women can judge badly, we can make incompetent judgments of value, and we can reject what we know to be of value in favour of a course of action which we recognize to be a mistake or a poor alternative. But the meaning of the term freedom is not defined here simply in terms of this absence of system or necessity linking insights with favourable judgments and linking judgments on the value of a possible course of action with the actuation of these values. "Man is not free because he can be unreasonable in his choices."[91] Rather, Lonergan's definition of freedom has as its central moment the actuation of a capacity for an emergent intelligibility to integrate or order an otherwise coincidental manifold of human skills. When a program of action has been conceived and implemented, regardless of the relative competence of the subject's critical evaluation of the worth of the program, and regardless of whether the subject decided to act in accordance with his or her critical evaluation, it is the distinct act of ordering his or her (or their) performance in accordance with an act of intelligence within a reflexively operative scheme which constitutes that actuated program as free. The distinctiveness of this type or class of act cannot be overstated. The operation which Lonergan comes to name "decision" in *Method* and which he sought to explain in *Insight*, chapter eighteen, is not knowledge of fact nor is it knowledge of value. It is an operation of ordering an otherwise coincidental manifold of skills in accordance with a cognitional act. And whether the cognitional act is merely a re-enactment of a time-worn tradition or whether it is an ingeniously conceived new way of solving an old problem, the act remains essentially free. The term freedom, in Lonergan's conception, designates the fact that such higher order emergent integrations of "will" have in fact occurred throughout human life and not the fact that they only correspond to judgments of value (themselves more or less badly performed) in accordance with statistical laws.[92]

This introduces the third and last qualification. The occurrence of an intelligent act integrating a manifold of performance skills qualifies that performance as essentially free. But there is a vast different between essential freedom and its various ranges of flexibility. And so in order to explain the apparent fact of levels or degrees of developed responsibility, and in order to account for the massively conditioned character of human life, Lonergan introduces a distinction between essential and effective freedom. "The difference between essential and effective freedom is the difference between a dynamic structure and its operational range."[93] Effective freedom is the measure of limitations and conditions, both immanent to the subject and proper to his or her historical environment, corresponding to the f-probable occurrence of *more diverse ranges* of acts and skills within the subject's operative repertoire.[94]

Effective freedom involves the external circumstances of the subject's life and the subject's own sensitive, intelligent and responsible states of habit, routine or development.[95] Lonergan notes briefly the way in which each of these types of conditions affects the subject's effective freedom. But an elaboration of the structure and the import of this presentation would be in order here. For while Lonergan's account of responsible practice focuses on the role of the practical insight in selecting among possible courses of action and in constituting an order in a subjective (or, as we will see in chapter six below, in an intersubjective) set of performance skills, the fact is that subjects are most usually limited in the range of possibilities open to them. In my view this distinction between essential and effective freedom can provide the key to understanding how social, economic, psychological, historical conditions can operate to shape and delimit the f-probabilities associated with classes of human performance without obliterating man's essential freedom. Furthermore this account explains how effective freedom, won principally through the conversions, and operative personally in the lives of subjects, constitutes the condition and the locus of social transformation.

In Lonergan's account of the practical, transformative skills in the dramatic pattern of experience, the human subject stands linked into a huge number of recurrence schemes which involve circles of events within his or her own envelope of skin and events of the more or less remote "external," biological, intersubjective, social, economic, historical environment. Such schemes includes the nutritional and respiratory cycles, the visual, auditory, tactile, olfactory cycles linking the coordination of muscles and organs to the various sensory responses, the social and linguistic cycles of gesture and role-taking, the economic cycles wherein recurrent actions link together with those of other members of an economy to yield circles of exchange, and historical cycles wherein the dreams of one generation become the routines of another for building the promise of the future. Like the carbon atom the human subject is ineluctably social. But unlike the carbon atom the human subject's sociality is operative on a number of complex, interlocking levels. For a number of the schemes linking the "inside" and the "outside" of this envelope have the curious ability to order or coordinate the routine functioning and interacting of other events and schemes. The most significant examples of such coordinating schemes are those involving the cognitional emergence of unities that integrate non-systematic manifolds of neural demand functions, thus constituting an order in what would otherwise be a cacaphony of sensory "experiences," or a hodgepodge of muscular movements. This immanent emergence occurs at first non-systematically for it is a structuration occuring spontaneously given the fulfillment of the necessary conditions. But as an emergence its f-probably systematized recurrence can be increased in the context of such developmental and intersubjective routines as pedagogy, parental example and apprenticeship. In this way the operative integrations in the practical life of a culture are drawn from the common font of a sedimented heritage of a succession of civilizations. The emergent integrations remain personal events inasmuch as the locus of their occurrence is the neural manifold of the subject and inasmuch as the fulfilling conditions need to occur and recur within the appropriate spatial and temporal range relative to the subject's neural manifold. But inasmuch as the integrations themselves are of classes, and the classes are common to subjects in cultures, the integrating acts that mediate and coordinate the routines, the anticipations, the memories and hopes of a culture are fully public.

The term essential freedom denotes the fact that the manifold of skills within the repertoire of any human subject is open to the possibility of such an emergent integration occurring in the context of a scheme of acts involving a selection among projected alternatives and modification through feedback cycles.[96] Because such integrations occur and recur in accordance with f-probabilities, the human subject is not locked into the determining constraints of biological, psychological or social conditioning. But because biological, psychological and social conditions are mediated to the neural manifold through the operation of countless recurrence schemes, such conditions operate to shift the f-probabilities associated with various classes of integrations. For this reason the subject is social. Furthermore the most significant fact about practically integrating skills is the way in which they function to transform subjective spontaneity, and thus to condition or shape the f-probabilities associated with the course of subsequent performance. Since the generally current practical routines of economy, society and polity will not be authored individually by the majority of subjects but will be established in accordance with the operative exigencies in each of these realms, there will be patterns in the flows of practical and theoretical insights in accordance with historical patterns in such exigencies. As operative routines shape daily experience such experience gives rise to corresponding insights. And as operative routines are themselves transformed in accordance with historically dynamic patterns in the transformation of economic, social and political life, such routines will mediate (both systematically and non-systematically) such patterns to the flows of cognitional acts of subjects. Such patterns of "conditioning" do not preclude essential freedom. For the capacity for emergent integration in a scheme involving cognitional projection, selection and feedback modification remains.

However, there also exists a set of skills wherein the subject can refine progressively the genesis of such operative integrations in accordance with his or her own reflexively transforming anticipations, in a scheme of intersubjective exchange wherein his or her own anticipations and those of another are assessed critically, and in the interests of the ongoing development of the capacity to constitute systematically his or her own subsequent capacities. The term "effective freedom" denotes the fact that the emergent integration of the subject's skills stands as an act within a set of acts wherein the subject can effect such an integration in one of a number of possible ways, and that the range of possibilities open to him or her at a point in time can be expanded or restricted, through the operation of social, historical, and psychological conditions as well as through the subject's developed skills of modifying or transforming his or her own "praxis," and subsequent lines of development in such "praxis."[97]

Because the emergent integrations are inertial (in the absence of intervening conditions) and because they reorder the subject's spontaneous engagement with his or her own environment, the practical, linguistic, cognitional skills of culture, once learned, recur spontaneously with the presence of fulfilling conditions. Consequently the practical routines of culture do not only proliferate, they also endure. But because the experiential life of subjects involves not only the recurring schemes of society, economy, polity, but also the random interactions among events in these schemes and events of the other "natural" routines of his or her environment, this experiential life will undergo a continual process of transformation. And so essential to the "welfare" of subjects will be a dynamic flexibility in their development and modification of skills. For this reason the notion of "effective freedom" pertains, in a minor way, to the social, economic, cultural conditions that restrict the proliferation of determinate practical forms. But in a major way effective freedom pertains to the developmental skills wherein subjects become capable of modifying their own skilled, practical spontaneity in accordance with the shifting exigences of culture on the move. And social, economic, cultural conditions remain relevant to this second, major, instance of effective freedom. But they will function to increase the f-probabilities associated with such dynamic, developmental skills only insofar as they enhance rather than supplant this reflexively operative flexibility. Conversely in this analysis the transformation of the social, economic, cultural conditions of life will exacerbate the problems of culture on the move to the extent that they are not directed towards increasing the occasion for and the f-probability of developing personally constitutive, integrative skills.

Such is Lonergan's distinction between essential and effective freedom. At its centre stands the emergent cognitional event integrating ranges of performance skills and the reflexively operative scheme of acts whose implementation shapes the content of this integration. In any learning process the role of this cognitional integration scheme is clear and obvious, not as "knowledge of facts" but as a cognitional anticipation or projection of a possible course of action, and a hit-and-miss process of ordering the elements of the skill in a feedback cycle of progressively refining stages until the elements "come together." Anyone who has learned recently to drive a car, to play "double stops" on a violin, to lay bricks, to write essays, to write poems, will remember the agonies associated with this cognitional anticipation and with its mediating role in assembling the succession of stages and identifying the elements to be integrated. Similarly in any practical or moral dilemma the role of this cognitional scheme in its linked set of operations stands clear and obvious. For a dilemma most usually demands a response in the absence of a clear differentiation of the superior alternative. But most profoundly, and perhaps least obviously, this cognitional scheme mediates the concrete application of socially current "praxis" to the ever-shifting conditions and situations of day to day living. Without the flexibility associated with the more or less restricted ranges of effective freedom the concrete practical implementation of the routines of culture could never occur. Indeed, because of the powerful way in which operative routines shape and orientate collective spontaneity, the concern for collective responsibility must turn to this conditioning relationship between operative routines and the f-probabilities associated with classes of insights and judgments of truth and value. But because the solutions to the continually arising problems of culture on the move requires the ongoing genesis of skills and the ongoing modification of practical routines in accordance with the shifting demands of randomly and systematically interacting conditions, this central role of the personal, emergent cognitional integration can never be supplanted.

It is in these terms that a first preliminary response to one of the most important critiques of Lonergan can be assembled. Charles Davis' article in *New Blackfriars*[98] is the most clearly developed and the most sharply formulated critique of Lonergan's notion of "praxis." And while a good deal of his article concerns aspects of Lonergan's thought which will be discussed more fully in chapters six and seven below, an initial response would be in order here to differentiate Lonergan's approach from the line of scholarship represented by Davis' approach.

Davis introduces two "key insights" that dominate the current discussions on the relationship between theory and practice. Since it is in the activity of human labour that human beings transform themselves and their modes of living,

... the question of praxis is in the first place the question of the dependence of ideas or consciousness upon the productive forces and relationships that constitute the basis of every human society.[99]

And since these productive forces and relations are themselves engaged in an ongoing transformation in the course of social, historical development,

... the question of praxis is in the second place the question of the dependence of our thinking and our judgments, the formation of our consciousness and our production of theories, upon the historical development of human society and upon the place where we find ourselves in that society.[100]

In the face of these two insights Lonergan,

> ... presents praxis as an affair of the subjectivity of the individual theologian, operating, seeming, independently of the material business business of society.[101]

Davis' reference here is to Lonergan's article "Theology and Praxis," published in the 1977 *Proceedings* of the Catholic Theological Society of America. And Davis reformulates a criticism of Fergus Kerr's in a direct response to Lonergan's 1977 essay.

> The very practical or praxis-oriented character of Lonergan's *Insight* and *Method in Theology* reveals the essential defect in his programme. The impetus of those writings is to launch people — and they have in fact launched many — upon a course of intellectual self-appropriation and the self-conscious articulation of religious conversion. But the programme is presented as an individual enterprise, as though it had been formulated and was available independently of economic conditions and social position. Whatever may be the theoretical acknowledgement of social conditioning — and that theoretical acknowledgement is made by Lonergan — it does not essentially affect the level of performance. We are told how to change our consciousness, but not how to change society, and the result is to make people think that the first action can be performed without the second. Nor does it seem necessary within a Lonerganian context to enquire into the social origins of Lonergan's thought and the social conditions required to interpret him correctly.[102]

Finally, in his concluding summary, Davis restates two problems in Lonergan's approach that are relevant to this preliminary consideration.

> (1) The primacy of praxis means that within the total context of human activities the theoretical interest or systematic pursuit of knowledge has a subordinate place and function. Granted that it has an integrity that must be respected, it itself must be limited and corrected by the practical activities by which human beings in society struggle to achieve a fully human existence. Those practical activities constitute praxis, which is the concrete embodiment of spirit as intelligence and love. Now, Lonergan's work, it seems to me, is skewed by an over-evaluation of the theoretical and, consequently, of the doctrinal. ...
>
> (2) Praxis is not an inner event, but the embodied activities of socially related men and women, whereby they struggle with nature as a reality independent of consciousness and with the sedimented, objectified products of past human action, in order to shape their world and themselves in their world. Knowledge or consciousness in general is not a reality apart from praxis, a realm or world of its own, proceeding purely by its own laws as an independent totality: it is an ele-

ment within praxis itself, so that modes of knowledge and forms of consciousness are to be understood in the context of the other elements and relationships that constitute praxis as a totality. However, what Lonergan offers us is essentially a philosophy of consciousness, in which the inner events or states of consciousness are always independent variables, of which everything else in human living and history is a function. What he says about the Church and the future of Christianity is representative, I think, of his general attitude to human affairs: "the perpetually needed remedy is not outer but inner."[103] That expresses a dichotomy the recent concept of praxis was designed to exclude.[104]

In my view there are two aspects to these criticisms. The first involves what I would consider to be errors in expressing Lonergan's intent. The second involves what I would suggest is a correct statement about Lonergan's work whose import needs to be re-emphasized in the face of a line of scholarship which, in my view, stands to complement and to carry forward but not to modify substantially Lonergan's work. In a nutshell I would say that Davis is not accurate in suggesting that in Lonergan's account the cognitional mediation of the subject's practical skills operates independently of the social, economic, historical context of experiences in which the subject is engaged. But he is right in indicating that in Lonergan's analysis the principal locus of social transformation is the transformation of the subject. For in Lonergan's view any analysis of social transformation which bypasses the responsible participation of subjects becomes a totalitarian repression of the subject. The norms of truth and value are immanent to the human subject as are the practical skills wherein these norms are made operative. Truth and value are not abstract, rather, they are concrete solutions to the concrete problems of human living. Consequently only the personal, skilled involvement of concrete subjects can meet the demands of human experiences. Social transformation demands attention to the conditions associated with increases in the f-probabilities associated with transformed subjectivity. And with this focus in attention the social, economic, historical conditions of culture need to be understood in the degree to which they increase or decrease the operative ranges of the authentic performance of subjects.

In contrast to the suggestion of Davis', Lonergan's account of the subjective locus and structure of cognitional acts admits of no independence from the "material business of society." It is the routine engagement with society which constitutes the experiential manifold of the subject. And while cognitional acts integrate this manifold, such integrations emerge in the manifold, linking or correlating the elements of the manifold, in accordance with more or less limited ranges of integrative possibilities. Insights do not come from beyond experience to impose their form upon experience. They are spontaneous structurations emergent in aggregates of experiential elements. Because of a curious flexibility in the human neural makeup this manifold can order or integrate in a wider or narrower variety of ways. In addition the reflexively operative or self-constituting structure of skilled performance results in the fact that the implementation of current routines of culture has the effect of ordering the experiential spontaneity of subjects. And in this way "the productive forces and relationships" of society exercise a massive (but not always decisive) influence upon recurrent subjective spontaneity and its subsequent flow of cognitional acts.

Lonergan's programme for self-appropriation will never proceed independent from "economic conditions and social position." This is so because the subject's social and economic context of experience is what constitutes the subject, and self-appropriation involves the subject coming to terms with him or herself. In addition self-appropriation involves the subject's self-assessment in the context of socially and historically dynamic but personally operative norms. Consequently the subject must come to terms with him or herself as a subject in social, political, economic history. Lonergan's insistence upon self-appropriation as a personal affair recognizes that norms are operative immanently to subjects. But subjects participate in the routines of history and so the concrete context for the operation and the development of such norms is the historical stream within which he or she stands.

With Davis, Lonergan would agree that the systematic pursuit of knowledge is a skill standing within the wider context of practical skills of human life and subject to the concrete effects that the operative forms of such skills have in ordering subjective spontaneity. Lonergan would also agree that the pursuit of knowledge must be integrated into a wider, global pursuit of "fully human existence." But like Davis, Habermas and Marx, Lonergan has devoted his life to *understanding* the overarching shape and structure of this human, historical question. And Lonergan understands this "higher viewpoint" to be a matter for theoretical intelligence in the service of global humanization.

While Lonergan's account of praxis recognizes the significant role of "inner events," the structure of Lonergan's account of praxis is that of the scheme of events, some of which occur within the subject's envelope of skin and some of which function to bring events of the subject's "external" environment within the immanent schemes of this envelope as materials to be transformed and integrated in accordance both with the exigences of the events' internal relations and with those of the habitual spontaneity of the subject's sensitive flow. Consequently in Lonergan's analysis there can be no such thing as a completely independent variable. Rather, the subject is inextricably involved in a set of interrelations with his or her environment such that the more or less developed exercise of certain skills within his or her repertoire can effect some ordering influence on the routine function of some of these schemes.

But Davis is correct in presenting Lonergan's enterprise as "an affair of the subjectivity of the individual [person]," with its focus upon "consciousness" and the "theoretical," in which "the perpetually needed remedy is not outer but inner." And the reason for this emphasis is Lonergan's discovery that the norms for human life are operative immanently in human subjects. More will be said on Lonergan's account of these norms, but what is significant here is their subjective locus. Lonergan's effort has been to differentiate an explanatory heuristic that could recognize the powerfully determining influences of dynamic patterns in the social conditions of life without repudiating the possibility of some measure of subjects shaping their lives in accordance with authentic practical performance. And while the concern of Davis has been with the social and ethical import of such determining influences, his concern has manifested itself in his developing his own theoretical account of the dynamic structure of this influence, precisely in the interest of subjects' participating in this shaping.[105] It would seem that Davis' own work shares Lonergan's appreciation of the practical import of theory.

But I would suggest that the central reason why Lonergan insists, perhaps at times to excess, on the personal locus of social transformation is because he understands the flow of life to be a matter of concrete solutions to the day to day problems of intersubjective living. Because such problems are concrete, only the relatively competent (authentic) exercise of subjective sets of skills can discern the immanent demands, the relevant truths, the value possibilities presented by such concrete contexts. Even though the operative routines of culture are generally common their adaptation and implementation in concrete situations demands the more or less creative interventions of subjects on the spot. It is in these routine adaptations to concrete circumstances that the current values of a culture are most regularly made operative. In Lonergan's view, it is only in the context of shifting trends in such concrete acts that societies are effectively transformed. This is not to say that environmental conditions, intersubjective routines, forms of economic ownership and control are irrelevant to such transformations. But they are relevant, profoundly, in the measure that they enhance the expansion of wide-scale responsibility in flexibly mediating the ongoing routines of culture.

Lonergan's approach needs to be expanded to include Davis' expressed attention to the conditioning effect of the operative routines and relations of history. But I would say that his concern for the concreteness of truth and value, the immanence of norms for their discernment and actuation, and thus the significance of expansions in the commonly operative ranges of effective freedom cannot be overemphasized. Without this emphasis, the attention to social conditions can slip easily into an obliteration of the subject.

Many of the elements in this discussion have anticipated topics that are dealt with in the following chapters. I have not discussed directly Lonergan's account of the foundation of moral and historical normativity. Neither have I discussed the structure of intersubjectivity, the operative patterns of historical and social transformations, nor the social and personal blockages which radically delimit the range of human agency. Charles Davis' critique of Lonergan addresses a number of additional topics which will be discussed in chapters six and seven. And so I will return to his analysis in the seventh chapter below. In my view, Lonergan's notion of value, worked out in *Method* and operative in *Insight*, chapter eighteen, can only be understood in terms of his account of the progress and decline of human history.[106] And so I will proceed to a discussion of the questions and issues relevant to this account.

FOOTNOTES - CHAPTER 5

1   Maurice De Wachter, "Interdisciplinary Bioethics: But Where Do We Start? A Reflection on Epochè as Method," *The Journal of Medicine and Philosophy* 7 (1982): 275-287.
2   B. J. F. Lonergan, S. J., *Grace and Freedom: Operative Grace in the Thought of St. Thomas Aquinas*, edited by J. Patout Burns, with an introduction by F. E. Crowe (London: Darton, Longman & Todd, 1971) (hereafter cited as *Grace and Freedom*). The original essays were first published in 1941-1942.
3   On the introductory, foundational nature of Lonergan's contributions to ethical theory, see *Insight*, p. 595; *Method*, p. 27. In his *Protestant and Roman Catholic Ethics* (Chicago: University of Chicago Press, 1978), James Gustafson notes, "The thought of Bernard Lonergan, S. J., has not yet been thoroughly applied to moral theology by others nor has Lonergan himself developed the implications of his thought for ethics and moral theology in a systematic way," p. 91. For more recent developments upon Lonergan's foundations in ethics, see Walter E. Conn, *Conscience: Development and Self-Transcendence* (Birmingham, Alabama: Religious Education Press, 1981); idem, "Moral Development: Is Conversion Necessary?" in Lamb, ed., *Creativity and Method*, pp. 307-324; Robert Doran, *Subject and Psyche: Ricoeur, Jung, and the Search for Foundations* (Lanham, Md.: University Press of America, 1980); idem, "Theological Grounds for a World-Cultural Humanity," in Lamb, ed., *Creativity and Method*, pp. 105-122; Bartholomew Kiely, *Psychology and Moral Theology: Lines of Convergence* (Rome: Gregorian University Press, 1980); Matthew L. Lamb, "The Production Process and Exponential Growth: A Study in Socio-Economics and Theology," in Lawrence, ed., *Lonergan Workshop*, vol. 1, pp. 257-307; David Roy, "Bioethics as Anamnesis," in Lamb, ed., *Creativity and Method*, pp. 325-338; Geoffry Price, "Politics and Self-Acceptance," in Lamb, ed., *Creativity and Method*, pp. 443-457; J. Raymaker, "The Theory and Praxis of Social Ethics," in Lamb, ed., *Creativity and Method*, pp. 339-352. This list is by no means complete.
4   See Lonergan, "Insight Revisited," in *A Second Collection*, pp. 276-278; Walter Conn, "Bernard Lonergan on Value," *The Thomist* 40 (1976): 243-257; F. E. Crowe, "An Exploration of Lonergan's New Notion of Value," *Science et Esprit* 29 (1977): 123-143; David F. Ford, " 'Method in Theology' in the Lonergan Corpus," in Corcoran, pp. 11-26. For Lonergan's own indications of developments beyond *Method*, see Lonergan, "Reality, Myth, Symbol," in *Myth, Symbol and Reality*, edited by Alan M. Olson (Notre Dame: University of Notre Dame Press, 1980), p. 37.
5   A number of authors have criticized Lonergan's work in ethics for failing to integrate an analysis of the various determining conditions of moral action. But this is by no means the only criticism that has been levelled at Lonergan's ethics. A full treatment of such criticisms will not be attempted here. I will address what I feel to be the most important arguments in 5.2 and 5.6 below. For a fuller range of criticisms of Lonergan's ethics, see Richard Roach, "Fidelity: The Faith of Responsible Love," unpublished Ph.D. dissertation, Yale University, 1974; idem, "Nature and Praxis," *Communio* 5 (1978): 252-274; William M. Shea, "The Stance and Task of the Foundational Theologian: Critical or Dogmatic?" *Heythrop Journal* 17 (1976): 273-92; Charles Davis, "Lonergan's Appropriation of the Concept of Praxis," *New Blackfriars* 62 (1981): 114-26; Fergus Kerr, "Objections to Lonergan's Method," *New Blackfriars* 56 (1975): 305-316; idem, "Beyond Lonergan's Method: A Response to William Mathews," *New Blackfriars* 57 (1976): 59-71; Nicholas Lash, "In Defence of Lonergan's Critics," *New Blackfriars* 57 (1976): 124-126; Charles Davis, "Lonergan and the Teaching Church," in McShane, ed., *Foundations of Theology*, pp. 60-75; Karl Rahner, "Some Critical Thoughts on 'Functional Specialties in Theology'," in McShane, ed., *Foundations of Theology*, pp. 194-196; David F. Ford, " 'Method in Theology' in the Lonergan Corpus," in Corcoran, ed., *Looking at Lonergan's Method*, pp. 11-26; Jean-Pierre Jossua,

"Some Questions on the Place of Believing Experience in the Work of Bernard Lonergan," in Corcoran, pp. 164-174; Elizabeth MacLaren, "Theological Disagreement and Functional Specialties," in Corcoran, pp. 73-87. More general criticisms, less directly relevant to Lonergan's ethics, include Leslie Dewart, *The Future of Belief* (New York: Herder and Herder, 1966); idem, *Religion, Language and Truth* (New York: Herder and Herder, 1970), particularly pp. 146-169; and Schubert M. Ogden, "Lonergan and the Subjectivist Principle," in McShane, ed., *Language, Truth and Meaning*, pp. 218-235. Responses to criticisms of Lonergan include the following: Donald Johnson, "Lonergan and the Redoing of Ethics," *Continuum* 5 (1967-1968): 211-220; Lonergan, himself, responds to Ogden in "Bernard Lonergan Responds," in McShane, ed., *Language, Truth and Meaning*, pp. 309-311, and to Dewart in "The Dehelleniztion of Dogma," in *The Future of Belief Debate*, edited by Gregory Baum (New York: Herder and Herder, 1967), pp. 69-91; McShane responds to Ogden in "The Core Psychological Present of the Contemporary Theologian," in *Trinification of the World*, edited by T. A. Dunne and J.-M. Laporte (Toronto: Regis College Press, 1978), pp. 84-96; William Mathews, "Lonergan's Awake: A Reply to Fergus Kerr," *New Blackfriars* 57 (1976): 11-21; Hugo Meynell, "On Objections to Lonergan's 'Method'," *The Heythrop Journal* 19 (1978): 405-10 (Meynell's response is to William Shea).

6 *Method*, pp. 27-30.
7 For a discussion of Marx's notion of labour, see chapter seven below.
8 *Method*, p. 27.
9 Ibid., pp. 27-8.
10 Ibid., p. 27.
11 See chapters three and four above, for the distinctive meaning of this word in Lonergan's work, particularly 3.2. I say "an element of randomness" for the curiosity of a child marks the distinct presence of system.
12 For a discussion of the precise meaning of f-probability, see chapter three above.
13 Ibid., p. 28.
14 Ibid., p. 6.
15 I would argue that it is this link between the performance of motor skills and the imaginative or cognitional genesis of meaning which is at the centre of Lonergan's definition of the terms "intend," and "intentionality." To perform an intentional operation is to fulfill the conditions for an event wherein an object becomes psychologically present to a subject, *Method*, p. 7. This psychological presence is in no way understood by Lonergan as a simple transposition of an "object" in the physical, material sense, to the "inside" of a subject. Rather meaning is an emergent integration in and of a subject in accordance with an immanent intelligibility, whose constitutive elements are mediated to a subject via a complex set of correspondences through the performance of the sensorimotor skills. What is distinctive about the mediating function of meaning is that more complex correspondences between groups of sensorimotor operations and imaginative and cognitional events can yield skills whose performance can make an object psychologically present without the physical proximity of the material object.
16 See chapter three above, particularly 3.2 and 3.3 for a discussion of the structure and the emergence of recurrence schemes and series.
17 See Lonergan's account of language and meaning in *Method*, pp. 70-71. I labour under no illusions that this account is complete. In fact there is a flexibility to language that allows a multiplicity of correspondences and, consequently, a much more complex pattern of combinations and correspondences both between words and their referents and also between words of ordered sets of words and other linguistic units. However without the relative durability of the more basic correspondences language would have no structure whatsoever. My point here is to argue that such correspondences exist and that their locus of occurrence is immanent to the human subject actively engaged in the performance of these complex sets of skills. See my responses to some of the relevant

criticisms in the following pages.
18. For much more on this, see *Method*, chapter three.
19. Ibid., p. 28.
20. Ibid.
21. See Lonergan's definition of the word "intend," in ibid., p. 7. See also note 15, this chapter above.
22. On doing mathematical puzzles and empirical inquiry, see McShane, *Wealth of Self*.
23. *Method*, p. 9.
24. Fergus Kerr, "Beyond Lonergan's Method," pp. 60, 68-69.
25. Nicholas Lash, "Method and Cultural Discontinuity," in Corcoran, pp. 127-143.
26. Edward MacKinnon, "Linguistic Analysis and the Transcendence of God," *Proceedings of the Catholic Theological Society of America* 23 (1968): 30.
27. Ibid., p. 31. For further criticisms along this line, see William Shea, p. 275; Patrick McGrath, "Knowledge, Understanding and Reality," in Corcoran, pp. 27-41.
28. *Method*, p. 255.
29. See, for example, the introduction to the work of de Saussure in John W. Van Den Hengel, *The Home of Meaning: The Hermeneutics of the Subject of Paul Ricoeur* (Washington: University Press of America, 1982), pp. 20-22.
30. Clearly there is much more to be said here. The point is that there is evidence of the fact of acts of cognitional emergence and the fact of recurrently structured sets of cognitional and responsible skills. As well there would seem to be evidence of the fact of recurrent patterns in the structuration and transformation of patterns of imagery whose import is felt upon cognitional acts. The attempt here is only to suggest emergent probability as the heuristic structure for relating the two sets of evident facts.
31. *Insight*, pp. 4, 9.
32. Ibid., pp. 191ff, 219.
33. Ibid., pp. 237-238, 604, 606.
34. This criticism has been expressed by Charles Davis, "Lonergan's Appropriation," p. 120.
35. It is this reflexivity of intelligence which liberates human life from determinism.
36. Geertz, *The Interpretation of Cultures*, p. 5.
37. R. G. Collingwood, *The Idea of History* (Oxford: Oxford University Press), pp. 217ff.
38. *Insight*, pp. 200ff, particularly p. 203.
39. See *Verbum* and *Grace and Freedom*. See also the opening remarks in chapter four above.
40. See *Understanding and Being*, pp. 313-314.
41. Alasdair MacIntyre, *After Virtue* (Notre Dame: University of Notre Dame Press, 1981).
42. See *Method*, pp. 30-34.
43. See chapter seven below.
44. On this difference between genetically and dialectically related insights, see *Method*, pp. 247, 236.
45. *Understanding and Being*, p. 325.
46. *Insight*, p. 178. On the generality and the limitations of common sense in its practicality, see *Understanding and Being*, p. 314.
47. See also *Insight*, pp. 179, 237.
48. *Understanding and Being*, pp. 315-316.
49. *Insight*, p. 179; see also "The Canon of Operations," pp. 74-78.
50. See Matthew L. Lamb, "Praxis and Generalized Empirical Method," in *Creativity and Method*, pp. 58-63.
51. David Tracy, "Theologies of Praxis," in Lamb, ed., *Creativity and Method*, p. 36.
52. On the meaning of the term "notion," see *Method*, pp. 287; *Insight*, pp. 352-357.
53. *Method*, pp. 29, 286.
54. See F. C. Copleston, *A History of Philosophy*, vol. 2, part 2 (Garden City, N. Y.: Doubleday, Image Books, 1962), pp. 94ff.

55  *Understanding and Being*, p. 314.
56  *Method,* p. 28.
57  *Insight*, p. 183.
58  Ibid.
59  Lonergan defines the term "conscious" by contrasting it with "unconscious," *not* with "sub-conscious." See *Insight*, pp. 320-321; *Method*, pp. 7-8.
60  *Insight*, pp. 183-4.
61  On the problems associated with conceiving the "inside" and the "outside" of the organism, see McShane, *Wealth of Self*, pp. 39-46.
62  *Insight*, pp. 183-4.
63  See *Method* here, p. 30.
64  *Insight*, p. 185.
65  Ibid., p. 184.
66  Ibid.
67  Ibid., pp. 184-185.
68  See *Method*, pp. 30ff. For a fuller account of the normative foundation of "value," see 6.6 below.
69  *Insight*, p. 185.
70  Ibid., p. 186.
71  Ibid., pp. 185-6.
72  Ibid., p. 187.
73  Ibid.
74  The notion of "intersubjectivity" is discussed in chapter six, 6.4.2, and chapter seven, 7.1 and 7.2 below.
75  *Insight*, p. 188.
76  Ibid.
77  Ibid., p. 181. The emphases are mine.
78  Ibid., p. 189.
79  Ibid., p. 190.
80  Charles Taylor, *Hegel and Modern Society* (Cambridge: Cambridge University Press, 1979).
81  Ibid., pp. 3-5. See also chapter two above, 2.1.
82  Herbert Marcuse, *Reason and Revolution*, second edition, with a "Preface: A Note on Dialectic" (Boston: Beacon Press, 1960; orig. ed., 1941), p. xiii.
83  See, for example, Ledger Wood, "Free-will," in *Dictionary of Philosophy*, edited by Dagobert D. Runes (Totowa, N. J.: Littlefield, Adams & Co., 1962), p. 112; Van A. Harvey, "Freedom of the Will," in *A Handbook of Theological Terms* (New York: Macmillan Publishing Co., Inc., 1964), pp. 101-103.
84  See chapter three above.
85  *Insight*, p. 617.
86  Ibid., p. 619.
87  See Patrick Byrne, "On Taking Responsibility," and "The Thomistic Sources."
88  See *Method*, pp. 9, 14, 74.
89  *Insight*, pp. 613, 619.
90  See Lonergan's own account of the shift from *Insight* to *Method* in "Insight Revisited," in *Second Collection*, pp. 276-278. See also Conn, "Bernard Lonergan on Value," and Crowe, "An Exploration," cited above.
91  *Insight*, p. 621.
92  See Ibid., pp. 619-621.
93  Ibid., p. 619.
94  Ibid., pp. 619-620.
95  Ibid., pp. 622-624.
96  See Ibid., pp. 616-619.

97 See ibid., pp. 619-633.
98 Davis, "Lonergan's Appropriation."
99 Ibid., p. 114.
100 Ibid.
101 Ibid.
102 Ibid., pp. 116-7.
103 Davis' reference here is to "The Future of Christianity," in *Second Collection*, p. 159, cited in Davis, p. 124.
104 Ibid., pp. 123-4.
105 See Charles Davis, *Theology and Political Society* (Cambridge: Cambridge University Press, 1980).
106 Evidence for this view is to be found in Lonergan's work. See *Insight*, p. 603; *Method*, pp. 52-55, 102, 117, 240.

# Chapter 6

# History, Ethics and Emergent Probability I

## 6.0 Introduction

Effective freedom and its correlate, the notion of value, are normative notions which demand both an explanation and an integration into an overall account of the dynamic orientation of world process. It is one thing to develop an account of the structure of a set of schemes of acts. It is something entirely different to distinguish their competent from their incompetent performance and to ground the meanings of the terms "competent" and "incompetent." There is clearly a flexibility to human intelligent performance, a flexibility which both allows and demands some criteria for selection among alternative courses of action. And associated with this flexibility there is a substantial ambiguity to human performance and its consequent impact on one's own life and the lives of others. Within one's experiential horizon this ambiguity arises when it is discovered that freely actuated performance can have disastrous effects, including the loss of one's own life and the mutilation of the lives and the living conditions of one's loved ones. And this immediate concrete experience is only the tip of an iceberg.

The history of ethics has included a variety of approaches towards grounding a theory of value or moral prescription.[1] As became clear in the first two chapters above, however one grounds an account of value or moral obligation, such a grounding will have a significance in relation to how one conceives the orientation of the course of human history. If individual morality is considered free and decisive for the direction of history, then the normative orientation of history will be grounded in the foundations of moral value. If, on the other hand, history is conceived as having a dynamic structure of its own, and an orientation (or an absence of orientation) of its own, then the appearance of freedom and the apparent relevance of moral action become problems that need explaining in terms of the two heterogenous foundations. Finally, if moral action is decisive for history and if all of history is conceived as lacking in direction, so that all change is simply change, then moral foundations are precluded and the search for criteria for action is pronounced vain.

Lonergan's approach to this complex of issues has been to try to meet both sets of questions at the same time with a single approach. And the reader may have guessed that this approach will appeal to his very distinctive notion of finality[2] as the foundation both for moral value and for historical progress. But before Lonergan's notion of value can be discussed in connection with his heuristic sketch of the structure and dynamism of human history, a nest of issues needs to be addressed. There exists a very large field of study called the philosophy of history. And within this field there are a number of debates concerning the possibility and the relevance of developing an overall account of the structure and dynamic orientation of history. In addition there exist some objections to defining human history in terms of the performance of acts of meaning. In the pages that follow, I will attempt to present and to respond to these debates and these objections. The goal throughout will be to clear the way for a presentation of Lonergan's notion of value and for a subsequent presentation of Lonergan's introductory account of the dynamic structure of human history. But if I have made a contribution towards clarifying some issues in the field of the philosophy of history, such contributions are to be counted as evidence for the heuristic and explanatory power of emergent probability.

## 6.1 Analytic or Critical Philosophy of History and the Speculative Philosophy of History

In his *Philosophy of History: An Introduction*,[3] W.H. Walsh sets out a few basic distinctions that will serve to identify some of the major sets of questions and concerns that are addressed in the relevant fields. Clearly contemporary philosophy of history is not a unity but an aggregate. And Walsh traces two roots in this aggregate to Vico in Italy, together with a line of thinkers from Herder to Hegel in Germany on the one hand, and to Dilthey, Rickert and Croce in the late nineteenth and early twentieth centuries, on the other. The two roots represent two positions in a debate that continues to rage over what constitutes a legitimate intellectual contribution to the study of history.[4]

Walsh's basic distinction is a commonly made one that Lonergan formulates quite simply as the distinction between history as written and history as written about.[5] As written about, history is the totality of past events and actions that historians seek to know and explain. As written, history is the account, explanation or narrative of these events or actions that the historian puts together. The collection of all such accounts comprises the corpus of historical writing and most frequently written history is in dialogue with or a commentary upon other works of written history. When conflicts arise among assessments as to what happened or how or why it happened — conflicts that cannot be resolved on this level of writing history — a further "meta-level" emerges which asks about the nature or process of historical writing and its relation to the history that is written about; what am I doing when I am writing history? Just as the philosophy of science can be an acceptable study of the procedures of scientists so too the philosophy of history can be an acceptable study of the procedures of the historian. And Walsh locates the divergence among the two schools or traditions in the philosophy of history on this further "meta-level." The two schools of philosophy of history constitute too different sets of questions that can be asked about the writing of history.[6]

In the critical or analytic school, the questions ask about the relation between history as a form of knowledge and other forms of knowledge. This tradition originated, according to Walsh, in Germany in the late nineteenth century and can be associated with names like Dilthey, Droysen, Ranke, Rickert, and Croce. As the field or discipline of historical writing expanded, the questions as to the appropriate methods and procedures for determining the relevant facts, for amassing evidence, for judging truth, and for interpreting both facts and the conclusions of other historians began to abound. Historians discovered that data was selected differently from age to age and from place to place, and that interpretations as to what data was relevant for an explanation reflected more the convictions and allegiances of historians than the horizons of the age being studied. Finally, the various historians and historical schools found themselves divided on what it was they were supposed to be doing. Does the historian simply narrate a course of events or does (s)he explain these events in terms of antecedent events or consequent outcomes? Can events and courses of events be classified? Are there operative patterns or laws to history? Is there an overall intelligibility to history as a whole?

At the limits of this first school of philosophy of history a set of questions begin to emerge which had horrified the working historians since the German idealists began developing their sweeping accounts of the overarching course of historical process.[8] Historians have feared that grand accounts of the meaning, purpose, *telos* of humanity and of the principal features or determinates of historical causation did violence to a careful empirical study of history. These broad questions about human nature and about the structure and the orientation of the whole of the history that is written about have been the concern of the second school of philosophy of history, the speculative school.[9] But their contemporary proponents, the speculative philosophers of history who have upheld a tradition since Vico, Herder, Kant, Hegel and Marx, argue that there is no getting around some implicit or explicit view on such fundamental questions. Walsh argues that contemporary answers to the questions raised by these speculative philosophers certainly need to emerge more carefully from a concrete study of empirical history. But in Walsh's view the theories of the great speculative thinkers can still operate as hypotheses which the historian can carry with him or her into the empirical study and which must be evaluated in terms of the contemporary data.[10]

To locate Lonergan's emergent probability within this vast field of questions and answers it would be helpful to begin with an image or analogy introduced in a talk that he gave at the Thomas More Institute in Montreal on September 23, 1960, entitled "The Philosophy of History."[11] Much of the material in this talk is reworked and refined in the eighth and ninth chapters of *Method in Theology*[12] But the "scissors analogy" remains relevant and suggestive.

Lonergan addresses himself to the two sets of questions which I have distinguished above as corresponding to the two schools of philosophy of history.[13] And to sketch a route through the first set, from the analytic or critical school, he introduces his often quoted analogy of the two-bladed scissors.[14] As is the case in the empirical sciences the historian operates not simply with data, with texts, with observation, with the testimonies of witnesses, with his or her own insights and judgments and those of others (the lower blade of the scissors) but also with a set of anticipations as to the shape or structure of the final account or explanation (the upper blade). In the natural sciences Galileo's set of anticipations was the axiomatic system of Euclidian geometry. With Newton it was a similar set of axioms, deductions, empirically verified constants and logically deducible, universally verifiable laws called mechanics. With Einstein and Heisenberg the introduction of notions like indeterminacy and discontinuity into the upper blade of method shattered the lawful determinism of Newtonian mechanics and changed radically the anticipations as to what a final explanation of physical processes would look like. The work of Monod, summarized in 2.2 above, reflects the impact of these revised anticipations.

In the field of historiography, whose methods were progressively refined through the contributions of analytic or critical philosophy of history since Ranke, Droysen and Dilthey, a wide sweep of types of "upper blades" emerged after the late nineteenth century. At one pole of the sweep stands a set of positions that emphasize historical relativity. And as an example, Johan Huizinga defines history as a people interpreting its past to itself.[15] Since the people interpreting are almost never the same as the people who lived this past, the interpretation will necessarily differ in orientation, in its selection of significant details, in its assessment of what is of value, from the lived world of the historical actors. Thus there will always be several histories and the horizon of the written history will be the horizon of the writer.[16]

To further illustrate what is involved in this "upper blade" of anticipations I will bring in a few more examples beginning from another pole of this sweep. In his little book *Laws and Explanation in History*,[17] William Dray reconstructs a model of historical explanation that was originally developed by Sir Karl Popper, perfected and presented for the philosophy of science by C.G. Hempel, and appropriated into the philosophy of history, to one degree or another, by such thinkers as Patrick Gardiner. According to Dray, the "covering law model" of historical explanation accounts for a historical fact or group of facts by "covering" it under a general law or explanation whose structure is that of a syllogism. The major premise of the syllogism is a generalization about lawful or necessary relations (or, in cases, "statistical" relations)[18] among types or categories of events or processes and initial conditions. The minor premise locates the historical facts as instances of the stated types or categories. And the effect of the covering law is to make the events logically deducible from the context of conditions and thus, at least in principle, predictable. According to Dray, the argument in this model of explanation is that all historical accounts implicitly make an appeal to such a covering law and that to link any event to a context of factors or determinations is necessarily to make an implicit claim to a lawful relationship between them.[19]

Dray's response to the covering law model is to reject the claim that historians always explain events in terms of covering laws. He argues that the historian is not really interested in events and processes as instances of general classes. Rather, he or she is concerned with their particularity.[20] To overlook the distinctive, the particular, the unique in historical events and processes and to seek only lawful relations among classes is to assume, according to Dray, that historical actors are not freely rational and that historical events are determined somewhat mechanistically.[21] Dray argues that the historian's intent is much more modest and that his or her account is a "colligation" (a term he borrows from Walsh) into a partial but nonetheless plausible account of a possible set of relations among the particular facts.[22]

W.B. Gallie[23] goes further along this line, back towards the relativity position, to argue that there is an essential and permanent contingency to historical processes that cannot be overlooked by the historian.[24] What the historian does is to narrate a succession of events by filling in the gaps between the facts and making a story. A story "follows" as a story precisely because the author sets up a theme at the beginning of the account so that the reader catches a glimpse of what might constitute a possible conclusion. Armed with such a theme the reader anticipates some events throughout the story and is surprised by others. The final outcome of the story is always unpredictable just as the historical events are unpredictable. So the reader is never confident that one or another outcome will necessarily prevail. Thus the reader is held in suspense throughout, anticipating the possible relationship between this event and the suggested outcome, wondering whether than event might push the course of action in another direction.[25]

Hayden White[26] comes full round to another formulation of a "relativist" position to argue that the overarching structures of the historian's narratives can be classified into four types and that these structures are rooted in the very structure of language itself.[27] Since there is no such thing as a completely "objective" account of what actually happened, the historian must choose the narrative structure that he or she will appropriate and integrate into the account.[28] If this choice is not made deliberately, the structure will be chosen spontaneously in accordance with prevailing cultural trends or with the author's own personal "story."[29]

We can see, in this set of positions, how implicit theories and assumptions from the speculative philosophy of history tend to be interwoven with attempts to work out some account of the method and enterprise of historiography. To develop an account of what the historian is doing and what he or she can expect to arrive at in writing history seems to require some position on what elements make up the history that is written about and how these elements are dynamically related. For Huizinga, the elements of the history that is written about can never be separated from the act of writing or constructing history.[30] And the authors of such acts are civilizations.[31] Furthermore a civilization's act of imposing a form on its own past in the light of its present is itself a significant determinant of that civilization's present activity.[32] The meaning that is the product of this historical remembering is a key element in the dynamics of the history that is written about.[33] But this activity of organizing and in-forming historical memory is always a restricted activity in which *present* concerns set the limits, select the data, and provide the organizing criteria for the historical writing.[34] Thus there will never be a single history of humanity.[35] Questions about the overall concrete shape and *telos* of *human history* are left open. And it would seem from Huizinga's view that such questions could never be answered on the basis of an appeal to historical evidence.[36] Huizinga's view of human cognition, as operative in historical writing, sets the foundation for his view of the elements of history, provides some insights into the structure and the dynamics of history, as written about, and excludes from the scope of the study of history speculative questions about the cyclic structure or the goal of the course of human events.[37]

For the covering-law modelist the "stuff" of history is events that are the outcomes of antecedent or simultaneous events, processes, laws and conditions.[38] Such events are of classes and such things as psychological and sociological laws (understood both as probabilistic and classical laws)[39] operate to determine the interrelations among antecedent events, conditions and processes and their consequent outcomes.[40] The historian can, to some extent, understand the events and processes of an age gone by precisely because such classes and laws either cut across cultures and ages or can be understood from a later perspective as generally operative within a bygone context.[41] Consequently he or she seeks to identify events as instances of classes and to draw upon whatever knowledge of laws and processes that is available from common sense and from such sciences as psychology, sociology, economics, etc., to explain what is, at least in principle, predictable about historical events.[42] The covering-law modelist admits the *possibility* of a macro-level explanation of the whole of human history, an explanation of the structure and the determinants of historical change. But because of the precision required by this model such macro-level explanations rarely fulfill the required tests of adequacy.⁴³ The most general characteristic of the covering-law model is its insistence upon explanation in terms of antecedent or simultaneous conditions.⁴⁴

Dray rejects the covering-law model because he holds that it is the uniqueness, the particularity alone that is significant about the events and processes of history.⁴⁵ Historical events are essentially non-classifiable (and if you want to be a covering-law modelist, according to Dray, you would pretty well need a separate class for every historical event).⁴⁶ History operates by contingent events converging and historical actors making rational, "undetermined" choices.⁴⁷ Thus complete explanation in terms of antecedent conditions would require the historian to know all the converging details and to foreknow the actors' free choices. This, of course, is impossible.⁴⁸ And so the best that the historian can do is to construct an approximate, incomplete picture or image of what possibly might have happened to bring about an event or outcome, on the basis of a partial knowledge of available facts and a speculation as to what the actors' motives might have been.⁴⁹ The historian has no illusions of explaining completely and his or her account makes no claim to identical correspondence with historical reality.⁵⁰ Dray's account of historical events emphasizes the future orientation of human rational action. Consequently his account of historical explanation involves the historian bringing his or her own self-knowledge into a judgment on where the historical actors might reasonably have been heading.

With Gallie and White the wider vision of the speculative philosophers of history comes into focus explicitly. But whereas the speculative philosophers claim that their theories about humanity, about historical change, about the goal of history are true of historical process, Gallie and White place such theories squarely within the minds of the historian. Gallie argues that the general, explanatory themes used by historiographers are a part of the historian's task of constructing a narrative that "follows" through the contingencies of historical events.⁵¹ And such themes can make no metaphysical claim on the "objective reality" of history.⁵² White argues that what the speculative philosophers and the historiographers alike are doing is projecting a "meta-historical" poetic structure — a structure that is rooted in the mind, in imagination, in language — onto the data of historical events.⁵³ The speculative philosophers have made such structures explicit but White argues that they remain implicitly operative in the work of historiographers.⁵⁴ Since no one structure is right or wrong the selection among structures remains to be made deliberately on the basis of "moral" or "aesthetic" criteria.⁵⁵ It is especially clear in White's case how a theory of cognition, based in the work of Kant, sets the foundation both for his account of historiography and of the enterprise of the speculative philosophers of history.⁵⁶

In each of these cases various answers to questions about the elements and the structure of the history that is written about were related integrally to the author's conception of the enterprise and the methods of historiography. And so Walsh's suggestion that the theories of the great speculative philosophers of history be understood and assessed by contemporary historians and philosophers is surely a good one. But is there not another angle or tack that can be taken on both sets of issues together? Is there not a basis in epistemology or cognitional theory to both sets of questions? An account of the substance and dynamic structure of historical events and processes is itself an act of knowing as are the procedures of historiography. Indeed there would seem to be some truth in conceiving intelligence as, in some way, constitutive of history. It becomes clear in the more "relativist" positions that what one conceives as the structure and the limits to acts of knowing history determines how one conceives what the historian is writing about. Writing at the end of the nineteenth century, Wilhelm Dilthey understood the integral connections among cognitional theory, one's conception of the substance and dynamic structure of history, and the enterprise and methods of historiography.

## 6.2 Wilhelm Dilthey

According to Michael Ermarth,[57] Wilhelm Dilthey's life was devoted to finding grounds for reconciling an appropriate knowledge of humanity and a belief in the foundations for human living with a newer form of knowledge of natural processes which was emerging with remarkable success from the application of the methods of the *Naturwissenschaften*. Dilthey had seen a marked shift occur in nineteenth century Germany. The first half of the century had been dominated by German Idealism with its emphasis upon the creative, originating, transformative power of mind. Human reality was conceived as decisively constituted by the operations of mind. And so the human sciences, with their sweeping generalizations which sought to bring all of reality under a single systematic viewpoint, were considered the sole adequate means for gaining access to this human reality. After 1850, however, a new, positivist approach began to gain dominance, an approach which emphasized the particular details of human life that could be discovered by applying the methods of the natural sciences. And here, mind and consciousness were not conceived as originating but as derivative of the external, natural world. Dilthey was convinced that the human sciences could still yield some knowledge of reality and that the successes of the natural sciences need not demand a reductionist view of mind. He wondered whether there was a route somewhere between the sweeping generalizations of the idealists and the concrete, reductionist explanations of the positivists. And so he sought to secure a methodological foundation for a newly conceived science of man, which would provide access to a comprehensive understanding of human history while still remaining a legitimate, grounded knowing.[58]

Dilthey's approach, according to Michael Ermarth, was to recognize the natural sciences as a legitimate way of knowing, but to demand a restriction in the field of knowledge to which the methods of the natural sciences would apply. Taking his clue from the great idealist philosophers, Dilthey asked whether the realm of human history, human value, human meaning was constituted differently from the realm of natural processes. And he found an answer in his distinction between inner lived experience of human conscious life and the outer sensory experience which provides access to the natural world. The human sciences have as their proper object of study the reality which is given directly to the mind as a coherent texture of relations and meanings.[59] And this inner lived experience is given directly to the mind as a coherent unity precisely because it is a product of mind itself. Dilthey seized upon an insight which had been formulated first by Giovanni Battista Vico, early in the eighteenth century. The mind can know directly what the mind has created. And so understanding in the human sciences is the reconstruction of mental life.[60] Consequently the methodology of the human sciences will have its foundations rooted in an adequate account of the workings of the human mind.[61] The "Fundamental Science," the foundations for a science of man, society and history, will be at once a psychology and an epistemology. For an empirical study of the laws that rule the human mind in its social, intellectual, and moral activity, will explain both the workings of mind and the nature of its products, human conscious historical life.[62]

Dilthey's turn was towards an empirical account of human knowing to ground a systematic method of knowing in the human sciences. Human knowing is spontaneously operative in its natural attitude of historical life experience.[63] And as such the activity of mind is constitutive of historical reality. Human understanding includes its objectification in language and gesture. And history is the manifold of relations that are constituted by such understanding. History is the process of objectification of *Verstehen*.[64] Thus Dilthey's "Fundamental Science" set the foundations for an account of the structure and dynamism of history, precisely because it is mind itself which is the author of historical process.[65]

There is certainly a great deal more than can be said about the work of Dilthey. And Michael Ermarth's book is a marvellous introduction to the many facets of Dilthey's life and his thought. But for the present purposes what is significant is that Dilthey understood the methodological implications for the study of history when history is conceived in terms of the mediating and constitutive acts of human meaning and human freedom. Acts of intelligence are not simply employed to understand human historical processes. Rather, they are, in some way, the significantly constitutive elements of those processes as decisively human. And so to work out a historiographical method will require a more basic explanation of the operation of mind in its mediation and its constitution of historical process. For it is this act of mind, operating in its myriad of concrete times and places, which the study of history seeks to explain.[66] There will be two "modes" of the operation of mind. In the spontaneous "natural attitude" mind understands and exteriorizes itself, thus constituting its object, historical life. And in the more refined attitude of inquiry in the human sciences understanding grasps the nature of its objectified operation in the natural attitude.[67] But the empirical study of the psychology of mind (a further refinement of this second mode of operation) will yield an understanding of the structure of mind's operation in both modes.

Lonergan would have some critical reservations about the way in which Dilthey set about working out his Fundamental Science. And Matthew Lamb has written a book on the similarities and the differences in the two approaches of Lonergan and Dilthey.[68] But what is relevant here is that Lonergan, like Dilthey, asks whether there can be any foundation for a single "upper blade" for history in general. In his 1960 Thomas More lecture, Lonergan notes than when it comes to writing a history in a particular field, say the history of mathematics, or the history of physics, there can be some agreement on historical explanations of the developments in the particular fields precisely because there is some agreement on how the operations of mathematics and physics currently are carried out. The data that is available on the various moments and advancements in the science constitute isolated points in the chronology, but the historian can fill in the spaces because he or she knows the current science and what is significant to its contemporary operation in its relevant fields of research and application.[69] The upper blade of a history of mathematics or a history of physics comes from the methods and procedures operating in present day mathematics and physics. And while philosophers of science still seem to be unable to agree upon a complete explanation of scientific knowing there remains, at the level of scientific practice, substantial agreement in many areas, on what procedures constitute appropriate experimental method and an appropriate foundation upon which to pronounce a hypothesis v-probably verified. What the historian of mathematics or science anticipates as a complete historical account or explanation of the particular field is the genesis of a set of procedures whose performance the historian must understand intimately before he or she sets about the historical task.

It would follow, then, that a general historiography would need to take its upper blade from something like a contemporary science of man and culture.[70] And here Lonergan is in agreement with Dilthey. Furthermore like Dilthey, Lonergan argues that what is essentially constitutive of human culture and history as human are the operations of human intelligence.

> There is an existential memory, that is constitutive of the people *qua* people, just as there is an existential memory constitutive of the personality *qua* personality. Again, the history of a people is an account, an interpretation of what the people were; but what the people were

was their own self-interpretation. A man is not just a thing. It's what he does. What he says, what he works for, is all function of his experience, his accumulated experience, understanding, judgment, his mentality, his way of thinking, what he approves of, and disapproves of, what he wants and doesn't want. His mental activities are the main determinants of all his actions and his mental activities include an interpretation, an idea of what he himself is and what he is for, — his nature and destiny. And as this is true of the individual so also it is true of the group.[71]

Lonergan agrees that at the basis of a critical and a speculative philosophy of history will lie a science of man whose foundation is rooted in an account of what is distinctively human about life, acts of meaning.[72]

### 6.3 Emergent Probability as an "Upper Blade" For a Critical Philosophy of History

Lonergan's proposal, then, for an answer to the problems encountered in the two schools of the philosophy of history will be that an overall science of man will develop a set of anticipations operative in the writing of history, that this science of man will be based in a theory of cognition, that the structure to the explanations in this science of man will be rooted in the operative structures of acts of knowing in both the classical and the statistical sciences,[73] and that such a science will recognize that historical events are transformed significantly with changes in the sciences of man which ground the popularly held anticipations of culture. Like Huizinga, Lonergan conceives the distinctive, constitutive element of human history, as written, to be acts of meaning, acts of understanding, judging and deciding. And, like Huizinga, Lonergan recognizes that such acts occur within a context or a horizon of anticipations, goals, projects, values, habits, routines, skills, roles, hopes, fears, drives, biases, etc., etc. Lonergan would agree that what is selected for a study by the historian, most usually corresponds to the concerns of a later age. And this foreign horizon of concern, far from constituting an obstacle to writing history, is its condition of possibility.[74] But Lonergan also recognizes that the orientation of the act of writing history is to transcend the limitations of this later horizon and to approach a correspondence or identity with an intelligibility immanent in emergent historical process. Consequently the historian's task is to achieve an *ecstasis*, or a standing out from his or her original horizon of concerns, and gradually to begin operating within a horizon of anticipations that is appropriate to the age or to the thinkers being studied. Thus while the historian chooses to study what he or she, in his or her own culture, deems significant, the study need not remain locked into the cultural horizon of the historian's own age.[75]

Like the covering-law modelists, Lonergan conceives acts mediated by meaning as events that occur in accordance with the fulfillment of an appropriate range of conditions and he conceives such events and conditions to be of classes. Classes of events recur and associated with this recurrence there is to be discerned an intelligibility that can be formulated as a "law." Laws are statistical as well as classical and it is the statistical laws that grasp and intelligibility that is operative in ranges of non-systematic aggregates of converging conditions.[76] History does not seek to explain events in their generality but in their particularity. Rather, it is psychology, sociology, economics, political science, and the like that explain events as instances of classes. History is interested in the particular, the concrete.[77] And so explanation in history will require an understanding of the classical laws operative in the recurring events and schemes and of the statistical laws associated with the fulfilling conditions for the more or less probable emergence of such events and schemes. But beyond these history will require the inverse insight that grasps individual occurrences as non-systematic divergences from statistical laws. At any historical moment a number of things possibly could have been going forward and at the moment the probabilities associated with the recurrence of appropriate ranges of conditions would narrow down that number. But what actually occurred did so in accordance with an aggregate of converging conditions that constituted a non-systematic divergence from the probabilities. And so while historical explanation will require an appeal to laws, such laws will not suffice to explain the historical events.[78]

Thus Lonergan agrees with Dray that the historian is interested in the concrete and the particular and that the concrete and the particular is not to be understood completely in terms of classical laws. But while a "colligation" is a possible account, Lonergan would draw upon the classical and statistical laws to narrow down the possibilities and to estimate the f-probabilities associated with a range of v-probable occurrences in an approach towards grasping a v-probable intelligibility immanent in historical process.[79]

With Gallie and White, Lonergan recognizes that there are overall structures or patterns operative in the oscillations between progress and decline, that these patterns conceivably could be classified, and that such patterns are surely operative in the imagination as anticipations of the long range course of one's life and that of one's culture and civilization. Lonergan would recognize careful classification of such anticipatory structures to be powerfully relevant to an understanding of a historical age and to one's understanding of oneself. But unlike White, Lonergan recognizes understanding to intend something more than an order in the mind or a structure to language. And Lonergan would argue that inasmuch as White intends to do something more than present an account of the structure of his own mind (inasmuch as White makes a historical claim about nineteenth century philosophers and historians) his own project reflects Lonergan's rejection of this narrower view of cognition.

Finally, Lonergan would add that historical events are transformed significantly in accordance with transformations in culturally operative theories on humanity and on historical process. As people in cultures live and act in accordance with anticipations about the nature of humanity, the structures of history, and the dynamics of progress and decline — anticipations which are shaped, generally, by the historians and theoreticians of the current or previous ages — their historical living comes to reflect the structure of such anticipations. The historian, equipped with the tools for an analysis of sciences of man and philosophies of history, will be in a position to understand the course of historical events in terms of transformations in culturally operative views drawn from such extant human sciences and philosophies of history. And a historical writing which reflects any advance upon the *status quo* in the science of man and the philosophy of history will have a profound effect on the future flow of events when it becomes widespread in the operative anticipations of culture. It is to this end of working out an advance upon current philosophies of history that emergent probability is proposed.

## 6.4 *History as Meaning*

There exist at least three fundamental problems with conceiving the structure and dynamism of history in terms of acts of meaning. My procedure here will be to develop some of the foundational notions operative in Lonergan's account of the structure of history and society in the course of meeting these problems. And so an initial presentation of the problems would be in order here.

First. While acts of meaning are certainly performed by human subjects, it can be argued that such acts are seldom, if ever, self-constituting or self-regulating. Rather, a myriad of "internal" psychic, affective and physiological processes of subjects exercise an overwhelming influence upon human intelligent activity, so much so that (in an extreme view) meanings are essentially derivative of such "internal" processes. Thus, history, conceived as decisively ordered by acts of subjects, is to be explained in terms of the patterns and regularities of subconscious life or, for example, in terms of repressed sexuality rather than in terms of subjectively constituted meaning.[81]

Second. While meanings are acts of human subjects, historical processes are rarely intended or foreseen by individuals. The battle plans of generals seldom explain the outcome of wars. In addition, the subtly but pervasively operative symbols and images of a society, of a culture, are rarely the result of acts of understanding of citizens of that society or culture. Thus Matthew Lamb criticizes Wilhelm Dilthey for not adequately handling "the larger systems in history which could not be understood as expressing a given individual's presence."[82]

Third. Meanings of individuals emerge in a social context in which the individual participates. But the individual's mode of participation in that context is, for the most part, determined by the economic structure of that society, its modes of production, its habitual routines, its traditional divisions among classes, its patterns of ownership and control over the institutions of society, etc., etc. It is not the meanings that determine the dynamic patterns of historical change but the operative relations of society and economy and the regular order in which such relations are transformed over the history of civilizations.[83]

In each of these three objections what is at issue is the extent to which subjective acts of intelligence, and more specifically one's own "interpretation" of oneself, are decisive in constituting the over-arching course of history. Lonergan recognizes that there is a truth to be grasped in each of the objections. But he would argue that at the extreme pole of each, the significance and indeed the possibility of human knowing and human responsible acting is either precluded or rendered insignificant for the course of human life. Lonergan would note that the very act of putting forward an extreme view, in each case, would involve the subject in a contradiction. For each objection itself intends a truth about human life which is not simply to be explained away in terms of inner or outer pre-conditions surrounding its author's cognitional activity. And each intends a decisive reversal of a long-standing history of misunderstanding, and thus each claims to be a significant contribution to man's development. But it is in coming to understand the truth intended by each objection that a fuller understanding of the role of cognitional and responsible activity in human society and history is to be gained.[84]

### 6.4.1 "Internal" Conditions and the Dramatic Subject: Dialectic and Dramatic Bias

The claim of the first objection is that "internal" psychic and emotional forces and processes operative at a subliminal level, function to condition, massively, intelligent and responsible activity, to the extent that much, if not all, of human freedom (understood here in terms of intelligent self-determination) is an illusion. To respond to this objection requires introducing Lonergan's notion of "dialectic."

> For the sake of greater precision, let us say that a dialectic is a concrete unfolding of linked but opposed principles of change. Thus, there will be a dialectic, if:
> (1) there is an aggregate of events of a determinate character,
> (2) the events may be traced to either or both of two principles,
> (3) the principles are opposed yet bound together, and
> (4) they are modified by the changes that successively result from them.[85]

In the dramatic pattern of common sense intelligence, Lonergan notes that there is operative a dialectical interaction between the spontaneous demands of neural patterns and processes, and the selection, integration and repression of such neural demand functions by the psyche through the conscious operations in the "basic pattern of experience." In such operations as seeing, hearing, wondering, understanding, an order or pattern is constituted in a manifold of neural events and processes. But such an order is not from nothing, for neural processes constitute an exigence for a certain range of ordering that leads to a correspondence between, for example, certain patterns of change in the optic nerve and certain acts of seeing.[86] Since acts of psychic integration which meet an exigence of the neural manifold never occur in accordance with hard and fast laws, there will generally occur acts in the basic pattern which miss their mark. Furthermore, Lonergan goes on to note that intelligent acts operate in terms of anticipatory structures, practical projects, and social relations of role, identity and status. Thus questions are not only met with incorrect answers, they often invite and encourage incorrect answers when the subject's projects and anticipations do not correspond to the demands of experience. Subjects do not only stop short of correct answers, they also reject correct insights in favour of incorrect ones, in the interests of other ranges of concerns. But because the complete neural manifold presents an exigence for an appropriate integration, intelligence will be driven back to the data, back to further questions as long as satisfactory answers are not found and settled upon.[87]

The two principles of change, the drive to psychic integration and the exigence of the nural manifold for appropriate integration, operate not only in harmony but also in opposition. Lonergan suggests that much fearful avoidance of questions and concerns, an unhappy subterranean life of questions, experiences and images, and some inhibited performance of psychically disturbed subjects has been explained in terms of the reordering of the neural and psychic manifolds around the repression of the "dramatic bias."[88] In the measure that repressed questions, experiences, and images arise in wider or narrower dimensions of life, the demand of the neural processes for appropriate integration will continue to drive more or less relentlessly towards surfacing in other areas of conscious life. Thus they operate more or less powerfully as a force or principle that warps the rest of the subject's life of experiences, insights, judgments and decisions.[89]

But the dialectical interaction between the ordering principle of psychic acts and the exigences of neural processes for appropriate order does not only manifest itself in dramatic bias and, at the extreme, psychic aberration.[90] For this dialectic drives the subject towards further questions, and further experience when insights fail to satisfy the demands of a question, towards images, music and art when the operative values of a culture cease to nourish, and towards getting in touch with the subject's own feelings when projects, routines, and relations of life become mechanical and unreal. But as life is constituted as much by failure as success the resultant aberrations of dramatic bias will manifest themselves as a principle of social and historical decline, which stands in opposition to the historical operation of the drive of universal finality.[91] Lonergan explains the historical principle of "individual bias" in terms of this dialectic. The historical manifestation of this principle of bias will be discussed in greater detail in the next chapter.[92]

In response to this first objection, then, Lonergan would argue that there certainly remain neural and affective events which constitute the conditions for cognitional and responsible operations and which function in patterns or schemes that distort and limit the effective range of these operations.[93] But such events and schemes of events do not order decisively and determine the cognitional and responsible acts. Rather, the neural and affective events and processes constitute a manifold to be ordered by such psychic operations. Because the ordering process involves the operation of two related but opposed principles of change the process will proceed dialectically as a linked set of changes in the intellect and in the neural manifold, such that each change conditions the occurence of the next. Each psychic integration of the neural manifold operates cumulatively on the materials presented by the previous acts and the combined effects of the linkage and opposition between the two principles both keeps the dialectical scheme operating circularly and keeps the subject either developing or, in the case of prolonged bias, declining until the repression either forces a reversal or destroys the subject. The cumulatively operating acts of integration recur in accordance with statistical laws. And in Lonergan's explanation it is the element of randomness, or absence of reason, at the centre of the statistical laws, which precludes a reductionist explanation and which accounts for the flexibility that dynamizes the operation of the dialectic.[94]

While precluding a reductionist account of acts of meaning, this notion of dialectic put forward by Lonergan makes room for an explanation of human action in terms of the operation of psychic aberration and opens the way for an account of historical events and processes in terms of bias. The difference between the operation of bias and the developing orientation of the dialectic is to be understood in terms of a difference in the f-probable frequency of occurrence of competently performed, cumulatively integrating acts of intelligence and responsibility. Shifts in such probabilities in the lives of individual subjects and in the recurring activities of societies and cultures could be explained in terms of changes in conditions associated with experiences and life routines. And a psychological study of the myriad of ways in which bias manifests itself could well prove a powerful explanatory tool in the hands of the historian. But such shifts in probability, Lonergan would argue, constitute expansions or contractions in the range of effective freedom. Far from precluding essential freedom such shifts in probability demand the notion of essential freedom and its dynamic structure as an emergent integration of a lower order manifold.[95]

### 6.4.2 The Schemes and Series of History and Society: Intersubjectivity and Dialectic

The claim of the next objection to conceiving history in terms of acts of meaning centers around the fact that no historical event or age would seem to correspond to any one person's act of meaning. People's intentions, insights, plans and projects are one thing. But the course of history is usually something quite different. If meaning is the term of a subjective act, then how are we to conceive history in terms of meaning when it is clear that historical patterns and structures would seem to be operative in historical ages whose subjects could not begin to think in terms of such patterns and structures?[96] To meet this objection requires an excursus of some length which will involve the development of some of Lonergan's clues in *Insight* and the introduction of some insights of Gibson Winter's from *Elements for a Social Ethic*. But an initial outline of the final response to this objection might help the reader through this excursus.

The following explanation of the overarching schemes and patterns of society and history in terms of a subjective account of the genesis of meaning will involve the heuristic structure of emergent probability. The responsible actions, projects, and routines of two or more individuals can link together to form an operative pattern or scheme in which all members participate intelligently and responsibly but which none need have devised and which none need understand completely for the scheme to operate. Such is the structure of the probably emergent scheme of recurrence. In this account the constitutive elements are acts of meaning (whether acts of knowing fact, or, far more regularly, intelligently integrated sets of performance skills). But the structures of society and history are constituted by the schemes in which the recurring classes of intelligent acts link together in a mutually conditioning pattern. And far from precluding the operation of individual acts of intelligence, such an explanation would require their habitual recurrence. This, in outline, is the response to this second objection. But to develop this notion of social and historical schemes will involve a discussion and development of the notion of "intersubjectivity."

In *Insight*, Lonergan points to evidence of a spontaneous, intersubjective bond, operative vitally and affectively, linking subjects together in a common field of experience.[97] In *Method* he introduces "intersubjectivity" as the "vital and functional" unity of subjects "that precedes the distinction of subjects and survives its oblivion."[98] As the spontaneous concern for another's welfare, as the spontaneous empathy with another's object of concern, and as the immediate grasp of the irreducible meaning of another's smile, the intersubjective "we" has its roots in the vital experiences of human subjects in the biological and aesthetic patterns but continues to operate as a condition for the whole range of intelligent and responsible acts of individuals and cultures.[99] But it is in Gibson Winter's *Elements for a Social Ethic* that we can find an account of the recurrent structure of intersubjective exchange among subjects.

Winter's account of the threefold structure of sociality, developed in *Elements*, did not draw upon Lonergan's work, but rather sought in the work of Alfred Schütz a corrective to an overly deterministic presentation of George Herbert Mead.[100] However, Mead's original account of the structure of gesture and response and Winter's reconstruction of Mead both explain the emergence of social identity in terms of a recurring set of acts which, once initiated, operate in a specific order of succession.[101]

Mead began with a view of the individual person which was developed in the tradition of behaviorism and pragmatic philosophy, and he sought to find how an individual's sense of identity came to be a social identity.[102] He developed a threefold pattern of gesture and response, in which an individual comes to see him or herself through the eyes of another person when he or she initiates a gesture, receives a response to the gesture, and in looking at him or herself through the eyes of the responding person interprets how the gesture must have looked to that other person. Mead argued that our sense of who we are emerges not so much in the picture we form of ourselves through our own acts but in the way that we see them through the eyes of others in the responses that they make to us.[103]

Winter found Mead's account unsatisfactory because it placed too much emphasis upon the socially determined character of our identity.[104] He argued that the response to one's gesture is followed not simply by an acceptance of the other's view of who we are or what we meant, but by a drive to what Winter calls "unification."[105] If another's response presents an image of who we are and what we meant that differs from what we intended by our gesture, we reflect on our original meaning and try to objectify our own image of ourselves that was implicit in this gesture. We compare this image with that presented by the other's response and seek to reconcile the two images with the other person. Thus the third stage or event in the threefold scheme is a drive to unification that conceivably could involve considerable further gesturing and responding until a unification is reached or until the reconciliation process is given up as beyond the resources of time and place.[106]

Winter explains this threefold structure of sociality in the terms and relations of a philosophical background that is somewhat different from Lonergan's. Nonetheless his account has the form of the scheme of recurrence.[107] Each stage functions as the fulfilling condition for the next stage and each stage is an event that can be classified irrespective of the particular meaning that it intends. The gesture always invites a response and we can all recollect personal experiences wherein responding to a gesture was almost impossible to avoid. The response is to the gesture, and it interprets the meaning of the gesture as well as invites its own confirmation or rejection as an adequate interpretation. And the drive to unification brings both the gesture and the response forward to reconcile them on two distinct levels: on the level of the coherence, the truth or the value in what the subjects intended, and on the level of the relative need for mutual confirmation and approval among the persons in dialogue.[108] The proper operation of the scheme requires the fulfillment of a determinate set of conditions: competence in the appropriate range of language, a certain antecedent interest and willingness to see the scheme through to unification, sufficient time and resources.[109] And the recurrent operation of the scheme sets the context and fulfills the conditions for the development of virtually all the social skills from the child's most primitive engagement with its mother's gestures of affection to the most sophisticated political maneuverings among heads of state. It is quite regularly in the context of this threefold pattern that sense and motor skills are learned. And the careful gesturing and responding of a sensitive educator can increase significantly the probabilities associated with the assimilation and adjustment developmental scheme described above.[110] By providing the student with the appropriate clues and by responding with affection and approval when a difficult discovery has been made or a group of operations has been performed successfully, the educator can significantly accelerate the rate of learning and development.

In Winter's reconstruction of Mead there can be discerned not only the structure of the recurrence scheme, but also a second instance of Lonergan's notion of dialectic. In the drive to unification there are operative two distinct principles of change that correspond to the two levels on which the gesture and response demand reconciliation.[111] The first principle is the drive towards intelligibility, towards truth, towards value. In Lonergan's terms, it is the drive of the transcendentals seeking higher order integrations of experiential data of the neural manifold into intelligible orders and into unified complexes of questions, and answers that meet the questions and lay them to rest. It is the drive to coordinate and integrate the manifold of skills within the subject's repertoire in the light of insights, judgments of truth, affective apprehensions of value and the grasp of possible courses of action that realize new human futures judged to be worthwhile. The second principle is the drive towards expression and confirmation of what is understood, judged, decided, with another person. It is the desire to understand and to be understood by another, to love and to be loved as a whole person. This second principle is linked to the first inasmuch as what we seek to share with another and to have understood by another is the content of an intelligent or responsible act. But it is opposed to the first because the drive to expression and confirmation wants a confirmation of the subject as a *whole person*, and not simply an approval of an intelligently grasped meaning. Thus while the initial gesture invites the approval of the other on the truth or value of what is expressed, the drive towards the intelligent grasp of truth and the affirmation and actualization of value is easily suppressed in favour of the more powerful and the more immediately felt need for the other's affection and approval. Similarly, the massive and exclusive cultivation of the cognitional skills can result in a person so relentlessly pursuing some knowledge that he or she runs roughshod over the feelings of others and finally isolates him or herself from the spontaneous care and concern of others.[112]

Though the effect of this operation of the three-stage, dialectically operative scheme can be the suppression of questions for intelligence or the alienation of oneself from others, the opposition between the two principles of change as frequently has the effect of driving the subjects to new data, to reformulations of questions, to more remotely related insights, to a reconsideration of the other's position or feelings, or to a rediscovery that other people truly care about one's welfare. And even more profoundly, this drive to unification leads to collaboration in the conception and execution of projects and to patterns of social interaction and organization that pursue a desired result which none could have achieved on their own.[113] This operation of the dialectic is fundamentally what Lonergan has conceived as the dialectic of community.[114] But with the introduction of Gibson Winter's threefold structure of sociality, the dynamic structure of the operation of this dialectic is clarified and expanded. The tension in the dialectic of community remains, as Lonergan has described it, the tension between "intersubjective spontaneity and intelligently devised social order."[115] But the introduction of Winter's scheme further explains the structure of the dialectical dynamism involved in the transition from a society characterized predominately by a vital, spontaneous, affective mutuality and a society in which this mutuality is operative in collaborative acts and schemes of practical intelligence that yield greater goods for all. The good of order[116] (the intrinsic worth of collaborating towards such further collaborative value) is sought, not originally out of the drive of intelligence but rather out of the drive towards mutuality, collaboration, the sense of approval one gets from belonging and participating in a group. The operations of intelligence are harnessed, first haphazardly, them systematically in service of this drive towards mutual confirmation and mutual love. But intelligence has its own immanent criteria and so the extension of the operations of practical intelligence into the realm of intersubjectivity is the introduction of a second principle or operator that is as uncompromising as the first. The drive towards unification with another needs to be a unification in accordance with the criteria of intelligence as well as a unification in a true, non-abusive care. And while compromise on the principle of cooperation and agreement might seem to yield the tumultuous consequence of anarchy and revolution a compromise of intelligence yields the equally destructive failure of poorly conceived plans and the distortions that ensue from "group bias."[117]

After this lengthy excursus, then, we can get back to the second objection that has been raised against a conception of human history in terms of operations of meaning. Again, this objection recognized the difference between individual acts of meaning and doing and the random or ordered interactions among such individual actions whose overall course or shape will most usually elude the grasp of acting individuals. From the perspective of this reconstruction of Lonergan's thought it is clear that such interactions do occur, that they constitute the shape or course of societies and of history and that they most often have a structure to their operation that is not understood completely by contemporaries of the society or historical age.[118] But as human, history consists of human subjects performing distinctively human acts. And from Lonergan's perspective what is distinctively human about these acts is that their regulative principle is not to be sought in antecedent conditions and environmental schemes but in the schemes immanent to the subject and in the intelligibilities that emerge in acts of knowing, judging and deciding; intelligibilities that are spontaneously learned and routinely performed by successive generations of a society, a culture, an economy. Consequently aggregates and patterns of interactions among human subjects are to be understood in terms of the cooperative schemes that link individual acts. Furthermore there can be discerned a pattern to the emergence and development of such societal schemes that can be understood in terms of the dialectical interplay between the dynamic orientation of intelligent, responsible acts (or their biased orientation in groups where a form of bias prevails), and the spontaneous drive to expression and unification that brings and keeps subjects acting together. In the context of this dialectical interplay between the two drives or principles, conceivably there could be a cumulative structure to the operations of societies and to history. And while this overall, cumulative structure moves towards "progress," towards events building upon the shoulders of previous events and schemes, the fact that the structure of the movement is dialectical also explains the possibility and the fact of both short and long term "decline."[119]

Thus there will be an overall intelligibility to the dynamic structure of intersubjective schemes. And there will be a further intelligibility associated with the pattern of emergence and development of such schemes. A concrete understanding of the schemes requires a grasp of the structure of cognitional acts and their dialectical interactions as well as a knowledge of the operative trends, skills and routines among the participating individuals. But while such intersubjective schemes and such patterns of development and decline will have an intelligibility, this intelligibility need not have been originated in the mind of one historical actor.

One further note would seem to be in order here regarding the subjective genesis of meaning and the spontaneously emergent schemes of society and history. It might seem that this account of society and history, as probably emergent schemes and series, would contradict a conception of history in terms of acts of meaning, on the one hand, and a subjective account of the genesis of meaning, on the other. For if the schemes, and the dialectical structure to the development of the schemes of society and history can emerge independently of any one subject devising and implementing them, then how could one possible call this history human meaning if meaning is conceived as the term of a subjective act?

(1) What is central to Lonergan's conception of history in terms of acts of meaning is the fact that the significant elements of human history are to be identified as humans performing distinctively human acts. Human life is overwhelmingly and inescapably mediated by language, by ideas, by symbols, by habits, skills, and by all the actions which require at least a minimal performance of operations or groups of operations of intelligence. It is in this sense that Lonergan affirms that the essentially constitutive events of human history are acts of meaning.

(2) But the sufficiently frequent recurrence of appropriate sets of acts of meaning and intelligently mediated performance skills, all other things being equal, fulfills the conditions for a further emergent intelligibility to world process (the schemes and dynamic patterns of development and decline of society and history). The constitutive events of these schemes and series are acts of meaning. And so an account of the genesis of such acts of meaning remains an essential part of the explanation of the schemes and series. And furthermore, in Lonergan's view, the dynamic structure to the emergence of such schemes and series stands in a relationship of isomorphism to a subsequent act of understanding which would grasp and affirm (thus intelligently actuating) the intelligibility immanent in such schemes and series. It is this relationship of isomorphism in the probably emergent structure of world process and in the probably emergent structure to acts of knowing which explains why knowing can know being and why an act of knowing concretely approaches a relationship of isomorphism with an intelligibility immanent in being.

(3) As intelligence expands its grasp of social and historical processes, more and more of human history comes within the regulative scope of human responsibility. For the dynamic schemes and series of history come to require, to a greater and greater extent, the understanding of such schemes and series as essentially constitutive elements of their regulation and finally their survival. When massive growths in human populations link the survival of larger and larger numbers of people to the survival of economic, industrial, political, social and cultural schemes, then it would seem that the human race has reached a point of no return. It is this awareness of the fragility of the current historical age, I would argue, which most power-

fully dynamizes Lonergan's urgent plea to conceive human history as essentially constituted by acts of intelligence and responsibility.[120]

### 6.4.3 *"External" Conditions and the Dramatic Subject*

The last of the three objections to conceiving history in terms of meaning, which were raised above, concerns the schemes and series of society and history as determinants of the intelligent activities of individual subjects. Whereas the second objection above concerned the role of individual acts of meaning in constituting the patterns and processes of society and history, this third objection asks whether the operations of such patterns and processes do not decisively condition subjective acts of meaning so that, in an extreme view, the self-regulating activity of intelligence and responsibility is precluded.

The elements for this response have been assembled. And so this response will be brief. In addition, in the following chapter, I will present a more detailed response to the most influential and articulate formulation of this objection.[121] And so many more details on this issue will be found there.

This account of Lonergan's work recognizes the emergence of patterns in the operation and development of an economy, a political society. And the conditions within which an individual grows, learns, chooses a career, organizes his or her life, understands him or herself will, in large measure, be set by the contemporary modes and relations of production, the contemporary patterns of circulation and accumulation of capital, and the class structures of the age.[122] But, once again, there remains operative an immanent dynamism and immanent criteria to the operations that distinctively constitute human activities as human. This operative principle is linked to the experiential exigence of the neural manifold in one dialectic, and it is linked to this exigence and to a further drive towards intersubjective mutuality in another dialectic. But with the performance of the intelligent and responsible skills there occurs an emergent integration of the materials of the intersubjective environment of the subject's life. Such an integration operates more or less competently in accordance with the subject's developed sensitivity to the demands of the experiential manifold and to the drive towards mutuality. But the ordering principle of intelligent and intelligently mediated acts is on the level of the psychic and not on the level of the neural. Consequently this account of the dynamic structure of such acts precludes a reductionist account of the import of economy and polity on the emergence of meaning. In fact it would seem that the schemes and series of contemporary economy and polity require the relatively developed performance of intelligent and responsible acts within wider ranges of flexibility.[123]

Furthermore, to understand the contemporary operation of economy and history, to identify the flaws in the current situation, to educate others and raise public consciousness of ills that demand redressing, and to implement changes in the structures of routines and in the policies that regulate such routines will require the performance of these cognitional and responsible operations. And such performance will constitute the essential element in the transformation of economy, polity and history. Efforts toward change will be intelligent and they will have a goal and a preconceived conception of the course of such change. The actual course of change will diverge from this goal either for better or for worse. For changes give rise to further changes that cannot be foreseen. But the continued application of intelligence and responsibility will be required either to evaluate this new course of history and to direct it in accordance with intelligent criteria or to refuse the mandate of intelligence and thus mobilize a principle for its own subsequent reversal.

In summary, then, Lonergan presents his notion of dialectic as an introductory analysis of a structure to the operation of historical process understood in terms of emergent probability. The dialectic operative between the exigence of a subject's neural manifold and the transcendental drive to ordering this manifold in the operations of the "basic pattern of experience" will constitute a recurrent structure in the development and decline of the subject's intentional operations. Since the subject is never an isolated subject the manifold will always consist of schemes that link him or her to the myriad of elements and processes of his or her "external environment." Consequently the neural manifold, the complete and total environment of the subject, will always be changing in accordance with the subtlest physical, biological and intelligent events occurring beyond the "confines" of his or her own envelope of skin. This dialectic, then, will itself constitute a structure of social and historical process. But in addition to this dialectic, there is an additional dialectic that links the structured occurrence of the operations of intelligence of two or more subjects with the spontaneous, vital and affective drive to mutuality and love between them. And so the two dialectics will operate as engines of social and historical change that function in continuity with the free, intelligent and reponsible operations of the subjects, in accordance with a dynamic pattern that need not be grasped and intended by any of the historical actors, and in a concrete context of conditions whose uniqueness and particularity does not violate the general dialectical structure.

This emergent probability heuristic, in my view, provides a powerful and distinctive framework for understanding the operations of human history in terms of human acts of meaning. As a generalized heuristic emergent probability recognizes human history as continuous in structure with the longer history of physical and biological evolutionary processes. However, the notions of randomness and emergence allow for, and indeed they explain, a discontinuity as well as a wider structural continuity between human history and physical, biological evolution. At the most basic level this discontinuity consists in the fact that human history is constituted by acts of meaning, and that the development of skills can fulfill the conditions for insights thus systematizing flows of classes of insights and adapting insights to concrete circumstances, thus transforming history. But given the fact of intelligent, responsible capacities, a set of intersubjective, social, economic, political schemes can emerge spontaneously in human societies in a pattern which bears remarkable similarity to the general evolutionary structure in physical and biological spheres. Thus a new intelligibility arises within human history which is no one's invention. Similarly social, historical conditions can shift the probabilities associated with recurring classes of meanings. These conditions can be fulfilled as a result of coincidental convergences, as a result of wider systematically operative trends in language, symbol and culture, or as a result of insight and responsible political action. And these shifting conditions can operate either to liberate humanity to effective freedom or to distort culture in a form of bias. Human responsibility can come to know bias, and promote the accelerated development of skills and conversions, thus adding a wider proliferation in flexibility and adaptability among human historical operators. And here, now, the parallels with physical evolution appear more and more remote. Finally emergent probability can be known as a heuristic and, in time, a theory of history can bring the dynamics of history under a further dimension of human responsibility when it is discovered that theory can embrace and nurture the random, the non-systematic, and that the norms for meaning, value and history are immanent to human subjects.

## 6.5 Ethics and History I: Progress and Decline

Just as Dilthey conceived that an epistemology and a psychology should set a foundation for a comprehensively conceived science of man which would study the structure of historical processes and set the tools and methods for the writing of history, so too Lonergan has built an account of the dynamic structure of history on the foundation of a theory of cognition. But what may not be immediately obvious is that Lonergan's account of the patterns and dynamism of history is at the same time an account of the criterion for an ethics, the criterion for distinguishing among more or less valuable courses of action. Upon reflection it would seem reasonable that some correlation should exist between a criterion of value and a criterion for historical progress and decline. But during the Enlightenment years a number of substantial concerns arose which resulted in the two sets of criteria being conceived independent from each other.[124] And in the work of Immanuel Kant we can see one example of an attempt to deal with this separation.

When Kant published the first of his essays on the philosophy of history in 1748, he had already published his *Critique of Pure Reason* three years earlier, and had worked out much of the material for the *Groundwork of the Metaphysic of Morals*, which would appear in print the following year.[125] And so when Kant asks how individual moral action relates to the overarching course of human history he formulates the question in terms of an account of moral action and the norm of morality that has been founded, for the most part, on his account of the autonomous operation of rationality. Kant's vision of moral man presented in the *Groundwork* and reflected in the essays on history, is of a self-creating creature who constitutes his own life through the free exercise of his rational will. The essence of Kant's notion of rationality is its autonomously constituting character. In the words of Yermiahu Yovel:

> In being autonomous, human reason must abide only by those universal rules it sets up by itself, and in which it can recognize the explication of its own subjective structure. Any other attitude will be "heteronomous" and thereby non-rational ... According to this theory, reason cannot be conceived of as a system of universal norms that subsist in themselves, but must be seen as constituted by the human subject.[126]

Thus the *Groundwork* begins with a presentation of the good will, the only thing that is unqualified good in and of itself, and the only thing that can ground the worth of any ends that come about through its exercise.[127]

There are a number of possible explanations for this strong emphasis on the autonomy and the subjectively constituting character of rationality in the work of Kant. In his first *Critique*, Kant sought a possible foundation for knowledge in *a priori* claims, claims whose truth value was independent from an appeal to experience. The reliability of truth claims whose truth rested on *a posteriori* appeal to experience had been shown by Hume to be unreliable and some foundation for certain knowledge had to be found that was not subject to the errors to which acts of perception were prone. Thus Kant looked to the structure of the mind itself for the source of the reliability and permanence of knowledge.[128]

George Kelly argues that Kant's work in ethics and in history takes up Rousseau's quest for a new beginning to history in a new foundation for morality. In the face of the corrupt course of history and tradition Rousseau proposed an ideal foundation for social order that required nothing more than the free, autonomous consent of rational men. According to Kelly, Kant championed Rousseau's moral voluntarism as a revolt against dogma and *status quo* politics and as a manifestation of what was most properly human.[129]

Charles Taylor argues that Kant's emphasis on the autonomy of rational morality is a revolt against an earlier Enlightenment view of man as driven by his desire or appetite to seek his own utility. Such a view of moral man, in Kant's view, was exactly contrary to true moral freedom because it precluded the decision that liberates the subject from the determining constraints of natural necessity.[130]

Whatever the reasons for Kant's concern for the autonomy of reason, the fact of his conception of rationality as autonomous remains clear. And so when Kant sets about investigating the relationship between the operation of rational morality and the overarching course of historical process he faces two sets of problems. First, if the exercise of human reason is free and autonomous, then how does this autonomy relate to the laws that govern the processes of nature and set the context in which man works out his life? Is man's reason a radical departure from nature? Or is he, in some way, in continuity with the biological laws that govern physical, vegetable and animal life?[131] Second, is there an overall shape or lawfulness to the course of human history, or is history an aimless aggregate of individual persons pursuing conflicting visions of duty? Is there an ideal way that societies can be conceived and organized so as to foster and coordinate individuals carrying out their duties? Is there an overall end or *telos* to human history and if so does it negate freedom and the autonomous exercise of free will?[132] It is these two sets of questions that are the concern of Kant's essays on the philosophy of history.

Writing almost two hundred years later, Bernard Lonergan works through these same sets of questions in his study of understanding, *Insight*. But while the philosophers of Enlightenment Europe were championing the radical discontinuities between the human exercise of intelligence and what was then conceived to be the "lawful" operation of the so-called "natural" processes of the material and social orders, Lonergan was writing in the wake of a massive scientific discovery of the continuites. Evolutionary theory since Darwin had come to think of man as evolving from the animal world and sharing many biological and social behaviour patterns with the higher animals. Psychological experimentation since Freud and Jung was uncovering vast regions of psychic life whose influence on the exercise of "reason" was both overwhelming and undeniable. Historians, cultural anthropologists, sociologists and scholars in theology and world religions were discovering the massive import of historical, cultural, and indeed since Marx, economic contexts for the prevailing meanings, themes, questions, concerns, symbols, values and styles of reasoning of any given time and place. And quantum mechanics and the statistical methods in the social sciences were progressively undermining a rigidly determinist conception of the "lawfully ordered" natural world, and were asking questions about the very meaning of the word "law."[133] Consequently Lonergan's question about the relationship between individual morality and the course of natural and human history is formulated with a notion of "ought" or "good" that is not defined purely in terms of what is autonomous or discontinuous in human rationality and morality but in terms of an overall account of the dynamic structure of world processes, both "natural" and human. The fact of continuity was, for the most part, taken for granted by Lonergan but it remained for him to develop his account of the structure of such world processes that left an open door for understanding the discontinuities: for randomness, for emergence, for freedom and thus for morality. How can the laws of physics and chemistry, the evolutionary structures of biological, zoological and human processes be understood so as to maintain the ground for generalization, for recurrence, for operative process, for continuity, while at the same time explaining the massive fact of contingency, of randomness, or newly emergent events, processes, and operators? This is the question which occupies the first five chapters of *Insight* and whose answers are integrated into Lonergan's theory of world process, emergent probability.

We have seen, above,[134] how Lonergan understands human acts of cognition, the development of skills, and the integration of groups of such skills in ordered patterns conceived by intelligence, in terms of the structured heuristic, emergent probability. The notion of human freedom was defined in terms of this intelligent integration of skills. And thus the apparent contradiction between human freedom and the operation of laws was, at least in principle, overcome. Again, human freedom is not conceived as randomness or the absence of restrictions but as the capacity for some intelligent self-regulation. Thus human freedom, the foundation for the possibility of moral action and thus an ethics, need not necessarily imply an indeterminism or a relativism. The problem that remains, then, is to determine how Lonergan conceives the criterion for discriminating among possible courses of action conceived by intelligence, and for judging some superior to others.

Most simply Lonergan develops this criterion for judging moral "good" in terms of the principles operative in his notions of historical progress and decline.

> Just as the counter-positions of metaphysics invite their own reversal by their inconsistency with intelligent and reasonable affirmation, so the basically similar counter-positions of the ethical order through the shorter and longer cycles of the dialectic of progress and decline either enforce their own reversal or destroy their carriers. Just as the heuristic structure of our knowing couples with the generalized emergent probability of the proportionate universe, to reveal an upwardly directed dynamism of finality towards ever fuller being, so the obligatory structure of our rational self-consciousness
> (1) finds its materials and its basis in the products of universal finality,
> (2) is itself finality on the level of intelligent and rational consciousness, and
> (3) is finality confronted with the alternative of choosing either development and progress or decline and extinction.[135]

Progress is the dynamic towards, and the structure of emergence and development as it is operative in human history. The essential elements recurring in all of Lonergan's discussions on progress are the notion of cumulation and the mediating operations of intelligence.[136] The mediating operations of intelligence are what constitutes and characterize world process as distinctively human history.[137] But it is the cumulative nature of development which constitutes the dynamic structure of progress. Consequently an analysis of the notions of progress and decline must begin with and focus upon the specific meaning of the terms emergence and development. The most complete treatment of these two terms is to be found in *Insight*, chapter fifteen, in the section on "The Notion of Development."[138] Anyone who is familiar with the range of materials covered in this section will understand that only a brief introduction can be attempted here.

> ... a development may be defined as a flexible, linked sequence of dynamic and increasingly differentiated higher integrations that meet the tension of successively transformed underlying manifolds through successive applications of the principles of correspondence and emergence.[139]

Schemes emerge and function when their conditions are fulfilled. And their functioning effects a higher order integration of lower order manifolds. The foundation of the *normative* dynamism of development is this relationship between the higher order integration and the lower order manifold. For the integration marks the presence of emergent system, emergent intelligibility, in a manifold of events whose recurrence is otherwise coincidental or non-systematic. Such an emergence is not necessarily the emergence of a new recurrence scheme. Rather, the routine functioning of older schemes can have the effect of regularly ordering the materials of a lower manifold. And Lonergan provides a number of examples of such emergent integrations.

> First, there is the already familiar principle of emergence. Otherwise coincidental manifolds of lower conjugate acts invite the higher integration effected by higher conjugate forms. Thus, in our account of explanatory genera, chemical elements and compounds are higher integrations of otherwise coincidental manifolds of subatomic events; organisms are higher integrations of otherwise coincidental manifolds of chemical processes; sensitive consciousness is a higher integration of otherwise coincidental manifolds of changes in neural tissues; and accumulating insights are higher integrations of otherwise coincidental manifolds of images or data.[140]

Most simply the normative dynamism of development is rooted in the relationship between being and non-being. A coincidental manifold exhibits an absence of system in its recurring events; an absence of intelligibility; an absence of "form." When the appropriate conditions are fulfilled the higher order integration of the manifold is the presence of system; the presence of intelligibility; the presence of "form." The difference between the two states of the manifold is precisely this presence or absence. The transition or dynamic structure of the movement from non-presence to presence is what is meant here by emergence. And what emerges is being (the term or object of a potential or actual act of intelligence). In each of his examples above, Lonergan is pointing to instances of the emergence of being from non-being. It would appear that the most basic, the most fundamental foundation for any normative or evaluative predication is conceived by Lonergan to be this dynamic relationship between being and non-being. Thus it is not coincidental that Lonergan's eighteenth chapter of *Insight* on "The Possibility of Ethics" begins a presentation of "The Notion of the Good" with the statement "As being is intelligible and one, so also it is good."[141] For without this most basic equation (or its opposite) any notion of norm or valuation is utterly precluded from the outset.

I think it is worth nothing here that the foundation of normative predication, within the context of Lonergan's analysis, is not simply this identity of being as good. Rather, a norm is a dynamic relationship and the possibility of such a dynamism is the possibility of emergence of being from non-being. Furthermore as we move progressively towards a distinctively moral or ethical normative foundation, a further number of elements need to be identified and distinguished.

The normative dynamism of development is not simply the fact that emergent and operative schemes can order a coincidental manifold. For "significantly different underlying manifolds require different higher integrations."[142] This was the point which was most relevant in the discussion of dialectic above.[143] The manifold is open to specific types of integrations in accordance with narrower or wider ranges of flexibility. In his "principle of correspondence," Lonergan expresses this fact that a manifold has an exigence for a specific form or range of forms of integrations, so that development is not simply a matter of any development in any direction.

> Thus, the chemical elements differ by atomic numbers and atomic weights, and these differences are grounded in the underlying manifold. Different aggregates of aggregates of chemical processes involve different organisms. Neural events in the eye and in the ear call forth different conscious experiences. Different data lead to different theories.[144]

But in addition to this exigence for appropriate integration, a manifold has a greater or lesser flexible range of possibilities. And so while development is directed it is not simply a matter of events following upon the recurrence of systematic processes. The presence of randomness in the manifold is the condition of possibility for the emergence of system. And in some cases this flexibility has the curious effect of promoting and sustaining continued development. This brings us to the final aspect of Lonergan's notion of development which is relevant for our purposes here.

> There follows at once a distinction between static and dynamic higher integrations. Every higher integration systematizes an otherwise coincidental manifold, but the systematization may be effected in two dif-

ferent manners. It is static when it dominates the lower manifold with complete success and thereby brings about a notable imperviousness to change. Thus, the inert gases lock coincidental manifolds of subatomic events in remarkably permanent routines. On the other hand, the higher integration is dynamic when it is not content to systematize the underlying manifold but keeps adding to it and modifying it until, by the principle of correspondence, the existing integration is eliminated and, by the principle of emergence, a new integration is introduced.[145]

The distinctive meaning of the term development involves this continued process of emergent integration which orders, but also transforms the manifold so as to call forth a new integration. In this manner the practical application of intelligence has the twofold effect of constituting an order both in the subjective and intersubjective repertoire of skills (thus ordering the subsequent course of events) and in the subject's routine or habitual spontaneity (thus constituting the subject's own affective and intelligent orientation to reality).[146] Practical activity changes the subject. And this change is the condition of possibility for the assimilation and adaptation developmental scheme involved in the acquisition of skills.[147]

The notion of progress is the distinctively human occurrence of this normative structure of emergence and development in a history of events whose constitutive characteristic is the mediating function of meaning. Progress consists in the continued emergence of being through the performance of the human acts of practical intelligence, within narrower or wider ranges of possibilities. The normative dynamism of progress is most fundamentally rooted in this relationship between being and non-being. But because of the profound import of the self-constituting operation of practical intelligence, progress in human history also means sustained and self-sustaining development. I would suggest that it is in these terms that we can gain a fresh, and perhaps an illuminating perspective on the question of the foundations of moral value.

## *6.6 Ethics and History II: The Foundations of Value*

This last section of chapter six begins where the fifth chapter left off, with a question about the foundation of value and its relationship to the overarching course of history. There would seem to be a spontaneous and habitual concern for selecting among alternate possible courses of action and for seeking out criteria for choosing appropriately. Is this spontaneous concern an intelligently grounded one? Even if clear criteria for selection remain to be found in concrete areas of moral life, can the search for criteria be expected to bear fruit at all? Or is the search to be pronounced vain? And if the search is not vain, then will deciding and living in the light of such criteria have any impact at all upon the overarching course of history?

Lonergan's discussions of "the human good" in *Insight*, chapter eighteen, and in *Method*, chapter two, link moral value with his notions of progress and decline.[148] But the two sets of texts deal with two different dimensions of the relationship between moral responsibility and the course of historical progress and decline. *Insight*, chapter eighteen, deals with the foundational elements operative in the dynamic structure of rational self-consciousness. Progress and decline are the objects of responsible choice, but they are also the dynamic orientation, the act of choosing itself. Consequently the criteria of progress and decline link the subject to the objective moral world inasmuch as a "terminal value"[149] is a true value when the subject appropriates the dynamism of progress immanent in the very act of choosing.[150] *Method*, on the other hand, speaks of historical progress and decline as proceeding from subjects who are themselves instances of originated value.[151] Here progress and decline are not so much a part of the choice of value as they are the result of a subject (and indeed a group of subjects) living their lives as authentic, self-transcending, "converted"[152] human persons, the originators of value. Consequently the discussion that follows will have two parts.

(1) In *Insight*, chapter eighteen, the focus is upon the structure of the act of responsible choice as the foundation for the criteria for choosing.

> For the root of ethics, as the root of metaphysics, lies neither in sentences nor in propositions nor in judgments but in the dynamic structure of rational self-consciousness. Because that structure is latent and operative in everyone's choosing, it is universal on the side of the subject; because that structure can be dodged, it grounds a dialectical criticism of subjects. Again, because that structure is recurrent in every act of choice, it is universal on the side of the object; and because its universality consists not in abstraction but in inevitable recurrence, it also is concrete.[153]

A person's act of integrating his or her own acquired skills to effect an ordering of a manifold of materials of an environment has the structure of an emergent integration of a lower order manifold. Furthermore even to conceive a course of action and to consider its relative merits in anticipation of performance is to give evidence that an emergent integration has already occurred at the level of cognition, and that a further dynamic orientation towards emergence is operative at the level of responsible action. It is not simply that a moral subject faces a choice between courses of action which will either realize or prevent emergence (or a sustained course of emergence in development). Rather, the very act of considering two alternatives is itself evidence that an emergence has already occurred. The "considering" has the dynamic structure of an emergence, and the act of choosing actuates a further emergence. The problem of moral value arises only insofar as an integrative act of conceiving two possibilities has already occurred. The responsible act of weighing the two alternatives is oriented towards a further emergence and this is constituted when the decision is made and the act is carried out. And so a decision as to whether to effect or to reject the normative orientation of development is itself an instance of such an orientation. If development is to be denied, either in a concrete case or as a general principle, it can only be denied through an instance of its own occurrence. And so the question arises as to whether a subject can reasonably repudiate something in principle that is actuated in the very act of repudiation.

It is this question that is at stake in Lonergan's queer and repeated insistence upon promoting the "positions" and reversing the "counterpositions."[154] In humans the events whose recurrence ensures routine operation throughout individual lives are not only the respiration of oxygen, the procurement and ingestion of food, the elimination of wastes, and the raising and caring of young. More significantly, they are the dialectical interplay between the subject's "interior" environment and his or her drive to order or coordinate that environment in accordance with psychic acts. In terms of emergent probability, what I am as human is a dynamically ordered set of physical, chemical, botanical, zoological schemes whose events include both occurrences within the spatial confines of a body, and events that occur beyond those confines. The complete set of processes that flow within and through me involves sets of higher integrations of manifolds of events that occur in accordance with exigent states of the manifolds. The relative correspondence of the integral pattern to the demands of the manifold either drives the psyche toward renewed attempts at integration or sets it to rest with the satisfaction of v-probable correspondence (only to find that the act of integration has given rise to a new form or instance of *Sorge*.) The dynamic operation of this dialectic is the structure of the scheme of judging value and deciding to act in the light of such judgments. And so the decision to affirm or to repudiate the principle of development, and to actuate or to refuse this principle in an act of progress or decline, is *a decision whose content seeks to approximate a correspondence with the operative structure of its own occurrence.*

When the content of a judgment or decision does not approximate such a correspondence with the intelligibility immanent in the structure of the performance of the act, the exigence of the neural manifold drives intelligence to keep raising further questions, attending to new data, adopting new perspectives. Lonergan's examples of the various types of efforts to dodge self-knowledge are put forward as evidence of the power of this drive towards correspondence.[155] And his account of the dramatic bias and its effects is an example of what distortions ensue when this drive is repressed or prematurely laid to rest.[156] The affirmation of a counter-position is understood by Lonergan as an occurrence of a cognitional or responsible event which seeks to order the experiential manifold of a subject in accordance with an order or a pattern which, if it were true, would prevent the cognitional or responsible event from occurring. The spontaneity of intelligence is to continue rejecting such incongruity until isomorphism is approached or until the operator is deformed in his or her capacity. And so the grasp and affirmation of positions constitute the development of the subject while the affirmation of counter-positions sets the subject on the road towards decline. Furthermore since practical acts in humans have the effect of constituting the spontaneity and the habitual orientation of successive acts of the subject, the choice of development not only avoids the deformations that ensue from bias but it also sets the orientation of the subject in anticipation of further instances and manifestations of development. This is the cumulative and progressive character of development which was discussed above. And in this fashion the choice of progress has the effect of constituting the subject as an instance of originating value.[157]

(2) If *Method* focuses on progress and decline as resulting or proceeding from the intersubjective activities of subjects who are, themselves, instances of originating value, this focus is in no way absent from *Insight*. The fact is that the self-constituting character of practical, responsible action is the central condition for the cumulative, and continually developing character of historical progress. And this explains why Lonergan sets terminal values as subordinate to originating value in his hierarchy of values.

> Again, terminal values are subordinate to originating values, for the originating values ground good will, and good will grounds the realization of the terminal values.[158]

Lonergan's introduction of the notion of "conversion" in *Method* raises the question of the role of gratuitous grace in effecting a change in a subject's orientation. And this topic will be discussed further in the next chapter. But notwithstanding the degree of our own cooperation in constituting ourselves as instances of originating value, there remains an interesting dialectical interplay between practical, responsible activity and the course of historical events that follows from this account. Inasmuch as the dynamics of development and bias are operative immanently in the human subject the relative prevalence of the one or the other will orient the subjects' spontaneity and his or her habitual judgments and decisions. Such spontaneity will be reinforced or redirected by responsible acts. And these responsible acts will have the effect of increasing or decreasing the f-probable occurrence of judgments and realizations of true terminal values. Meanwhile the acts themselves will contribute to or present obstacles to the emergence of historical progress. And whatever they do, they will certainly change historical conditions to a greater or lesser degree, thus placing the subject in a new set of historical circumstances with a new set of practical problems to solve. Immanently operative development and bias find their influence felt on intersubjective, historical progress and decline, and vice versa. And the mediator or regulator is the subject who possesses the remarkable ability to monitor, in a cybernetic-like fashion, "internal" and "external" environmental events and processes by v-probably approaching a cognitional actuation of the intelligibility immanent in both sets of data, and ordering both manifolds in accordance with an emergent "projection" of a possible course of action in the light of such cognition. The immanent norm for selection is the dynamic towards growth and development operative in the human subject. And the nature of truly human growth is such that a person can choose long-term progress in history even when such a choice leads to the short-term destruction of the person himself or herself.

The affirmation of progress over decline is fundamentally at the root of the notion of value. And persons as originators of value are the engines of historical progress and decline. Were progress and decline only predicates of history and not immanently operative in the human subject, then responsible, moral action would be purely a matter of conformity to an extrinsic norm. Were they operative only immanently and not in history, then moral activity would not make a difference to the course of historical events. Morality would be irrelevant. Lonergan's approach, to try to explain both at once, in terms of generalizable heuristic, provides the bare bones of a possible explanation which may well bear some fruit if applied to the study of humanity and history.

There remains the fact that while individuals will choose progress or decline, the course of a society and of history is never simply the result of one person's choice. It follows that there will certainly be coincidental aggregates of converging decisions and actions. And human society and human history will exhibit considerable evidence of randomness or absence of system. But randomness is never simply randomness. Rather, it is the condition of possibility for the emergence of higher order recurrence schemes which integrate lower order events into orders and routines, and regularly order the materials of the lower order in recurring patterns. Does this mean that there will be patterns or cycles in intersubjective, social and historical events? Lonergan's brief discussion of the three biases in chapter seven of *Insight* is his attempt to sketch a response to the great speculative philosophers of history on this question of the order(s) of history.

FOOTNOTES - CHAPTER 6

1. In his book *After Virtue* (Notre Dame: University of Notre Dame Press, 1981), Alasdair MacIntyre presents a fascinating account of the recent history of theories of value since the Enlightenment. He contrasts this history with an older Aristotelian approach whose rejection, during the fifteenth to seventeenth centuries, set Enlightenment Europe on its search for new foundations. Additional surveys of ethical theories include E. Leroy Long, Jr., *A Survey of Christian Ethics* (New York: Oxford, 1967); and William K. Frankena, *Ethics* (Englewood Cliffs, N.J.: Prentice-Hall, Inc., 1963). See also chapter two above.
2. See chapter four, 4.6 above.
3. W. H. Walsh, *Philosophy of History: An Introduction*, revised edition (New York: Harper & Row, Publishers; Harper Torchbooks, 1967; original 1951).
4. Ibid., pp. 1-28.
5. Ibid., p. 16; *Method*, p. 175.
6. Walsh, pp. 16-17.
7. Ibid., pp. 17-25, 30-47, 97ff.
8. Ibid., pp. 63-71.
9. Ibid., pp. 26-28.
10. Ibid., pp. 27-8.
11. B. J. F. Lonergan, "The Philosophy of History," introductory lecture at the Thomas More Institute, Montreal, September 23, 1960. (Mimeographed).
12. *Method*, pp. 175-234.
13. Lonergan, "The Philosophy of History," p. 9. Lonergan divides this essay into three topics: "history," "philosophy of," and "philosophy of history." In considering the third topic he distinguishes philosophy of "history as written" and philosophy of "history as written about." He admits that the former is what he was discussing under the first topic when he was distinguishing "occasional," "technical," and "explanatory" history. In terms of Walsh's classifications above, the analytic or critical school examined historical writing with a focus on the writing. This corresponds to Lonergan's philosophy of "history as written." Walsh's speculative school examined historical writing with a focus on the nature of man, the structure of historical "causation," the goal of history. The focus here was on the history that is written about insofar as these classifications and hypotheses spontaneously inform the historian's acts of historical writing. This is precisely what Lonergan deals with in his philosophy of "history that is written about."
14. Ibid., pp. 4-5. Lonergan introduces the scissors analogy in his discussion of "explanatory history." His distinction between "technical history" and "explanatory history" is based upon his distinction between understanding and judgment, in *Insight*. And explanatory history corresponds to his "functional specialty," "history" in *Method*, chaps. 8 and 9. Explanatory history seeks to explain "what is going forward" from point to point, from age to age, see pp. 5-6.
15. Johan Huizinga, "A Definition of the Concept of History," in *Philosophy & History: Essays Presented to Ernst Cassirer*, edited by R. Klibansky and H. J. Paton (New York: Harper & Row, Publishers; Harper Torchbooks, 1963; original edition 1936), pp. 1-10, particularly p. 9. Huizinga's actual definition runs as follows: "History is the intellectual form in which a civilization renders account to itself of its past," p. 9. This reference to Huizinga is found in Lonergan's essay, "The Philosophy of History," pp. 3-4. But Lonergan does not introduce Huizinga and "relativism" as a type of "upper blade." He discusses relativism as a trend in "technical history" whereas the scissors analogy only comes in with an "explanatory history" which tries to fill in the gaps between historical moments. However, my point here is that even in technical history there are operative, spontaneously, anticipations about the shape and structure of the explanan-

dum, the "history that is written about." I do not think that this point, or my discussion of Huizinga in a context quite distinct from that found in Lonergan's essay, stand contradicted by Lonergan's treatment in his essay or in *Method*.
16   Huizinga, pp. 5-7.
17   William Dray, *Laws and Explanation in History* (London: Oxford University Press, 1957).
18   Hempel distinguishes "deductive-nomological" from "probabilistic-statistical" covering laws; see "Reasons and Covering Laws in Historical Explanation," in *The Philosophy of History*, ed. Patrick Gardiner (Oxford: Oxford University Press, 1974), pp. 90-92.
19   Dray, pp. 1-3. Carl Hempel published a response to Dray's criticisms in his article "Reason and Covering Laws in Historical Explanation."
20   Dray, pp. 44, 47.
21   Ibid., pp. 110, 135, 154.
22   Ibid., p. 135.
23   W. B. Gallie, *Philosophy and the Historical Understanding* (London: Chatto & Windus, 1964).
24   Ibid., pp. 30-43, 102, 125.
25   Ibid., pp. 23-28, 45-49, 71, 105.
26   Hayden White, *Metahistory: The Historical Imagination in Nineteenth-Century Europe* (Baltimore: The Johns Hopkins University Press, 1975).
27   Ibid., pp. ix-xi, 7-9 , 29ff.
28   Ibid., pp. xi-xii, 12-19, 23-29.
29   Ibid., p. xii. This is, by no means, a complete introduction to White's work. He distinguishes chronicle, story, mode of emplotment, mode of argument, mode of ideological implication. He discusses story along lines similar to Gallie. He draws on Northrop Frye for his four modes of emplotment: satire, romance, comedy, tragedy. He introduces mode of argument along the lines of Hempel's covering law model but then presents four explanatory paradigms drawn from Stephen Pepper: formist, organicist, mechanist and contextualist. He discusses ideology under four categories drawn from K. Mannheim: anarchism, conservatism, radicalism and liberalism. He proceeds to integrate all of these sets with the four types of literary styles: metaphor, metonymy, synechdoche, and irony. The bulk of the book is then devoted to analysing the speculative philosophers of history and the historiographers of nineteenth-century Europe in an effort to argue that all were operating with an implicit or explicit philosophy of history of the speculative kind.
30   Huizinga, p. 10.
31   Ibid., p. 9.
32   Ibid., p. 8.
33   Ibid., pp. 7, 8.
34   Ibid., p. 7.
35   Ibid., pp. 9, 10.
36   Ibid., p. 10. The reader may detect an implicit contradiction here in Huizinga.
37   Ibid., p. 10.
38   Hempel, p. 90.
39   Ibid., pp. 90-91. Hempel's appeal to probabilities differs significantly from that of Lonergan, see 6.3 below. Hempel applies f-probabilities to estimate the "likelihood" of individual cases. See chapter three, 3.5 above, for this specific meaning of "likelihood."
40   See C. G. Hempel, "The Function of General Laws in History," *The Journal of Philosophy* 39 (1942): 36-38, 40-41.
41   See ibid., pp. 38, 40-41, 44, 47-48.
42   Ibid., pp. 46-48.
43   Ibid., pp. 42, 43-44.

44  This comes out most strongly in Hempel's response to Dray's explanation by appeal to rational reasons, see "Reasons and Covering Laws," pp. 98-105.
45  Dray, p. 44.
46  Ibid., p. 39.
47  Ibid., chap. 5.
48  See ibid., pp. 104, 110.
49  See ibid., pp. 135, 154.
50  See ibid., pp. 110, 164.
51  Gallie, pp. 94-101.
52  Ibid., pp. 125, 155-161.
53  White, pp. ix-xii.
54  Ibid., pp. xi, 29.
55  Ibid., pp. xi-xii.
56  White's cognitional theory and its basis in the work of Kant are made explicit in Peter Munz, *The Shapes of Time: A New Look at the Philosophy of History* (Middletown, Conn.: Wesleyan University Press, 1977), particularly pp. 13-21.
57  Michael Ermarth, *Wilhelm Dilthey: The Critique of Historical Reason* (Chigago: University of Chicago Press, 1978).
58  Ibid., pp. 15-19.
59  Ibid., pp. 93-97.
60  Ibid., p. 250.
61  Ibid., p. 97.
62  Ibid., pp. 142-149.
63  Ibid., pp. 157-8, 245.
64  Ibid., pp. 266-271.
65  Ibid. pp. 245, 265-271.
66  Ibid., pp. 249, 256-7, 266, 271, 274, 276, 285.
67  Ibid., pp. 245ff.
68  Matthew Lamb summarizes Dilthey's contributions in four points. First, Dilthey understood that what constitutes history is human acts of meaning, the operations of human subjects who are present to themselves as acting subjects. Second, human cognitional acts are "openly and dynamically patterned in structurally recurrent and related functions or operations." Third, the world of history is the interaction among many instances of human interiority and so "any historical objectification is the expression of that interiority, and as such is understandable." Fourth, there therefore stands a possibility of integrating all systems and contexts of human activity in terms of a growing and ever-refining account of the structures and operations of acts of interiority. See Lamb, *History, Method and Theology*, p. 352. But Lamb also sees some serious problems in Dilthey's work. Dilthey's cognitional theory was based, finally on the work of Kant. And just as Kant severed the correspondence relationship between the content of acts of cognition and the objects intended by such acts in the natural sciences, so too with Dilthey, historical knowledge was never self-transcending, never oriented towards an object that might not be the work of another's mind. All historical knowledge had to be understood in terms of worldviews and the ongoing march of worldviews finally collapsed into historicism, see ibid., pp. 353-356.
69  Lonergan, "The Philosophy of History," pp. 4-6. The point here is not that contemporary philosophers of science have a complete and acceptable *account* of the operations of cognition as they are performed in scientific explanation but that the experimental and explanatory procedures can be learned by a scientist and their essential performative elements identified in textbooks.
70  It is relevant to note here that Lonergan distinguishes between "occasional history," "technical history," and "explanatory history." This last "explanatory history" is not a history of historiography but a history of humanity. And so what is explained is the

genesis of the current historical situation. The difference between "technical history" and "explanatory history" is a difference like that between individual events and the flow of events in a continuum. "Explanatory history" seeks to grasp the interrelations among the events, the dynamic course of events, the overarching movement of "what was going forward" in society, in civilizations. Consequently the "upper blade" appropriate to such an "explanatory history" would be rooted in an account of contemporary human, social, economic, political, psychological activity. Like Dilthey, Lonergan argues that what is distinctively human about all of this activity is that its constitutive elements are meaning. See ibid., pp. 4-7, 10-11. See also note 14 above, this chapter.

71  Ibid., p. 11.
72  Potential problems in this view are treated in 6.4 below.
73  See ibid., pp. 9-14. See also *Method*, pp. 225ff.
74  See *Method*, pp. 187, 214-233.
75  See ibid., pp. 187-196, 217, 231-233.
76  Ibid., pp. 226, 230.
77  Ibid., pp. 179-180, 219, 229-230.
78  See 4.4. above.
79  See *Method*, p. 226. Even more significantly, in *Method*, Lonergan emphasizes the historian's own self-knowledge and his or her "conversions" as the conditions for such a grasp; see pp. 217-218.
80  See ibid., p. 225-233.
81  Lonergan discusses the import of "sub-conscious" psychic phenomenon on acts of meaning in a brief note on Freud in *Insight*, pp. 203-206. The context for his discussion is not an analysis of the structure of history, but his discussion is nonetheless relevant. See also *Insight*, p. 622.
82  Lamb, *History, Method and Theology*, p. 354. See also *Method*, pp. 178-180.
83  This objection to conceiving history in terms of originating acts of meaning clearly can be associated with the name of Marx. A more detailed discussion of Marx is found in the seventh chapter, 7.5 below, and so this brief discussion will not treat Marx's work directly. For the present purposes, see *Insight*, pp. 251, 622ff.
84  In his "Philosophy of History" lecture, Lonergan has a very interesting note on "dialectic" that is relevant here. Each of the three "objections" introduced here is a "counterposition" which, if worked out fully in all of its implications, becomes a "position," see pp. 11-12. It is in this spirit or working the objections into "positions" that they will be treated here.
85  *Insight*, p. 217.
86  Anyone who has examined the art works of M. C. Escher has witnessed a dramatic example of these two principles operative in acts of seeing. See M. C. Escher and J. L. Locher, *The World of M. C. Escher* (New York: Harry N. Abrams, 1971). Similarly anyone who changes the lenses in their eyeglasses or who mistakenly puts on another's glasses finds the tension between these two principles painfully obvious.
87  *Insight*, pp. 217, 189-191.
88  Lonergan cites the work of Wilhelm Stekel as an example, ibid., pp. 200-203.
89  Ibid., pp. 191-199.
90  See ibid., pp. 217, 189-191.
91  See 4.6 above, and 6.5 and 6.6 below.
92  See particularly 7.2 below.
93  See *Insight*, pp. 622ff.
94  Ibid., pp. 205-206.
95  See 5.6 above.
96  An objection similar to this has been raised against Collingwood's account of historical action as rational or reasonable. See W. H. Dray, *Philosophy of History* (Englewood Cliffs, N. J.: Prentice-Hall Inc., 1964), pp. 10-13.

97  *Insight*, pp. 212-213.
98  *Method*, p. 57.
99  Ibid., pp. 57-61. I would suggest that this intersubjective spontaneity is what Gibson Winter calls the prior "we," the prior relatedness, the "We-relation" that precedes the communicative process; see *Elements*, pp. 93 ff. Most simply, this relatedness is rooted in the fact that many recurrence schemes are not confined to the "inside" or the "outside" of an organism but are constituted by circular chains or clusters of events which cycle materials or "in-formation" from the "exterior" environment of the organism to its "interior" environment and back again. See *Randomness*, pp. 220ff, and *Wealth of Self*, pp. 39-46.
100  See *Elements*, pp. 14-33, particularly pp. 23-33. See also the first pages of the "Introduction," chapter one above.
101  See ibid., pp. 19-22, 99-109.
102  Ibid., pp. 14ff, 23ff, 32.
103  Ibid., pp. 14-33, particularly 19-22.
104  Ibid., pp. 23-33, 99-100.
105  Ibid., pp. 99-104.
106  Ibid., pp. 99-109.
107  There is some evidence that Lonergan noted this recurrence scheme structure in Winter's reconstruction of Mead. See *Method*, pp. 256, 357 and note that the structure of his account and his terminology are remarkably similar to his account of "skills" in *Method*, pp. 27-30. See also 5.1 above.
108  See *Elements*, p. 105. "This analysis of the 'We-relation' involves two dimensions – 'impulse to confirmation of being' and 'impulse to meaning' – which can be separated only analytically."
109  I would suggest that some recent work of Jürgen Habermas focuses on the range of conditions necessary for the proper operation of this intersubjective scheme of gesture and response. See "What is Universal Pragmatics?" in *Communication and the Evolution of Society*, translated by Thomas McCarthy (Boston: Beacon Press, 1979), pp. 65ff. "Institutionally unbound speech acts owe their illocutionary force to a cluster of validity claims that speakers and hearers have to raise and recognize as justified if grammatical (and thus comprehensible) sentences are to be employed in such a way as to result in successful communication. A participant in communication acts with an orientation to reaching understanding only under the condition that, in employing comprehensible sentences in his speech acts, he raises three validity claims in an acceptable way." These claims are to the "truth" of propositions, to the "appropriateness" of norms or values, and to the "truthfulness" of the subject's intentions, pp. 65-6.
110  See chapter five, 5.1 and 5.2 above.
111  *Elements*, p. 105.
112  Lonergan discusses this dialectic under the subtitles "Intersubjectivity and Social Order," "The Tension of Community," and "The Dialectic of Community," in *Insight*, pp. 211-218. In his analysis of the dialectical structure in which the two principles of human intersubjectivity and practical common sense are at once linked and opposed, Lonergan gives the impression that by human intersubjectivity he means simply feelings that need to be curbed by intelligence. "The two principles are linked, for the spontaneous, intersubjective individual strives to understand and wants to behave intelligently; and inversely, intelligence would have nothing to put in order were there not the desires and fears, labours and satisfactions of individuals," pp. 217-218. But in his discussion of intersubjectivity, Lonergan makes it clear that he is referring here to "a sense of belonging together [which] provides the dynamic premise for common enterprise, for mutual aid and succour, for the sympathy that augments joys and divides sorrows," p. 212. If there is a fault to Lonergan's presentation, I would argue that it is his disproportionate emphasis upon the principle of intelligence in each dialectic and his tendency

to play down the exigence toward appropriate integration in the lower order manifold. See also 7.2 below.
113 See *Insight*, pp. 212-214.
114 Ibid., pp. 217-218.
115 Ibid., p. 214.
116 On the "good of order," see also 7.1 below, and ibid., pp. 213-214. See also *Method*, pp. 49ff.
117 See *Insight*, pp. 212-214. On "group bias," see 7.4 below, and *Insight*, pp. 222-225.
118 A perfect example here would be the international economy.
119 The specific meanings of the terms "progress" and "decline" are discussed in 6.5 and 6.6 below. See also 7.6 below.
120 This urgency is reflected clearly in Lonergan's accounts of the "General Bias" and its "longer cycle of decline," in *Insight*, pp. 225-242. This is treated in chapter seven, 7.6 and 7.7 below.
121 See 7.5 below.
122 In an odd little comment that would seem to be directed towards the thought of Marx, Lonergan discusses the relationship between the dialectic of community and the individual dialectic of the subject. "Accordingly, one might say that a single dialectic of community is related to a manifold of individual sets of neural demand functions through a manifold of individual dialectics. In this relationship, the dialectic of community holds the dominant position, for it gives rise to the situations that stimulate neural demands and it moulds the orientation of intelligence that preconsciously exercises the censorship," *Insight*, p. 218. I would suggest that Lonergan is giving a qualified assent here to a specific way of understanding the priority of "base" to social, cultural "superstructure." For more on this, see 7.3, 7.4, 7.5 below.
123 See *Insight*, p. 218.
124 For more on this, see Alasdair MacIntyre, *After Virtue*.
125 See chapter two, 2.1 above.
126 Yovel, *Kant and the Philosophy of History*, p. 13. See also pp. 15, 18.
127 Immanuel Kant, *Groundwork of the Metaphysic of Morals*, pp. 61-62.
128 See Justus Hartnack, *Kant's Theory of Knowledge*, pp. 12-14.
129 George Armstrong Kelly, *Idealism, Politics and History: Sources of Hegelian Thought* (Cambridge: Cambridge University Press, 1969), pp. 15-16.
130 Charles Taylor, *Hegel and Modern Society* (Cambridge: Cambridge University Press, 1979), pp. 3-5.
131 This is the question addressed in the first seven theses in the "Idea of a Universal History from a Cosmopolitan Point of View," in *On History*, pp. 12-20. It is also the central question throughout "Conjectural Beginnings of Human History," in *On History*, pp. 53-68. See Despland, pp. 21ff, 30ff.
132 On this second question, see Despland, pp. 42-51.
133 A glance through the index of *Insight* reveals the impact of these influences.
134 See chapter five above.
135 *Insight*, p. 603.
136 See *Insight*, pp. xiv, 231, 234, 303-304, 392-393, 603.
137 See 6.4 above.
138 *Insight*, pp. 451-458.
139 Ibid., p. 454.
140 ibid., p. 451.
141 Ibid., p. 596.
142 Ibid., p. 451.
143 See 6.4.1 and 6.4.2 above. See also 7.2, 7.4 below.
144 *Insight*, p. 451.
145 Ibid., p. 452.

146  See 5.5 above.
147  See 5.1 above.
148  See *Insight*, p. 603; *Method*, p. 53.
149  A "terminal value" is an object for possible choice, see *Insight*, p. 601.
150  See *Insight*, pp. 603-604 and the discussion that follows.
151  *Method*, pp. 53ff.
152  On the conversions, see *Method*, pp. 237-244. See also Lonergan, *"Reality, Myth, Symbol,"* pp. 34-37.
153  *Insight*, p. 604.
154  *Insight*, pp. 387-390, 624-625; see also *Method*, pp. 251-254.
155  Ibid., pp. 599-600.
156  Ibid., pp. 191-206. See also 6.4.1 above, and 7.2, 7.4, 7.6 below.
157  Ibid., p. 601.
158  Ibid.

# Chapter 7

# History, Ethics and Emergent Probability II

## 7.0 Introduction

In the seventh chapter of *Insight* Lonergan enters into a conversation with Hobbes, Kant, Hegel, Marx, with proponents of the liberal thesis of automatic progress and, generally, with the entire field that has been called the speculative philosophy of history. His goal, like theirs, is to identify the structural elements and processes on which to build a theory of society and history and with which to chart general, overall patterns of historical change. Lonergan's style in writing does not begin by reconstructing the history of the theories and insights of the authors with whom he is conversing. And so it is often difficult to understand why he raises and answers the questions that he does. Sometimes in a summary or a passing reference Lonergan leaves a clue indicating the name of a thinker with whom his conclusions are allied.[1] Other times he summarizes a position with which his findings can be contrasted.[2] Generally, though, Lonergan's approach is to raise the circle of questions that frame the limits of his topic and to isolate the terms and relations that define implicitly the central insights.[3]

A number of excellent collections or summary reviews have been edited or written on the contributions of the great speculative philosophers of history.[4] And so no attempt will be made here to summarize these contributions. There are, however, at least two particular sets of theories that seem to have been decisive in influencing the way in which Lonergan framed his questions on history and its relationship to individual morality. The first of these finds its expression in the work of Thomas Hobbes, the second in that of Karl Marx. There is some evidence in *Insight* that Lonergan developed his notion of the good of order in response to Hobbes and his notions of the group bias, general bias and the shorter and longer cycles of decline in response to Marx. And so in an effort to introduce Lonergan's application of the general heuristic, emergent probability, to an analysis of the dynamic structure of society and history, I will proceed by comparing and contrasting Lonergan's insights with some of those of Hobbes and Marx. As was my procedure earlier, I will not enter into debate with interpreters of Hobbes and Marx but will draw from some recognized exponents of their works in an effort to clarify the work of Lonergan.

The relationship between individual morality and the overarching course of history has been a central issue throughout the course of debates in the speculative philosophy of history. Lonergan's work has been criticized in this regard for placing too much emphasis on the import of individual intelligence and responsibility.[5] Whereas Marx's work has focused on the economic structures as a condition limiting the individual's intelligent and responsible acts Lonergan has been criticized for disregarding such conditions. This criticism has been met, in part.[6] But in the discussion of individual and group bias it should become clear that Lonergan recognizes the import of Marx's intent and, indeed, concludes with a somewhat more pessimistic analysis of the current situation than Marx himself would have envisioned.

## 7.1 The Good of Order and Social Structure: Lonergan and Hobbes

In the thirteenth chapter of *Leviathan*, part one, Thomas Hobbes begins his consideration of the social state of man.[7] On his own man could achieve some limited success in securing the objects of his desire, in securing his own happiness or "felicity." But placed in the permanent and inescapable company of other men who are all equally matched in skill, intelligence and strength, the pursuit of the objects of desire becomes a permanent state of competition for the same things. Thus, social life is the permanent state of struggle or war among equally matched opponents for the same, scarce objects of desire. To achieve any worthwhile goal is simply an invitation for someone to come and take it away. And since worth is a comparative term men need not even want the same things for them to stand in conflict. For whatever their possessions, their relative superiority or inferiority in their respective states of felicity will always be an object of competition.[8] Thus, in the words of Michael Oakeshott:

> There is a radical conflict between the nature of man and the natural condition of mankind; what the one urges with hope of achievement, the other makes impossible.[9]

Man's deliverance from this permanent state of all out war rests in his fear of death. And so out of fear men are willing to transfer the right to the exercise of their own free will, in specific matters, to a third party, the "Commonwealth," who will exercise this right on their behalf and who will enforce each man's commitment to his contracted restrictions. Hobbes thus conceives social order as the necessary constraint upon each individual's free pursuit of his or her own desires, in the interest of securing the basic conditions for any pursuit of personal happiness.[10]

The power of Hobbes' theory of social order has been immeasurable. His conception of society as a constraint upon the individual's exercise of his natural rights and freedoms has prevailed in a line of social and political theory that continues to this day.[11] In the view of C. B. Macpherson, Hobbes' theory of political obligation is rooted in an implicit social theory of a possessive market society.[12] And in Macpherson's view, the historical conditions for such a possessive market society were, in fact, met between the seventeenth century and the mid-nineteenth century.[13] The individual in this society is seen as "the proprietor of his own person or capacities, owing nothing to society for them," as sole owner of himself, as part of no larger social whole, as one whose freedom consists in independence from the wills of others.

> Society consists of relations of exchange between proprietors. Political society becomes a calculated device for the protection of this property and for the maintenance of an orderly relation of exchange.[14]

In response to the various theories about the meaning of Hobbes' use of the term "nature of man" Macpherson argues that what Hobbes was doing was describing the behavior of men in a particular type of society.[15] He draws out explicitly some of the elements of this type of society and contrasts it with two other types of society in an effort to argue that Hobbes' political theory remains untenable in a historical age where the conditions of the possessive market society no longer prevail.[16]

Macpherson's brief account serves to highlight the essential elements of Hobbes' social and political theory. Man is essentially and perpetually in conflict or competition with his or her fellow man, and capable of securing the minimum conditions for commodious living only through the transfer of personal rights to an all powerful sovereign.[17] In his "Introduction" to the Penguin edition of *Leviathan*, Macpherson calls Hobbes the "analyst of power and peace." For more than any other his concern was dominated by the fear of civil war and the control of power which could secure some lasting relief from its hideous threat.[18] But in contrasting some of the characteristics of the possessive market society with two alternatives, Macpherson indirectly draws attention to some more basic characteristics of the structure of societies in general. If Macpherson is correct, then concurrent with the competition of man against man, there is operative an intricate set of relations of exchange and cooperation in Hobbes' marketplace. And I would suggest that Lonergan's intent in his notion of the "good of order" is captured in his description of this possessive market model.

> Without any authoritative allocation of work or rewards, the market, responding to countless individual decisions, puts a price on everything, and it is with reference to prices that the individual decisions are made. The market is the mechanism through which prices are made by, and are a determining factor in making, individual decisions about the disposal of energies and the choice of utilities.
>
> Exchange of commodities through the price-making mechanism of the market permeates the relations between individuals, for in this market all possessions, including men's energies, are commodities. In the fundamental matter of getting a living, all individuals are essentially related to each other as possessors of marketable commodities,

including their own powers. All must continually offer commodities (in the broadest sense) in the market, in competition with others.[19]

While the operation of the possessive market society involves the alienation and exchange of the individual's right and capacity to labour in a competitive framework of relations, such competition is not the essential characteristic of societies, but a distinctive characteristic of this particular type of society in a more basic system of *cooperative* relations. The exchange relations which trade goods for goods or goods for money, the system of expectations in which prices are fixed in accordance with supplies, demands and the negotiating skills of participants, the divisions of labour, the cultivation of skills, the dates, locations, physical layouts of the marketplaces, all the essential routines whose functioning constitutes the market structure, are more or less tacit, cooperative schemes involving wide-scale agreement among members of a society. In drawing attention to the social model upon which Hobbes allegedly drew, Macpherson has set the stage for a more comprehensive account of the elements of social and political structure. I would suggest that Lonergan's account of "the good of order" was cast as a response to a narrower view, like that of Hobbes', which conceived the struggle for power as the central, defining foundation for an analysis of social and political structure.

In chapter seven of *Insight*, Lonergan develops a complementary account of the structure of social processes that aims at righting a distortion in this view of society. Society certainly operates as a constraint upon individuals, as a constraining condition into which individuals are born and raised, as an imposition upon the individual's exercise of freedom, and as a contracted compromise that seeks to secure the minimum conditions for public order. But society is also collaboration in the achievement of ends that none could secure on his or her own. And it is to this dimension of social order that Lonergan turns in his account of the "good of order."

In the terms of the last chapter's presentation of Gibson Winter's threefold structure of sociality, intersubjective exchange proceeds in three stages: with the gesture, the response and the drive to unification.[20] The unification that is sought between two subjects is on two levels: on the level of the truth or the value in the meaning intended by the gesture and on the level of mutual confirmation of the two subjects as subjects. The structure of the drive towards unification is dialectical. The two principles of the dialectic are the two drives of the subjects towards intelligent grasp, reasonable affirmation and responsible decision on the content of the gesture and the response, and towards mutuality in personal expression and confirmation. In the primitive, intersubjective community the bonds that unite the members of the family or tribe as the foundation for interpersonal exchange, are not the products of acts of intelligence, but they precede such acts as a condition for their occurrence. And so in the dialectic of gesture and response it is the spontaneously apprehended drive toward mutual respect and approval with, for example, a mother or father, that tends to prevail as the operator in the drive towards unification.

But as acts of practical intelligence begin to yield more and more palpable success in securing advantages in living, the immanent criteria of intelligence are given more and more sway in the dialectic of social exchange. The authority of social relations and roles begins to give way to the authority of practical success when the fruits of such success begin to be felt in war, in hunting and in agriculture. And when experiments in the division of labour begin to produce craftsmen who can devote their total time to the pursuit of their craft, their achievements become cumulative. Children learn the skills of their fathers and mothers and carry the development of those skills forward with their own innovation. Gradually the community realizes that it is worthwhile to provide such craftsmen with the food, clothing and shelter they require to pursue their craft. For the fruits of their labour increase the gross product of the whole community. Thus the dialectical drive towards unification among subjects begins to demand the demonstrations of practical intelligence to complement and to found the roles and the authority of intersubjective spontaneity. With this trend there begins to emerge a new notion of "the good" in which the talents, roles, and contributions of each are measured not in terms of some antecedent image or tradition of social order but in terms of their practically demonstrable contributions to the good of all. The undeniable success of practical intelligence becomes an operative principle in the dialectical drive towards the unification among subjects. And mutual respect and admiration becomes respect for competence and admiration for socially valuable skill.[21]

Once again, it must be emphasized that Lonergan recognizes the truth in Hobbes' claim.[22] Society is not all cooperation and collaboration. It is also constraint and coercion. But while Hobbes' principle datum was the fact of competition for scarce goods, Lonergan's central datum was the fact of collaboration towards hitherto unknown goods.[23] Social process is not entirely the one or the other. And so an account based solely on the one or the other will lead to a distortion in one's understanding of society. Furthermore it will lead to a distortion in one's direction of society, for an account of the structure of a social process will constitute a foundation for a science of the direction of social process, for a political theory.[24]

What Hobbes understood and expressed well in his *Leviathan* was the spontaneous orientation of the subject to pursue his or her own individual desires and the negative, constraining aspect of the dialectical tension that ensures between this individual pursuit and the intelligently emergent common good. Hobbes conceived the spontaneous pursuit of individual felicity to be the "natural" state of man. But Lonergan recognizes Hobbes' own passionate concern for the good or order to be no unnatural accomplishment. And Hobbes' achievement was a responsible act in which Hobbes transcended his own vital desires and fears. Consequently Lonergan's method of proceeding begins by taking Hobbes' own drive towards the practical realization of value as an equally "natural" state of man and then accounting for the human phenomena that Hobbes describes in these chapters of *Leviathan*, part one, as an earlier stage in an ongoing personal and/or social development or as one or another form of "bias."

## 7.2 Individual Bias

Lonergan calls individual bias the distortion in the development of an individual's intelligence and the consequently ensuing distortion in his or her whole affective and experiential orientation which results from the refusal to choose the good of order over the individual's egoistically centered desires and fears.[25] Such egoism is not to be confused with the individual's desire for his or her own development in virtue, in wisdom and in ultimate happiness.[26] Rather, egoism is the exclusion of the immanent drive of intelligence to participate, dialectically, with the drive towards spontaneous, intersubjective unification in the pursuit of the common good.[27] It is the refusal to raise and to meet the further questions that arise in the design and execution of one's own projects. And such a refusal constitutes a circumscription of one's own horizons of concern and a limitation that one sets on the range of concerns to which one will open oneself. The intelligence is given free play within the boundaries set by personal desire. But beyond these confines practical intelligence is simply ruled out.[28]

The quest for the good of order was conceived as the dialectically structured drive towards the unification of two principles, the operative principle of intelligence and the principle of mutuality.[29] Consequently individual bias will manifest itself as contradicting both principles. As a deformation of intelligence, individual bias contradicts the drive of intelligence to raise and answer the relevant further questions. And as a violation of the demands of intersubjectivity, the individual bias suppresses the spontaneous concern for approval of and approval by others. In addition, since the spontaneous drive of intelligence actually involves its own dialectic operating between an exigence in the neural manifold and a drive to order that manifold, the bias will also constitute a distortion in the experiential orientation of the whole subject. Thus, when Lonergan calls individual bias or egoism "an interference of spontaneity with the development of intelligence," his presentation here is somewhat misleading.[30] It might seem, from this presentation, that knowing seeks an autonomy from the distorting influences of the other human passions, appetites, feelings and drives. And so in this view the individual bias would be another instance of the intrusion of "affectivity" into the proper exercise and development of autonomous rationality. But this view stands in contradiction to the thrust of my interpretation of Lonergan's account of the dialectical interaction of intelligence with experiential exigence, on the one hand, and with the principal of mutuality in the dialectic of community, on the other.[31]

What intelligence seeks to achieve is not a flight from experiential spontaneity or affectivity, rather, an integration of such affectivity. The neural manifold changes with changes in the subject's environment. And operations in "the basic pattern of experience" seem to order the neural manifold in accordance with a set of anticipations immanent in the question and in subjective spontaneity on the one hand, and with an intelligibility immanent in the environment manifesting itself as an exigence in the neural manifold, on the other. Thus the drive of intelligence involves the tension between two principles seeking resolution in the adequacy of an appropriate integration of a human person, in the context of a flexibly recurring scheme of acts. The individual bias, then, is not so much an intrusion of the biological or aesthetic, affective or intersubjective spontaneities into the proper development of intelligence, but the failure to integrate properly the demands of the neural and intersubjective exigence with the anticipations of a question, in a scheme of acts involving understanding, judgment or decision. The individual bias is, ultimately, an intelligent, responsible act that does violence to the demands of personal and intersubjective experience. And it does so by failing to carry out its own mandate.

If carried on long enough the refusal to raise and to answer the appropriate questions will result in distortions not only in the horizon within which intelligence operates but also in the experiential and intersubjective routines of the whole person. These experiential routines are the basis for the subject's practical interrelations with his or her environment. And so as they become more and more distorted the probabilities for adequate integration become lower and lower. Distorted experience becomes the foundation for distorted understanding and praxis and the bias sets the subject on an accelerating course of decline.

However, while individual bias is operative in society, the recurrent deformations that follow from operative "social structures" can in no way be attributed to the individual bias. For while individual bias occurs extremely frequently there are not recurrent patterns or trends associated with stable f-probabilities in identifiable classes of individual bias. And when such recurrent patterns and classes arise then the bias is no longer to be explained in terms of the refusal of the "good or order" but in terms of deformations in the operative notions of what would constitute such order and in how it is to be achieved. In his account of the dissolution of the possessive market structure in the nineteenth century, Macpherson notes that the development of class consciousness, political articulation, and a vision of alternate social and economic relations among the working class resulted in their becoming aware that the existing "order" was neither necessary nor in the service of their interests. Thus was lost their sense of equal participation in the marketplace. Furthermore with the universal franchise and the perpetuation of consciously operative class division, the general sense of cohesion, necessary for the functioning of the possessive market structure, was also lost.[32] This account illustrates well the fact that operative orders need to be known as in fact "good." Bias can be operative recurrently in classes to marshall power in the service of group interests which do not serve the wider common good. But as long as such is known to be the case (and evidence is never long in arising) the fact of order ceases to be the "good or order." Lonergan's account of the group bias shows that structural parallels exist between the individual bias and the group bias. But the difference lies in the fact of system operative in the genesis and maintenance of f-probably recurrent classes of deformations in notions of what constitutes the "good of order." And while power is an accelerator, power is not the central issue in this account.

## 7.3 The Practical Intelligence as Historical

In the twenty pages on "Group Bias" and "General Bias," Lonergan's emergent probability becomes a foundation for a theory of historical dynamics. In these pages the sketch of the structure of historical change which so far has remained heuristic and suggestive takes on some flesh. After discussing the two biases and their corresponding cycles of historical decline, Lonergan briefly sets his account in opposition to that of Marx.

> To ignore the fact of decline was the error of the old liberal views of automatic progress. The far more confusing error of Marx was to lump together both progress and the two principles of decline under the impressive name of dialectical materialism, to grasp that the minor principle of decline would correct itself more rapidly through class war, and then to leap gaily to the sweeping conclusion that class war would accelerate progress. What, in fact, was accelerated was major decline which in Russia and Germany leaped to fairly thorough brands of totalitarianism.[33]

This presentation is, without a doubt, not what one could call a sensitive analysis of Marx's thought. But in spite of its scathing dismissal of Marx's proposed solution for the reversal of historical decline, this passage betrays a profound concern for a solution to the problem to which Karl Marx was passionately dedicated.

Like Marx, Lonergan understands clearly the integral relationship between an account of human nature and a theory of social and historical process. It is certainly true that Lonergan conceives the performance of acts of intelligence and responsibility to be the constitutive elements of human nature as human. But there is evidence in *Insight* that Lonergan shares with Marx the view that the broad range of human life involves not so much the theoretical operation of intelligence in the intellectual pattern of experience but the practical application of common sense intelligence to the transformation of "material" conditions of society, culture and economy.

Common sense is practical. It seeks knowledge, not for the sake of the pleasure of contemplation, but to use knowledge in making and doing. Moreover, this making and doing involve a transformation of man and his environment, so that the common sense of a primitive culture is not the common sense of an urban civilization, nor the common sense of one civilization the common sense of another. However elaborate the experiments of the pure scientist, his goal is always to come closer to natural objects and natural relationships. But the practicality of common sense engenders and maintains enormous structures of technology, economics, politics, and culture, that not only separate man from nature but also add a series of new levels or dimensions in the network of human relationships.[34]

Man's most primitive as well as his most developed activities consist of the recurrent practice of applying human ingenuity and effort to the available materials of life and converting these materials to the satisfaction of physical needs and of culturally and economically created desires, appetites and values. Such activity not only transforms the conditions of life. It also creates such conditions so that in time the environment in which men and women live and work is constituted predominantly by the fruits of previous acts of intelligent "production."[35] Thus, Lonergan conceives the practical operation of intelligence in its "labour" or "production" to be the motive power of history has human.[36]

Lonergan also recognizes that what is most significant for a proper study of human nature and history is the concrete, historical performance of the acts of practical intelligence by human subjects. Ideas are not begotten by ideas, but by human subjects developing and executing cognitional and cognitially-mediated skills in concrete contexts of historical materials and conditions. Lonergan has sought to understand the structure of the schemes of acts wherein such ideas and such practical activities are born. Marx, on the other hand, has focussed most predominantly upon the historical and economic conditions surrounding the performance of specific classes of such acts. And, as will be discussed in greater detail below, this difference in orientation is a significant element in the differences between Marx's and Lonergan's accounts of history and the human prospects. But the two thinkers share a profound appreciation for the concrete genesis of acts of practical intelligence.

The constitutive elements of societies, in Lonergan's analysis, are "the pattern of relations of a social order."[37] The operative distinctions between modes or forms of labour, the fields of skills corresponding to such forms, the functional distinctions between productive sectors of an economy, the current classifications of income groups and the distinctions between functioning contributions to political process all constitute the terms and relations which define implicitly the operative routines of schemes of a society. And while such operative terms and relations are themselves the products of countless instances of the practical application of intelligence, the context of such conditions into which all of us are born and raised has the overwhelming effect of shaping and adapting human spontaneity in accordance with its own needs and exigences.

> In a school, a regiment, a factory, a trade, a profession, a prison, there develops an ethos that at once subtly and flexibly provides concrete premises and norms for practical decisions. For in human affairs the decisive factor is what one can expect of the other fellow. Such expectations rest on recognized codes of behaviour; they appeal to past performance, acquired habit, reputation; they attain a maximum of precision and reliability among those frequently brought together, engaged in similar work, guided by similar motives, sharing the same prosperity or adversity.[38]

As was discussed earlier, Lonergan's notion of intersubjectivity and his account of society and history as constituted by human acts of intelligence by no means implies that all insights are the genesis of novelty or that the pattern of insights constituting a social order is the product of one subject.[39] For the most part, the course of a person's development consists of his or her grasping the dominant meanings of the culture and actuating the currently accepted practical forms of labour and social comportment. And while every form of activity represents the fruit of some intelligent adaptation to the conditions of life or some ingenious solution to a practical problem, the complete set of practical insights and the consequent patterns of interactions among such operative insights is seldom, if ever, understood by any one person. Consequently the operative set of practical relations and routines which constitutes any society and any economy will remain, for the most part, operative implicitly, hidden from the understanding of its citizens, and a powerful determinant in shaping the ideas emerging in that milieu. In a very significant sense, then, Lonergan recognizes that the relations which structure a society and an economy operate to shape and adapt the sensitive spontaneity and the practical intelligence of that society in accordance with the smooth attainment of its own social and economic ends.[40]

The course of society and history, in Lonergan's analysis, proceeds as practical activity gives rise to new sets of conditions and problems and then seeks subsequently to adapt to these conditions and solve their problems. As was noted above, the possibility for social order rests in the fact that individuals will perform practical operations which link up with those of others to form flexible schemes yielding goods which otherwise could not have been achieved.[41] And it should be clear now that such schemes operate to condition the emergence of further insights and practices which perpetuate their smooth functioning. But the actuation of such events and schemes changes environmental conditions, and eventually there occurs a sufficiently great set of changes as to require an adaptation of the events and routines of the society and economy. At this point the tendency of the social whole to adapt new insights and practices in accordance with its sustenance and its perpetuation begins to operate as an obstacle to its own survival. For the sufficiently changed conditions no longer call for minor adaptations in the routines of the society. They call for major changes in its constitutive terms and relations.

## 7.4 Group Bias

In the above presentation of Lonergan's notion of intersubjectivity I suggested that two dialectics are operative immanently in the living out of man's nature as distinctively human. The first involves the tension between the exigence of the subject's experiential basis in the events and schemes of his or her neural manifold and the intelligent and responsible drive to integrate that manifold in acts of understanding, judgment, and most profoundly practical, moral activity. The second dialectic involves the tension between the first dialectic and the spontaneous drive to unification with other human subjects as subjects, in the mutuality of respect, care and love. The individual bias occurred when the human subject so circumscribed his or her horizon of personal desires and goals that the drive of intelligence and responsibility was stopped or cut short. In the face of an experiential exigence demanding further questions to be answered, a broadened sensitivity to more remote realms of experience and finally an expansion of that horizon within which intelligence functions, the spontaneous dynamism of intellect is laid to premature rest. The result of this failure of intelligence and responsibility is a reordering of the experiential manifold, a censorship of its exigencies and a repression of the relevant neural demands until they either forced their way back into conscious life or deformed the habitual operations of the subject.

When the social and economic routines that are constitutive of a society begin to meet changing conditions which demand substantial changes in their operative structures, there occurs a rising frequency of instances of bias in the intelligent, responsible operations of subjects. But unlike the individual bias this instance of bias is not merely the result of individuals restraining the mandate of intelligence in the interest of personal gain. Rather, the "group bias" results when the second dialectic, operative immanently in men and women, undergoes a recurrent distortion. And the drive towards mutuality with members of the social group takes precedence over the demands of practical intelligence and responsibility.

When changes in the environment of a society's operation begin to demand structural changes in the relations which constitute that society then the dominant groups in that society face the prospect of significant threats to their established gains and interests. Thus members of the group circumscribe their own horizons of interests as over against mounting evidence that such is not the more general good. And bias begins to operate.⁴² But because the interests which are defended by the dominant group are those of a class or group of people the drive towards solidarity within the group will begin to operate massively and effectively to preclude habitual attention to the defects in its horizons. Thus the conditions surrounding the wide-scale genesis of insights and responsible action that seek the good of the whole of society are precluded (i.e. regular experiential contact with the suffering of the marginalized, and the habitual raising of questions concerning the relevance of this experience to the restructuring of the whole society or economy). The intelligent and responsible acts of the group settle their accounts with the drive toward intersubjective mutuality within the group before consulting the exigence of the experiential data on the whole of society. And the common insights, values and expectations of the group operate spontaneously as a horizon within which intelligence meets the data of experience.⁴³

The fact that the dominant classes possess control results in their increased ability to mobilize insights that promote their own interests. Corresponding to this success is the failure of marginalized groups to make operative the acts and routines which would promote their own welfare.⁴⁴ Thus the course of social development

> ... does not correspond to any coherently developed set of practical ideas. It represents the fraction of practical ideas that were made operative by their conjunction with power.⁴⁵

The tension between the partial insights operatively constitutive of the social whole and the experiential exigence of the conditions of social and economic life which demand a restructuring of the social whole (a restructuring which would favour the whole of society and not simply the dominant groups) manifests itself in a tension between the dominant and the marginalized social groups and a visible distortion or aberration in the routines of social and economic life. This distortion eventually becomes great enough to be visible to all and the tensions between the groups begins to manifest itself in class unrest. This combination of evident distortion and class unrest becomes a principle for social and historical change that awaits the catalysis of an individual like Marx to be actuated.⁴⁶

Clearly Lonergan shares Marx's (and Hegel's) appreciation of the fact that history moves forward as the distortions of any age fuel the engines for their own reversal. But in Lonergan's view, an end to this cycle of domination cannot consist in a transformation of historical conditions. The historical cycle which results from the group bias and its tendency to effect its own reversal by mobilizing the neglected interest and insights of the marginalized is conceived by Lonergan to be an ongoing shorter cycle of alienation and short-lived liberation. Once the marginalized groups come to power their own attempts to structure the whole of society in accordance with the partial insights of their own perspective eventually suffer the same distortions due to the group bias for which their predecessors were ousted. The basis for this conviction, that the group bias is not to be overcome immanently, is rooted in Lonergan's basic conception of the problem operative in the group bias. And here he differs with Marx in his assessment of the form and the import of historical, economic conditions for acts of "production," and of the role of subjective agency in effecting historical change. And so in order to understand as precisely as possible the locus and the nature of these differences I will draw upon some reliable sources to summarize, very briefly, Marx's analysis of the human situation and its prospects for solution.

## 7.5 Marx and the Cycles of History

Clearly considerable debate reigns on Marx's intended meanings regarding such terms as "forces of production," "relations of production," "base," and "superstructure." And various authors understand such terms in their interrelations with other among Marx's terms and notions, in their attempts at explaining what Marx might have meant.[47] Consequently since more or less significant variations among such acts of understanding reign in current literature on Marx, my very brief presentation will necessarily involve some selection and a modest concern with general directions in current interpretations of his work.

At the centre of Marx's account of the problem in the current historical human situation stands his notion of "alienation."[48] The essentially human act is man's production of himself and his life through the act of labour. But the way in which this labour is carried out, and thus the way in which this labour functions to promote the workers' own well-being, is not set by the labourer him or herself but through historical processes. So if the conditions that shape and surround this act of labour have the effect of diminishing the worker's well-being, and if the social and economic relations specifying the mode of distribution of the fruits of his or her labour have a similar effect, then man's essential act of producing himself and his life is "alienated." This alienation is twofold. The worker encounters the fruits of production as an alienated force operating to diminish his interests. And the alienated act of production contradicts the essential goal of the fundamentally human act of self-production, and thus the worker is alienated from himself or herself. In a capitalist society the control, not only over the fruits of production, but also over the very act itself, is "made over" to another person. And so the very act of production becomes "objectified," made into an object of exchange, and subjected to the relations and forces of market exchange which specify the form of such exchange with more or less complete disregard for the intrinsic relationship of the work to the well-being of the worker.

In the view of William Shaw[49] the determining factor in setting the historically operative conditions for the current degree of alienation will be the reigning "productive forces." Such productive forces include the tools and means used in the production process, the objects produced, the means and elements of the transportation of such objects, the tools and buildings, the labour power itself with its operative forms and levels of knowledge and skill, the current scientific and technological achievements, and the degree and forms of cooperation among workers.[50] The productive forces not only specify the structure of the workplace and the forms of work, they also determine the relations among men and women, the social relationships, the relationships of ownership and control over the forces which shape the work forms and determine the distribution of its fruits.[51] The productive relations shape the forms and distributions of property and historically the productive relations have always resulted in class divisions with their corresponding points of view and ideologies.[52] Shaw's argument is that "the productive forces are the motive and determining factor in history,"[53] and that the advance and expansion of such forces is the central factor in transforming all other aspcts of man's dialectical engagement with his world.[54] In this way the conditions surrounding the exercise of labour, the productive forces and, derivatively, the relations of production, determine the ongoing shape of history as most essentially human. The history of humanity, thus, will be the history of the changes and developments in such productive forces.

The structure of this history is dialectical. And this dialectic involves the fact that every historical reality is at the same time a negation of possibilities which drives towards reversal. In the capitalist society this negation takes the form of alienated labour.

> Alienation has taken its most universal form in the institution of private property; amends will be made with the abolition of private property.[55]

In Nicholas Lash's view the concrete dialectic operative in industrial capitalism involves the fact that the class which controls the forces and relations of production does so in accordance with interests that are alien and oppressive to the worker. Thus the key to reversing the state of alienation involves finding a group or class whose interests coincide with the general interests. Lash notes that "there could only be such a class if it had, in fact, *no* 'particular' interest, nothing particular to defend, to cling on to." And in nineteenth century Europe this class was the industrial proletariat.[52]

The dynamism of history comes to a special, unique point with the emergence of the industrial proletariat. For with the arrival of a class "which has to bear all the burden of society without enjoying its advantages, which is ousted from society and forced into the sharpest contradiction to all other classes," the conditions are finally fulfilled for the reversal of the human history of alienation. With the capacities for social organization of a highly developed industrial society the possibility of bringing the conditions surrounding the exercise of labour under human control finally arises. In addition with the current industrial capacity the possibility of eliminating material need finally arises. And with the industrial proletariat there emerges a class whose complete impoverishment leaves it without any particular interests to defend. Thus for the first time in history the class interests of one group corresponds to the interests of all humanity. As the excesses of the ruling classes increase it simply becomes a matter of time before such excesses fuel the revolution of the proletariat. And when the workers' control over the conditions surrounding the exercise of their own labour is finally complete man will, for the first time in history, be able to live and work in accordance with his nature, free from domination, with the exercise of his labour operating in accordance with his own interests.[57] Such, at least, is the analysis of Nicholas Lash.[58]

William Shaw's analysis of the means for reversal of the condition of alienation downplays what he calls a "rather romantic attachment to the proletariat" in Marx's earlier works. In his view the engine for reversal is purely and simply the degree of conflict between the productive forces and the ownership relations, generating (derivatively) class conflict.[59] The proletariat is capable of redressing the condition of alienation because they and only they (historically) are

> motivated to implement the solution (namely, social control of production) that will provide economic stability, and [...] in a position to carry out such a resolution.[60]

However, Shaw is no less convinced that Marx envisaged this transformation to be complete, inevitable and permanent in its creation of a classless society.[61]

The import of Marx's anticipation of a complete transformation of history, through the transformation of control over the forces of production, cannot be underestimated. In a somewhat extreme,[62] but well argued view, Allen Buchanan provides evidence that in Marx's view the structure of economic and social relations (after the revolution) will be such that principles of justice for production and distribution will no longer be required.

> The superiority of this new mode of production will not lie in institutions by which society recognizes and protects each individual's claim to a share of control over production and, derivatively, to a share of the goods produced. Its superiority will consist, instead, in the fact that it is a form of social organization in which no one will find it necessary to press such claims, nor to rely upon an institutional apparatus to recognize and enforce them.[63]

While the implications of Buchanan's account of the link beween currently operative notions of justice and rights and the structure of *essentially competitive* economic and social systems are extremely provocative,[64] my point here is to illustrate the degree to which Marx's thought emphasizes the dependence of social, economic routines on the conditions surrounding their exercise. With the transformation of these conditions the central problem of the human condition, alienated labour, will disappear. In the words of John Plamenatz:

> Marx says very little about the communist society of the future, but he does say enough to make it clear that it will have a managed economy in a sense in which not even the most custom-bound of preindustrial societies has one. It will regulate production so as to ensure that men and women are free, that human capacities are fully developed, and human needs fully satisfied.[65]

It is at this point that we are in a position to highlight what I would argue are the central and essential differences between Lonergan's account of the human situation and that of Marx. Marx recognized that the conditions surrounding the acts of production of any age are the result of a dialectical interplay between the acts of production of the previous age and the negations in social life which the effects of such acts generate. While Marx urged men and women to assume responsibility for history, his explanation of the determinants of this history placed no emphasis upon the degree to which subjective agency authors these determinants. For his account focuses almost exclusively, and certainly in the main, upon such determinants as shaped in a dialectic whose locus of operation is extrinsic to the human subject. Lonergan's account of the group bias, the dialectic of community, and the shorter cycle of decline seeks to understand the human exercise of practical responsibility as conditioned, significantly, by dialectically operating determinants. But in his account the *locus* of the operation of such historical determinants and dialectics is immanent to the human subject, historically effective as a shift in f-probabilities associated with the recurring acts of practical intelligence which mediate the schemes of society, history and economy. Because the relationship between the emergent integrations of practical skills and the experiential manifolds of subjects is not purely systematic, but a relationship of an f-probable emergence, the operation of the group bias will not be completely decisive. Rather, there remains room for some measure of human agency. The subject's experiential manifold is irreducibly social, and historical, as are the schemes in which his or her integrations participate as mediating events. And so the incremental measure of the subject's exercise of this responsible agency will constitute the significant agency for systematic historical change towards progress. All other dialectical changes in the long run will be non-systematic.

As a result of Lonergan's conception of the historical role of subjective agency, the "problem" in the human condition is only derivatively a matter of conditions surrounding the exercise of practical responsibility. Principally the issue is the distinction between authentic (competent) and inauthentic (incompetent) performance. And the issue of conditions arises in the context of asking how to increase the f-probabilities associated with conversions from inauthentic to authentic performance. Like Marx,

Lonergan's approach accommodates and demands attention to the schemes of economy, society, and polity which shape human spontaneity, and increase or decrease the f-probabilities associated with humanly transformative emergence. But in Lonergan's view if this order of priority is inverted, the subject is obliterated.

Marx looked forward to a final resolution to the essential problem in the human condition, operative on the level of the problem, as an end to the possibility of human misery. Lonergan anticipates no such resolution. For in his view the acceleration of the shorter cycle only exacerbates a greater and more fundamental problem in the human situation, the general bias. But before proceeding to a discussion of the general bias a few points could be made more precisely in response to a published critique of Lonergan which appeals to a modification in Marxist theory.

In his article "Beyond Lonergan's Method," Fergus Kerr suggests that Lonergan fails to deal with the fact that theological ideas do not come out of a vacuum but are rooted in a believing community with its modes and structures of activities and relations. The history of Christian theology has been immersed in a milieu of class conflicts and this has perennially affected theology. Kerr suggests that we must come to terms with this class struggle explicitly in our theology. And his suggestion is that a proposal for doing theology that prescinds from any reference to this class struggle must be flawed essentially.[66] I think we can respond to Kerr with three important points that re-emphasize Lonergan's essential difference from Marx.

(1) Kerr draws upon Wittgenstein to contrast solving philosophical issues "by the intervention of a man of genius," with changing social order.[67] I will take the liberty of understanding Kerr to mean that the focussed attention on the concrete social conditions surrounding the genesis of theological and philosophical ideas would better serve the cause of humanization than a concern for personally understanding and developing cognitional and responsible skills. Fundamentally, the question boils down to whether the significant problems and routines of human life are or are not concrete in their particularities. If they are, and Lonergan would insist that they are (but we need not defer to Lonergan's advice, for the evidence is available), then the ongoing flow of solutions to such problems will require some element of personally developed cognitional and responsible skills for their concrete resolution. If there is a systematic blockage operative in society, preventing or distorting this development, then this blockage will require attention in the form of social analysis and social transformation. But the route towards this analysis and transformation requires a theoretical analysis of the nature of the problem and the route towards its solution. And if this theoretical analysis does not admit that the problem is a blockage or a distortion in the development and the exercise of cognitional and responsible skills, then the problem will most probably be exacerbated. I would suggest that this insistence upon the concrete character of the elements

of daily life animated Lonergan's concern with the significance of human agency and human interiority.

(2) An attention to class struggle is mediated by a theoretical analysis of the elements and structure of class differentiation and class struggle. To the extent that this theoretical analysis is correct, its implementation in a concrete study of historical conditions will yield an understanding and a set of possible solutions. Lonergan has contributed to such an analysis and an account based on his work differs from that of Marx in that it recognizes the operation of two distinct dialectics whose locus of operation is immanent to a human subject who is inextricably locked into a huge number of intersubjective, social, biological, historical schemes. Because these dialectics are operative immanently, the norms for their f-probable resolution are likewise immanent. And so attention to social conditions becomes attention to conditions for increasing the f-probabilities of conversions. There is no question that Lonergan was concerned with the f-probabilities of conversions.[68] And I would suggest that a dialectical analysis of the contemporary enterprise of theology, with attention to the intersubjective conditions for the conversions is urgently needed.

(3) The question of how we are to attend to the class struggles which set the context for our doing philosophy and theology raises the very important problem of expectations. For if we expect that such struggles are to be resolved somewhat quickly then we will approach the problem very differently than if we recognize the fulfilling conditions to require some centuries or millennia. Explicit in Marx's analysis was an impatience rooted in the conviction that a revolution can transform the conditions that give rise to the problems.[69] One might ask, in Lonergan's terms, whether drastic measures might be implemented in the interest of conditioning an increase in f-probably developed responsibility and authenticity. And the answer would involve recalling that the foundation of moral and historical normativity is operative immanently in subjects, as a demand for integration of an operative dynamic in its intentional term. Thus the question arises whether a subject can perform an act whose concrete form or structure is a repudiation of the dynamic immanent in its emergence.[70] The answer, I would suggest, is that at least two forms of bias would ensue, the individual bias and the group bias. For the subject involves him or herself in a contradiction or counter-position in the act. And performance operates publicly to ratify its universalization and reversal, thus launching the group bias. Consequently the problem of widespread conversions becomes considerably more complex from the point of view of Lonergan's analysis. For the actual doing of theology raises the very foundational theological problem of the group bias and the longer cycle of decine. If Lash is right and Marx is actually doing theology,[71] but committing errors in Christian theology in the absence of self-knowledge, then one needs to ask how far these errors have penetrated one's anticipations.

I will raise one further point here. One might ask whether Lonergan's notion of feeling as intentional response to value, if integrated completely into a discussion of the group bias, might modify an assessment of the dominant role of cognitional acts in the dynamics of historical progress and decline.[72] If the feelings can be intentional responses to value then could feelings that are cultivated through art, literature, imagery, poetry, education, music or architecture be understood as significant agents for cultural transformation, which minimize or bypass the role of concrete intelligent acts? Are not feeings so operative in history, and does not a recognition of their operation demand a substantial modification of one's account of historical dynamics?

The response, I would suggest, demands recalling that while a certain class of feelings respond to value, they do so non-systematically. In other words these particular feelings are not themselves the criterion of value, they are indicators which as easily indicate false values as true. It is the judgment of value that pronounces the value as true and thereby orders or integrates the energy of the feelings.[73] And so to the extent that a concrete value (and all values are concrete) has not been judged true, by anyone, the feeling which intends it will operate only coincidentally as a principle of progress. However, once judged true a value can become public. It can be celebrated, sung, dramatized. And such art does in fact shift the f-probabilities associated with the widespread dissemination of the value by mobilizing the feelings of a culture whose members need not themselves perform the judgment of value.[74] But because values are concrete, as are the exigences of human situations, there will always be an element of responsible discernment, on the part of individual subjects, who seek to realize the value in particular times and places. And so while music and art increase the f-probabilities of recurrence of the value they do not systematize its recurrence. Only the developed authenticity and competence of concrete subjective practical skills will effect such a systematization.[75] Thus the account of the role of subjective agency in history in *Insight* remains substantially unchanged. However, I hope I have indicated how it might be developed.

## 7.6 *General Bias and Historical Decline*

### 7.6.1 *Preliminary Clarifications: Intellect and Will*

General bias is the statistical fact that the problems of human living most frequently exceed the developed capacities and skills of human subjects to meet them.[76]

> Besides the bias of the dramatic subject, of the individual egoist, of the member of a given class or nation, there is a further bias to which all men are prone. For men are rational animals, but full develop-

ment of their animality is both more common and more rapid than a full development of their intelligence and reasonableness. A traditional view credits children of seven years of age with the attainment of an elementary reasonableness. The law regards as a minor anyone under twenty-one years of age. Experts in the field of public entertainment address themselves to a mental age of about twelve years. Still more modest is the scientific attitude that places man's attainment of knowledge in an indefinitely removed future.[77]

The greatest problem involved in coming to understand what Lonergan is trying to grasp and express with his notion of "general bias" concerns the meaning of the expression "full development of their intelligence and reasonableness." There is some evidence within *Insight* and in a later remark of Lonergan's that in writing *Insight*, Lonergan was undergoing a development in his view of "intelligence and reasonableness" as it relates to moral action.[78] In his 1941 and 1942 articles in *Theological Studies* on St. Thomas Aquinas' notion of "operative grace" (the articles which have since been collected into the volume entitled *Grace and Freedom*), Lonergan works out Thomas' view of the relationship between intellect and will in terms of a faculty psychology approach.[79] This, of course, was the approach of Thomas. And it would seem from his treatment of "The Notion of Will" in *Insight*, chapter eighteen,[80] that Lonergan maintained the basic distinction between intellect and will that is rooted in this faculty psychology approach. But there is also some considerable evidence in *Insight*, chapter eighteen, that Lonergan had already modified his conception of the role of "intellect" in moral action to the point where a more traditional distinction between "intellect" and "will" (a distinction rooted in a faculty psychology approach) was no longer tenable. By the time of *Method in Theology* (1972) Lonergan had come to casting his analysis in terms of an "intentionality analysis" approach that was sufficiently different from the older approach as to require a rejection of the older term "will."

> Again, [decision] is not to be conceived as an act of will. To speak of an act of will is to suppose the metaphysical context of a faculty psychology. But to speak of the fourth level of human consciousness, the level on which consciousness becomes conscience, is to suppose the context of intentionality analysis. Decision is responsible and it is free, but it is the work not of a metaphysical will but of conscience and, indeed, when a conversion, the work of a good conscience.[81]

In *Grace and Freedom*, Lonergan points to a discovery of Dom Lottin's as an important moment in explaining Thomas' account of the relationship between intellect and will. The challenge to Thomas presented by the Parisian Averroists' doctrine of determinism was the occasion for Thomas' own refinement in his understanding of the operation of the will. If the specification and the exercise of the act of will are both caused by intellect, then free will is finally precluded. For the will would then be activated by anything that occurs to intellect. Thomas' response to this dilemma was to specify four presuppositions necessary for an act of free will:

... (A) a field of action in which more than one course of action is objectively possible; (B) an intellect that is able to work out more than one course of action; (C) a will that is not automatically determined by the first course of action that occurs to the intellect; and, since this condition is only a condition, securing indeterminacy without telling what in fact does determine, (D) a will that moves itself. All four are asserted by St. Thomas but with varying degrees of emphasis at different times.[82]

Following Aristotle, St. Thomas took for granted a faculty of will, distinct from the faculty of intellect, with a distinct object of desire, the good in general.[83] And in an effort to develop an explanation of free, moral action he affirmed both a link between the two faculties and a distinction in their operation.

Finally, while it was always maintained that the will is not determined by the intellect, it is only in the *De malo* and the *Prima secundae* that one finds an explicit answer to the question: What does determine the will? As we have seen, Aristotelian passivity of appetite is then transcended and the freedom of man yields place to the freedom of the will; in consequence, attention is concentrated on the negative factor that the will is not determined by the intellect, and on the positive factor that the will moves itself and in this self-motion is always free either to act or not act.[84]

The point to be observed here is that for Thomas intellect and will are presupposed, from the outset, to be the two distinct categories in whose terms the problem of freedom is to be resolved.[85] There is some clue in these passages that intellect performs different types of functions with respect to different types of objects when it conceives and judges truths of fact, on the one hand, and when it conceived and judges possible courses of action, on the other. But nothing more is made of this clue either by Thomas or by Lonergan in *Grace and Freedom*. The problem of freedom is not to be resolved in terms of a radical set of differences in types or levels of "conscious" operation each involving some role of intelligent emergence. It is to be resolved in terms of a distinct category, the will.

In *Insight*, chapter eighteen, considerably more is made of the different types of conscious operations, all involving intelligence, and the distinct objects towards which they move.

The detached, disinterested, unrestricted desire to know grasps intelligently and affirms reasonably not only the facts of the universe of being but also its practical possibilities. Such practical possibilities include intelligent transformations not only of the environment in which man lives but also of man's own spontaneous living. For that living exhibits an otherwise coincidental manifold into which man can introduce a higher system by his own understanding of himself and his own deliberate choices. So it is that the detached and disinterested desire extends its sphere of influence from the field of cognitional activities through the field of knowledge into the field of deliberate human acts.[86]

It is generally recognized that in the *Verbum* articles Lonergan discovered St. Thomas to be working with a view of intellect which recognized not one but two distinct types of operations, the operations of insight or understanding and the operation of judgment. It would appear that in *Insight* Lonergan was on the verge of a further discovery, a discovery which would eventually expand the older faculty psychology distinction between intellect and will into a series of circularly operating schemes involving something like fourteen distinct acts progressing cumulatively towards transformations on at least four distinct levels and on two further sublevels.[87] The first piece of evidence which seems to have struck Lonergan was Thomas' observation that intellect can not only have insights and make judgments about matters of fact, it can also have insights and make judgments about practical courses of action which are not yet fact. The twofold scheme of insight and judgment is operative in each case, but in *Insight* Lonergan takes great pains to point out the radical differences in the intention of the questions and the status of the answers in each pair of operations.

However, while the speculative or factual insight is followed by the question whether the unity exists or whether the correlation governs events, the practical insight is followed by the question whether the unity is going to be made to exist or whether the correlation is going to be made to govern events. In other words, while speculative and factual insights are concerned to lead to knowledge of being, practical insights are concerned to lead to the making of being. Their objective is not what is but what is to be done. They reveal, not the unities and relations of things as they are, but the unities and relations of possible courses of action.

There follows another important corollary. When speculative or factual insight is correct, reflective understanding can grasp a relevant virtually unconditioned. But when practical insight is correct, then reflective understanding cannot grasp a relevant virtually unconditioned; for if it could, the content of the insight already would be a fact; and if it were already a fact, then it would not be a possible course of action which, as yet, is not a fact but just a possibility.[88]

The practical insight and its corresponding reflection do not head towards truth. Rather, they head towards value. "Now it is in rational, moral self-consciousness that the good as value comes to light, for the value is the good as the possible object of rational choice."[89] But values do not remain as objects of understanding and judgment. Beyond the practical insight and its corresponding judgment lies the actuation of the value, the execution of the course of action. It is in his account of the "decision" that Lonergan tries to integrate this developed set of distinctions into an overarching faculty psychology framework of intellect and will. And, in so doing, Lonergan shows up the serious inadequacy of this older framework. For by now Lonergan had discovered that beyond the levels of experience, understanding and judgment, there lies not a single operation of "will" but three distinct types of operations, the practical insight, practical reflection (what, in *Method*, terminates in the judgment of value), and the decision.[90] It is in *Method* that Lonergan focuses on the distinctiveness of the practical reflective operation to highlight the way in which judgments of value integrate the spontaneous orientation of the subject towards value in feelings.[91] But in *Insight* practical reflection had already been noted as a distinct operation.

> Secondly, though the reflection heads beyond knowing to doing, still it consists simply in knowing. Thus, it may reveal that the proposed action is concretely possible, clearly effective, highly agreeable, quite useful, morally obligatory, etc. But it is one thing to know exactly what could be done and all the reasons for doing it. It is quite another for such knowledge to issue in doing.[92]

From the very beginning of his eighteenth chapter, Lonergan recognizes that the will is not discontinuous with intellect, but a further, distinguishable function of intellect itself.

> ... the goodness of being comes to light only by considering the extension of intellectual activity that we name deliberation and decision, choice and will ... Further, willing is rational and so moral.[93]

But it would appear that Lonergan's inclination to cast his analysis in the terms of the faculty psychology *distinction* between intellect and will prevailed over this insight into the continuity. And so he beings his account of will with the more traditional analogy of sensitive hunger.

> Will, then, is intellectual or spiritual appetite. As capacity for sensitive hunger stands to sensible food, so will stands to objects presented by intellect.[94]

There is a sense in which this analogy to sensitive hunger remains true through both *Insight* and *Method*. For appetite is understood by Lonergan as a dynamic orientation of a whole human person to take up environmental materials and to transform them or integrate them in the performance of a skill.[95] But the problem with this traditional analogy is that it also evoked the traditional conception of will as ordered towards the object of intellect. *The faculty psychology approach began with a categorical distinction between intellect and will and argued to will's independence from intellect, on the one hand, and to its orientation towards the objects of intellect, on the other. In "Insight," Lonergan had assembled all the materials for conceiving will as a set of distinct acts and schemes of acts, involving some occurrence of an emergent integration, on the one hand, and all ordered towards an object which is distinct from the object of the "speculative" operation of intelligence, on the other.* With his framework of emergent probability Lonergan had set the grounds for conceiving "will" in a radically new way, as a part of a larger recurring skill or scheme of acts whose developed performance yields a more or less intelligent integration of the (biological, aesthetic, affective, intelligent, reasonable, intersubjective, historical) experiential materials of a human subject and which is oriented towards the grasp, the affirmation and the actuation of courses of action which transform and constitute both the subject and his or her environment. All of these elements are present in *Insight*, chapter eighteen. But the traditional faculty psychology approach tended to prevail in Lonergan's attempts to specify the precise function of the "will" precisely because the context of his analysis was the traditional scholastic question of the independence of the will from the determining constraints of rational necessity.[96] So he defines the will as "an exigence for self-consistency in knowing and doing."[97] And in so doing he obscures both the *continuity* of intelligence in its various functions throughout the whole operation of "will" and the distinctiveness of "will's" own object.

> But the rationality of decision emerges in the demand of the rationally conscious subject for consistency between his knowing and his deciding and doing ... But the final enlargement and transformation of consciousness consists in the empirically, intelligently, and rationally conscious subject
> (1) demanding conformity of his doing to his knowing, and
> (2) acceding to that demand by deciding reasonably.[98]

When it is understood that by "knowing" Lonergan does not mean knowing truth but "knowing" the value of a possible and probable course of action, his definition begins to ring true. And when it is understood that the object of this "demand for conformity" is the comprehensive integration of the enormous manifold of skills of the person or people involved in accordance with this "projected" course of action, then the act of will begins to appear less as the passive submission of humanity to the imperious demands of intellect and more as the heroic work of intelligent devotion and love creatively cultivating and actuating the fragile directives of truth and value.

All of this brings us back to the issue of the general bias. On the basis of the above evidence it would be fair to conclude that when Lonergan speaks of "full development of their intelligence and reasonableness" his intended meaning would be obscured badly by contrasting "intelligence and reasonableness" either with "willing" or with sensitive spontaneity. The general bias does not apply solely to knowledge of facts but more generally to the cultivation of intelligently mediated spontaneously operative skills on all levels of what Lonergan subsequently comes to call "conscious intentionality." I would suggest that what Lonergan had in mind in writing his account of the general bias was something that he came to call in *Method* a problem of "horizons," where the word "horizons" designates both the limitations in what one can conceive as possible, and the limitations in developed capacities and skills which usually go hand in hand with an earlier stage in development, with a deficiency in experiential range or with a distortion in operational authenticity.[99] And so even though Lonergan would seem to define willing as seeking conformity to knowledge and even though he seems to characterize the basic problem in the human condition in terms of insufficient knowledge, I would argue that both of these expressions tend to diverge from, rather than converge upon his emergent probability conception of humanity and world process in *Insight*.

### 7.6.2 General Bias and Decline

The general bias concerns the insufficiently developed and infrequently actuated capacities and skills of intelligent, responsible knowing and doing.[100] The normal routines of human life are massively constituted by the common and more or less novel mediating activities of theoretical and practical intelligence. Such activities are performed in accordance with developed capacities and within the confines of corresponding cultural, economic, social, historical conditions and limitations. The simple fact about human life that is expressed in the notion of general bias is that the problems encountered most regularly throughout human life demand a general level of developed capacities and skills in excess of that which is commonly operative. This fact is true not only of aggregates of persons, but also of the course of any one person's life. And the consequence of this fact is that human attempts to order human life in accordance with the immanent norms of developed intelligence quite regularly fail. Finally, by specifying the essential problem in the human condition as insufficiently developed skills, this view paints a substantially gloomier picture than that of Marx. This view certainly lends itself to a consideration of the social, cultural, economic and psychological conditions surrounding the development and exercise of skills. But unlike Marx's view, Lonergan's view permits no shortcuts around the basic requirement that each and every human being acquire, develop and exercise the relevant capacities and skills. This, I would argue, is the reason for Lonergan's endless preoccupation with "the subject." For I can never acquire or exercise a skill for another person.[101]

Lonergan's account of the human condition in terms of the general bias does not rest with noting the recurrent fact of failure. Rather, he goes on to discuss the particular characteristics of failure which result from the operation of the general bias and the historical consequences of its impact. Most simply, the distinctive characteristic associated with the operation of the general bias is the restricted horizon or viewpoint within which com-

mon sense (practical) intelligence operates.
> The lag of intellectual development, its difficulty and its apparently meagre returns bear in an especial manner on common sense. It is concerned with the concrete and the particular. It entertains no aspirations about reaching abstract and universal laws. It is easily led to rationalize its limitations by engendering a conviction that other forms of human knowledge are useless or doubtfully valid. Every specialist runs the risk of turning his specialty into a bias by failing to recognize and appreciate the significance of other fields. Common sense almost invariably makes that mistake; for it is incapable of analyzing itself, incapable of making the discovery that it too is a specialized development of human knowledge, incapable of coming to grasp that its peculiar danger is to extend its legitimate concern for the concrete and the immediately practical into disregard of larger issues and indifference to long-term results.[102]

Lonergan's call for a higher viewpoint, a wider perspective on man and history within which to understand the specialized operations of common sense, recalls Dilthey's efforts to set the groundwork for his fundamental science of man. And Lonergan is explicit in conceiving his higher viewpoint as analogous, in intent, to Marx's historical theory.

> So far from granting common sense a hegemony in practical affairs, the foregoing analysis leads to the strange conclusion that common sense has to aim at being subordinated to a human science that is concerned, to adapt a phrase from Marx, not only with knowing history but also with directing it. For common sense is unequal to the task of thinking on the level of history. It stands above the scotosis of the dramatic subject, above the egoism of the individual, above the bias of dominant and of depressed but militant groups that realize only the ideas they see to be to their immediate advantage. But the general bias of common sense prevents it from being effective in realizing ideas, however appropriate and reasonable, that suppose a long view or that set up higher integrations or that involve the solution of intricate and disputed issues.[103]

The historical consequence of the operation of the general bias is the emergence of a dynamic trend that stands in opposition to the drive of finality towards successively higher emergent integrations. Lonergan calls this inverse trend "the longer cycle of decline." And the central characteristic of this trend is the "neglect of ideas to which all groups are rendered indifferent by the general bias of common sense."[104] The reason why the general bias yields this trend is to be understood in terms of the fact that history is constituted by meaning.[105] The insights made operative in one age set the conditions for life in the next age. If common sense is generally prone to restricting its horizons of operation to the realm of the immediate and practical, then the alternating cycles of group bias consistently will fail to discover and to implement the insights that would serve the good of all. For the group bias turns the operation of intelligence to serve the interests of the group. In addition, since the data base of common sense is the common experience of life in that age, every narrow viewpoint of common sense that is made operative will set the experiential range of the successive age. As long as common sense excludes insights that are relevant to understanding and directing the whole of life (the distinctive characteristic of common sense's operation), it will bequeath upon the next generation an ever-narrowing data base for the discovery and regulation of human affairs.[106]

Like the other biases, the general bias is not merely negative. It is not only an exclusion of complete insights. Rather, like the other biases the general bias involves the subject in a dialectical tension with the exigencies of his or her intersubjective experience. The partial insights of common sense result in a distortion of the subject's experiential manifold. And so subsequent insights and practical decisions begin conforming more and more to the distorted experiential base. But the general bias involves its own peculiar form of distortion, a distortion that is more serious than those of the other biases. For insufficiently developed intelligence with its shrunken or delimited horizons does not grasp the need for growth. And as ever-narrower points of view gain wider and wider acceptance, insufficiently developed intelligence pronounces theoretical issues to be irrelevant. The result is that common sense not only finds itself insufficiently developed, it also judges further development to be impossible or irrelevant.

The cycle of decline has a number of distinct implications. And Lonergan's presentation of these implications is cast as a dramatic monologue which mounts from a technical restatement of the elements of the longer cycle, through the history of the growing irrelevance of religion and philosophy to a graphic portrayal of the barbarism of Hitler's Germany. One could speculate on the names, dates, places and events to which Lonergan alludes. And in some cases little imagination would be required. But throughout the monologue Lonergan's principal target is that particular form of insufficiently developed intelligence which manifests itself in a repudiation of intelligence. The narrowed horizons of common sense practicality with its short-term preoccupation with solving the problems at hand using the immediately available tools gives rise to a commonly operative theory which judges the theoretical issues, the general of ultimate good, the foundations of truth, to be irrelevant speculation. And to illustrate this narrowing of horizons in the field of political philosophy, Fred Lawrence quotes Leo Strauss in identifying Machiavelli as a key figure in the history of this shift towards short-term practicality:

> The initiator of the shift from the medieval synthesis into that succession of lower syntheses characteristic of socio-cultural decline was Machiavelli who, in the fifteenth chapter of his odd little book, *The Prince*, wrote the fateful words: "... many have imagined republics

and principalities which have never been seen or known to exist in reality; for how we live is so far removed from how we ought to live, that he who abandons what is done for what ought to be done will rather learn to bring about his own ruin than his preservation. A man who wishes to make a profession of goodness in everything must necessarily come to grief among so many who are not good. Therefore it is necessary for a prince who wishes to maintain himself to learn how not to be good, and to use this knowledge and not use it according to the necessity of the case."[107]

The general bias with its longer cycle of decline concerns the failure of the development of intelligence in its various schemes of operation with its respective transformations. Intelligence which neglects or refuses to understand itself places an insurmountable obstacle in the path of its long range development. And since common sense intelligence looks to the data of contemporary experience for the source of its insights, the mounting exclusion of theoretical insights on man from the normal range of experience gives rise to the growing conviction that such insights are neither possible nor relevant. It is claimed that the truth about humanity is not to be found in an analysis of his capacities or her potentialities. Rather, it is to be discovered in generalizations from common performance. And when such generalizations are put forward as the only plausible norms for subsequent performance, then every subsequent stage is bound to conform to the past age's incomplete understanding of itself. The only norms for intelligent performance are current or recently past general performance. And so intelligence, both in its speculative and in its regulative or moral operations, becomes "radically uncritical." For it has rejected its own immanent norm of "progress," in favour of the extrinsic and arbitrary norm of current practice.[108]

### 7.6.3 Sinful Man and Human Agency

Now it would seem that this view of the human situation places considerable emphasis upon the role of subjective human agency in social and historical success and failure. And it might seem that in spite of his rather pessimistic account of the human situation, nonetheless Lonergan views the problem in the human situation as one which demands a response at the level of human agency and one for which human agency is an adequate response. Professor Gustafson might argue that such a view lies open to a critique from a Protestant theologian for misconstruing the state of human sinfulness.

In his *Protestant and Roman Catholic Ethics*, Professor Gustafson notes that a basic difference in their respective approaches to human sinfulness has traditionally separated Catholic and Protestant theologians. Quite generally, the theologians of the Roman Catholic tradition have tended to conceive man in terms of his origins in God and in terms of his natural orientation towards God and towards his own highest good:

> The ultimate end of humans is God; ... Humans are also naturally inclined toward their natural end or good; thus there is a ground for a natural morality available to the knowledge of all rational persons.[109]

This view of the continuity between the natural order and the divine order, combined with a recognition of some capacity of intelligence to guide moral action towards this end has led to a conception of moral action, in the Catholic tradition, as contributing towards salvation.

> To be properly oriented toward the natural good is one dimension of being properly oriented toward God. Thus a frame is set in which specific infractions of the natural moral order, specific sins, are salvifically deleterious, and right moral acts (in accord with the natural moral order) are salvifically beneficial.[110]

In Professor Gustafson's view, this overall conception of morality and its continuity with salvation (in combination with other factors) tended to shift attention toward particular *sins* as concrete acts and away from *sin* as a basic condition of man.

> To Luther, as it has to many Protestants since the time of the Reformation, this preoccupation with avoiding sins for the sake of salvation sounded like 'works-righteousness'. It sounded as if salvation is earned on the basis of meritorious works rather than received as a free gift of God's grace.[111]

The Reformers viewed the state of the human condition to be not so much a matter of man's more or less direct orientation towards God as man having turned his back on God and not trusting him. Original sin turned man against God, perverting his desires and distorting his reason.[112] And since this original fault was not a moral fault but a religious fault, the only appropriate correction can be an act of God.

> If sin is basically unfaith, a lack of trust in God, the antidote had to be faith or trust in God. No moral rectitude could achieve faith; to be properly oriented toward the natural moral good did not set one on a course toward salvation. Faith had to be a response to the free gift of God's grace. Grace was strongly perceived to be mercy, and not so much the rectification, redirection, and fulfillment of nature.[113]

There is a sense here in which the Reformers viewed the state of human condition as beyond the capacities of men to rectify, in any significant way, through the development and exercise of natural abilities. Only the free and gracious initiative of God can make a difference in this condition. And man participates in the rectification, not by moral rectitude, but by responding with trust in God's gratuitous activity. The moral action of which man is capable flows as an effect or a consequence of God's gift of righteousness.[114]

It is clear that Lonergan's emphasis upon the upward dynamism of finality, his general preoccupation with cognitional and responsible skills, and most of all his account of the human condition in terms of the relative insufficiency of these developed cognitional and responsible skills place him soundly within the Catholic tradition as Gustafson has characterized it. The question remains, however, whether Lonergan, in his somewhat novel, emergent probability conception of intelligent and responsible activity, still remains open to the Reformers' charge of "works-righteousness" and their accusation that Catholics have tended to ignore the essentially theological dimension of sin.

It is essential to recall that the general bias is fundamentally a statistical law.[115] The relative insufficiency and infrequency of developed capacities and skills is an f-probability for which there is no further explanation in terms of, for example, corrupted nature. To introduce an element such as *essentially* corrupted nature would be to explain human reality as sufficiently different in structure to be discontinuous with an explanation of world process which satisfies the canon of parsimony. In addition such an explanation would require that human goodness be explained in terms of God's selective dispensation of grace. And whether such a doctrine of election could ever avoid the pitfalls of a gnostic stratification of humanity into the "children of light" and "the children of darkness" remains to be seen. In any case Lonergan would argue that introducing such a radical discontinuity as *essentially* corrupted human nature is neither necessary nor is it unconditionally warranted by the data on human life. His account of the dramatic bias, the egoist bias and the group bias all explain not only the failure of intelligence but also its intermittent and habitual perversion in individuals and groups. And the intimate dialectical relationship between the intellect and the experiential manifold which it orders, allows a distorted intelligence progressively to distort the whole range of human performance so that human spontaneity in all spheres of action becomes perverse. The structure of these biases explains the Reformers' perverse human nature. The structure of history wherein one generation's insights establish the conditions for the activity of the next explains how perversity continues and accelerates. And the statistical fact of the general bias explains the proliferation of the perversion.

But while the general bias is fundamentally a statistical law, there remains the possibility of occurrence of a systematic element that is in continuity with finality, which would increase the f-probability of developed "competence." And this, I would argue, is what *Insight*, chapter twenty, on "Special Transcendent Knowledge" is all about. Furthermore, this would explain Lonergan's development of the notion of "conversion" in *Method in Theology*. The general relationship of *Insight's* account of understanding and its biases, to *Method's* account of the religious subject and his or her conversions can be conceived as a relationship of systematically operative skills to the conditions associated with their f-probably developed performance. The ever-widening circles of intelligent, reasonable and responsive schemes of acts are the systematically operative skills. The developmental stages of growth and, more profoundly, the conversions with their corresponding graces are the conditions whose fulfillment results in the jump in f-probabilities of competent performance. This, too, I would argue, could be the clue to understanding and integrating the respective emphases of the Catholic and Protestant accounts of morality and human sinfulness. But before these insights can be developed a basic presentation of the possibilities for the reversal of the general bias is required.

## 7.7 The Possibility for Reversal: History, Ethics and Religion

### 7.7.1 The Higher Viewpoint, Cosmopolis, and Moral Impotence

The root of the problem in the human condition, the general bias, is understood by Lonergan as an insufficient development and a corresponding insufficiently frequent actuation of the human capacities and skills for intelligent knowing and doing. The consequence of this insufficient development is a deformation or bias in common sense intelligence's habitual operation. The direction of this bias is towards short-term practicality, and its preoccupation with immediately realizable solutions using immediately available means and commonly available experiential resources. Because the world of experience of any historical age is, for the most part, constituted by the insights that were made operative by the previous generations, this bias towards short-term practicality results in an ever-narrowing series of horizons. As common sense becomes more and more practical, the range of experiential data and insights that are deemed relevant to human life shrinks to include only those elements that can be discovered and verified in a appeal to current practice. Since the insights that order and regulate human life emerge from the experiential data base on man which that age recognizes as relevant, the ever-shrinking ranges of practical insights will bequeath upon successive generations ever-shrinking experiential ranges. And the major upshot of this trend is intelligence's rejection of the need for development and its despair of the possibility of development. As intelligence progressively is judged irrelevant to human life there arises a growing preoccupation with the environmental and interior determinants of human life. Corresponding to this growing conviction there arises a growing appeal to the use of force either to ensure and secure those determinants which are thought essential to the routine operation of existing social schemes, or to realize those determinants which are thought to be capable of transforming social life. Such is the longer cycle of decline.

The possibility for the reversal of this bias and its longer cycle consists in reversing this deceleration in the development of intelligent capacities and skills and promoting accelerated development. In opposition to the short-term practicality of intelligence, Lonergan proposes a "higher viewpoint" on man and history from whose perspective common sense, with its virtues and its deficiencies, can be understood.[116] Such a higher viewpoint would be something like what Vico, Marx and Dilthey sought to develop: an integrated theory of man and history which would grasp man's fundamental and essentially human capacities and which would explain their positive and negative contributions to the dynamism of human history. But Lonergan insists that the central element of this higher viewpoint must be the discovery that intelligently mediated operations play the chief role in the constitution of culture and history and that because intelligence has its own immanent norms, norms which cannot be forced or externally conditioned, there is no alternative to the widescale development of responsible subjects. If a higher viewpoint is to meet the general bias and its longer cycle of decline it must grasp the route towards this development and it must affirm both its possibility and its necessity.

In Lonergan's analysis, the route towards progress requires the recognition that if intelligence and responsibility contain their own immanent norms, then progress can be cultivated only through the growth of the whole human person. Human progress can never be realized merely through the transformation of social or economic life conditions or through the imposition of the rule of force. Quite the contrary, in this analysis of the human situation, force can and must play but a minor role. For inasmuch as intelligent acts and intelligent development have the structure of a probably emergence of a higher-order integration, the condition of possibility for this emergence is a sufficient randomness.[117] In human life the form of this randomness is liberty, the opportunity for trial and error accumulation of skills, and a sufficiently wide range of opportunities for the application and cultivation of skill and creativity.[118] Environmental conditions and the exercise of force play a role in reversal insofar as they promote rather than supplant this assimilation and adjustment growth scheme.[119]

The role of culture in reversal is to embrace and to reflect this higher viewpoint on human life and human history and to critique any deformations in common sense intelligence in the interests of its liberation from short-term practicality. But first culture itself needs to undergo this very liberation. As long as the general vias has its strangle-hold on culture then culture only accelerates the decline. Consequently culture must understand the elements of the higher viewpoint.[120]

It is to this higher viewpoint on man and history that Lonergan gives the name "cosmopolis." It is not altogether clear precisely what Lonergan intends by cosmopolis. But three of its functions can be summarized. (1) Cosmopolis seeks to express and make operative the ideas on man and history that are rendered inoperative by the general bias of common sense. In contrast to common sense's short-term practicality, cosmopolis proclaims a wider perspective on man and champions those dimensions of human life that are not immediately practical. Cosmopolis must witness publicly to the possibility of such ideas being made operative in society and culture without appeal to the use of force.[121] (2) Cosmopolis has the critical function of exposing, ridiculing and falsifying the deformations in common sense's exclusively practical concern for day-to-day living. Far from repudiating the practical orientation of intelligence such a critical function operates in the interests of practical intelligence. For it is common sense's exclusive preoccupation with short-term practicality that results in its own ultimate destruction.[122] (3) Cosmopolis develops its higher viewpoint on man on the basis of a critical analysis of history. And to carry out its tasks cosmopolis needs continually to be engaged in the critical study of historical origins and historical responsibilities. Thus while cosmopolis is a development of intelligence it is not merely another specialized field for the operation of common sense. Rather, it is a development of intelligence beyond common sense from whose perspective the historical operations and limitations of common sense could be understood, and from whose perspective common sense's positive and negative contributions to the whole historical process can be understood.[123]

In a very general sense cosmopolis includes the very project which Lonergan has begun in his own life's work. It concerns a developed understanding of those operations which distinguish human life as, in a limited but nonetheless essential sense, self-regulating or self-constituting. It concerns an account of human history as essentially constituted by human acts of intelligence and it concerns the specific ways in which the horrors and deformations of human life are to be explained in terms of the limitations and perversions of these acts. It concerns the fact that such a grasp of the limitations of intelligence can lead to a subsequent reduction in the impact of such limitations and to a development in the competent operation of intelligence. But it also concerns the fact that such a grasp of the limitations of intelligence leads to a fuller and richer appreciation of the limitations of the human condition. For to grasp the possibility for the reversal of the general bias is also to grasp that the fulfillment of the conditions for such a reversal appears unlikely.[124]

Clearly cosmopolis is conceived by Lonergan to be the foundation of the possibility for the reversal of decline. But if his presentation would have ended with *Insight*, chapter seven, Lonergan would have left us with an account of the human situation whose central problem, intelligence's inability and refusal to develop, could only be resolved if the human situation were to undergo significant structural change. For clearly, cosmopolis is the very thing that the bias of common sense precludes. However, his account of the possibilities for the reversal of decline does not end with *Insight*, chapter seven. And it is clear in chapters eighteen to twenty that Lonergan recognizes that as long as the analysis is restricted to man, the sufficiently widespread proliferation of cosmopolis must be considered unlikely.[125]

It is certain that Lonergan appreciates the dilemma that his presentation leaves for man. For in his subsection of chapter twenty entitled "The Existence of a Solution," he defines what he means by the human "problem." "First of all, I have employed the name, problem, in a technical sense, so that it is meaningless to speak of a problem for which no solution exists."[126] If Lonergan's analysis of the human situation and his introduction of the notion of cosmopolis as the condition for reversal are to be something more than a counsel of despair then his intended meaning needs to be re-examined. And I would suggest that a first clue in this re-examination is to be found at the end of chapter eighteen.

> Earlier, in the chapter on Common Sense as Object, it was concluded that a viewpoint higher than the viewpoint of common sense was needed; moreover, that X was given the name, cosmopolis, and some of its aspects and functions were indicated. But the subsequent argument has revealed that, besides higher viewpoints in the mind, there are higher integrations in the realm of being;
> 
> . . .
> 
> Finally, whether the needed higher integration has emerged or is yet to emerge, is a question of fact. Similarly, its nature is not an object for speculation but for empirical inquiry. Still, what can that empirical inquiry be? Since our metaphysics and ethics have been developed under a restriction to proportionate being, we have to raise the question of transcendent knowledge before we can attempt an investigation of the ulterior finality of man.[127]

It becomes perfectly clear in chapters nineteen and twenty that the viewpoint higher than common sense, to which corresponds the higher integration in the realm of transcendent being, demands grappling, finally, with the question of God.

### 7.7.2 Religion and the Human Sciences: The Limits and Demands of Intelligence in The Face of Moral Impotence

At this point, I would suggest that we stand at a most subtle, a most central and a most complicated moment in Lonergan's work. And it would be worthwhile, here, to step back and to survey the issues that are at stake by introducing another work which leads us to a similar moment. In 1974, Robert Heilbroner published his penetrating and controversial book, *An Inquiry into the Human Prospect*.[128] And his summary statement of the human situation, especially with regard to man's natural capacities and propensities, bears some resemblance to Lonergan's analysis of the general bias and its longer cycle of decline.

To these obstacles we must add certain elements of the political pro-

> pensities in "human nature" that stand in the way of rational, orderly adaptation of the industrial mode in the directions that will become increasingly urgent as the distant future comes closer. ... The bonds of national identity are certain to exert their powerful force, mobilizing men for the collective efforts needed but inhibiting the international sharing of burdens and wealth. The myopia that confines the present vision of men to the short-term future is not likely to disappear overnight, rendering still more difficult a planned and orderly retrenchment and redivision of output.[129]

Heilbroner recognizes here that the common sense exercise of practical intelligence (operating at a lesser rather than at a greater degree of competence) will be the constitutive element in forging the future. He notes the accelerating trend towards the exercise of political force as fears and insecurities prevail.[130] He notes the role of the "group bias" with its corresponding blindness to the common good. And he closes with the characteristic limitation of common sense, "the myopia that confines the present vision of men to the short-term future." This is not to suggest that Heilbroner shares Lonergan's analysis of the central conditions for the reversal of the contemporary state of man. For Heilbroner identifies such conditions as (1) "governments capable of rallying obedience far more effectively than would be possible in a democratic setting,"[131] and (2) a new "collective bond of identify with those future generations."[132] However, Heilbroner is insightful in noting that the human condition, with all its inherent limitations and deformations is not to be expected to change. His somewhat "conservative" insistence on the "limits to the possibilities for change"[133] contains a critique both of the liberal view of the "self-made man"[134] and of the "radical" view with its "expectations that are founded to a large extent on the dynamics of socio-economic change."[135] The point here is that like Lonergan, Heilbroner rules out of court both a naive view of human possibilities and an expectation of immanent change in the structure of the human condition.

In his "Final Reflections on the Human Prospect," Heilbroner indicates what we can reasonably expect in the middle- to long-range future. And it is here that some of the characteristics of Heilbroner's own "higher viewpoint" come to light. Since appropriately creative responses will not be forthcoming in time we can expect "the outbreak of wars arising from the explosive tensions of the coming period." Or we might expect such environmental crises as "large-scale fatal urban temperature inversions, massive crop failures, resource shortages" to result from our failure to mobilize sufficient technological and political initiative. But in either case Heilbroner conceives such crises as operating as "negative feedbacks" to "reduce the growth rates of the surviving nation-states and thereby defer the danger of industrial asphyxiation for a period," or to "slow down economic growth and give a necessary impetus to the piecemeal construction of an ecologically and socially viable social system."[136] In short, Heilbroner views man as standing within a grand-scale, dialectically operating, environmental equilibrium "feedback-loop" system.[137] While man's attitudes, his political will, his intelligence and his creativity are unable to adapt themselves to known but future threats to his long-term survival, the structure of this ecological system is sufficiently benevolent towards man as to force such changes in our attitudes and our actions in time for survival. Heilbroner explicitly takes issue with Meadows' and Forrester's expectations in *The Limits to Growth*[138] and with the British authors' hopes expressed in "Blueprint for Survival,"[139] that an "appeal to collective foresight" might avert immanent disaster. But he shares in a much more profound and subtle way, those authors' conviction that world process is not finally and completely hostile to humanity's long-term survival.

Heilbroner's "higher viewpoint" conceives world process as operating with the structure of what Lonergan calls "recurrence schemes with defensive circles."[140] Within this equilibrium feedback scheme Heilbroner sees human intelligence as, for the most part, conditioned by the operative environmental forces, and reflecting humanity's conditioned survival responses.[141] Consequently he asks how we can best live with the somewhat drudgerous, tumultuous, and burdensome lifestyle that will be forced upon the future generations in their efforts to adapt to extremely difficult living conditions. He answers by proposing the myth of Atlas.

In these half-blind gropings there is, however, one element in which we can place credence, although it offers uncertainty as well as hope. This is our knowledge that some human societies have existed for millennia, and that others can probably exist for future millennia, in a continuous rhythm of birth and coming of age and death, without pressing toward those dangerous ecological limits, or engendering those dangerous social tensions, that threaten present-day "advanced" societies.

. . .

At this last moment of reflection another figure from Greek mythology comes to mind. It is that of Atlas, bearing with endless perseverance the weight of the heavens in his hands. If man is to rescue life, it must first preserve the very will to live, and thereby rescue the future from the angry condemnation of the present.[142]

The "angry condemnation of the present" has been the result of intelligence's and imagination's somewhat unsuccessful attempts to dominate natural process.[143] Heilbroner attributes to this "Promethean spirit" not only the cause of the present dilemma but also the root of the death wish which leads modern man to ignore, and, indeed, self-indulgently to accelerate those conditions which lead towards the tumultuous future of the planet.[144] But man need not resign himself to a future of complete self-destruction. And the foundation of Heilbroner's hope is a fact about man; "the elements of fortitude and will from which the image of Atlas springs."[145] Like all of world process man is oriented towards *survival* in an equilibrium system of forces and counter-forces. If our restless spirit of aggressive creativity has resulted in our disturbing an equilibrium on the planet, then this drive towards survival will surface when the counter-forces of war, climatic changes, food and resource shortages lash back to restore the balance. While Heilbroner conceives the myths of Atlas and Prometheus to be "immense projections of our own hopes and capabilities" which are "cast on the screen of our imaginations," he nonetheless recognizes the spirit of "fortitude and will" to be a true and powerful dimension of humanity "from which the image of Atlas springs."[146] Man is oriented towards survival, but survival will be possible only if we abandon "the lethal techniques, the uncongenial lifeways, and the dangerous mentality of industrial civilization itself."[147] The conditions along the road towards survival will call forth that will and that determination for survival which is a profound part of what we are as human. We can project this dimension of ourselves into our imaginations and into the collective imaginations of future generations, as a myth about man and the cosmos, the myth of Atlas. And such projections can reinforce our determination and our will to survive, and shape our attitudes to conform to the life conditions of the difficult age to come.

What is Heilbroner doing here?

I would suggest that Heilbroner has taken a first giant step back from the massive rejection of religion that followed upon Marx's, Feuerbach's and Freud's discovery that religion emerges in a concrete, human, historical and psychological context of events and operations. He has encountered the limits which knowing must transcend if it is to face the most profound and the most terrifying realities of human life. He has discovered that a higher viewpoint is demanded by intelligence if man is to allow the immanent criteria of intelligence full reign in human life. And while Heilbroner may reject the subsequent question of truth which is equally demanded by intelligence, and while he may restrict his horizon of data on human life to exclude the concrete experiences of transcendence operative within life, nonetheless, he has come face to face with the terrible question to which God is an answer. I would suggest that Heilbroner's courageous confrontation with the possibility that world process may, in fact, be hostile or indifferent to humanity, is a perfect example of the way in which a higher viewpoint on humanity, on history, on world process inevitably raises the question of ultimate meaning, of transcendent knowledge, of religion, of God.[148]

I do not know whether Heilbroner would be offended at the suggestion that his concerns and his approach in *The Human Prospect* bear many of the characteristics of religion. My intent here is not to offend by suggesting that Heilbroner's presentation shares with traditional religions characteristics that he would wish to reject as a personal stance on life. Rather, my intent is to respect and to admire Heilbroner's seriousness and his comprehensive vision and to point to his concerns as an instance of a somewhat renewed and perhaps more original meaning for the word "religion." Furthermore my intent is to appeal to Heilbroner's own "higher viewpoint" as an illustrative example of what is entailed in Lonergan's notion of cosmopolis.

In the face of a future prospect so terrible as to involve a possible end to the human race, Heilbroner's horizons expanded to include questions about the nature of humanity, the benevolence of world process, and the grounds and limitations for hope in the future of humanity. His last chapter ends with a set of speculations on the overarching structure of world process, our place in this structure, the role of intelligence and imagination and the root of suffering, human obtuseness and corruption in this structure. His speculations appeal to experiential data within human life. And while his speculations go well beyond the limitations of the data his own rejection of mistaken views suggests that the data on human experience is sufficient to warrant a critical appraisal of possible higher viewpoints. Whether Heilbroner's analysis stands up in such a critical appraisal is not my direct concern here. I would venture to say that some of his insights would be rejected or significantly modified were they subjected to a dialectical analysis that appealed to some empirically verifiable insights on cognitional acts. However, my goal here is to indicate that a higher viewpoint on humanity, on human history, on world process, on our orientations, our ends, our grounds for hope, is the inevitable result of a line of questioning which begins with the profound experience of human limitations and pushes to the limit intelligence's demands for answers which satisfy its own immanent criteria. Far from exceeding the limits of empirical intelligence such a higher viewpoint is forced upon us by empirical intelligence itself. And as Heilbroner well understands, intelligence is none the less ruthless in its demands for correct answers and for adequate data, even if it grasps its own limitations in this realm of transcendent knowledge.[149]

I would suggest that Lonergan used the word, cosmopolis, in *Insight*, chapter seven, in an effort to point towards this dimension within human experience, this set of questions and answers about transcendent being which is Heilbroner's concern in his final chapter of *The Human Prospect* and which arises inevitably in a resolute attempt to understand human possibilities and human limitations within history. I would suggest that he knew that all serious questioning about human life, historical origins, and grounds for human hope must necessarily lead to questions about relatively or absolutely transcendent being regardless of how one might answer these questions.[150] But I would also suggest that he used the word, cosmopolis, at this point, early in *Insight*, in order to prevent the confusions and misunderstandings that words like "transcendent being," "grace," and "God" generally evoke. His goal was to point towards those dimensions of God's operation within human life to which religious experience responds and about which religion and theology ask and answer questions. And his strategy was to avoid misleading the reader with references to traditional religious answers and practices.

It is not clear to me whether Lonergan understood cosmopolis to be coextensive with the full range of religious, philosophical and theological knowledge of transcendent being. It would appear that the questions about God which are raised and answered in *Insight*, chapter nineteen, are conceived explicitly by Lonergan to be a prelude to a discussion of the objective correlate to the higher viewpoint, cosmopolis, namely faith, hope and charity. His critical realist cognitional theory demands that a higher viewpoint in the mind can arise only by virtue of a corresponding higher integration in the realm of being.[151] And from Lonergan's concluding paragraphs in chapter eighteen of *Insight*, it becomes clear that while the higher viewpoint in the mind is what he designates by the term, cosmopolis, the higher integration in the realm of being is the transformation of the human subject resulting from God's gift of grace.

Earlier, in the chapter of Common Sense as Object, it was concluded that a viewpoint higher than the viewpoint of common sense was needed; moreover, that X was given the name, cosmopolis, and some of its aspects and functions were indicated. But the subsequent argument has revealed that, besides higher viewpoints in the mind, there are higher integrations in the realm of being; and both the initial and subsequent argument have left it abundantly clear that the needed higher viewpoint is a concrete possibility only as a consequence of an actual higher integration.

Finally, whether the needed higher integration has emerged or is yet to emerge, is a question of fact. Similarly, its nature is not an object for speculation but for empirical inquiry. Still, what can that empirical inquiry be? Since our metaphysics and ethics have been developed under a restriction to proportionate being, we have to raise the question of transcendent knowledge before we can attempt an investigation of the ulterior finality of man.[152]

For the present I think we can conclude reasonably that in *Insight*, Lonergan intended the notion of cosmopolis to lead to the question of God, to the arguments about God developed in chapter nineteen, and, most significantly for my purposes here, to God's "solution" to the apparent impasse presented by his analysis of the human situation, which he works out in chapter twenty, "Special Transcendent Knowledge."

It would be beyond the scope of this study to examine Lonergan's conclusions about God which are worked out in *Insight*, chapter nineteen, and to evaluate how his answers to theological questions stand in relation to those of Marx and Heilbroner. I think it is safe to note Nicholas Lash's observations that Marx was, in fact, engaging in theological speculation.[153] And from the brief exposition of Heilbroner's *Inquiry*, above, I think it is safe to conclude that his "higher viewpoint" on the human prospect includes answers to questions about "the ultimate dimension" which Fred Streng identifies as a central characteristic of religions. What is of interest here is how Lonergan conceives the solution to the human situation and how this solution stands in continuity with the earlier chapters of *Insight* and, at the same time, sets the stage for a shift in his attention in *Method* and in the bulk of his works written after *Insight*.[154]

### 7.7.3 God's Love as the Wholly Transcendent Solution Operative Immanently in the Lives of Subjects

In his "Epilogue" to *Insight*, we get an indication as to what Lonergan understood himself to be doing in chapter twenty, and how he conceived the whole of *Insight* as a bridge between the human sciences and theology. Still such human science would offer, not an adequate understanding of its proper aspect of human activity, but only the measure of understanding possible from the scientific viewpoint. For an adequate understanding reveals the manner in which man can remedy the evil in his situation. But the solution to man's problem of evil has been seen to lie, not in a human initiative, but in an acceptance of the solution that God has provided; and while empirical human science can lead on to the further context of the solution, the systematic treatment of the solution itself is theological. In a word, empirical human science can become practical only through theology, and the relentless modern drift to social engineering and totalitarian controls is the fruit of man's effort to make human science practical though he prescinds from God and from the solution God provides for man's problem.

My second suggestion is the obverse of the first. Grace perfects nature both in the sense that it adds a perfection beyond nature and in the sense that it confers on nature the effective freedom to attain its own perfection.[155] A glance through the index to *Insight* reveals onto two entries beside the word, "grace." One might be led to conclude, from this, that Lonergan was not concerned with grace, in *Insight*, but with the solution(s) to the human problem which could be initiated by man. However, Lonergan's remarks above, as well as his conclusions on cosmopolis, summarized earlier, would suggest that he saw no possible solution that could be secured on the basis of purely human initiative. Consequently his analysis of "The Heuristic Structure of the Solution" in chapter twenty must be understood as an analysis of the locus of the operation of grace. It should become clear that Lonergan understands the operation of God's grace, in its capacity to transform human subjects, to be the condition of possibility for the development and the fully competent operation of human intelligence and responsibility.

His analysis of the structure of the solution begins with the fact of the goodness of being. Like all facts Lonergan's judgment here is an insight into the data of human experience which is pronounced v-probably true. And his proof is an extrapolation of the structure of proportionate being into the realm of transcendent being.[156] But since Lonergan has ruled out the possibility of a solution at the level of purely human agency, this fact requires the introduction of further elements of his "higher viewpoint."

Fifthly, the solution can consist in the introduction of new conjugate forms in man's intellect, will, and sensitivity.

For such forms are habits.
...
because man's living is prior to learning and being persuaded, it is without the guidance of knowledge and without the direction of effective good will; as long as that priority remains, the problem remains. The solution, then, must reverse the priority, and it does so inasmuch as it provides intellect, will, and sensitivity with forms or habits that are operative throughout living.

Seventhly, the relevant conjugate forms will be in some sense transcendent or supernatural.[157]

In accordance with the structure of emergent probability, the higher order conjugate forms are integrations in and of a lower order manifold in dialectical tension with an exigence of that manifold. Like all higher order integrations these habits are in no way a departure from the events and routines of the manifold but they are an ordering of the sensitive drives, passions, feelings, anticipations, habitual insights, values, outlooks, practical routines, skills, and aspirations of the human person.

Eighthly, since the solution is a harmonious continuation of the actual order of the universe, and since that order involves the successive emergence of higher integrations that systematize the non-systematic residues on lower levels, it follows that the relatively transcendent conjugate forms will constitute a new and higher integration of human activity and that that higher integration will solve the problem by controlling elements that otherwise are non-systematic or irrational.[158]

What is this higher order integration which will constitute a solution to the problem of the general bias and its longer cycle of decline? In Lonergan's view it is the habit of "charity" in which the "will" is ordered towards God, in which this habitual love of being manifests itself in an ordering of the intellect, and in which the overall effect on the subject is a transformation in the orientation of one's complete spontaneity. The solution consists in an inversion of the priority of living over knowing how to live. For with charity, the capacity of practical intelligence to devise and to implement courses of action which realize true value rests no longer simply upon the capacity of developed intelligence, but now upon the affective, intelligent and responsible spontaneity of the subject to seek and realize the good.

In the thirteenth place, then, the appropriate willingness will be some type or species of charity. ...

Again, a man or woman knows that he or she is in love by making the discovery that all spontaneous and deliberate tendencies and actions regard the beloved. Now as the arm rises spontaneously to protect the head, so all the parts of each thing conspire to the good of the whole, and all things in all their operations proceed to the realization of the order of the universe.[159]

I would suggest that the deficiencies pointed out above in Lonergan's retention of the older, faculty psychology distinction between intellect and will, show up again when Lonergan states that "good will follows intellect."[160] It might seem as if Lonergan were presenting an intellectualist account of grace by affirming that an act of intelligence needs to precede an act of love and that grace is, first and principally, a good insight. But his meaning, I would suggest, is better understood by noting that with charity the will follows the *"desire of intellect."*

> For good will follows intellect, and so it matches the detached, disinterested, *desire of intellect for complete understanding*; but complete understanding is the unrestricted act that is God; and so the good that is willed by good will is God.[161]

The point Lonergan is making here is that just as intelligence, in its appetite for understanding and truth, is oriented towards God, so too practical, responsible intelligence "follows" the earlier stages or operations in the complete skill of intelligent, responsible human living in this *hunger for God*. Whereas the actual operations of understanding and judging truth may be performed either competently or incompetently, charity is the orientation of practical, responsible living in accordance with the *ultimate desire* of intelligent humanity, irrespective of the subject's failures, defects, biases, or incomplete development in some or all aspects of the overall range of skills. Consequently while the charitable will "follows" the "desire" of intellect in the sense that it shares its orientation towards God, it need not, and in fact does not, "follow intellect" in the temporal sense of awaiting the correctly judged insight. And for this reason Lonergan can conclude that good will has the subsequent effect of functioning as the condition of possibility for the perfection of intelligence.

> In the fourteenth place, besides the charity by which the will itself is made good, there will be the hope by which the will makes the intellect good.
>
> For intellect functions properly inasmuch as the detached and disinterested desire to know is dominant in cognitional operations. Still this desire is merely spontaneous. It is the root of intelligent and rational self-consciousness, and it operates prior to our insights, our judgments, and our decisions. Now if this desire is to be maintained in its purity, if it is not to suffer from the competition of the attached and interested desires of man's sensitivity and intersubjectivity, if it is not to be overruled by the will's connivance with rationalizations,

then it must be aided, supported, reinforced by a deliberate decision and a habitual determination of the will itself.[162]

I have discussed above, some of the problems associated with Lonergan's insistence that "the detached and disinterested desire to know" stands in contrast and in competition with "the attached and interested desires of man's sensitivity and intersubjectivity."[163] Whereas this mode of expression might seem to lead one to conclude that knowing stands opposed to the other human and intersubjective desires, and that those other desires constitute an intrusion into the proper operation of intelligence, I have suggested that Lonergan's analysis understands knowing as an act of coordinating or integrating these other desires and that the integration effected by knowing (most particularly knowing value) seeks an isomorphism with a structured dynamism operative in all of human spontaneity.[164] However, Lonergan's subsequent analysis of belief and faith, in *Insight*, does place considerable emphasis upon the role of knowledge in the reversal of the longer cycle of decline.

There is needed in the present a universally accessible and permanently effective manner of pulling men's minds out of the counter-positions, of fixing them in the positions, of securing for them certitude that God exists and that he has provided a solution which they are to acknowledge and to accept. ...

Now the argument outlined above goes to prove that there is no probability of men generally moving from the counter-positions to the positions by immanently generated knowledge. On the other hand, as far as the argument goes, it reveals no obstacles to the attainment of truth through the communication of reliable knowledge.[165]

It is clear that his focus here upon the importance of knowledge (particularly knowledge of value) in reversing the longer cycle of decline is a focus upon knowledge as a communal, cultural, historical, religious inheritance and that within the context of his analysis of charity, the condition of possibility for the appropriation of this knowledge in "belief" is a transformation of the "will" in love.[166] However, while I am convinced that the role of knowledge in reversing the general bias cannot be underestimated I would say that his analysis of the route towards reversal, in *Insight*, remains to be complemented by a fuller study of the role and nature of conversions, the massive effect of symbols, cultural traditions, economic and social modes of life and work, and, most generally, the various ways in which human spontaneity, patterns of action, and profound feelings aroused by literature can shift the f-probabilities of virtuous action in cultures in the absence of immanently generated or responsibly appropriated knowledge of fact. Lonergan's work in *Method* marks a first step in the direction of this complementary study.[167]

One final word needs to be said here on the particular way in which charity constitutes a reversal to the historical cycle of decline generated by the general bias.

> Now the will can contribute to the solution of the problem of the social surd, inasmuch as it adopts a dialectical attitude that parallels the dialectical method of intellect. The dialectical method of intellect consists in grasping that the social surd neither is intelligible nor is to be treated as intelligible. The corresponding dialectical attitude of will is to return good for evil. For it is only inasmuch as men are willing to meet evil with good, to love their enemies, to pray for those that persecute and calumniate them, that the social surd is a potential good. It follows that love of God above all and in all so embraces the order of the universe as to love all men with a self-sacrificing love.[168]

How this dialectical attitude of "will" would translate into concrete economic, political, social programs of action remains to be discovered in an analysis of history and an in-depth study of the economic, political, social problems of our times. Lonergan's account here focuses only upon *the structure* of a solution which would stop the ever-accelerating cycles in which progressively deformed cultural patterns of experience become the data base for progressively shrinking ranges of insights on human life, and such shrinking ranges of insights become implemented as the practical routines of the subsequent cultures. The root of this cycle of decline is common sense's tendency to generalize insights from common experience. As actual experience becomes more and more deformed common sense develops theories that ratify the deformations, it despairs of the possibility of broader explanations of human potentials, and it pronounces the rule of force as the only corrective for the deformations. The dialectical attitude of "will," on the other hand, breaks the ever accelerating cycle of decline because it refuses to respond in kind to the fact of evil. The "will" transformed by love refuses to accept the fact of evil as the whole story, it refuses to explain the totality of life on the basis of an appeal to the massive proliferation of evil, and it refuses to base its practical response upon a despair of man ever rising above the corruption of common practice.[169]

Lonergan conceives the charitable "will" as practical intelligence's gracefull refusal to act in accordance with common sense's generalizations from corrupt practice. It is the refusal to meet evil with evil, to meet aggression merely with the punitive rule of force. It is, more positively, humanity's willingness to respond to the fact of evil with an act of love, to look to the historical evidence of such benevolence as an integral part of the foundation for a science of man, and to base the programs of action of a society upon a political theory which anticipates graceful benevolence and which is itself animated by such benevolence. What we find in *Insight*, chapter twenty, is the completion of Lonergan's analysis of cosmopolis, begun in chapter seven. With the transformation of the "will" (clearly a misleading term) in an act of charity, practical intelligence is liberated from its bondage to the experience of corrupt practice, and theoretical intelligence is given an orientation and a data base upon which to understand and act towards realizing new human possibilities. While the solution is the liberation and the orientation of intelligence towards truth and value the condition of possibility for this operation of intelligence is not itself an act of intelligence, the fruit of human initiative, but an act of grace which orders human intelligence and responsibility while at the same time respecting its essential freedom.

*Insight*, chapter twenty, is clearly the transition to Lonergan's book on theology, the book which Lonergan set out to write when he began *Insight*, and which he had to leave until *Method*. There is no doubt in my mind that Lonergan understood a theology to be the only adequate foundation for a science of man. And if I am right in noting the novelty of his emergent probability foundations for a theology, then it is clear that Lonergan did not conceive such a theology to be a completed enterprise. I would say that his life's work was devoted to laying foundations for a theology that could take seriously the procedures and the discoveries of the nineteenth and twentieth century natural and human sciences. And his call for a theology to provide a foundation for a renewed human science was born of the conviction that any other approach would paralyze human science with a heuristic and a foundation that progressively stifled that of man which is most distinctively human, his and her drive towards self-transcendence, towards God.

## FOOTNOTES – CHAPTER 7

1. For example, *Insight*, p. 227.
2. For example, ibid., p. 215.
3. See chap. three above, 3.2 on "implicit definition."
4. Among them are Patrick Gardiner, ed., *Theories of History* (Glencoe, Ill.: The Free Press, 1960); Hans Meyerhoff, ed., *The Philosophy of History in Our Time* (Garden City, N. Y.: Doubleday, 1959); Karl Löwith, *Meaning in History* (Chicago: University of Chicago Press, 1949); Dray, *Philosophy of History*; Walsh, *Philosophy of History: An Introduction*.
5. See particularly Davis, "Lonergan's Appropriation"; Kerr, "Beyond Lonergan's Method."
6. See above, 5.2, 5.6, 6.4.2, and 6.4.3.
7. Thomas Hobbes, *Leviathan*, edited with an introduction by Michael Oakeshott (Oxford: Basil Blackwell, 1957).
8. See Oakeshott's "Introduction," in Hobbes, pp. xxxiv-xxxv. See also Hobbes, pp. 80-84.
9. Oakeshott in Hobbes, p. xxxv.
10. Oakeshott in Hobbes, pp. xxvi-xxix; Hobbes, pp. 84-113.
11. See C. B. Macpherson, *The Political Theory of Possessive Individualism: Hobbes to Locke* (London: Oxford University Press, 1975; originally published 1962), pp. 88, 91, 264-265, 272. For Macphersons's criticisms of the generality of Hobbes' view of society as essentially and ineluctably competitive, see p. 100.
12. For Macpherson's reconstruction of the qualified relevance of Hobbes' view, see pp. 105-106.
13. Macpherson, pp. 61-2, 272-3.
14. Ibid., p. 3.
15. Ibid., pp. 29, 45-6.
16. Ibid., pp. 46-61, 273ff.
17. Ibid., pp. 53-61, 70-71.
18. Macpherson, "Introduction," in *Leviathan*, by Thomas Hobbes (Harmondsworth: Penguin Books, 1968), pp. 9-10.
19. Macpherson, *Political Theory*, p. 55.
20. See 6.4.2 above.
21. Lonergan's discussion of this material is in *Insight*, pp. 211-214.
22. See *Insight*, p. 215.
23. Ibid., p. 213. One might suggest that Lonergan's account here is similar to what Marx does in his account of the forces and relations of production. On Marx, on this similarity, and on differences in the two approaches, see 7.5 below.
24. Fred Lawrence argues that such a distortion is evident in the political theory of Machiavelli and he charts the influence of this distortion through subsequent political theorists. Fred Lawrence, "Political Theology and 'The Longer Cycle of Decline'," in *Lonergan Workshop*, vol. I, pp. 239-243.
25. See *Insight*, pp. 218-222.
26. See ibid., pp. 218-219.
27. See ibid., p. 221.
28. Ibid.
29. See 6.4.2 above.
30. *Insight*, p. 219. Charles Davis criticizes the apparent implications of Lonergan's account here in "Lonergan's Appropriation," pp. 118-19, 120-22.
31. See ibid., pp. 217-218. See also chap. 6, 6.4.1, 6.4.2 above.
32. Macpherson, *Political Theory*, pp. 272-4.
33. *Insight*, p. 235.
34. Ibid., p. 207. See also my account of history as meaning, 6.4 above.

35 Ibid., pp. 207-9.
36 It is this practical application of intelligence which, for the most part, constitutes history as "meaning," and which is intended in Lonergan's account of history as meaning; see 6.4 and 6.3 above. Again, acts of intelligence need not be the genesis of novelty but rather, more frequently, they are the subject's intelligent integration of skills within his or her repertoire in accordance with an order or pattern common to a society; see 5.3 above.
37 *Insight*, p. 222; see also pp. 213-214.
38 Ibid., p. 222; see also p. 216.
39 See 6.4.2 and 7.1 above.
40 *Insight*, pp. 222-23.
41 See 6.4.2 and 7.1 above.
42 *Insight*, p. 223.
43 This restriction of horizons is the meaning that Gibson Winter intends by the word "ideology." See *Elements*, p. 67.
44 *Insight*, p. 224.
45 Ibid.
46 Ibid., p. 225.
47 See, for example, G. A. Cohen, *Karl Marx's Theory of History: A Defence* (Oxford: Clarendon Press, 1978).
48 This summary account of "alienation" is drawn from Herbert Marcuse, *Reason and Revolution*, pp. 273-280. This account of Marcuse's is neither original nor without considerable support. The relevant texts of Marx are the "Economic and Philosophical Manuscripts of 1844," and *The German Ideology*; see Robert C. Tucker, *The Marx-Engels Reader*, second edition (New York: W. W. Norton, 1978), pp. 70-81, 84-85, 117-125, 149-200. See also Nicholas Lash, *A Matter of Hope: A Theologian's Reflections on the Thought of Karl Marx* (London: Darton, Longman and Todd, 1981), pp. 40-45, 170-175, 186-7. For an extended discussion of the human situation and alienation, see John Plamenatz, *Karl Marx's Philosophy of Man* (Oxford: Clarendon Press, 1975), chaps. IV-VI.
49 William Shaw, *Marx's Theory of History* (Stanford, Calif.: Stanford University Press, 1978).
50 Ibid., pp. 10-27.
51 These are the "relations of production," ibid., pp. 27-42.
52 Ibid., pp. 42-50.
53 Ibid., pp. 54-5.
54 Ibid., pp. 53-82. See also Cohen, pp. 134-174.
55 Marcuse, p. 282.
56 Lash, pp. 45-6, see also pp. 244-5. Lash's account draws upon *The German Ideology*.
57 See Lash, pp. 45-7, 186-8, 240-1, 244-5.
58 See also Marcuse, pp. 291, 288.
59 Shaw, p. 109, 155-6.
60 Ibid., p. 112. See also Allen Buchanan, "The Marxian Critique of Justice and Rights," in *Marx and Morality*, pp. 296-7.
61 See Shaw, p. 113.
62 I say extreme because others argue that Marx's thought includes the possibility of justice; see, for example, Jeffrey Reiman, "The Possibility of a Marxian Theory of Justice," in *Marx and Morality*, pp. 307-322. Whether this latter view demands admitting that Marx was incorrect in his account of the sources of interpersonal conflict remains to be seen. See Nielsen, "Introduction," in *Marx and Morality*, pp. 12-13.
63 Buchanan, p. 283. See also pp. 279, 288.
64 See my discussion of Macpherson's critique of Hobbes, 7.1, 7.2 above.
65 Plamenatz, p. 160. See also Nielsen, "Introduction," pp. 12-13.

66  Fergus Kerr, "Beyond Lonergan's Method," pp. 70-1.
67  Ibid., p. 64.
68  See, for example, *Method*, pp. 237-244, 130-131, 283-4; "Theology and Praxis," pp. 14-16.
69  On the philosophical and theological problems associated with this impatience, see Lash, chapters 17 and 18.
70  See chapter six, 6.6 above.
71  See note 69 this chapter above.
72  In his article, "Lonergan's Appropriation," Charles Davis suggests that while *Method* turns to feelings, religious love and to the distinct transcendental notion of value, and while these notions correct the overly intellectualist stance of *Insight*, still Lonergan's account of the human situation in *Insight* would be transformed significantly if these notions were integrated into a revised account; see pp. 120-123.
73  One might ask here whether Lonergan's account of the happy conscience is, fundamentally, an account of practical intelligence whose authentic or responsible performance is known through a feeling. See, for example, *Method*, pp. 35, 268-9. Indeed is not such a feeling the foundation of competent performance in all intelligent acts in this view? The answer, I would suggest, involves distinguishing among classes of feelings, noting that one particular class accompanies competent intelligent performance in the intellectual pattern, and another accompanies responsible performance in the dramatic pattern (i.e. all feelings are not of a kind), and recognizing that these particular classes of feelings intend objects of their operations authentically performed and not vice versa. The fundamental criterion is not the feeling but authentic performance. Thus Lonergan has spent his life understanding the dynamic structure of authentic performance.
74  This is, fundamentally, the grounds for Lonergan's notion of "belief" and his distinction of "belief" from "faith." See *Insight*, pp. 703-721.
75  I am in no way using the words "competent" and "incompetent" here in any "techno-rationalist" sense. Rather, an analogue would be the professional concert violinist who can become and remain competent only through a lifetime's passionate devotion to skill and beauty. The qualifier to this analogate would be the fact that competence in the area of human responsibility requires an additional psychological and religious "conversion" which the musician may or may not require.
76  See *Insight*, p. 693, re "statistical fact."
77  Ibid., p. 225.
78  Frederick Crowe and Walter Conn place considerable emphasis upon the changes in Lonergan's notion of "value" that are evident in works written after *Insight*. See Crowe, "An Exploration," and Conn, "Bernard Lonergan on Value." The analysis which follows provides some evidence that these changes were going on while *Insight* was being written.
79  *Grace and Freedom*, pp. 93ff.
80  See also *Insight*, chap. 20.
81  *Method*, pp. 268-69; see also pp. 121-22. Crowe and Conn place the significant moment of Lonergan's change with his 1968 Aquinas Lecture, *The Subject*. Conn, "Bernard Lonergan on Value," pp. 247ff; Crowe, "An Exploration," p. 127.
82  *Grace and Freedom*, p. 95.
83  See Copleston, *A History of Philosophy*, vol. 2, part 2, pp. 94ff, particularly p. 99.
84  *Grace and Freedom*, p. 96.
85  This fact is powerfully evident throughout Lonergan's account of the development of the state of the question on freedom and grace leading up to Thomas. For St. Augustine, the facts of human freedom of the will and of God's divine operation were taken as given and the problem was one of reconciling their apparent mutual exclusion, *Grace and Freedom*, pp. 2-4. Similarly through the work of St. Anselm and Peter Lombard,

the efforts were to render coherent the efficacy of grace in rendering man free and the starting point for the questions was always the distinction of intellect from will and the way in which grace operates on the will, pp. 6, 9-10.

86 *Insight*, pp. 598-9.
87 In Chapters 2 and 6 of *Wealth of Self*, McShane distinguishes the act of questioning from the insight which answers the question, on the one hand, and from the act of formulation which further refines the insight in a subsequent set of questions and answers. These three acts appeal to and seek to order or integrate the "data" of "experiential acts," when the term "experiential acts" means simply any set of human experiences which stands in relation to a "what question" which asks about its "nature." These four types of acts are complemented by a further set of three acts, the "is-question," the insight and the formulation, which when completed yield a v-probable answer to the question of truth. These acts are then duplicated at the "responsible level" when the questions ask not about the facts of reality but about the value of possible courses of action. "Experience," (the first type of act) is not duplicated on the responsible level but the remaining six are. And these thirteen are completed by a final act of decision.
88 *Insight*, pp. 609-610.
89 Ibid., p. 601.
90 Ibid., pp. 609-616. See *Method*, pp. 35, 36-41, 268 for the development in Lonergan's analysis of "practical reflection" and for the distinctions that Lonergan retains. See also McShane, *Wealth of Self*, pp. 48-49.
91 *Method*, pp. 36-41.
92 *Insight*, p. 611.
93 Ibid., pp. 596, 598.
94 Ibid., p. 598.
95 See, for example, *Method*, p. 13 on the "eros of the human spirit."
96 *Insight*, pp. 614-15.
97 Ibid., p. 599.
98 Ibid., p. 613. Davis is correct in criticizing the position implied in these quotations, "Lonergan's Appropriation," pp. 118-119, 120-21. My attempt to reconstruct Lonergan's intended meaning has sought to meet these criticisms by noting that his intention must diverge from this implication.
99 See *Method*, pp. 235-37, 237-44.
100 Since Lonergan's notion of development places principal emphasis upon the higher order transformations in one's horizons, one's attitudes, one's spontaneity, one's values which result from a conversion to a more comprehensive integration of the materials of life, his analysis of the "systematic exigence," the "theoretical differentiation of consciousness" takes on a new meaning. For the point of a higher viewpoint on life is not so much its ability to yield further knowledge on life but its effect upon our habitual capacities and spontaneity, to carry out responsibly the business of culture.
101 See *Insight*, p. 632.
102 *Insight*, pp. 225-6.
103 Ibid., pp. 227-8.
104 Ibid., p. 226.
105 Again in his response to E. MacKinnon, Lonergan recognizes the public character of meaning and the conditioning role of this public meaning for acts of individuals. Individual's acts of meaning are most usually the grasp and practical implementation of this public inheritance of culture. See *Method*, pp. 254-57.
106 *Insight*, pp. 226-8.
107 Lawrence, "Political Theology," p. 239.
108 The difference between common sense's successive generalizations from ever-shrinking ranges of current practice and a more critical "theoretical" operation of intelligence

which seeks to understand man, not simply as he currently behaves, but as he could be, as that to which he could aspire, rests, most fundamentally, in the range of "data" about man to which intelligence opens itself. In its resolute concern for immediate practicality common sense rules out any experience which would not seem to be immediately relevant to the project at hand and which would not seem to be immediately verifiable in an appeal to common practice. See *Insight*, pp. 176-181, 228-232, and chap. five above. On intelligence's immanent norm of "progress," see 6.5 and 6.6 above.

109 Gustafson, p. 7.
110 Ibid.
111 Ibid., p. 8.
112 Ibid., p. 62.
113 Ibid., p. 9.
114 Ibid., p. 11.
115 See *Insight*, pp. 693-4. On the specific meaning of "statistical law," see chap. three above.
116 *Insight*, pp. 233ff.
117 See chapters three and four above on the meaning of "randomness" and its role in emergence. See also Lonergan's notion of "liberty" in *Insight*, pp. 234-5. This notion is integrally linked to the role of "trial and error" in the accumulation and development of practical skills. See chap. five above.
118 *Insight*, p. 234.
119 The analysis of how, exactly, a restructuring of social, historical and economic conditions can play a role in progress, remains, clearly, beyond the scope of this analysis. I would suggest that Charles Davis' article, "Lonergan's Appropriation," is a call for Lonergan's analysis to be extended to include a consideration of such a restructuring. My presentation here is oriented towards showing that Lonergan's foundations do not preclude such an extension. I would suggest that the limited but profound contribution of Lonergan's analysis to the vast field of current literature on the import of social, economic, cultural, psychological, conditions for human life rests in this insight that such conditions must be oriented towards promoting subjective authenticity, development, conversion, responsibility rather than bypassing or precluding them.
120 *Insight*, pp. 236-238.
121 Ibid., pp. 238-239.
122 Ibid., pp. 239-40.
123 Ibid., pp. 240-241.
124 See ibid., pp. 690-692.
125 Ibid., pp. 690, 691, 692, 693, 694.
126 Ibid., p. 694.
127 Ibid., p. 633.
128 Robert L. Heilbroner, *An Inquiry into the Human Prospect*.
129 Heilbroner, pp. 131-132.
130 In fact Heilbroner laments that force may well be the only solution, p. 110.
133 Ibid., p. 110.
132 Ibid., p. 115.
133 Ibid., p. 118.
134 Ibid., p. 119.
135 Ibid., p. 117.
136 Ibid., pp. 132-133.
137 This term was coined by Jay W. Forrester. See *Principles of Systems*, second preliminary edition (Cambridge, Mass.: MIT Press, 1968), pp. 1-5 to 1-10.
138 Donella H. Meadows, Dennis L. Meadows, Jörgen Randers and William W. Behrens, III, *The Limits to Growth*, second edition (New York: New American Library; a Signet Book, 1974).

139  Edward Goldsmith, ed., *Blueprint for Survival* (New York: Houghton Mifflin, 1972). See Heilbroner, p. 133.
140  See *Insight*, p. 118; see also 3.3 above.
141  See Heilbroner, p. 133. See also pp. 104, 106, 107, 109, 110.
142  Ibid., pp. 141, 143-144.
143  Ibid., p. 142.
144  Ibid., pp. 142-143.
145  Ibid., p. 144.
146  Ibid., p. 144.
147  Ibid., p. 138; see also pp. 139-140.
148  In his account of religion, Frederick J. Streng shows how ultimate concerns which are authentically religious can emerge in a context which bears little resemblance to those of the traditional religions: "People today are often conscious of their 'conditionedness'; that is, they are aware of their limits and recognize that they must make decisions that can bring important changes in their lives. Within this consciousness, they wrestle with the larger questions of truth, reality, meaning, and the problems involved in living a full life. Many ask what is really true, and what is the purpose of life, thereby pondering in the most comprehensive way what it means to *be*. When people make demands on themselves and others in the name of a transpersonal and transcultural force (or forces), when they perceive facets and images of life that expose the source of life, wisdom and joy or when they become aware of modes of consciousness that transform common events into moments of extraordinary significance, they are probing the ultimate dimension. The fact that these perceptions may occur outside of traditional religious life makes them no less 'ultimate' for those who experience them." This dimension of religion is by no means the whole of religion, and Streng goes to considerable lengths to discuss the social, the institutional, the symbolic, dimensions of religions. The point here is that Heilbroner's concern bears significant characteristics of ultimate concern. *Understanding Religious Life*, second edition (Encino, Cal.: Dickenson Publishing Company, Inc., 1976), p. 5; see also pp. 2, 7, 8.
149  In spite of considerable uncertainty regarding his analyses of ongoing world processes and their possible outcomes, Heilbroner found himself, one year after the publication of his *Inquiry*, firm in his conviction that the structure of his analyses and the overall shape of his long-range predictions remained valid. In his postscript, "Second Thoughts on the Human Prospect," Heilbroner goes to great pains to marshall intelligible arguments in favour of his original conclusions, even in the face of a shifting data base. See Heilbroner, pp. 154-162. While one might be inclined to call such resolute conviction "ideology," my point here is not the content of his conclusions but the relentless *drive* of his intelligence towards a "higher viewpoint." Whether or not such a drive is always "ideological" depends upon whether the content should ever be judged true. This was Lonergan's concern in *Insight*, chap. 19.
150  See *Method*, pp. 101-3.
151  A full exposition of Lonergan's argument here is surely beyond the scope of this study. The whole of *Insight* is devoted to marshalling empirical evidence on cognitional acts and developing arguments on the basis of this evidence towards the v-probable conclusion that knowing does, in fact, know being, that being is the condition of possibility for such knowledge, and that knowing is an interrelated scheme of acts whose responsible performance results in the gradual conversion or transformation of undifferentiated human experiential events, into the objects of wonder, into the objects of imaginative and affective response, into insights, both fruitful and silly, into questions which ask about the truth of these insights, into judgments which settle these questions, into widely imaginative projects for action, and into the execution of projects that are judged worthwhile. In a very bare outline his argument here runs as follows. The structure of being shows evidence of higher order transformations of lower order

manifolds. Explanatory knowing proceeds as experiential data is converted from experiential conjugates (correlative data whose meaning is expressed by appeal to the content of some experience) to explanatory conjugates (correlative data defined implicitly in relation to each other by insights). And the fact of explanatory conjugates on a "higher order" of terms and relations is evidence of such a higher order integration in the realm of being (whatever such an integration might turn out to be) precisely because of knowing's spontaneous and resolute orientation towards being. This fact can only be denied by making an implicitly operative appeal to its truth. And while imagination can conjure up wild and wooly possibilities imagination is itself only one step in the wider scheme of acts of intelligently knowing human experience. The overwhelming presence of experiential data which raise questions about the structure and the benevolence of being perenially drives intelligence to possible answers which are necessarily higher viewpoints on man and world process. The fact that such higher viewpoints are held by those who seem to deny traditional answers to the question of God makes the evidence for this fact all the more convincing. To deny an objective correlate to this higher viewpoint would be to deny the whole knowing process which led one to arrive at this viewpoint on life or at any viewpoint on anything. See *Insight*, pp. 79-82, 255ff, 348ff, 437ff.

152 *Insight*, p. 633.
153 Lash, *A Matter of Hope*, pp. 252, 258-259.
154 On this shift in attention, see Charles Davis, "Lonergan's Appropriation," pp. 121-22.
155 *Insight*, pp. 745-746.
156 Ibid., pp. 641, 655, 657-658, 694.
157 Ibid., pp. 696-697.
158 Ibid., p. 697. See also pp. 723ff.
159 Ibid., p. 698.
160 Ibid.
161 Ibid., italics are mine.
162 Ibid., p. 701.
163 See 7.2, 7.6.1, 6.4.2, 5.3 above.
164 See 6.5 and 6.6 above on the relationship between "finality," historical progress and decline, and the foundations of value. What is interesting about Lonergan's analysis of intentionally-oriented feelings, in *Method*, pp. 30-34, is that here he opens the door towards understanding the human person as dynamically oriented towards truth and value in a variety of ways. In addition, the cultivation of human feelings and habits, either through the structures, the inheritance, the education of a culture, or through one's own discipline has the further effect of operating as an experiential exigence to shift the f-probabilities of insights and judgments of truth and value.
165 *Insight*, pp. 702-3.
166 Lonergan's definition of "belief" is quite distinctive. He distinguishes "faith" from "belief" and defines belief as the judgment to accept or to implement a truth or a value, not on the basis of an immanently generated cognitional act which assembles conditions linking insights to the data of personal experience, but on the basis of the judgment that another is a reliable authority or master. See *Insight*, pp. 702-720.
167 Contrary to Charles Davis, in "Lonergan's Appropriation," pp. 121-23, I would argue that such a development and complementary work would not affect substantially Lonergan's account of the general bias. Because reality is concrete the problem remains the insufficient f-probability of practical intelligence (responsibility). For only concrete subjective agency through practical intelligence can discern and implement values concretely in a world of shifting experiential exigences. Faith transforms the situation by transforming the subject into a person intent upon realizing good irrespective of the concrete circumstances which invite the generalization of evil. Belief comes in not only as belief of fact but more significantly as the communal cultivation and transmission of attitudes and practical skills oriented towards love. Such attitudes and skills do not

bypass concrete practical intelligence, they are its actuation, they enable its development and they transform its orientation. The issue, once again for Lonergan, is a concern for dynamic rather than static operators. Conversion, the complete transformation of the person, is to be understood after the analogy of "implicit definition" (see chap. one above), wherein a higher integration (in this case a set of relations operative at the fourth level of intentional consciousness) transforms the experiential and cognitionally mediated spontaneity of the subject by clustering and orientating the elements of the experiential manifold about a new centre. This transforms all subsequent intelligent and practical anticipations. Furthermore love does not alleviate the basic problem in the human situation, the necessity of doing before knowing how to do it. Love enables man to live with him or herself without accelerating decline.

168 *Insight*, p. 699.
169 Lonergan's analysis of charity, hope, faith and mystery is much richer than this brief introduction would suggest. See *Insight*, pp. 700-701, 724-5, 727.

# Epilogue

The expressed goal of this study has been to understand Lonergan's heuristic, emergent probability, as the underlying dynamic structure unifying his treatment of ethics in *Insight*, chapters six and eighteen and *Method*, chapter two, and his discussions of human history in *Insight*, chapters seven and twenty. In addition, my intention has been to show how emergent probability can operate as a structured heuristic for explaining evolutionary, historical and ethical events and processes, which opens on to a realm of being that is disproportionate to human knowing (transcendent being) and which admits the essential relevance of transcendent being for a solution to the core problem in human history, the general bias. To this end my order of proceeding has been to present the central terms and relations of emergent probability, as laid out in *Insight*, chapters one through four, and then to discuss these central terms and relations as they are operative implicitly or explicitly in the stated chapters on ethics and history.

Some work has been done on Lonergan's ethics and on his philosophy of history. However, none has treated explicitly the import of his notions of randomness, statistical laws, direct and inverse insights, recurrence schemes, and emergence as foundational for understanding the integral relationships linking his work in these two fields. It is emergent probability which explains the meaning of Lonergan's term, sublation. And while many authors have noted the term sublation as a key concept throughout his work since *Method*, few have adverted directly to the precise meaning of this term as it is worked out in the first chapters of *Insight*. In addition, I would suggest that since emergent probability was the explicitly stated heuristic operative throughout Lonergan's sketches of ethical foundations and historical dynamics in *Insight* and *Method* my treatment here has contributed to a more precise understanding of Lonergan's intended meanings there. Where particular preoccupations, questions and challenges guided Lonergan's formulations in these chapters, I would suggest that emergent probability constitutes the proper hermeneutical context for distinguishing the appropriate line of interpretation from those more immediately suggested by various instances of stylistic or rhetorical excess. Where some such excesses or inadequate conceptual formulations have led to obscurities or contradictions in his thought I have sought to suggest clarifications that would be in line with his more generally expressed intent. Finally, inasmuch as Lonergan's emergent probability is itself an original heuristic for unifying a foundation in ethics with a theory of evolution and human history, my exposition and clarification of Lonergan's thought constitutes an original contribution to the field of social ethics.

In general, the key to understanding how the terms and relations of emergent probability are operative in Lonergan's account of history as meaning and in his curious account of the solution to the moral and religious problem in human history is to be found in his explanation of the structure of practical intelligence. Randomness, classical laws, statistical laws, recurrence schemes, and emergence interrelate in the dynamic structure of practical knowing and doing. And these elements distinguish Lonergan's account of practical intelligence from an older approach which has its roots in a medieval faculty psychology. Rather than beginning with a distinction which isolates various human "faculties," Lonergan centres on evidence of a curious, spontaneous structuration with unifies events and elements of a random manifold of sensory, affective, appetitive routines and processes which are mediated to the human central nervous systems, from the inside, and the outside of the subject's envelope of skin by a wide rang of cyclically operative recurrence schemes. This spontaneous structuration (integration) occurs non-systematically, in accordance with coicidental convergences in the manifold of randomly interacting neural events and processes (the neural manifold). But the f-probable frequency of recurrence of classes of such structurations can be increased with the acquisition and development of skills which link ranges of acquired sensorimotor skills to such integrative events in emergent recurrence schemes.

Originally these spontaneous integrations are the groups of sensory data which yield the intentional presence of sensible unities. And because of the vast systems of correspondences in which sensory receptors cycle and recycle "in-formation" to the neural manifold, such structurations stand in some correspondence with unities in the subject's experiential field. But in addition to such sensory unities the human neural manifold has the wider flexibility to accommodate more intricate sets of correspondences among such sensory unities, and more significantly, to generate somewhat "synthetically" further intricate correspondences and integrations in the imagination.

This flexibility is the condition for the occurrence of a totally new and much more powerful, higher order event, the insight. Like the more basic integrations of sense the insight can stand in a recurrence scheme of sensorimotor, imaginative and intelligent events and skills, such that the developed competence in effecting the recurrence of the scheme of questions, anticipations, attention to experiential "data," trying out integrative possibilities and modifying questions, can increase substantially the f-probabilities of further insights in determinate fields of life. Again, the integrative event is a spontaneous convergence of events in a randomly interacting manifold rather than a cog in a clockwork of systematically unified classical processes. And so the skill linking the events of the scheme never guarantees the insight's occurrence. However, the ("horizontally") recurring scheme can shift the f-probabilities of the recurrence of the insights which emerge ("vertically") to re-order the experiential manifold thus transforming the developed skill and the subject's entire spontaneity.

In addition to skills linking questions, anticipations, images, clues and insights, there also emerge further series of schemes in which the subject adopts a new posture with respect to insights and asks about their adequacy in integrating available experiential elements, their perfection in accommodating relevant but more remote data, their efficiency in streamlining cognitionally integrative unities, and their heuristic power in opening up new experiential vistas. And so the wider series of schemes of intelligence orient the subject "upward" with an immanent norm which is a product of the series' own dynamic structure of interrelations. While such schemes and series set the subject in relation to his or her environment with a hunger, an appetite for knowledge of fact, more significantly they facilitate the subject's engagement with the materials of life with an ability to *constitute* a set of relations both in his or her "internal" and "external" environments, in accordance with the pattern or order emergent in the cognitional events. Thus an intelligibility is introduced onto the scene of world process which is to be explained not completely in terms of systematically or randomly interacting environmental conditions but essentially (if not completely) in terms of the internal terms and relations of the cognitional event. The subject can effect an order or pattern in his or her own repertoire of skills and, again, the integrative events occur and recur in accordance with statistical laws. But when the systematic links among the events in the cognitional and practical skills become habitual, and when the subject's repertoire of acquired insights, questions and skills is in some sense appropriate to the exigences of the experiential data, then the f-probabilities of the cognitional and practical emergent events increase substantially. Such is the structure of practical intelligence.

Because human beings do not operate in isolation but rather live in close proximity to each other, the cognitional events and skills of one person fall within the range of experience of another. And so the dialectic operative between the experiential exigencies of a subject and the immanent norm in the interrelated cognitional schemes is complemented by a second dialectic. For the presence of another person in one's life is the introduction of a distinct integrating principle. Humans have the very curious capability of taking on, almost wholesale, a structured attitude, a disposition, a skill, a linked set of operations, an integrated cognitional unity (either intellectual or practical) of another person. And Gibson Winter has appealed to a notion from George Herbert Mead, the notion of role-taking, to explain how this appropriation occurs. We seem to have the ability to assume the "viewing" perspective of another person, and to take on, as it were, the "picture" of ourselves and the world as it is "seen from their eyes." Because of this curious capacity, the content or objects of intelligent operations (and most significantly those of practical intelligence) are most usually the currently operative meanings, symbols, habits, skills, values, anticipations of a commonly shared culture. For the presence of another person as a distinct integrating principle within the experiential horizons of a subject increases the f-probabilities of the cognitional integrations of that other person occurring within the experiential manifold of the subject. And so a double dialectic ensues, the dialectic between the subject's own experiential exigences and the immanent norms of his or her own (usually practical) intelligence, and a dialectic between such exigences and those integrations he or she does or does not personally effect on the one hand, and the integrations that another would seem to have effected, on the other. Because the role-taking occurs with an extremely high f-probable frequency humans are social in a distinctively human sense. Because the role-taking is hardly ever complete and because it sits in a dialectical relationship with other immanently operative capacities and skills this sociality includes a communal tension.

Once children have reached a very basic level of competence in the acquisition and implementation of linguistic skills, their lives are, for the most part, shaped in accordance with immanently generated cognitional acts of practical intelligence even though such acts remain, in the greatest measure, the more or less modified reactuation of the meanings, values, concerns and anticipations of the common culture. But because each cognitional event modifies the subsequent spontaneity of the subject, and because the field of society includes systematic and random interactions among such events, both the subjective and the objective poles of social life are in constant flux, undergoing successive transformations which modify the experiential exigences of subjects' lives. One generation's solutions to the problems of living are learned by the next. And these solutions constitute the habitual spontaneity of that next generation. But in the interim the exigences of life have changed as the various solutions implemented by that previous generation collided with each other and with the events of the environment. In addition, events constituted by individual subjects have linked with those of other subjects in mutually conditioning groups or schemes. And while individuals have responded to the apparent recurrences in their social environment by making their needed contribution to the schemes on cue, no one has devised the schemes and no one has understood their overall functioning structure. Thus society and human history have been and continue to be constituted by acts of meaning even though novel insights into the data of experience remain rare and no one has grasped the immanent intelligibility operative at any point in world process. In the main, historical trends are to be understood in terms of the f-probable recurrence of classes of popular practical insights. And the emergence, stability, and demise of such statistical trends are to be explained more regularly in terms of the absence or refusal of novel discovery, and in terms of the power of the intersubjective drive towards mutuality, than in terms of insights in the intellectual pattern of experience.

While the capacity for role-taking and the drive towards mutuality with other subjects fulfills the conditions for huge leaps forward in the rates at which subjects can learn and become the sedimented products of the trial and error discoveries of previous cultures, this social principle is not without its pitfalls. For in itself this principle is uncritical. Intersubjective life is constantly in a state of flux, but publicly available meanings and routines remain adequate only as long as other things have remained equal. Because human living problems are concrete, what is needed is a flexibly operative, doubly dialectical skill in which subjects regularly consult a wider range of human experiences and insights relevant to more remote members of humanity. But because communally and socially operative events of practical cognition shape the spontaneity and the heuristic anticipations of subjects, such consultations are what the drive to mutuality tends to preclude. And so a group bias emerges, reinforcing the deformations in the operative insights of the group until the evidence of such deformations becomes obvious to all. At this point the obvious experiential exigences are mobilized as a principle for the reversal of decline and they remain operative until their own deformations begin their own reversal.

In the short run these cycles of decline and progress operate self-correctively. But in the long run they promote an additional and far more serious form of decline whose origins are rooted in what Lonergan calls the general bias. As with the group bias, the general bias is operative in the subject's dynamic structure of common sense intelligence. But because the general bias is rooted in the simple fact that practical intelligence creates more problems than it can solve, its effects are not limited to groups, cultures, or factions. As the insights of one age set the experiential routines of another age, the data for the insights of that subsequent age shrink to include only those partial insights which were made operative earlier. What intelligibility can be discerned in social historical processes is limited to what remains operative and reasonable from the earlier age. And since intelligence seeks to verify its insights in the data of daily experience the succession of ages will mark a diminishing body of intelligible experiences. As the ages display, to greater and greater degrees, an absence of intelligibility, intelligence is judged progressively irrelevant for handling the routines of culture. And the only possible solution to the general bias, intelligence's appeal to more remote evidence on life's possibilities, is more and more ruled out of court. Thus there follows a longer cycle of decline in which appeal to practical and theoretical intelligence is supplanted by an appeal to the use of force.

In his account of the solution to the problem of the general bias and its longer cycle of decline, Lonergan focuses upon the dialectically structured drive of explanatory and practical intelligence as the locus of the operation of a distinct principle — a wholly transcendent principle — and as the mediator of the fruits of this salvific principle. This is so because human history has as its distinctively human component the mediating acts of practical intelligence. Were the solution to prescind entirely from such human acts, human history would cease to be human for essential freedom would be precluded. But the salvific principle remains wholly transcendent in the sense that it in no way relies upon immanently generated knowledge (either theoretical or practical). Such immanently generated knowledge is what the general bias precludes. And it remains wholly transcendent in the additional sense that an account of its structure and its relation to proportionate being requires a distinctive type of inverse insight.

As with all movements to a "higher viewpoint" the first dimension of this inverse insight is the grasp that the available tools for the explanation of the relevant data are inadequate. The anticipations of an intelligibility operative at the level of historical process, systematizing historical events towards progress (or even towards survival) are replaced by the realization that a social surd is a constitutive element of the structure of historical process. There is an absence of intelligibility in the routines and processes of history, not simply because of the fact of randomly interacting classical laws, but also because common sense intelligence is regularly inadequate to its challenges. To understand this defect in common sense requires moving beyond common sense to a higher viewpoint in which the structure and role of common sense can be understood. This much Marx, Dilthey and Heilbroner understood.

But the inverse insight also grasps that because common sense is unable to recognize its inadequacy, the problem of human living is moral impotence. Only a widespread f-probable frequency of highly developed personal growth could reverse the general bias with its longer cycle of decline. For the locus of history is human subjects and historical progress demands widespread subjective growth. But such growth is precisely what the general bias both precludes and reverses. The problems of human living are concrete and manifold and constantly in a state of flux so no other solution but widespread personal development will meet their shifting exigences. And yet such development is not only infrequent, it is increasingly so. For common sense is resolutely empirical and the evidence for its generalizations are common practice.

However, the history of human life would seem to be a history in which decine is not the whole story. And so the inverse insight grasps that the whole story is not simply beyond the range of common sense, it is not simply the fact of moral impotence, but it is also disproportionate to any human knowing. And because a higher order integration can emerge and operate wherever a non-systematic manifold occurs, the inverse insight operates as a pivot for the turn to a wholly transcendent solution operative in the realm of human living, systematizing the manifold without bypassing or precluding the essential freedom which characterizes human life, and rendering such freedom effective by liberating it from the constraints of bias.

While an explanation of the human situation in the theoretical differentiation of consciousness involves this threefold inverse insight, the operation of the solution to the human problem does not await this inverse act of intelligence. In fact what intelligence grasps in this "higher viewpoint" is that the solution is already operative in human life, retarding the rate of decline and maintaining the possibility for the reversal of decline. But since the solution does not supplant practical intelligence, but rather demands its cooperation, the role of theoretical and practical intelligence remains vital for the long-term survival of the planet.

The general structure to the solution to the human problem is in line with the structure of all insights, all "higher viewpoints," all emergent schemes. The solution is a spontaneous structuration occurring in the lives of subjects, ordering the non-systematic manifold of experiential anticipations, orientations, and habitual inclinations (on the fourth level of intentional consciousness) in accordance with a wholly transcendent principle, a principle which (in the face of experiential evidence which would argue against its immediately practical expedience) refuses to return evil with evil. By defining implicitly the subject's entire range of practical anticipations about a new centre of terms and relations the "conversion" effectively liberates practical intelligence from the progressive enslavement to the general bias. And so far from precluding essential freedom, the solution presupposes essential freedom and renders practical intelligence effectively free. Finally, since acts of practical intelligence progressively modify the subject (and the intersubjective field) in accordance with the trends implicit in their structure (trends toward progress or decline), this liberation will be cumulative, conditioning a more thorough grasp both of practical possibilities and of self-knowledge in the theoretical differentiation of consciousness.

Lonergan's account of the solution in *Insight*, chapter twenty, includes a long excursus on "belief." And in this excursus his emphasis upon the communication of reliable knowledge would seem to place intelligence at the centre of the solution to the problem which intelligence itself created. And so in *Method* his concern is with the "conversions" which reorientate the subject in a spontaneously emergent structuration. But the solution in *Insight* begins with an account of an event which would seem to bear remarkable similarity to his account of religious conversion in *Method*.

> Moreover, to will the good of a person is to love the person; but God is a person, for he is intelligent and free; and so good will is the love of God. Further, good will matches the detachment and disinterestedness of the pure desire to know, and so good will is a love of God that is prompted not by a hope of one's own advantage but simply by God's goodness.
>
> Again, a man or woman knows that he or she is in love by making the discovery that all spontaneous and deliberate tendencies and actions regard the beloved. ...
>
> Again, the order of the universe includes all the good that all persons in the universe are or enjoy or possess. But to will the good of a person is to love the person; and so to will the order of the universe

because of one's love of God is to love all persons in the universe because of one's love of God.[1]

The subsequent account of "belief" is set in the context of his discussion on how the "will" (what he comes to call fourth level intentional consciousness in *Method*) transforms the orientation of understanding towards the grasp of the truth regarding transcendent knowledge. But the condition of possibility of such a grasp is the prior liberation of "will" in love. And so the basic structure of Lonergan's account of the solution remains unchanged from *Insight* to *Method*.

Beyond an initial sketch of the structure of a problem and its solution lies the extremely complex task of consulting and integrating the wealth of concrete knowledge on social, political, economic, historical, religious life which currently is available from the natural and human sciences. But this integration will proceed dialectically and Gibson Winter's account of social ethics in *Elements* is an example of such a dialectical analysis, not simply in search of expanding knowledge of human affairs but also in search of foundational contributions and deformations in the theories and methods which give rise to such knowledge. Because of the creative, synthetic character of that spontaneous structuration which is discovery, empirical knowing is never locked completely into the constraints either of theoretical anticipations or of limited data. And so dialectic can proceed both in the search for new data and new theories (armed with a novel heuristic) and in anticipation of major or minor modifications to one's heuristic (confronted with the overwhelming power of new evidence). It is with this ongoing dialectic in view that I have sought to understand and to present what I would suggest is a rather novel approach to the problems of ethics, history and society. And if my critical exposition of this aspect of Lonergan's work contributes to this ongoing dialectic, even as a step towards its own further clarification or modification, then my intent will have been fulfilled.

## FOOTNOTES - EPILOGUE

1   *Insight*, pp. 698-699.

## BIBLIOGRAPHY

Albertson, James. Review of *Insight* by Bernard Lonergan. *The Modern Schoolman* 35 (1958): 236-244.
Barbour, Ian C. *Issues in Science and Religion.* New York: Harper & Row, Publishers, Harper Torchbooks, 1966.
Barden, Garret. Review of *Randomness, Statistics and Emergence* by Philip McShane. *Philosophical Studies* 20 (1971): 344-6.
Barrow, John D., and Silk, Joseph. "The Structure of the Early Universe." *Scientific American* 242 (April 1980): 118-28.
Becker, Carl L. *The Heavenly City of the Eighteenth-Century Philosophers.* New Haven: Yale University Press, 1932.
Berger, Peter L. *The Sacred Canopy.* Garden City, N. Y.: Doubleday, Anchor Books, 1969; originally published 1967.
Blackwell, R. J. Review of *Randomness, Statistics and Emergence* by Philip McShane. *The Modern Schoolman* 49 (1971-1972): 89.
Boughey, Arthur S. *Strategy for Survival.* Menlo Park, Calif.: W. A. Benjamin, Inc., 1976.
Bowker, John. "Did God Create this Universe?" In *The Sciences and Theology in the Twentieth Century*, pp. 98-126. Edited by A. R. Peacocke. Stocksfield, England: Oriel Press, 1981.
Brennan, Anne Marie Martin. "Bernard Lonergan's World View: Emergent Probability and the God-World Relation." Unpublished Ph.D. dissertation, Columbia University, 1973.
Buchanan, Allen. "The Marxian Critique of Justice and Rights." In *Marx and Morality. Canadian Journal of Philosophy*, supplementary volume VII, pp. 269-306. Edited by Kai Nielsen and Steven C. Patten. Guelph, Ont.: Canadian Association for Publishing in Philosophy, 1981.
Burch, William R., Jr., and Bormann, F. Herbert, eds. *Beyond Growth: Essays on Alternative Futures.* Yale University: School of Forestry and Environmental Studies Bulletin No. 88. New Haven: Yale University, 1975.
Bury, J. B. *The Idea of Progress.* New York: Dover Publications, 1955; originally published 1932.
Byrne, Patrick H. "God and the Statistical Universe." *Zygon: A Journal of Science and Religion* 16 (1981): 345-363.
_____. "Lonergan and the Foundations of the Theories of Relativity." In *Creativity and Method*, pp. 477-494. Edited by Matthew L. Lamb. Milwaukee: Marquette University Press, 1981.
_____. "On Taking Responsibility for the Indeterminate Future." In *Phenomenology and the Understanding of Human Destiny*, pp. 229-238. Edited by Stephen Skousgaard. Lanham, Md.: University Press of America, 1981.
_____. "The Thomist Sources of Lonergan's Dynamic World View." *The Thomist* 46 (1982): 108-145.
Cacòpardo, Rocco. "A Study of Ongoing Social Processes." Unpublished Ph.D. dissertation, Brunel University, Uxbridge, Middlesex, 1974.
Childress, James F. "The Identification of Ethical Principles." *Journal of Religious Ethics* 5 (1977): 39-68.
Churchman, C. West. "A Philosophy for Complexity." In *Futures Research: New Directions*, pp. 82-90. Edited by Harold A. Linstone and W. H. Clive Simmonds. Reading, Mass.: Addison-Wesley, 1977.
Churchman, C. West, and Mason, Richard O., eds. *World Modeling: A Dialogue.* North-Holland/TIMS Studies in Management Science, Vol. 2. Amsterdam: North Holland Publishing Company, 1976; New York: American Elsevier Publishing Company, Inc., 1976.
Cohen, Gerald A. *Karl Marx's Theory of History: A Defence.* Oxford: Clarendon Press, 1978.
Cole, H. S. D., Freeman, Christopher, Jahoda, Marie, and Pavitt, K. L. R., eds. *Thinking About the Future: A Critique of the Limits to Growth.* London: Chatto & Windus for

Sussex University Press.

Collier, Andrew. "Scientific Socialism and the Question of Socialist Values." In *Marx and Morality, Canadian Journal of Philosophy*, supplementary volume VII, pp. 121-154. Edited by Kai Nielsen and Steven C. Patten. Guelph, Ont.: Canadian Association for Publishing in Philosophy, 1981.

Collingwood, R. G. *The Idea of History*. Oxford: Oxford University Press, 1946.

Conn, Walter E. "Bernard Lonergan on Value." *The Thomist* 40 (1976): 243-257.

_____. *Conscience: Development and Self-Transcendence*. Birmingham, Alabama: Religious Education Press, 1981.

_____. "Moral Development: Is Conversion Necessary?" In *Creativity and Method*, pp. 307-324. Edited by Matthew L. Lamb. Milwaukee: Marquette University Press, 1981.

Copleston, F. C., S.J. *A History of Philosophy*. Vol. 2: *Mediaeval Philosophy*. Part 2: *Albert the Great to Duns Scotus*. Garden City, N. Y.: Doubleday & Company, Inc., Image Books, 1962.

Corcoran, Patrick, ed. *Looking at Lonergan's Method*. Dublin: The Talbot Press, 1975.

Crowe, F. E. "An Exploration of Lonergan's New Notion of Value." *Science et Esprit* 29 (1977): 123-143.

Curran, Charles E., and McCormick, Richard A., S.J., eds. *Readings in Moral Theology*. No. 2: *The Distinctiveness of Christian Ethics*. New York: Paulist Press, 1980.

Davis, Charles. "Lonergan and the Teaching Church." In *Foundations of Theology*, pp. 60-75. Edited by Philip McShane. Dublin: Gill and Macmillan, 1971.

_____. "Lonergan's Appropriation of the Concept of Praxis." *New Blackfriars* 62 (1981): 114-26.

_____. *Theology and Political Society*. Cambridge: Cambridge University Press, 1980.

Despland, Michel. *Kant on History and Religion*. Montreal: McGill–Queen's University Press, 1973.

Dewart, Leslie. *The Future of Belief*. New York: Herder and Herder, 1966.

_____. *Religion, Language and Truth*. New York: Herder and Herder, 1970.

De Wachter, Maurice A. M. "Interdisciplinary Bioethics: But Where Do We Start? A Reflection on Epochè as Method." *The Journal of Medicine and Philosophy* 7 (1982): 275-287.

Doran, Robert M. *Subject and Psyche: Ricoeur, Jung, and the Search for Foundations*. Lanham, Md.: University Press of America, 1980.

_____. "Theological Grounds for a World-Cultural Humanity." In *Creativity and Method*, pp. 105-122. Edited by Matthew L. Lamb. Milwaukee: Marquette University Press, 1981.

Doughty, Mark. "This Impossible Universe." *The Tablet* 235 (September 19, 26, 1981): 906-908, 928-930.

Douglas, Mary. *Natural Symbols*. New York: Random House, Pantheon Books, 1981.

Dray, William H. *Philosophy of History*. Englewood Cliffs, N. J.: Prentice-Hall, Inc., 1964.

_____. *Laws and Explanation in History*. London: Oxford University Press, 1957.

Encel, Solomon, Marstrand, Pauline K., and Page, William, eds. *The Art of Anticipation*. London: Martin Robertson, 1975.

Ermarth, Michael. *Wilhelm Dilthey: The Critique of Historical Reason*. Chicago: University of Chicago Press, 1978.

Escher, M. C., and Locher, J. L. *The World of M. C. Escher*. New York: Harry N. Abrams, Inc., Publishers, 1971.

Everett, William W. "Vocation and Location: An Exploration in the Ethics of Ethics." *Journal of Religious Ethics* 5 (1977): 91-114.

Flanagan, Joseph, S.J. "From Body to Thing." In *Creativity and Method*, pp. 495-508. Edited by Matthew L. Lamb. Milwaukee: Marquette University Press, 1981.

Ford, David F. " 'Method in Theology' in the Lonergan Corpus." In *Looking at Lonergan's Method*, pp. 11-26. Edited by Patrick Corcoran. Dublin: The Talbot Press, 1975.

Forrester, Jay W. *Principles of Systems*. Second preliminary edition. Cambridge, Mass.: MIT Press, 1968.

_____. *World Dynamics*. Second edition. Cambridge, Mass.: Wright-Allen Press, Inc., 1973; original edition 1971.
Fowles, Jib, ed. *Handbook of Futures Research*. Westport, Conn.: Greenwood Press, 1978.
Frankena, William K. *Ethics*. Englewood Cliffs, N. J.: Prentice-Hall, Inc. 1963.
Freeman, Christopher. "Malthus With a Computer." In *Thinking About the Future*, pp. 5-13. Edited by H. S. D. Cole, Christopher Freeman, Marie Jahoda, and K. L. R. Pavitt. London: Chatto & Windus for Sussex University Press, 1973.
Gadamer, Hans-Georg. *Truth and Method*. New York: The Seabury Press, 1975.
Gaine, J. Review of *A Matter of Hope* by Nicholas Lash. *The Month* 15 (February 1982): 67.
Gale, George. "The Anthropic Principle." *Scientific American* 245, No. 6 (December 1981): 114-122.
Gallie, W. B. *Philosophy and the Historical Understanding*. London: Chatto & Windus, 1964.
Gardiner, Patrick, ed. *Theories of History*. Glencoe, Ill.: The Free Press, 1960.
Geertz, Clifford. *The Interpretation of Cultures*. New York: Basic Books, 1973.
Giddens, Anthony. *New Rules of Sociological Method*. London: Hutchinson, 1976.
Gilkey, Langdon. "Empirical Science and Theological Knowing." In *Foundations of Theology*, pp. 76-101. Edited by Philip McShane. Dublin: Gill and Macmillan, 1971.
Goldsmith, Edward, ed. *Blueprint for Survival*. New York: Houghton Mifflin, 1972.
Greenberger, Martin, Crenson, Matthew A., and Crissey, Brian L. *Models in the Policy Process*. New York: Russell Sage Foundation, 1976.
Gustafson, James M. *Protestant and Roman Catholic Ethics: Prospects for Rapprochement*. Chicago: University of Chicago Press, 1978.
Habermas, Jürgen. *Communication and the Evolution of Society*. Translated by Thomas McCarthy. Boston: Beacon Press, 1979.
Hartnack, Justus. *Kant's Theory of Knowledge*. Translated by M. Holmes Hartshorne. New York: Harcourt, Brace & World, Inc., Harbinger Books, 1967.
Harvey, Van A. *A Handbook of Theological Terms*. New York: Macmillan Publishing Co., Inc., 1964.
Heelan, Patrick A. "The Logic of Framework Transpositions." In *Language, Truth and Meaning*, pp. 93-114. Edited by Philip McShane. Notre Dame: University of Notre Dame Press, 1972.
_____. "A Realist Theory of Physical Science." *Continuum* 2 (1964): 334-342.
Heilbroner, Robert L. *An Inquiry into the Human Prospect*. With "Second Thoughts" and "What Has Posterity Ever Done for Me?" New York: W. W. Norton & Company, Inc., 1975; originally published 1974.
Hempel, Carl G. "The Function of General Laws in History." *The Journal of Philosophy* 39 (1942): 35-48.
_____. "Reason and Covering Laws in Historical Explanation." In *The Philosophy of History*, pp. 90-105. Oxford: Oxford University Press, 1974.
Hesse, Mary. "Lonergan and Method in the Natural Sciences." In *Looking at Lonergan's Method*, pp. 59-72. Edited by Patrick Corcoran. Dublin: The Talbot Press, 1975.
_____. "Retrospect." In *The Sciences and Theology in the Twentieth Century*, pp. 281-295. Edited by A. R. Peacocke. Stocksfield, England: Oriel Press, 1981.
Hobbes, Thomas. *Leviathan*. Edited with an introduction by Michael Oakeshott. Oxford: Basil Blackwell, 1957.
Hough, Joseph C., Jr. "Christian Social Ethics as Advocacy." *Journal of Religious Ethics* 5 (1977): 115-134.
Hughes, Barry B. *World Modeling*. Lexington, Mass.: Lexington Books, 1980.
Huizinga, Johan. "A Definition of the Concept of History." In *Philosophy & History: Essays Presented to Ernst Cassirer*, pp. 1-10. Edited by R. Klibansky and H. J. Paton. New York: Harper & Row, Publishers, Harper Torchbooks, 1963; originally published 1936.
Humphreys, John. "What, if Anything, is Probability?" *Horizons* (a journal of the students of Milltown Institute of Philosophy and Theology, Dublin) 7 (Summer 1973): 91-103.

Jantsch, Erich, and Waddington, C.H., eds. *Evolution and Consciousness: Human Systems in Transition*, Reading, Mass.: Addison-Wesley Publishing Company, 1976.
Jantsch, Erich. "Evolution: Self-Realization Through Self-Transcendence." In *Evolution and Consciousness*, pp. 37-70. Edited by Erich Jantsch and Conrad H. Waddington. Reading, Mass.: Addison-Wesley Publishing Company, 1976.
_____. "Modeling the Human World: Perspectives." In *World Modeling: A Dialogue*, pp. 89-96. Edited by C. W. Churchman and R. O. Mason. Amsterdam: North Holland Publishing Company, 1976.
Johnson, Donald H. "Lonergan and the Redoing of Ethics." *Continuum* 5 (1967-1968): 211-220.
Jossua, Jean-Pierre. "Some Questions on the Place of Believing Experience in the Work of Bernard Lonergan." In *Looking at Lonergan's Method*, pp. 164-174. Edited by Patrick Corcoran. Dublin: The Talbot Press, 1975.
Kamenka, Eugene. *The Ethical Foundations of Marxism*. London: Routledge and Kegan Paul, 1962.
Kant, Immanuel. *Groundwork of the Metaphysic of Morals*. Translated and analysed by H. J. Paton. New York: Harper & Row, Publishers, Harper Torchbooks, 1964.
_____. *On History*. Edited with an Introduction by L. W. Beck. Translated by L. W. Beck, R. E. Anchor, and E. L. Fackenheim. Indianapolis: Bobbs-Merrill Company, Inc., 1963.
Kaufman, Gordon D. "Nuclear Eschatology and the Study of Religion." *Journal of the American Academy of Religion* 51 (March 1983): 3-14.
Kelly, George Armstrong. *Idealism, Politics and History: Sources of Hegelian Thought*. Cambridge: Cambridge University Press, 1969.
Kerr, Fergus. "Beyond Lonergan's Method: A Response to William Mathews." *New Blackfriars* 57 (1976): 59-71.
_____. "Objections to Lonergan's Method." *New Blackfriars* 56 (1975): 305-316.
Kiely, Bartholomew M., S.J. *Psychology and Moral Theology: Lines of Convergence*. Rome: Gregorian University Press, 1980.
Kohlberg, Lawrence. *Essays on Moral Development*. Vol. I: *The Philosophy of Moral Development*. New York: Harper & Row, 1981.
Kohls, Gerald V. "The Evolutionary Source: A Study of Evolution Based on the Philosophy of Bernard F. Lonergan." Unpublished Ph.D. dissertation, University of Fribourg, Switzerland, July 1969.
Kristol, Irving. "Rationalism in Economics." In *The Crisis in Economic Theory*, pp. 201-218. Edited by Daniel Bell and Irving Kristol. New York: Basic Books, 1981.
Kroger, J. "Polanyi and Lonergan on Scientific Method." *Philosophy Today* 21 (1977): 2-20.
_____. "Theology and Notions of Reason and Science: A Note on a Point of Comparison in Lonergan and Polanyi." *The Journal of Religion* 56 (1976): 157-161.
Kuhn, Thomas S. *The Structure of Scientific Revolutions*. Second edition, enlarged. *International Encyclopedia of Unified Science*. Vol. 2, No. 2. Chicago: University of Chicago Press, 1970; original edition 1962.
Lamb, Matthew L., ed. *Creativity and Method: Essays in Honour of Bernard J. F. Lonergan, S.J.* Milwaukee: Marquette University Press, 1981.
_____. *History Method and Theology: A Dialectical Comparison of Wilhelm Dilthey's Critique of Historical Reason and Bernard Lonergan's Meta-Methodology*. AAR dissertation series 25. Missoula, Montana: Scholars Press, 1978.
_____. "Praxis and Generalized Empirical Method." In *Creativity and Method*, pp. 53-77. Milwaukee: Marquette University Press, 1981.
_____. "The Production Process and Exponential Growth: A Study in Socio-Economics and Theology." In *Lonergan Workshop*, Vol. 1, pp. 257-307. Edited by F. Lawrence. Missoula, Montana: Scholars Press, 1978.
_____. "Towards a Synthetization of the Sciences." *Philosophy of Science* 32 (1965): 182-191.
Lash, Nicholas. "In Defence of Lonergan's Critics." *New Blackfriars* 57 (1976): 124-126.

_____. *A Matter of Hope: A Theologian's Reflections on the Thought of Karl Marx.* London: Darton, Longman and Todd, 1981.
_____. "Method and Cultural Discontinuity." In *Looking at Lonergan's Method*, pp. 127-143. Edited by Patrick Corcoran. Dublin: The Talbot Press, 1975.
Lawrence, Fred, ed. *Lonergan Workshop.* Vols. 1 to 5. Missoula, Montana and Chico, California: Scholars Press, 1978, 1980, 1982, 1983, and 1985.
_____. " 'The Modern Philosophic Differentiation of Consciousness' or What is Enlightenment?" In *Lonergan Workshop*, Vol. 2, pp. 231-279, Chico, Calif.: Scholars Press, 1981.
_____. "Political Theology and 'The Longer Cycle of Decline'." In *Lonergan Workshop*, Vol. 1, pp. 223-256. Missoula, Montana: Scholars Press, 1978.
Linstone, Harold A., and Simmonds, W. H. Clive. "Epilogue." In *Futures Research: New Directions*, pp. 253-263. Reading, Mass.: Addison-Wesley, 1977.
_____, eds. *Futures Research: New Directions.* Reading, Mass.: Addison-Wesley, 1977.
Lonergan, Bernard, J. F., S.J. "Bernard Lonergan Responds." In *Language, Truth and Meaning*, pp. 306-312. Edited by Philip McShane. Notre Dame: Notre Dame University Press, 1972.
_____. "The Dehellenization of Dogma." In *The Future of Belief Debate*, pp. 69-91. Edited by Gregory Baum. New York: Herder and Herder, 1967.
_____. "The Example of Gibson Winter." In *A Second Collection*, pp. 189-192. London: Darton, Longman & Todd, 1974.
_____. *Grace and Freedom: Operative Grace in the Thought of St. Thomas Aquinas.* Edited by J. Patout Burns, with an Introduction by Frederick E. Crowe. London: Darton, Longman & Todd, 1971.
_____. *Insight: A Study of Human Understanding.* Revised students' edition. New York: Philosophical Library, 1958; London: Darton, Longman & Todd, 1958.
_____. *Method in Theology.* New York: Herder and Herder, 1972.
_____. "The Philosophy of History." Introductory lecture at the Thomas More Institute, Montreal, Sept. 23, 1960. (Mimeographed).
_____. "Reality, Myth, Symbol." In *Myth, Symbol and Reality*, pp. 31-40. Edited by Alan M. Olson. Notre Dame: University of Notre Dame Press, 1980.
_____. *A Second Collection: Papers by Bernard J. F. Lonergan, S.J.* Edited by William F. J. Ryan, S.J., and Bernard J. Tyrrell, S.J. London: Darton, Longman & Todd, 1974.
_____. "Theology and Praxis." *Catholic Theological Society of America Proceedings* 32 (1977): 1-16.
_____. *A Third Collection.* Edited by F. E. Crowe. New York: Paulist Press, 1985.
_____. *Understanding and Being.* Edited by Elizabeth A. Morelli and Mark D. Morelli. New York: The Edwin Mellen Press, 1980.
_____. *Verbum: Word and Idea in Aquinas.* Edited by David B. Burrell. Notre Dame: University of Notre Dame Press, 1967.
Long, E. Leroy, Jr. *A Survey of Christian Ethics.* New York: Oxford, 1967.
Loveridge, Denis L. "Values and Futures." In *Futures Research: New Directions*, pp. 53-64. Edited by Harold A. Linstone and W. H. Clive Simmonds. Reading, Mass.: Addison-Wesley, 1977.
Löwith, Karl. *Meaning in History.* Chicago: University of Chicago Press, 1949.
MacIntyre, Alasdair. *After Virtue: A Study in Moral Theory.* Notre Dame: University of Notre Dame Press, 1981.
MacKinnon, Edward M., S.J. "Cognitional Analysis and the Philosophy of Science." *Continuum* 2 (1964): 343-368.
_____. "Linguistic Analysis and the Transcendence of God." *Proceedings of the Catholic Theological Society of America* 23 (1968): 28-44.
MacLaren, Elizabeth. "Theological Disagreement and Functional Specialties." In *Looking at Lonergan's Method*, pp. 73-87. Edited by Patrick Corcoran. Dublin: The Talbot Press, 1975.

McGrath, Patrick. "Knowledge, Understanding and Reality." In *Looking at Lonergan's Method*, pp. 27-41. Edited by Patrick Corcoran. Dublin: The Talbot Press, 1975.

McLelland, D. Review of *A Matter of Hope* by Nicholas Lash. *Tablet* 235 (December 19-26, 1981): 1266.

Macpherson, C. B. "Introduction." In *Leviathan* by Thomas Hobbes. Edited with an introduction by C. B. Macpherson. Harmondsworth: Penguin Books, 1968.

_____. *The Political Theory of Possessive Individualism: Hobbes to Locke*. London: Oxford University Press, 1975; originally published 1962.

McShane, Philip. "The Core Psychological Present of the Contemporary Theologian." In *Trinification of the World*, pp. 84-96. Edited by T. A. Dunne and J. M. Laporte. Toronto: Regis College Press, 1978.

_____. "The Foundations of Mathematics." *The Modern Schoolman* 40 (1962-3): 373-387.

_____, ed. *Foundations of Theology: Papers from the International Lonergan Congress, 1970*. Dublin: Gill and Macmillan, 1971.

_____. "Insight and the Strategy of Biology." *Continuum* 2 (1964): 374-388.

_____, ed. *Language, Truth and Meaning: Papers from the International Lonergan Congress, 1970*. Notre Dame: University of Notre Dame Press, 1972; Dublin: Gill and Macmillan, 1972.

_____. *Randomness, Statistics and Emergence*. Dublin: Gill and Macmillan, 1970.

_____. *Wealth of Self and Wealth of Nations*. Hicksville, N. Y.: Exposition Press, 1975.

Marcuse, Herbert. *Reason and Revolution*. Second edition, with a "Preface: A Note on Dialectic." Boston: Beacon Press, 1960; original edition 1941.

Mason, Richard O. "The Search for a World Model." In *World Modeling: A Dialogue*, pp. 1-9. Edited by C. West Churchman and Richard O. Mason. Amsterdam: North Holland Publishing Company, 1976.

_____. "A World Issue Debate: On Assumptions Underlying World Models." In *World Modeling: A Dialogue*, pp. 97-106. Edited by C. West Churchman and Richard O. Mason. Amsterdam: North Holland Publishing Company, 1976.

Mathews, William. "Lonergan's Awake: A Reply to Fergus Kerr." *New Blackfriars* 57 (1976): 11-21.

_____. Review of *Randomness, Statistics and Emergence* by Philip McShane. *The Heythrop Journal* 13 (1972): 319-321.

Meadows, Dennis L., Behrens, William W. III, Meadows, Donella H., Naill, Roger F., Randers, Jørgen, and Zahn, Erich K. O. *Dynamics of Growth in a Finite World*. Cambridge, Mass.: Wright-Allen Press, Inc., 1974.

Meadows, Dennis L., and Meadows, Donella H., eds. *Toward Global Equilibrium: Collected Papers*. Cambridge, Mass.: Wright-Allen Press, Inc., 1973.

Meadows, Donella H., Meadows, Dennis L., Randers, Jørgen, and Behrens, William W. III. *The Limits to Growth*. A Report for the Club of Rome's Project on the Predicament of Mankind. Second edition. New York: New American Library, Signet Book, 1974; original edition 1972.

Melchin, Kenneth R. "Gibson Winter on Ethics and Social Science: Elements and Four Later Articles." *Gnosis* (A journal of philosophic interest, Concordia University, Montréal, Québec) Vol. 2, No. 2 (Spring 1981): 51-64.

Meyerhoff, Hans, ed. *The Philosophy of History in Our Time*. Garden City, New York: Doubleday, 1959.

Meynell, Hugo A. *An Introduction to the Philosophy of Bernard Lonergan*. New York: Barnes & Noble, 1976.

_____. "On Objections to Lonergan's 'Method'." *The Heythrop Journal* 19 (1978): 405-10.

Miles, Ian. "The Ideologies of Futurists." In *Handbook of Futures Research*, pp. 67-98. Edited by Jib Fowles. Westport, Conn.: Greenwood Press, 1978.

Miles, John A., Jr. "Jacques Monod and the Cure of Souls." *Zygon* 9 (march 1974): 22-43.

Miller, J. Hillis. "The Limits of Pluralism, III: The Critic as Host." *Critical Inquiry* 3 (1977):

439-447.
Monod, Jacques. *Chance and Necessity: An Essay on the Natural Philosophy of Modern Biology*. Translated by A. Wainhouse. New York: Random House, Vintage Books, 1972; original French edition 1970.
Munz, Peter. *The Shapes of Time: A New Look at the Philosophy of History*. Middletown, Conn.: Wesleyan University Press, 1977.
Newton-Smith, W. Review of *Randomness, Statistics and Emergence* by Philip McShane. *Bibliography of Philosophy* 18 (1971): 34.
Nielsen, Kai. "Introduction." In *Marx and Morality. Canadian Journal of Philosophy*, supplementary volume VII, pp. 1-17. Edited by Kai Nielsen and Steven C. Patten. Guelph, Ont.: Canadian Association for Publishing in Philosophy, 1981.
Nielsen, Kai, and Patten, Steven C., eds. *Marx and Morality. Canadian Journal of Philosophy*, supplementary volume VII. Guelph, Ont.: Canadian Association for Publishing in Philosophy, 1981.
Nisbet, Robert. *History of the Idea of Progress*. New York: Basic Books, 1980.
O'Connor, R. Eric, S.J. "A Dialogue on Learning Mathematics." In *Creativity and Method*, pp. 509-525. Edited by Matthew L. Lamb. Milwaukee: Marquette University Press, 1981.
_____. "From a Mathematician." *Continuum* 2 (1964): 313-15.
O'Donovan, Leo J. "Emergent Probability and the Method of an Evolutionary World View." *The Personalist* 54 (Summer 1973): 250-273.
_____. "Evolution as a Systematic Concept in Recent Catholic Thought." Unpublished Th.D. dissertation, Westfälische Wilhelms Universität, Münster, 1971.
_____. "Lonergan: Emergent Probability and Evolution." *Continuum* 7 (1969-70): 131-142.
Ogden, Schubert M. "Lonergan and the Subjectivist Principle." In *Language, Truth and Meaning*, pp. 218-235. Edited by Philip McShane. Notre Dame: University of Notre Dame Press, 1972.
Ossowska, Maria. *Social Determinants of Moral Ideas*. Philadelphia: University of Pennsylvania Press, 1970.
Outka, Gene, and Reeder, John P., Jr., eds. *Religion and Morality*. Garden City, N. Y.: Doubleday, Anchor Press, 1973.
Pannenberg, Wolfhart. "History and Meaning in Bernard Lonergan's Approach to Theological Method." In *Looking at Lonergan's Method*, pp. 88-100. Edited by Patrick Corcoran. Dublin: The Talbot Press, 1975. Reprinted without substantial change as "History and Meaning in Bernard Lonergan." *The Irish Theological Quarterly* 40 (1973): 103-114.
Peacocke, A. R. "Chance and the Life Game." *Zygon* 14 (December 1979): 301-322.
_____. *Creation and the World of Science*. Oxford: Clarendon Press, 1979.
_____, ed. *The Sciences and Theology in the Twentieth Century*. Stocksfield, England: Oriel Press, 1981.
Pitcher, Alvin, and Winter, Gibson. "Perspectives in Religious Social Ethics." *Journal of Religious Ethics* 5 (1977): 69-90.
Plamenatz, John. *Karl Marx's Philosophy of Man*. Oxford: Clarendon Press, 1975.
Pollard, Sidney. *The Idea of Progress*. Harmondsworth: Penguin Books, 1971.
Potter, Ralph B., Jr. "The Logic of Moral Argument." In *Toward a Discipline of Social Ethics*, pp. 93-114. Edited by Paul Deats, Jr. Boston: Boston University Press, 1972.
Price, Geoffry L. "Politics and Self-Acceptance." In *Creativity and Method*, pp. 443-457. Edited by Matthew L. Lamb. Milwaukee: Marquette University Press, 1981.
Quay, P. Review of *Randomness, Statistics and Emergence* by Philip McShane. *Review for Religious* 30 (1971): 30.
Rahner, Karl. "Some Critical Thoughts on 'Functional Specialties in Theology'." In *Foundations of Theology*, pp. 194-196. Edited by Philip McShane. Dublin: Gill and Macmillan, 1971.
Raymaker, John. "The Theory and Praxis of Social Ethics." In *Creativity and Method*, pp. 339-352. Edited by Matthew L. Lamb. Milwaukee: Marquette University Press, 1981.

Reiman, Jeffrey H. "The Possibility of a Marxian Theory of Justice." In *Marx and Morality. Canadian Journal of Philosophy,* supplementary volume VII, pp. 307-322. Edited by Kai Nielsen and Steven C. Patten, Guelph, Ont.: Canadian Association for Publishing in Philosophy, 1981.

Ricoeur, Paul. "Hermeneutics and the Critique of Ideology." In *Hermeneutics and the Human Sciences*, pp. 63-100. Translated and edited by John B. Thompson. Cambridge: Cambridge University Press, 1981.

Riley, Philip B. and Fallon, Tim, eds. *Religion and Culture: Essays in Honor of Bernard Lonergan, S.J.* Albany, N. Y.: SUNY Press, forthcoming 1986.

Roach, Richard R. "Fidelity: The Faith of Responsible Love." Unpublished Ph.D. dissertation, Yale University, 1974.

_____. "Nature and Praxis." *Communio: International Catholic review* 5 (1978): 252-274.

_____. "A New Sense of Faith." *Journal of Religious Ethics* 5 (1977): 135-154.

Roy, David. "Bioethics as Anamnesis." In *Creativity and Method*, pp. 325-338. Edited by Matthew L. Lamb. Milwaukee: Marquette University Press, 1981.

Ryan, Denis. Review of *Randomness, Statistics and Emergence* by Philip McShane. *The Furrow* 22 (1971): 596-598.

Schotland, Richard. "Meteorology and Climatology," pp. 40-65. In *Collier's Encyclopedia*, William D. Halsey, editorial director. New York: Crowell-Collier Publishing Company, 1964.

Shaw, William H. *Marx's Theory of History*. Stanford, Calif.: Stanford University Press, 1978.

Shea, William M. "The Stance and Task of the Foundational Theologian: Critical or Dogmatic?" *Heythrop Journal* 17 (1976): 273-92.

Stassen, Glen H. "Editorial Notes." *Journal of Religious Ethics* 5 (1977): 1-7.

_____. "A Social Theory Model for Religious Social Ethics." *Journal of Religious Ethics* 5 (1977): 9-38.

Streng, Frederick J. *Understanding Religious Life*. Second edition. Encino, Calif.: Dickenson Publishing Company, Inc., 1976.

Suppe, Frederick. *The Structure of Scientific Theories*. Second edition. Edited with a Critical Introduction and Afterword by F. Suppe. Urbana, Ill.: University of Illinois Press, 1977.

Taylor, Charles. *Hegel and Modern Society*. Cambridge: Cambridge University Press, 1979.

Thomas, John Heywood. Review of *Randomness, Statistics and Emergence* by Philip McShane. *The Clergy Review* 56 (1971): 310-312.

Tracy, David. "Theologies of Praxis." In *Creativity and Method*, pp. 35-52. Edited by Matthew L. Lamb. Milwaukee: Marquette University Press, 1981.

Tucker, Robert C., ed. *The Marx-Engels Reader*. Second edition. New York: W. W. Norton & Company, Inc., 1978.

Van Den Hengel, John W., S.C.J. *The Home of Meaning: The Hermeneutics of the Subject of Paul Ricoeur*. Washington, D. C.: University Press of America, 1982.

Vertin, Michael. "Maréchal, Lonergan, and the Phenomenology of Knowing." In *Creativity and Method*, pp. 411-422. Edited by Matthew L. Lamb. Milwaukee: Marquette University Press, 1981.

Voegelin, Eric. *Anamnesis*. Translated and edited by Gerhart Niemeyer. Notre Dame: University of Notre Dame Press, 1978.

_____. *The New Science of Politics*. Chicago: The University of Chicago Press, 1952.

Von Foerster, Heinz. "The Curious Behavior of Complex Systems: Lessons from Biology." In *Futures Research: New Directions*, pp. 104-113. Edited by Harold A. Linstone and W. H. Clive Simmons. Reading, Mass.: Addison-Wesley, 1977.

Waddington, C. H., F.R.S. *Tools for Thought*. New York: Basic Books, 1977.

Walsh, W. H. *Philosophy of History: An Introduction*. Revised edition. New York: Harper & Row, Publishers, Harper Torchbooks, 1967; original edition 1951.

Watson, Gerard. "A Note on Lonergan and a Greek Conception of Science." In *Looking at Lonergan's Method*, pp. 55-58. Edited by Patrick Corcoran. Dublin: The Talbot Press,

1975.

Weber, Max. *From Max Weber: Essays in Sociology*. Translated, edited, and with an Introduction by H. H. Gerth and C. Wright Mills, New York: Oxford University Press, 1946.

White, Hayden. *Metahistory: The Historical Imagination in Nineteenth-Century Europe*. Baltimore: The Johns Hopkins University Press, 1975.

Winter, Gibson. *Elements for a Social Ethic*. New York: The Macmillan Company, 1966.

———. "Introduction: Religion, Ethics, and Society." In *Social Ethics: Issues in Ethics and Society*, pp. 1-17. London: SCM Press Ltd., 1968; New York: Harper & Row, Publishers, 1968.

———. *Liberating Creation: Foundations of Religious Social Ethics*. New York: Crossroad, 1981.

Wood, Ledger. "Free-Will." In *Dictionary of Philosophy*, p. 112. Edited by Dagobert D. Runes. Totowa, N. J.: Littlefield, Adams & Co., 1962.

Yamane, Taro. *Statistics: An Introductory Analysis*. Third edition. New York: Harper & Row, Publishers, 1973.

Yovel, Yirmiahu. *Kant and the Philosophy of History*. Princeton: Princeton University Press, 1980.

DEC 3 1 1988